Poetry *Writers'*
YEARBOOK
2008

Edited by Gordon Kerr & Hilary Lissenden

A & C Black • London

Second edition 2007
A & C Black Publishers Limited
38 Soho Square, London W1D 3HB
www.acblack.com

© 2006 A & C Black Publishers Limited

ISBN 978–0–7136–8469–8

A CIP catalogue record for this book is available from the British Library.

Typeset by QPM from David Lewis XML Associates Ltd
Printed and bound in Great Britain by William Clowes Ltd, Beccles, Suffolk

Contents

Poetry Writers' Yearbook 2008

POETRY COMPETITION

Enter the *Poetry Writers' Yearbook 2008*
poetry competition and you could win:

- a cash prize of £300, or £500 of A&C Black books
- publication of your poem on the A&C Black website
- publication of your poem in the
Poetry Writers' Yearbook 2009
- publication of your poem on **writersservices.com**

. All you have to do is write a poem of no more than 30
lines, on the theme of **'Desire'** and visit our website at
www.acblack.com/poetrycompetition for full details of
how to enter by email and register your details online.

The closing date is 30th June 2008.

Good luck!

Poetry Writers' Yearbook 2007
Poetry Competition

THE WINNING POEM

Congratulations to the winner of the 2007 competition, Michael J Woods, of Worcester, UK. His poem, *Callow End*, was chosen by the judge, *Poetry Yearbook* editor Gordon Kerr.

Michael J Woods' poem is reproduced here
with the kind permission of the author:

CALLOW END

Cows, mist-drowned, merge with sheep
in this soft focus Malverns morning.
Powick church has shivered out of night.
The sun is a white-hot coin struck
in the mint of the sky, unquenchable
and incensed by vapour from the fields.
Nothing is not what it seems as the river floods
and water strains to wed itself to land.
The horizon shimmers like the inside of a forge
or quivering air around the after burner
of the low flying jet that sometimes scuds the hills.

Taking the bend, I see the village announce itself
in what seems to be a claim to wisdom;
the sign is bald - blocks of black on white.
But this isn't Italy. It doesn't warn with a red slash
that its limits have been reached. So, I sweep
beyond its parish pale, apparently boundless
but sensing the car break some meniscus
as it passes deep magnetic fields.

In this winter's wet and ice it's odd to think
the hedges hangar what will fledge and fly.
So, I signal, put my foot down and roll the car
over the camber to avoid the wash of what might
overtake me. A rear-view glance is all it takes
to show the whole reflected shrinking scene -
less substance than accident, and the open road ahead.

Foreword

A poem is a piece of public art, and I've long been of the opinion that the poem ends not with its completion, but with its publication. It's in the anticipation of the poem being made public that we discover its final form – in the art or trick of standing back and looking at your poem as if it were someone else's, or as if someone else were reading it. This gives us the distance and bravery to make unsentimental decisions, to 'murder our darlings'; the patience to polish and refine; the impetus to discover the tiny shifts of tone and sense that turn a good line into an unforgettable one ... to do the things, in other words, that make the poem something worth giving, worth reading.

'Publication', though, is a much-misunderstood word. It really just means 'someone else reading your poem'. Whatever brings this about – an email group, a workshop, a website, a poster, a pamphlet, a reading, a recording, a book – is publication. This book is a guide to making your work public, and a map of all the routes you can take to that end.

The late 1980s and early 1990s were boom-and-bust years for poetry. Promoters (and perhaps the poets themselves) simply overestimated the public appetite for it. Poetry was never the 'new rock 'n' roll', nor ever could be. Some people made investments that were never returned; the poetry bays disappeared from the bookshops; publishing was forced to contract dramatically; and the whole scene plunged into a time of hand-wringing and self-examination.

Luckily, the loss of shelf-space in the shops coincided with the emergence of Internet publishing. This has matured rapidly from its somewhat shaky beginnings, and there are now many excellent websites where it's as tough to place work as for the best magazines – which is as it should be. Additionally, self-publication boasts a long and noble history (a fact which many had forgotten), and this was the right time to reclaim it. Poetry slams and live readings grew in popularity. Slowly, sensibly, and by increments, poetry began to rebuild a large and interested audience.

No doubt posterity will judge our poetry as harshly as ever, but I don't think there can ever have been a more interesting time to write the stuff. Yet its changing role in society means that definitions of poetry are harder to fix than ever. Some insist that we must have a poetry equal to, and reflective of, the uncertainty of the times; others feel that we must follow an almost impersonal, Neo-Classical approach now that Romanticism has reached its dead end. Some believe that poetry must take advantage of the remarkable new advances in IT and multimedia; others feel that rap and performance poetry have much to teach the page-bound poet about reconnecting to an audience. And some think that the only way forward in such a time is for the poet to pursue their individual path alone, outside all schools and trends. As a result, the range of outlets for poetry is now vast – and equally bewildering.

Mercifully, we have this *Poetry Writers' Yearbook* to guide us, and effectively turn a minefield into a garden. Not only will you quickly find the groups, readings, publishers, festivals and competitions that cater for your kind of poetry; you'll also find many other avenues to explore that will change the way in which you think about your own work. *Poetry Writers' Yearbook* is not only a guide to 'the business end' of poetry, but also an introduction to the community of poets: perhaps more than any other artistic group, poets rely on one another for feedback, support, advice and encouragement in what can often be (and perhaps *has* to be) a lonely and often deranging business.

So get yourself on the map – not to schmooze or to network, but simply to keep the company of other poets, which is still the best way to improve your craft in what, next to music, is the most brutally technical of artistic disciplines. Besides, all the poetry editors I know are in touch with many other poets, and rely on their enthusiastic recommendation as the most reliable way of tracking new talent. I once heard about a particular author from three different sources ... *before* she had had a single poem published. The community forms a grapevine, a big jungle telephone primed to jangle wildly at the arrival of genuine poetic talent (still as rare a thing as ever); being part of it is a far surer and quicker way of making a name for yourself than adding another manuscript to a publisher's already Alpine slush pile. More to the point, it's a happy and rewarding end in itself.

At the end of the day, though, the only thing that makes anyone a poet is their becoming very, very good at composing verses. All those who are, conspicuously, are also individuals for whom a love of poetry comes first, and the idea of being a poet a very distant second. This *Yearbook* also contains a wealth of information on how to best approach the poet's best teacher: poetry itself.

Don Paterson

Introduction
Reading, writing, learning, being

The poet **George Szirtes**, whose first collection was published in 1979, examines what it means to be a poet, and how and why we write poetry. He casts his eye over the poetry world of the early 21st century – noting the opportunities afforded by technology, and finding reasons to be cheerful in the number of writing courses on offer today, as well as the volume of entries for poetry competitions.

To be a poet: is that the same as writing a poem, or maybe a dozen? If so, there are hundreds of thousands of poets in the country, if not more; perhaps millions – people who have at some time or other felt that the appropriate thing to do in respect of this or that experience or memory or desire was to take a piece of paper and try to write it down in a form that had lines, a steady rhythm and, usually, rhyme. This feeling may have come upon them in their youth and perhaps persisted on an intermittent basis; even, in some cases, into old age. They might have liked the lyrics of some song, or sung hymns, or laughed at some particularly adroit piece of wit whose sharpness was provided by rhythm or rhyme. Or maybe they felt that there was some peculiar, ritual, commemorative power in verse: such verses could be seen on gravestones and on monuments. Or it was simply that the emotional power of the experience, memory or desire was such that ordinary talk, ordinary writing, couldn't capture it – and capturing it, or at least representing it in some way, was important. Poetry was that form, and always has been. Poetry is that instinct finding a shape in language. And not only in language, but in action too. It isn't that there are sensitive people who understand poetry (a small minority) and insensitive people who don't (the vast majority), for almost everyone who at some time or other has uttered, "Sheer poetry!" or simply gasped, "Wow!" at a bird soaring, a footballer swerving or any act that seems perfect in itself, understands poetry in the most visceral sense.

The desire to commemorate, celebrate, mourn or gasp "Wow!" is the stuff of poetry. That is why poetry can never die, and why it is at the very beginning of writing and speaking and singing. Unless this is understood as the basis on which the whole structure of poetry stands, we may as well give up. The state of poetry in the country is therefore as it ever was: central, vital, and partly hidden.

A private art

Partly hidden because, as Geoffrey Grigson said, poetry is in some respects a private art. Private not only in the sense that it is written out of keenly personal sensibility – all the arts have their origins in the solitary mind wandering about the unknown world of language and experience – but in that most poetry, even when read by, or read to, or spoken or sung to hundreds or even thousands of people, is addressed to a mind as solitary and ambient as itself. There is communal experience, of course: the cabaret, the slam, the rally, events that act as important public confirmations of communality. And yet, it seems to me that even in those conditions, at some level there is a seeking of what theologian Martin Buber called "the I-Thou communion". Something that moves from depth to depth and implies, as did Rilke's sonnet on the Archaic Torso of Apollo, that you must change your life. Depth needn't be the same as solemnity, of course. It may come as a form of serious existential play, but depth it is, the echo deep and wide.

This is, of course, a personal view, not an attempt to point to a hierarchy among kinds of poetry. It is offered as one possible reason why poetry is a hidden art: it addresses the hidden. It takes concentration. It makes demands but it rewards enormously. The demands are not necessarily those of 'difficulty' but of attention – attention to the true articulation of all those experiences, memories and desires I have already mentioned. Such attention is at a premium everywhere. Often it is at its greatest when most needed, and it tends to be needed more in poverty, in trouble, in discomfort, where truth and the desire for meaning are more pressing. Fat, comfortable societies don't need it: what they want is distraction and entertainment. Words are dirt cheap.

Nevertheless, there are cultural differences even among fat and comfortable societies replete with entertainments. This is not the place to undertake a serious description of British society and its attitudes to art. Art as news, art as personality, art as entertainment, art as a nice big noise has no real problem here. People have no problems with verse either, provided it turns on some of the ready taps and gives us nice, ready, warm feelings. But there is, and has long been, a kind of emotional embarrassment, particularly in English society, which prefers the impersonal to the personal, the non-verbal to the verbal, and is afraid of boring the pants off someone else by betraying something about itself. This is partly a product of the complex class system, the tradition of empiricism and the fear of pretension – or worse still, of being perceived as pretentious – but whatever it is, it does constitute a cultural pattern.

Such ingrained cultural patterns have considerable virtues. People are less liable to being told nonsense, or to fall under the spell of demagogues. There is at some level a great bottom of good sense that rejects cant. On the other hand this mindset can lead to a certain blandness, in turn producing a stylised reaction in which the cult of the rough is turned into a series of approvable gestures. There are also the approved eccentrics, of course – the lovably barking, who eventually become 'national treasures'; but even so, these establish a fairly low level of tolerance for the kind of art that poetry can be at its best.

But times and generations change. The poetry I grew up with is different from the poetry I came to some sort of maturity with, and is different again now as I move towards 60. I grew up at the end of post-war romanticism, in the world of the Movement, the Group and of Alvarez's *The New Poetry* on the one hand and the Beats and the Mersey Sound on the other. I came to my first adulthood in writing at the time of the *New Review*, of Lowell, Plath, Berryman, moving towards Hamilton, Heaney, Longley and Harrison. I found myself to some extent in Mahon. I arrived in one boat with the Martians. The kind of approach to formality I found myself using in the 80s is fairly general parlance now: I see it in O'Brien, Paterson, Donaghy, Farley and many others. That's just literary history, and ten years from now it will be different again.

What has changed, and changed greatly, is the interest in learning to write poetry. In the last five years or so more than 50 MAs in Creative Writing have sprung up, all desperate to fill their places and mostly with enough applicants to do just that. And beyond that there are the expanding short courses offered by organisations like the Arvon Foundation, which now has four centres to work from, as well as external courses run from universities and other colleges. Whether this is a result of an aspirational leisured middle-class; of the acceptability of borrowing and living in debt; of the desire to supplement a communal and individual spiritual space; of years of degrees in arts administration; of crafty funding initiatives by central and regional arts bodies; or of a genuine awakening in the art of poetry is hard to say. Probably something of each. Having worked often as a tutor for Arvon, and been both tutor and examiner on MA courses, I am pretty sure that they can be extremely worthwhile and interesting. In teaching through reading they are also serving the broader purpose of creating an intelligent, involved matrix of readers-and-writers which may well bear fruit in the future. It is not simply the egotistical satisfaction of the individual at stake: when a course is properly conducted and understood, it encourages a critical awareness of daily language and the forms it employs.

It is a different story in publishing, reviewing and book-buying. People write more but read less, they say. Few publishers of poetry can get by without grants, and the getting of grants is a long, tortuous, managerial process that may entail filling in forms of 40-odd pages and answering questions driven by different agendas. In return for these grants the publisher can publish a number of volumes that sell in their hundreds rather than their thousands, partly because the big book chains store very little poetry, preferring to pile high and sell cheap, and partly because the books (when they appear) are not always noticed. Not that this is so different from the situation when I started. My first book from Secker and Warburg in 1979, *The Slant Door*, was expected to sell about 700 copies at best. It won the Faber Prize so it might have sold a few more, I don't remember now, but it wouldn't have made a substantial difference. Secker was a mainstream publisher working without funding; its poetry list was supported by the most successful items on the fiction list. No big sales of money then either. However the book was reviewed on the day of its appearance – in the *New Statesman*, if I remember right.

There were many more independent bookshops then. The best of them displayed and sold literary magazines, set up or advertised events and welcomed as much poetry as they could. Poetry at the sales end was better supported. Sales improved still further when books or poets got on to schools' or universities' syllabuses.

It also helped that there were more magazines and periodicals that published poems and reviews. *The Observer*, the *Sunday Times*, the *Sunday Telegraph* and others had a certain amount of regular space for both. Poetry was more a part of the literary conversation. That is not to say it is entirely peripheral now – *The Guardian* does its level best to keep the conversation going – but serious general magazines such as *The Listener* and *Encounter* are gone, and the *TLS* publishes far fewer poems or reviews of poetry than it did.

This represents a serious loss, but there are some gains too. New magazines have appeared and there is the whole Web to play on. The Internet and computer technology generally have made and continue to make a significant contribution to the publication, discussion and sale of poetry. Though vast and formless at first – like an infinitely large tobacconist's window; one that displayed anything anyone cared to put in it – the Web is on the way to developing a proper literary society of its own. Magazines appear, as do newspapers. Bloggers have created a new political space, and the use of links has enabled various meetings of minds in poetry (as in much else). The infinitely large tobacconist's window remains, but sections of it are talking to each other. Nor is it only the young and the geeky driving the process: email is used by people of all ages and needs no great sophistication, so poems circulate by email, from poet to friend to tutor or student to editor and publisher, and may appear on your screen rather than on a piece of paper. News travels fast.

Eventually, though, it is still the book that matters. The new technology allows books to be set and edited quickly, and even printed to order, bypassing the chain-stores of the big book companies. I expect this to expand, and many publishers and literary agents believe that books of poetry and other serious literature will be often produced and made available in this way.

The process is quite exciting at this stage: it is like being at the birth of a new culture that is technological but not impersonal.

Despite the push in the 80s onwards to get poetry, or rather poets, 'out of the poetry ghetto' and into factories, supermarkets, surgeries and oilrigs, the last 20 years have not produced a surge in poetry-buying. The best initiatives have, I suspect, been strictly non-managerial and non-institutional. The most successful individual act of genius has probably been *Poems on the Underground*, of which there have been several series now. The secret, I think, is that this addresses the potential reader in the best one-to-one way, as part of daily life. The tube isn't a social mode of transport: it is often uncomfortable; there may not be enough elbow room to open a newspaper, and the traveller is both physically and psychologically in an in-between state. As a reader, he or she comes across the poem as an object of brief personal contemplation. The poem is caught in a fascinating attention space. There is nothing else to do, there is no communal dynamic. There, among all the advertisements with their commercial language, is this entirely other language addressing another aspect of the human condition. One could well have short poems on bookmarks, serviettes, tickets, tube maps. There is a potential readership for such things.

For ordinary books of poetry, leaving out most bookshops, there is Internet shopping and the Poetry Book Society, a small but important organisation that acts not only like a book club but also as a magazine and a maker of reputations through its Choices, Recommendations and prizes.

And lastly there is the great expansion in prizes, quite wealthy prizes, from £500 to £10,000, for books and for individual poems. These have been instrumental in familiarising the work of a number of writers, some of them little-known before the award of the prize. It is in judging these that one discovers how many people write poetry. The entries come in their hundreds and thousands.

And this takes us back to the beginning, to the reasons why all kinds of people write poetry and think it appropriate to do so. To be a poet, however, is more than writing the occasional poem. The desire is not the deed; the recognition of the possibility of grace is not the achievement of grace. Poetry is a vocation, a delight, a discipline, a kind of necessity, an ache, occasionally a terrible pain. There isn't such a thing as a poet's career with a specific job description, promotion scheme and pension. The one thing certain is that being a poet in the sense of being engaged in the pursuit of writing poetry, trying to embody ever deeper, ever more complex experiences, memories and desires – in fact, ever more of life – in ever better poems is something quite distinct from whatever public success or status the person who is a poet may achieve or fail to achieve as a person. "Poetry begins in delight," said Frost, "and ends in wisdom." There is certainly the hope of wisdom – if nothing else, the wisdom of understanding what it means to articulate life in language.

This is what it is like being alive, says the poem. Speak it, sing it, whisper it.

Sheer poetry.

George Szirtes was born in Budapest in 1948 and came to England as a refugee in 1956. His poems began appearing in national magazines in 1973 and his first book, *The Slant Door*, was published in 1979, winning the Faber Memorial prize the following year – the first of many prizes including the TS Eliot Prize for Reel (Bloodaxe) in 2005.

Markets for poetry
A publisher writes

Does poetry ignore its audience? Do poets seeking publication often neglect the great poetic tradition that has gone before them, and pay scant attention to the poetry being written and published around them? **Neil Astley**, Editor at Bloodaxe, is the man who has to sift through all those manuscripts sent in hope. But he accuses the poetry world of often neglecting its duties, and reminds the poet firstly that s/he has an audience, and secondly that the road to publication is, indeed, a rocky one.

While a poet may not write *for* other readers, it's the *readership* that justifies publication. All editors are flooded with submissions of poetry from people whose desire to be published is greater than their desire to write well or to communicate – which must involve reading the work of poets from all periods. Few however seem to grasp that if you don't read poetry, you can't expect to be able to write poetry of any value; poetry that other people will want to read.

I would say that 95 per cent of the submissions I receive are unsuitable for book publication, for one of the following five reasons:

1. The so-called poet does not read poetry

This is the main reason for the rejection of most manuscripts. If you do not read much contemporary poetry, or if you write poetry "as a hobby", I'm unlikely to be interested in your work. You may disagree, but I believe that no one can write poetry of quality unless they read other poets and are in touch with the literary culture. I think you need to read poetry from all periods as well as contemporary poetry, and to have both an awareness and a *love* of English poetry from Shakespeare to Shapcott. If you also read other English-language poetry and poetry in translation or in the original language, so much the better. But if your knowledge of poetry stops at the beginning of the 20th century, don't even bother sending your work to any publisher or magazine. In poetry terms, you are an anachronism. If you don't talk like a person from the 18th or 19th century, why should you write like one?

Likewise, if you think your own work is much better than what today's poets have to offer the reader, and believe that publishers should see this – publishing you regardless of all the problems they have in marketing and disseminating poetry, because you are the real thing – forget it. You are deluded. You are out of touch not only with contemporary poetry, but also with the readers who buy (or don't buy) poetry books and are a truer test than even the poetry editors and reviewers.

2. It's a case of premature ejaculation

Before you even think about putting a book together, you should be submitting poems to magazines and pamphlet presses. Such a 'track record' is not used by publishers as a guarantee of quality, but as an indication that the writer has spent time building up a publishable collection. Trying to publish a book before you have had work taken by magazines is viewed by publishers as thinking you can run before you can walk. In sporting terms it would be like a Sunday afternoon footballer expecting to be picked to play for

England. I use the football metaphor deliberately here, because this kind of ignorance – which often borders on arrogance – is displayed more by young male writers than by women.

3. The poet is trying the wrong publisher

Don't submit to publishers unless you've read their books, or to magazines unless you're familiar with the kind of work they publish. Every imprint is different, and you will not be able to publish much unless you research the field and send to the publishers or magazines whose output you like and respect. The books I publish are those I respond to as a reader, and what interests me most is subject matter, breadth of vision and engagement with language. I look for an original voice and poetry showing a lively interplay of intellect and emotion. Technique has to be a *given* if a writer is expecting to publish a book: before I even begin to read and absorb a manuscript, I register immediately whether or not the work is well-crafted. If it's prose chopped into lines, or rhyming verse with no metre or rhythmical sense (the two most common crimes against poetry committed by unpublished writers), it goes straight back into the envelope. I have very wide taste – from traditional to postmodern – but there are publishers whose editors are only interested in certain kinds or schools of poetry.

4. The poet needs help, not publication

I can't offer detailed criticism of poetry submitted for publication. That's not the publisher's 'job'. But there are organisations offering critical services, writers' courses, workshops and mentoring, some of these via the Poetry Society. The Arvon Foundation's residential week-long writers' courses in Britain, based in Yorkshire, Devon, Scotland and now Shropshire, have been tremendously important, as has the Poetry School in London, and there are now postgraduate creative writing programmes at several universities – notably at East Anglia, City University and Goldsmiths College in London, Lancaster, Sheffield Hallam, Newcastle, Warwick, and the
Oscar Wilde Centre at Trinity College Dublin. Many poets who have published their first collections over the past two decades have benefited from working with established writers on their manuscripts by one or other of these methods.

5. It's a matter of sheer numbers

At Bloodaxe I receive around a hundred manuscripts, samples or letters offering collections every week. That's 5000 poets a year wanting to be taken on by just one publisher. Bloodaxe publishes 30 or so new books of poetry a year, but only one or two of those will be first collections: we have a stable of more than 200 already-published poets with new books coming out every month, as well as poets from America, Europe and the Commonwealth whose work we want to introduce to our readers. But along with all the other poetry publishers, Bloodaxe has had to reduce its output of new titles because the bookshops have been drastically reducing their ordering and stock range of poetry.

Apart from Bloodaxe, there are now only four other publishers in Britain actively publishing and distributing new books of poetry in significant numbers: Picador, Faber, Cape and Carcanet (including the Oxford/Carcanet list with separate Oxford University editors); in Ireland there is Gallery Press. None of the other commercial publishers has any commitment to new poets; Chatto only publishes Chatto poets and Harvill only publishes Paul Durcan, while Penguin publishes paperback editions of books originated by other publishers, or new books by really famous poets. Of the other small or specialist British poetry presses, only Anvil, Arc, Enitharmon, Flambard, Peterloo and Smith/Doorstop have active poetry lists, but are able to take on very few new poets. Peepal Tree concentrates on Black and Asian writers, and especially poetry (and fiction) from the Caribbean, while Seren has reverted to publishing only poets from Wales. Avant-garde or modernist poets are served by Shearsman and Salt (whose books are produced on a print-on-demand basis).

There are many presses producing pamphlets, including several recent ventures (notably Donut, Flarestack and Tall Lighthouse), but other small presses – such as Rockingham, Shoestring, Waywiser and Worple – produce only occasional collections in book form, mostly by writers with some kind of track record of publication. The only new imprints producing poetry in book form are Smokestack in Middlesbrough and a first-collection imprint run by *The Rialto* magazine. There are many poets in Britain who used to publish with commercial and specialist poetry publishers who no longer have their books in print, and who now have no possibility of having their new work taken on by those imprints which are still active. Many of those who rely upon readings or schools or community work for their livelihood have been resorting to self-publication (either getting printers to produce their books and then storing them, or using print-on-demand publishers and selling from a website).

The main reason why the poetry publishers have had to cut back is the rationalisation of the UK book trade which followed the demise of the Net Book Agreement, when the bookshops were forced to compete with the supermarkets for their share of the bestseller market. The big chains have been doing what they call 'professionalising' their operations: this means telling publishers they will only stock their books if they give them a minimum of 50 per cent discount, which is unviable for the short print run economies of specialist areas of cultural publishing such as poetry. The main bookshops are stocking less and less poetry, concentrating mainly on better-selling titles such as anthologies and 'selecteds' by big-name authors. As a direct result of this, all the poetry publishers have reduced their output of new titles. But most haven't helped themselves or their poets. Continuing to package their books to appeal only to an intellectual elite has severely disadvantaged them in the marketplace. If readers find a book cover visually unappealing, they won't pick up the book. And if the back cover blurb is a piece of literary criticism more concerned with craft than with content, new readers will be put off. Reducing print runs has also meant that many poetry publishers have had to increase their cover prices, which in turn has further affected their sales. But an even more damaging cause of the downturn in poetry sales has been the huge gulf which exists between poetry publishing and the grassroots readership.

Readers don't have access to the diverse range of poetry being written, not just in Britain, but around in the world, because much of the poetry establishment – including many publishers and reviewers – has become narrowly based, male-dominated, white, Anglo-centric and skewed by factions and vested interests. Too often, poetry editors think of themselves and their poet friends as the sole arbiters of taste, only publishing writers whom they think people *ought* to read and depriving readers of other kinds of poetry that many people would find more rewarding. Publishers and writers who address a broader readership are attacked by elitist critics for 'dumbing down', but receive overwhelming support from readers as well as from the more intelligent poets. Publishers have also been unresponsive to much poetry by women (who comprise over two-thirds of poetry's readership) as well as to writing from Britain's rapidly growing ethnic population. Ignoring the readership would be commercial suicide in any other field, but this malpractice in poetry publishing and reviewing has survived into the 21st century because of what one might call 'academic protectionism'.

A recent report in *The Observer* quoted the latest statistics: sales of poetry in Britain last year sank to 890,000 books, the worst performance in years, while sales of fiction soared to nearly 46 million books. The only British poetry publisher whose sales have been increasing is Bloodaxe – and that's because we've been reaching a broader readership through imaginative, anti-elitist marketing which ensures that we are connecting with the readership at grassroots level. And as if to show how inept the poetry community is in reaching a wider audience, the bookshop statistics for sales during the week of National Poetry Day in October over the past five years show that sales of poetry books actually go *down* in that week, when the media are giving contemporary poetry its biggest publicity boost of the whole year. Whatever interest in poetry that activity creates, it isn't something that's making people want to *read* more poetry books. While poetry has been receiving more feature coverage in the press, the amount and quality of serious review coverage has declined. And because it's often three or four months before the reviews start appearing in the papers, by the time you see the reviews and are prompted to go and look for the book in the shop, many titles may have been returned because without the publicity they haven't sold any copies.

Too many poetry reviews in national newspapers are written by poets or critics who don't review the books for the reader of the newspaper, but instead discuss their content in minute and acutely critical detail in terms which are only comprehensible or of interest to academics or other poets. They use the same critical language and terms of reference when reviewing for a newspaper as for a specialist poetry magazine, weaving strings of quotations broken up by slashes into a text-linked commentary which means nothing to anyone who hasn't already read the book. Many of these reviews read like potted academic essays. Even dedicated poetry-readers find them difficult to follow. Positive reviews written in this inappropriate critical jargon don't encourage potential readers to seek out the books; they put them off.

But few people seem to care about the poor reader now, or about choice and range of titles. The monster of Thatcherism may have been vanquished in Britain but the dragon's curse has paralysed many areas of our culture, from supermarket-style bookselling to the performance-related criteria of university management (the poets of Oxford University Press's former poetry list being just the latest casualties: their books didn't make a loss, but they didn't make enough profit).

Poets write poetry. Publishers sell it. Readers buy the books and read them. Poetry doesn't sell purely on merit, especially in the current commercial climate – it has to be marketed to reach its potential readership. While a poet may not write *for* other readers, it's the *readership* that justifies publication. Any poet who thinks otherwise is a deluded egotist, and most readers aren't actually interested in reading poetry written out of such an arrogant mindset. All of which brings me full circle back to where I started this piece: that publishers publish for readers, not to serve the vanities of poets or to follow poetical orthodoxies and fashions. But if you are a passionate *reader* of poetry – and don't just want to write the stuff – and even more importantly, if you really do have something to *say* in your work, and a distinctively original way of saying it, your conviction and persistence may eventually result in you having a book published. Wanting to write must come before wanting to be a writer. But don't underestimate the difficulties. It is a very difficult field to break into.

Neil Astley is Editor of Bloodaxe Books, a not-for-profit limited liability company supported by Arts Council England, specialising in publishing the best contemporary poetry.

The long and winding road to publication

Publisher **Alex Macmillan** explains the difficulties that await the poet attempting to get published. All is not lost, however, as he explores the different outlets that do exist for poets.

Dozens of independent presses scattered across the British Isles publish hundreds of poets and broadly represent the range of contemporary poetry being written, as well as reflecting the poetic tastes of editors. The publishing activities of these presses are diverse: many specialise in publishing periodic magazines featuring several poets; some publish magazines and individual collections; others publish pamphlets and magazines; a few publish pamphlets; many publish on the Internet, and so on. Most of the printed magazine presses are available mainly through subscription, and if they are displayed in bookshops, their availability in retail outlets is limited. The publishing landscape for aspiring and established poets is as confusing as it is diverse. Numerous publishing opportunities appear to beckon, yet it is difficult to get work published even in magazines, and the process – even after acceptance of work – is often time-consuming. And post-publication, a poet's life may not change radically.

Poetry collections and pamphlets from independent presses are rarely available on high-street retail bookshelves. Most are easier to find through publishers' dedicated websites or consortia of small presses like Inpress or Independent Northern Publishers.

Templar Poetry has established a poetry press in response to the often difficult publishing and working environment that poets encounter when they seek wider exposure of their work. Although it may seem perverse, this is an appropriate moment at which to establish an independent press with innovative approaches to publishing poetry. Revolutions in print and communication technologies enable small publishing organisations to operate alongside larger ones in publishing new authors into wide markets, and reach their readers and audiences effectively. Furthermore, the new technologies provide independent publishers with exciting opportunities to transmit the best new writing, in diverse styles and new formats. Templar Poetry, for example, will be publishing its first pamphlet with a CD audio insert in October, and plans to offer the option of simultaneous text and audio publication to all its authors from 2007.

For most aspiring poets seeking publication of their work, there are a range of pressures (some perceived, others imagined) from within poetry's celestial circles and academies, collectively defining who is the 'real thing' and who is not. Some of these camps hold on to an elitist position that emerged from modernism and several modernist poets, whose influence and power is still assiduously maintained, often with a chilling and overbearing 'authority'. Some would argue that it is like a poison preventing poetry from developing a much wider and more popular following. The elitists are often linked to various academies and groups of one persuasion or another, and can hold specific and sometimes narrow views of what 'ought' to be regarded as 'real' poetry. Unfortunately for writers of poetry, poetry is not a broad church exercising wide tolerance for the range of 'poetries' that are written and published, which collectively represent the genre. Aspiring new poets find themselves writing and submitting their work in a fraught environment where they struggle through a labyrinthine critical system dependent on extensive peer review, in the quest to seek the 'validity' (or otherwise) of their work.

Sadly, the journey rarely encourages hope and aspiration. One high-profile annual national competition aimed at young new poets explicitly tells winners to dumb down any poetic career expectations, and expect to maintain a day job as well – as TS Eliot did for most of his career. However, in a world where sports practitioners are paid handsomely for playing even the most obscure sports badly, it is not unreasonable to advocate that good new poets be offered the opportunity to earn a reasonable income as working poets. It is also true that the most substantial poetry market (with a handful of high-profile exceptions) in published poetry comes from the work of poets whose poetry has apparently become more important after their death. There is much work to be done by poets, publishers, and both the published and the broadcast media to work together in raising the public profile and recognition of the best contemporary poetry – bringing more poetry back into the living language of our culture, and enabling poets to earn a fair and appropriate reward for their work.

Conventional wisdom suggests several routes to publication. The most commonly held is the road taken by developing a track record of magazine publication, perhaps achieving some success in major open competitions, and pamphlet publication – leading finally to the publication of a full collection. Another possible route to publication is through attending creative writing courses or workshops, which are now widely offered by universities and colleges as well as by dedicated poetry writing organisations like the Arvon Foundation and The Poetry School. Information on poetry writing courses and workshops is available on the Internet and is also often advertised in public libraries. The Poetry Society, The Poetry Library in London, and the Scottish Poetry Library provide extensive information with links on their respective websites for practising poets.

Most magazine publishers recommend that poets read their magazines prior to submission, to establish whether or not their style of poetry is likely to fit in with the published poets. Submissions to some magazines gain almost instant responses one way or the other; others take months or even longer to respond; and some expect writers to submit several times before serious consideration is given to their work. It is hard work submitting to magazines and it is best to keep a record. Many will be upset if you submit the same poem or poems simultaneously to other magazines or competitions and then receive simultaneous offers of publication. Poets should do their homework on their submission strategies and appreciate that magazines are often keen to discover new writers first. They should also temper their judgement in the knowledge that it is difficult to get accepted in the first instance. Some magazines have single editors; others have several readers who will decide which poetry to accept and publish. Some pay nominal amounts for publication; others not at all – however, poets should always retain copyright of their work. Most magazines indicate reading times for submissions, but a realistic strategy is probably to choose a few magazines and send poems to them on several occasions. Do not expect a critique of your work on its return; a brief pithy remark expressing some level of interest may occasionally encourage you to submit again.

Poetry competitions run all year round, and single poem competitions are numerous; details are readily available from Internet search engines. There are several dedicated poetry websites, such as **Poetrykit**, which list most of the competitions with closing dates, and give links to appropriate websites that provide access to entry forms and competion rules. These competitions do not usually lead to wider publication, but some single-poem competitions have substantial cash prizes and are widely 'respected' in the poetry world. The biggest of these competitions include the National Poetry Prize, The Arvon Prize (biennial), The Academi Cardiff International Competition, and the Bridport Prize.

Poets who have accumulated a body of work may opt to submit to pamphlet competitions, where their work will usually be read by poets with significant national or international reputations. If judged to be of sufficient quality, their work may be put forward for publication as a small collection or pamphlet. This is often regarded as a first step towards publishing a full collection. The entry fees for these competitions tend to be higher than for single-poem competitions, but the potential outcomes in terms of publication and career development are more extensive.

Writers who have arrived at a point where they are confident that they have a substantial body of work which merits consideration for publication as a full collection should research the publication opportunities available and consider which publishing house might look at their work. This should involve an awareness of the published poets of any given publishing house: too many writers do not appear to read contemporary poetry. Individual publishers, large and small, usually post submission guidelines and information on their websites, but these tend to vary and writers should always check the current submission situation with any preferred publishers. Larger poetry publishers such as Faber, Cape, Picador and the large independents like Bloodaxe and Carcanet vary in their submission policies, and writers should look at their websites or contact the relevant poetry editor when they are considering submission (do not always expect rapid responses, even to minor questions). One poet I am aware of with an impressive 'track record' submitted work to one of the larger independents and waited for almost three years for a negative response. This poet has subsequently been published elsewhere, but such a response timescale is not unusual, and is certainly detrimental to the development of new poets and public access to their work. Their work may be several years 'out of date' by the time it is published. Poets, even if they are very very good indeed, need to take the view that if you can't go through an obstacle, go around it – water does.

Alex Macmillan is Managing Editor of Templar Poetry, a new independent press which publishes contemporary poetry and facilitates and promotes wider access to poetry in the community. Templar Poetry aims to bring a refreshing and unfettered approach to publishing poetry, and is committed to ensuring that poetry engages with new readers. To find out more, or to submit your work, visit **www.templarpoetry.co.uk**.

Publishers UK and Ireland

The poetry publishing world is like an iceberg: seven-eighths of it takes place beneath the surface, with dozens of small presses publishing sometimes only a handful of books a year. It has to be said that the few major publishers showing above the surface still do not publish a huge number of new poets. Therefore, it pays to carry out some research before sending off the manuscript you have been sweating over for years. Investigate what kind of poetry a publisher is interested in, and ensure that they are happy to receive material. An email or a letter in advance could save everyone time and prevent you from having any misplaced optimism about being published. Submissions should *always* be accompanied by an sae if a response is required.

Abbey Press

Courtenay Hill, Newry, Co Down,
Northern Ireland BT34 2ED
tel 028-3026 3142 *fax* 028-3026 2514
email adrianrice@earthlink.net
website www.geocities.com/abbeypress
Editor Adrian Rice

A fast-growing literary publisher with a strong poetry list. Also publishes biography, memoirs, fiction, history, politics and academic titles. Since 1997 has published 15 poetry books, including works from major Irish poets like Michael Longley and Brendan Kennelly.

Acair

7 James Street, Stornoway,
Isle of Lewis HS1 2QN
tel (01851) 703020
email info@acairbooks.com
website www.acairbooks.com
Contact Norma Macleod

Publishes all categories of fiction and non-fiction for children in the Gaelic language. Adult books relating to the Gaidhealtachd, history, music, poetry, biography, environmental studies, Gaelic language.

Acorn Book Company

PO Box 191, Tadworth, Surrey KT20 5YQ
email info@acornbook.co.uk
website www.acornbook.co.uk

An independent publisher specialising in small, high-quality editions. Publishes haiku and minimalist poetry and literature in translation.

Agenda Editions

The Wheelwrights, Fletching Street, Mayfield,
East Sussex TN20 6TL
tel (01435) 873703
email editor@agendapoetry.co.uk
website www.agendapoetry.co.uk
Editor Patricia McCarthy

A small independent poetry publishing press run in tandem with *Agenda Poetry Journal*. It publishes small, individual collections by poets considered by the editor to be worthy of promoting.
    Submission details Send hard copies in a folder, each page numbered and with name, address and email clearly marked.

Akros Publications

33 Lady Nairn Avenue, Kirkcaldy,
Fife KY1 2AW
website www.akrospublications.co.uk

Publisher of poetry in paperback and pamphlet format.

Alison Allison

Double Dykes, Elm Row, Galashiels TD1 3HT
tel (01896) 753728
email alisonallisondouble@yahoo.co.uk
website www.scottish-pamphlet-poetry.com
Contact Alison Allison

A Scottish pamphlet publisher.

Angel Books

3 Kelross Road, London N5 2QS
tel 020-7359 3143
email woodangel@ukonline.co.uk
Contact Anthony Wood

Anvil Press Poetry

Neptune House, 70 Royal Hill,
London SE10 8RF
tel 020-8469 3033 *fax* 020-8469 3363
email anvil@anvilpresspoetry.com
website www.anvilpresspoetry.com
Director Peter Jay

Founded by Peter Jay in 1968. Anvil Press Poetry is England's longest-standing independent poetry publisher. It publishes the best of English-language poets: Martina Evans, AB Jackson, Dennis O'Driscoll, Greta Stoddart, Dick Davis, James Harpur, Michael Hamburger and others. In addition, Anvil's backlist includes several Nobel prize laureates and has a deserved reputation for poets in the international canon (Apollinaire, Baudelaire, Bei Dao, Goethe, Hikmet, Lorca, Neruda, Seferis, Tagore, etc.). Publishes about 12 new titles annually. For those who wish to familiarise themselves with the flavour of the list, Anvil's 30th anniversary anthology, *The Spaces of Hope*, gives a perfect starting point.

Arc Publications

Nanhome Hill, Shaw Wood Road, Todmorden, Lancashire OL14 6DA
tel (01706) 812338 *fax* (01706) 818948
email arc.publications@btconnect.com
website www.arcpublications.co.uk
Editor Tony Ward

Publishes new and established writers from the UK, English-speaking, international poets, and bilingual translation editions.

Submission details Submissions are not encouraged, but all must include publishing history and be familiar with type of work normally published. No electronic communication and no response unless an sae is included.

Arehouse

72 Sedgwick Street, Cambridge CB1 3AL
email arehouse@cambridgepoetry.org
website www.cambridgepoetry.org/arehouse.htm
Editor Neil Pattison, Sam Ladkin

Argyll Publishing

Glendaruel, Colintraive, Argyll PA22 3AE
tel (01369) 820229
email info@argyllpublishing.co.uk
website www.argyllpublishing.com
Contact Sean Bradley

Argyll Publishing was established in 1992; from its base in Glendaruel it produces a general list of titles. It has a fiction/poetry imprint, Thirsty Books.

Arrowhead Press

70 Clifton Road, Darlington,
Co Durham DL1 5DX
website www.arrowheadpress.co.uk
Poetry Editor Joanna Boulter

A small press specialising in the publication of quality books and pamphlets of contemporary poetry. Aims to provide a platform for poets to cross the difficult gap between magazine publication and first pamphlet or full collection. This does not, however, preclude publication of more established authors.

Submission details Submit by post, including a brief biography and publishing history. You must already have been published in reputable magazines or have had a pamphlet published.

Atlantean Publishing

38 Pierrot Steps, 71 Kursaal Way,
Southend-on-Sea, Essex SS1 2UY
email atlantean publishing@hotmail.com
website www.geocities.com/dj-tyrer/atlantean_pub.html
Editor DJ Tyrer

A non-profit small press seeking poetry in all styles, lengths and genres for inclusion in its magazines and collections. It also produces solo-poet broadsheets and chapbooks.

Submission details Unsolicited submissions accepted via post (with sae) or email. Poet receives complimentary copies as payment.

Avalanche Books

130 Oxford Street, Totterdown,
Bristol BS3 4RH
tel 0117-377 0007
email deborahgaye@blueyonder.co.uk

Specialises in cutting-edge, high-quality poetry.

Bad Press

email badpress@gmail.com
website http://badpress.infinology.net

Publishes conceptually uncompromising, linguistically innovative, and politically informed poetry.

Barque Press

c/o Andrea Brady, 70a Cranwich Road,
London N16 5JD
email info@barquepress.com
website www.barquepress.com
Contacts Andrea Brady, Dr Keston Sutherland

Founded by Andrea Brady and Keston Sutherland in 1995; since then, has published more than 30 chapbooks and four perfect-bound books. Published poets are from the UK, the US, France and Canada. In addition to these text-based publications, it has produced four CDs, which include spoken-word performances by a variety of artists alongside improvisational music.

Between the Lines
14 Lyncroft Gardens, Ewell, Surrey KT17 1UR
tel 020-8393 7055
email btluk@aol.com
website www.waywiser-press.com/imprints/
betweenthelines.html
Contact Philip Hoy

Produces book-length interviews with established poets of note, chosen by an editorial board. Has published 14 volumes to date, including in most not just the interview, but also a career sketch, a comprehensive bibliography, career-spanning critical quotations and, in more recent volumes, a gallery of photos.

Bewrite Books
32 Bryn Road South, Ashton in Makerfield, Wigan, Lancashire WN4 8QR
website www.bewrite.net

Founded in 2004. Since its inception, this editorially driven publishing house has released more than 20 paperback titles a year, in several genres (each backed by eBook versions).

Birlinn Ltd
West Newington House, 10 Newington Road, Edinburgh EH9 1QS
tel 0131-668 4371 *fax* 0131-668 4466
email info@birlinn.co.uk
website www.birlinn.co.uk
Managing Director Hugh Andrew

Publishes a wide range of books of Scottish interest. Its Polygon imprint publishes modern and classic Scottish poetry, including Liz Lochead and Norman MacCaig, in addition to anthologies.

Biscuit Publishing
email info@biscuitpublishing.com
website www.biscuitpublishing.com
Contact Brian Lister

Founded in 2000 by the Lister family. Publishes mainly fiction, some non-fiction, and very occasionally poetry.

Submission details All publications are by Biscuit prize winners, or by selected authors approached and commissioned by Biscuit. See website for details.

Black Spring Press Ltd
Curtain House, 134-146 Curtain Road, London EC2A 3AR
tel 020-7613 3066 *fax* 020-7613 0028
email enquiries@blackspringpress.co.uk
website www.blackspringpress.co.uk

Specialises in the contemporary, as well as breathing new life into neglected classics. Since 1985 it has produced work by Nick Cave, Anaïs Nin, Charles Baudelaire, Kyril Bonfiglioli, Carolyn Cassady and Leonard Cohen, among many others.

Blackstaff Press
4c Heron Wharf, Sydenham Business Park, Belfast BT3 9LE
email info@blackstaff.com
website www.blackstaffpress.com
Contact Stefan Baxter

Launched in Belfast in 1971, Blackstaff Press is now regarded as one of Ireland's foremost publishers. Over 750 titles have been published, covering a wide range of subjects. The Press provides an important platform for creative writers and artists; its contribution to cultural life is recognised in the generous assistance it receives from the Arts Council of Northern Ireland. Blackstaff books are produced to the highest standards by a prize-winning team of editors and designers, and professional in-house marketing staff ensure effective sales distribution throughout the world.

Submission details Submit 10-12 poems with covering letter and short biography. See website for more details.

Bloodaxe Books Ltd
Highgreen, Tarset, Northumberland NE48 1RP
tel (01434) 240500 *fax* (01434) 240505
email editor@bloodaxebooks.com
website www.bloodaxebooks.com
Directors Neil Astley, Simon Thirsk

Poetry, literary criticism. Send sample of up to a dozen poems with sae. No email submissions or correspondence. No disks. Founded 1978.

Bluechrome Publishing

PO Box 109, Portishead, Bristol BS20 7ZJ
tel (07092) 273360
email anthony@bluechrome.co.uk
website www.bluechrome.co.uk
Editor Anthony Delgrado

Established in 2002 as an independent publisher of poetry and some fiction. Has published a wide range of styles. Poets include: DM Thomas, James Kirkup, Alexis Lykiard, Rupert Loydell and Kevin Bailey.

Submission details Submission guidelines can be found on the website; submissions by email are preferred.

Bogle L'Ouverture Press

PO Box 2186, London W13 9QZ
tel 020-8579 4920
email bogle.louverture@btinternet.com
Contact EL Huntley

Mainly interested in work giving a positive stance to the African diaspora.

Bradshaw Books (Tigh Filí)

tel ++353 21 4509274
email info@tighfili.com
website www.tighfili.com
Contact Máire Bradshaw

Bradshaw Books provides an outlet in publishing for new names in poetry. It has published many previously unknown writers who have gone on to greater success.

Brindin Press

Drake Wood, Devonshire Avenue, Amersham, Buckinghamshire HP6 5JF
tel (01494) 726214 *fax* (01494) 432281
email brindinpress@aol.com
website www.brindin.com

A not-for-profit operation that maintains the Brindin Press website.

Submission details Submit by post or email.

The Brodie Press

c/o Department of English,
University of Bristol, 3/5 Woodland Road,
Bristol BS8 1TB

email thebrodiepress@hotmail.com
website www.brodiepress.co.uk
Contact Tom Sperlinger

A small independent press, which publishes individual volumes of poetry and anthologies. Aims to give new writers a voice and to allow established writers the opportunity to undertake unusual or experimental projects.

Jonathan Cape

The Random House Group,
20 Vauxhall Bridge Road, London SW1V 2SA
tel 020-7840 8400 *fax* 020-7828 6681
website www.randomhouse.co.uk
Editor Robin Robertson

Robin Robertson presides over one of the UK's most exciting poetry lists, including Anne Carson, John Burnside, Michael Symmons Roberts, Sharon Olds, Michael Longley and Peter Redgrave.

Carcanet Press Ltd

4th Floor, Alliance House, 28-34 Cross Street, Manchester M2 7AQ
tel 0161-834 8730 *fax* 0161-832 0084
email info@carcanet.co.uk
website www.carcanet.co.uk
Director Michael Schmidt

Poetry, *Fyfield* series, Oxford Poets, translations. Founded 1969.

Cargo Press

The Annex, Penhaver House, Cliff Road, Gorran Haven PL26 6JN
tel (07813) 930827
email info@cargo-press.co.uk
website www.cargo-press.co.uk
Contact Derek Hines

Cargo Press is a small press based in Cornwall. It publishes limited editions of poetry and *belles-lettres* to a very high standard.

The Celtic Cross Press

Ovins Well House, Lastingham,
York YO62 6TJ
tel (01751) 417298
email info@celticcrosspress.com
website www.celticcrosspress.com

Prints and publishes limited editions of fine books. Publishes poetry and short works of prose, hand-printed by letterpress, on fine paper and bound in full cloth covered boards. Each copy is numbered and signed.

Chapman Publishing

4 Broughton Place, Edinburgh EH1 3RX
tel 0131-557 2207
email chapman-pub@blueyonder.co.uk
website www.chapman-pub.co.uk
Contact Joy Hendry

Founded in 1986, Chapman Publishing sprang from the idea that poets published in *Chapman Magazine* were not getting a voice in poetry collections. Poetry remains at the heart of the company, with books by Dilys Rose, George Gunn, Magi Gibson and Janet Paisley among recent titles.

Submission details Priority is given to poets published in *Chapman Magazine*. Other writers are unlikely to be considered.

Chatto & Windus

The Random House Group,
20 Vauxhall Bridge Road, London SW1V 2SA
tel 020-7840 8400 *fax* 020-7828 6681
website www.randomhouse.co.uk

Publishes a small amount of poetry.

Cinnamon Press

Meirion House, Glanyrafon, Tanygrrsiau,
Blawnau Ffestiniog LL41 3SU
tel (01766) 832 2112
email jan@cinnamonpress.com
website www.cinnamonppress.com
Contact Jan Fortune-Wood

Small press publishing mainly poetry, including first collections. Holds annual competitions to select first collections for publication. Also publishes *Coffee House Poetry Magazine*.

Submission details Submit 10 poems with covering letter and writing credits, initially. See website for full details.

Clo Iar-Chonnachta

Indrebhan, Co Galway, Ireland
tel ++353 91 593 307
email cic@iol.ie
website www.cic.ie

Located in Connemara, Galway, publishing books primarily in Irish.

Clutag Press

PO Box 154, Thame OX9 3RQ
email mervynlinford@aol.com
website www.clutagpress.com
Contact Andrew McNeillie

Established in 2000 to issue Clutag Poetry Leaflets, by established and emerging poets.

Cois Life

62 Páirc na Rós, Ascaill na Cille,
Dún Laoghaire, Co Bhaile Átha Cliath, Éire
tel (01) 2807 951
email eolas@coislife.ie
Contact Dr Caoilfhionn Nic Pháidín

Cois Life was established in 1995 to publish literary and research works in the Irish language. Publishes books for learners of Irish, for young people and also plays, fiction and poetry.

The Collective Press

c/o Penlanas Farm, Llantilio, Y-fenni,
Gwent NP7 7HN
tel (01873) 859559
email through website
website www.welshwriters.com
Coordinator John Jones *Editor* Frank Olding

A not-for-profit organisation supported by the Welsh Arts Council and staffed by volunteers. Main aim is to promote and publish contemporary poetry without regard to race, religion or profit.

Submission details Postal submissions only.

Comma Poetry Press

3 Vale Bower, Mytholmroyd,
West Yorkshire HX7 5EP
tel (07792) 564747
website www.commapress.co.uk/poetry
Contact Ra Page

Set up to discover and promote the best in new British poetry, as well as to support established poets, through anthologies and single poet collections.

Community of Poets & Artists Press

26 St Mildred's Avenue, Minnis Bay,
Kent CT7 9LD
tel (01843) 842780
email bennetta.artco@virgin.net
website www.artistspress.co.uk

Printmakers and publishers with an increasing focus on printing and publishing original artwork and poetry/text. The press is based in Kent, and produces special-edition fine books, artists' books and hand-sewn collections. Has an online poetry magazine and exhibition space. Produces a poetry journal, *Community of Poets*.

Crocus Books

Commonword, 6 Mount Street, Manchester M2 5NS
tel 0161-832 3777
website www.commonword.org.uk

The publishing imprint of Commonword and Cultureword. Publishes paperback poetry and fiction reflecting the diverse talents of North West writers, and bringing those talents to a national audience.

David Paul Books

25 Methuen Park, London N10 2JR
tel (07958) 991121 *fax* 020-8444 8698
email info@davidpaulbooks.com
website www.davidpaulbooks.com

Publishes books and translations of Jewish and international interest, including fiction, history, memoir and poetry.

Dedalus Poetry Press

13 Moyclare Road, Baldoyle, Dublin 13, Ireland
email editor@dedaluspress.com
website www.dedaluspress.com
Contact Pat Boran

Poetry from Ireland and around the world.
Submission details Always include sufficient return postage and a self-addressed envelope with your work, together with a short covering letter giving details of previous publications. Expect a response time of approximately 3 months.

Deliberately Thirsty

Argyll Publishing, Glendaruel, Argyll
email thirstybooks@hotmail.com
website www.deliberatelythirsty.co.uk

Poetry imprint of Argyll Publishing.

Diamond Twig

PO Box 279, Newcastle upon Tyne NE6 5ZE
tel 0191-276 3770

email diamond.twig@virgin.net
website www.diamondtwig.co.uk
Contact Ellen Phethean

A women's press based in North East England. Publishes poetry and short stories for new women writers with a Northern connection.
Submission details Always write or email before submitting. Does not accept unsolicited material.

Dionysia Press Ltd

127 Milton Road West,
7 Duddingston House Courtyard,
Edinburgh EH15 1JG
Contact Denise Smith

Submission details Submit MSS of circa 100 pages or less; no less than 65 pages.

Doghouse

PO Box 312, Tralee GPO, Tralee Co Kerry, Ireland
tel ++353 6671 37547
email doghouse312@circom.net
website www.doghousebooks.ie
Contact The Editor

Founded in 2003 to publish poets and short-story writers who are Irish-born or usually resident in Ireland, and who have established records in the small presses, journals, magazines, etc.
Submission details Send 4 hard copies of full manuscript (40-60 poems) with CV and publishing credits.

Donut Press

PO Box 45093, London N4 1UZ
email donutpress@hotmail.co.uk
website www.donutpress.co.uk
Editorial/Sales Andy Ching

Small poetry press publishing 2 pocketbooks per year and occasional full collections.
Submission details Submissions by post, accompanied by sae.

Dreadful Night Press

82 Kelvin Court, Glasgow G12 0AQ
tel 0141-339 9150
email dreadfulnight1@aol.com
website www.scottish-pamphlet-poetry.com

A Scottish pamphlet publisher.

Driftwood Publications
5 Timms Lane, Freshfield,
Merseyside L37 7DW
tel 0151-525 0417 *fax* 0151-524 0216
email janet.speedy@tesco.net
Contact Janet Speedy

Attempts to provide outlets (books, readings,
etc.) for poets whose work has been hitherto
neglected – new or established poets who are
no longer on the lists of larger presses. "Poetry
for the page more than for the stage."
  Submission details Unsolicited manuscripts
welcome.

Earlyworks Press
45 Robertson Street, Hastings,
Sussex TN34 1HL
website www.earlyworkspress.co.uk

Produces at least 3 anthologies a year, based on
its Open Competitions, plus at least one special
genre challenge. Altogether, this gives an
opportunity for 50-100 writers and illustrators
to publish in book form.

Egg Box Publishing
25 Brian Avenue, Norwich NR1 2PH
tel (01603) 470191
email mail@eggboxpublishing.com
website www.eggboxpublishing.com
Editor Alexander Gordon Smith, Nathan
Hamilton

Publishes first collections by some of the best
new poets around the country. Also runs
Eggbox magazine.
  Submission details Submissions should be
accompanied by a brief biography. No email
submissions.

Enitharmon Press
26B Caversham Road, London NW5 2DU
tel 020-7482 5967 *fax* 020-7284 1787
email info@enitharmon.co.uk
website www.enitharmon.co.uk
Director Stephen Stuart-Smith

Poetry, literary criticism, fiction, translations,
artists' books. Founded 1967.
  Submission details No unsolicited MSS. No
freelance editors or proofreaders required.

Equipage
Jesus College, Cambridge CB5 8BL
email equipage@cambridgepoetry.org
website www.cambridgepoetry.org/
equipage.htm

Editor Rod Mengham
Small press operating out of Cambridge.

Essence Press
8 Craiglea Drive, Edinburgh EH10 5PA
email jaj@essencepress.co.uk
website www.essencepress.co.uk
Contact Julie Johnston

Publishes small editions of poetry, some
handbound, with emphasis on landscape and
the natural world.
  Submission details Send a hard-copy sample
of work, with sae.

Etruscan Books
28 Fowler's Court, Fore Street, Buckfastleigh,
Devon TQ11 0AA
email etruscan@macunlimited.net
website www.seaham.i12.com/etruscan
Contact Nicholas Johnson

Poetry publisher with a book club.

Everyman – see The Orion Publishing Group Ltd

Faber and Faber Ltd*
3 Queen Square, London WC1N 3AU
tel 020-7465 0045 *fax* 020-7465 0034
website www.faber.co.uk
Chief Executive & Publisher Stephen Page,
Commercial Director David Tebbutt, *Editorial
Directors* Lee Brackstone, Walter Donohue,
Julian Loose, Belinda Matthews, *Sales Director*
Will Atkinson, *Publicity Director & Associate
Publisher, Original Arts* Rachel Alexander,
Marketing Director Jo Ellis, *Production Director*
Nigel Marsh, *Rights Director* Jason Cooper,
Head of Children's Fiction Julia Wells

High-quality general fiction and non-fiction,
children's fiction and non-fiction, drama, film,
music, poetry. Unsolicited submissions
accepted for poetry only. For information on
poetry submission procedures, ring 020-7465
0189, or consult the website. No unsolicited
MSS.

Fal Publications
PO Box 74, Truro, Cornwall TR1 1XS
tel (07887) 560018
email info@falpublications.co.uk
website www.falpublications.co.uk

Editor Victoria Field

An award-winning small press based in Cornwall, publishing books by such writers as DM Thomas, Victoria Field, Jane Tozer and Angela Stoner. Books have a strong visual identity and all have a clear connection with Cornwall.

Submission details No unsolicited submissions. Enquire by email first.

Feather Books

PO Box 438, Shrewesbury,
Shropshire SY3 0WN
tel (01743) 872177
email john@waddysweb.freeuk.com
website www.waddysweb.freeuk.com/
Contact Rev John Waddington-Feather

Publisher of Christian poetry, music and drama. With its associate company, Moorside Words and Music, it also produces CDs/cassettes and audio-books.

Fighting Cock Press

45 Middlethorpe Drive, York YO24 1NA
Editor Pauline Kirk

Very small non-profit-making press, specialising in high-quality poetry and short prose from the north of England.

Five Leaves Publishing

PO Box 81, Nottingham NG5 4ER
tel 0115-969 3597
email info@fiveleaves.co.uk
website www.fiveleaves.co.uk
Contact Ross Bradshaw

Small publisher, specialising in social history, regional writers and Jewish secular culture. Collections include: *Red Sky at Night: An Anthology Of Socialist Poetry*.

Submission details All work is commissioned. No unsolicited submissions.

Five Seasons Press

41 Green Street, Hereford HR1 2QH
tel (01432) 261100
email books@fiveseasonspress.com
website www.fiveseasonspress.com
Contact Glenn Storhaug

Publishes a few carefully produced titles each year, in collaboration with poets who fuss over

the sound and etymology of every word. Parallel-text translations are always of interest.

Submission details Send letter (not email) with an account of the proposed book's structure, and no more than 6 sample poems/pages. See the website for further guidelines.

Flambard Press

Stable Cottage, East Fourstones, Hexham, Northumberland NE47 5DX
tel (01434) 674360 *fax* (01434) 674178
email flambardpress@btinternet.com
website www.flambardpress.co.uk
Managing Editor Peter Lewis *Deputy Editor* Will Mackie

Publishes poetry and literary fiction, but only 4-5 books of poetry a year. Consider proposals from everywhere, but has a particular interest in writers living in the north of England. Good track record of magazine and/or pamphlet publication normally required. Founded 1990.

Submission details Only hard-copy submissions of a sample of 10-15 poems with sae will be considered; these should be accompanied by a short biographical note and list of previous publications. Preliminary letter advisable. No phone calls, emails or faxes. See website for further information.

Flarestack Publishing

41 Buckley's Green, Alvechurch, Birmingham B48 7NG
tel 0121-445 2110
Editor Charles Johnson

Flarestack has been publishing stapled A5 pamphlet collections by new poets since 1995. Poetic excellence and coherence override commercial viability and the whims of poetic fashion. Combining simple production methods with an eye for colour and style, each pamphlet is carefully designed as an individual hand-crafted object with its own look.

Flax Books

PO Box 751, Lancaster LA1 9AJ
tel (01524) 62166
website www.litfest.org

Digital and print publishers showcasing writers from Lancashire and Cumbria. Launched by Litfest. Aims to highlight contemporary voices from this diverse region of England.

Flipped Eye Publishing Ltd
tel 0845-430 9517 *fax* 0845-430 9518
email books@ flippedeye.net
website www.flippedeye.net

Formed in Ghana by a group of schoolfriends in a bid to start a literature revival in the country. The UK company was established in 2001. Aims to produce consistently high-quality fiction, non-fiction and related products, with a focus on poetry; also, to raise the profile of performance and oral literature as legitimate and viable forms of artistic interpretation and learning.

Forward Press Ltd
Remus House, Coltsfoot Drive, Woodston, Peterborough PE2 9JX
tel (01733) 898105
email info@forwardpress.co.uk
website www.forwardpress.co.uk
Head of Imprints Steve Twelvetree

Founded in 1989 by poet Ian Walton, the company has published more than 900,000 original poems. Sees itself as a bridge to publication, rather than a barrier, giving everyone the opportunity to see their work in print. Writing initiatives include: Anchor Books; Poetry Now; Strong Word; WomensWords; Triumph House; Spotlight Poets; New Fiction; Young Writers; Need2Know; Writers' Bookshop; and Pond View.

Submission details Submit a maximum of 3 poems per theme, each no more than 30 lines in length. Write name and address on each piece of work. Alternatively, email to inbox@forwardpress.co.uk.

The Frogmore Press
42 Morehall Avenue, Folkestone, Kent CT19 4EF
tel (07751) 251689
website www.frogmorepress.co.uk
Contact Jeremy Page

The Frogmore Press was founded in 1983 and publishes poetry and prose by new and established writers. *The Frogmore Papers* appears biannually in March and September, and the Frogmore Poetry Prize (est. 1987) is awarded annually and paid in guineas.

Submission details Submissions should be made by post with sae. No more than 6 poems.

Frontier Publishing
Windetts, Kirstead, Norwich NR15 1EG
website www.frontierpublishing.co.uk
Contact J Black

Publishes *The Green Book of Poetry*, established in 1986. Occasional poetry publishers with interests in other subjects, such as Art History.
Submission details Submit by post, with sae.

The Galdragon Press
2B Church Road, Stromness, Orkney KW16 3BT
email galdragonpress@ntlworld.com
website http://homepage.ntlworld.com/galdragonpress
Contact Anne Thompson

A Scottish pamphlet publisher.

The Gallery Press
Loughcrew, Oldcastle, Co Meath, Republic of Ireland
tel 049-854 1779 *fax* 049-854 1779
email gallery@indigo.ie
website www.gallerypress.com
Editor/Publisher Peter Fallon

Poetry, drama, and occasionally fiction – by Irish authors only at this time. Founded 1970.

Godstow Press
60 Godstow Road, Wolvercote, Oxford OX2 8NY UK
tel (01865) 556215 *fax* (01865) 552900
email info@godstowpress.co.uk
website www.godstowpress.co.uk

The aim of Godstow Press is to sing the Orphic song, through books of fiction, poetry and non-fiction, as well as through CDs.

Gomer Books
Gwasg Gomer, Llandysul, Ceredigion SA44 4JL
tel (01559) 362371 *fax* (01559) 363758
email gwasg@gomer.co.uk
website www.gomer.co.uk

Wales's largest independent publisher, publishing books from Wales, about Wales, in Welsh and in English. Produces more than 120 new titles every year, for children and adults, in both languages.

Greville Press

6 Mellors Court, The Butts,
Warwick CV34 4ST
website www.haroldpinter.org/poetry/
poetry_greville.shtml

Publishes well-designed pamphlets and, over
the years, some very big names including
Harold Pinter, George Barker, WS Graham and
many others.

HappenStance

21 Hatton Green, Glenrothes, Fife KY7 4SD
email nell@happenstancepress.com
website www.happenstancepress.com
Contact Helena Nelson

A pamphlet and chapbook imprint originated
in 2005 and run by Helena Nelson.
Happenstance features first collections and is
interested in poets from across the UK, while
maintaining an emphasis on those based in
Scotland, or with Scottish connections.

Submission details Unsolicited submissions
accepted. Send at least 12 (but no more than
20) poems with sae. Do not staple poems. Put
name and address on every sheet.

Hard Pressed Poetry

37 Grosvenor Court, Templeville Road,
Templeogue, Dublin 6, Eire
website http://gofree.indigo.ie/~hpp/frame.html
Contact Billy Mills

A small press which publishes poetry that you
won't often find in your local bookshop.

Headland Publications

38 York Avenue, West Kirby, Wirral,
Merseyside L48 3JF and Ty Coch, Llansfwrog,
Ruthin, Denbighshire LL12 2AR
tel 0151-625 9128
email gladysmarycoles@hotmail.co.uk
Contact Gladys-Mary Coles

A quality literary press with high production
standards, publishing individual collections of
poetry and anthologies.

Submission details Send a preliminary letter
of enquiry before submitting.

Hearing Eye

Box 1, 99 Torriano Avenue, London NW5 2RX
email hearing_eye@torriano.org
website www.torriano.org/hearing_eye/

Publishes poetry and also hosts poetry readings
in London.

Heaventree Press

PO Box 3342, Coventry CV1 5YB
email info@heaventreepress.co.uk
website www.heaventreepress.co.uk
Contact Jonathan Morley

A not-for-profit West Midlands-based
independent publisher, dedicated to promoting
the arts in Coventry and the surrounding area,
and specialising in anthologies and pamphlets
of new literature. Set up by local young poets as
a community venture.

Hilltop Press

4 Nowell Place, Almondbury, Huddersfield,
West Yorkshire HD5 8PB
Contact Steve Sneyd

Founded in 1966, Hilltop Press is a specialist
publisher of science fiction and dark fantasy
poetry collections and anthologies – including
some reprinting of significant past work in the
field, along with texts about it. Does not have a
website, but Hilltop Press publications are
listed and can be purchased at **www.bbr-
online.com/catalogue**.

Submission details Submit a small selection of
relevant work or an extract, if a long poem.
Must be accompanied by sae.

Hippopotamus Press

22 Whitewell Road, Frome,
Somerset BA11 4EL
tel (01373) 466653 *fax* (01373) 466653
email rjhippopress@aol.com
Editors Roland John, Anna Martin

Poetry, essays and criticism. Publishes *Outposts
Poetry Quarterly*. Welcomes poetry submissions
from new writers; work should be sent by post.
Specialises in first full collections by poets who
have established a reputation in mainstream
poetry magazines. Founded 1974.

Honno Welsh Women's Press

Canolfan Merched y Wawr, Vulcan Street,
Aberystwyth SY23 1JH
tel (01970) 623150 *fax* (01970) 623150
email post@honno.co.uk
website www.honno.co.uk

Editor Caroline Oakley

An independent co-operative press run by women and committed to publishing the best in Welsh women's writing.

Submission details Only considers for publication the work of women who are Welsh, living in Wales, or have a significant Welsh connection. Not actively seeking poetry submissions.

Hub Editions
Longholm, East Bank, Wingland,
Sutton Bridge, Spalding, Lincolnshire PE12 9YS
Contact Colin Blundell

Small poetry publisher.

Independent Northern Publishers
Aidan House, Sunderland Road,
Gateshead NE8 3HU
tel 0191-212 0354
email cristae@zoom.co.uk
website www.northernpublishers.co.uk
Contact Crista Ermiya

A group of book and magazine publishers based in North East England. The group includes: Mslexia, Liar Inc, Other Poetry, Flambard, Iron Press, Diamond Twig, Vane Women, The Word Foundation, Mudfog, Arrowhead, and Biscuit Publishing.

Iron Press
5 Marden Terrace, Cullercoats, North Shields, Northumberland NE30 4PD
tel 0191-253 1901
email seaboy@freenetname.co.uk
website www.ironpress.co.uk
Contact Peter Mortimer

Iron Press was established in 1973, since when it has brought out a regular programme of new poetry, fiction and drama.

Submission details Does not welcome unsolicited submissions; please make telephone contact first.

Katabasis Press
10 St Martin's Close, London NW1 0HR
tel 020-7485 3830
website www.katabasis.co.uk
Contact Dinah Livingstone

Publishes down-to-earth and utopian poetry and prose from home and abroad.

Submission details No unsolicited manuscripts.

Kernow Press
Bude Haven, 18 Frankfield Rise,
Tunbridge Wells, Kent TN2 5LF
Contact Bill Headon

Publishes limited small editions.

Kettillonia
24 South Street, Newtyle, Angus PH12 8UQ
tel (01828) 650615
email james@kettillonia.co.uk
website www.kettillonia.co.uk
Contact James Robertson

Set up in 1999, Kettillonia publishes occasional publications in pamphlet form only (no full-length books). Specialises in new, original, Scottish work.

Submission details No unsolicited submissions; send initial letter or email before submitting.

King's England Press
Cambertown House, Commercial Road,
Goldthorpe Industrial Estate, Rotherham,
South Yorkshire S63 9BL
tel (01484) 663790
email Steve@kingsengland.com
website www.kingsengland.com
Contact Steve Rudd

Only publishes children's poetry.

Submission details No unsolicited proposals.

Koo Press Poetry
19 Lochinch Park, Aberdeen AB12 3RF
email koopoetry@btinternet.com

An independent small press based in Aberdeen, and primarily publishing poetry chapbooks. Its main objective is to provide the poet with a bridge between magazine publication and a full-length poetry collection.

KT Publications
16 Fane Close, Stamford,
Lincolnshire PE9 1HG
tel (01780) 754193
Editor Kevin Troop

Looking for *new* material for publication. Copies are sold to authors at a reduced price. Founded 1989.

Submission details Submit by post with sae and covering letter.

Lapwing Productions

1 Balysillan Drive, Belfast BT14 8HQ
Contact Dennis Greig, Catherine Greig

In business for 15 years, an independent, non-grant-aided publisher, specialising in small first collections. Produces a saddle-stitched pamphlet format of up to 44 pages; 'book' format is 48 pages upwards. All work hand-printed and hand-bound. Writers get 20 complimentary copies and extra copies at 50% of cover price.

Submission details Send an introductory letter plus 6 sample poems as well as a brief biography. For books, as above, but send a larger selection of poems.

The Lilliput Press

62-63 Sitric Road, Arbour Hill, Dublin 7, Ireland
tel ++353 (01) 671 16 47
website www.lilliputpress.ie
Contact Antony Farrell

Has some 250 titles under its imprint; these encompass art and architecture, autobiography and memoir, biography and history, ecology and environmentalism, essays and literary criticism, philosophy, current affairs and popular culture, fiction, drama and poetry – all broadly focused on Irish themes.

The Littoral Press

10 Prail Court, Vesta Close, Coggeshall, Essex CO6 1QG
tel (01376) 564859
email mervynlinford@aol.com
website http://mysite.wannado-members.co.uk/mervyn_linford/press.htm
Contact Mervyn Linford

Publishes a limited number of poetry collections, all of which have to be on the theme of 'Nature and the Spirit'. Publication is a partnership deal. All profits (if any) go to the funds of the Littoral Press. Littoral is a not-for-profit organisation; all work is voluntary and unpaid.

Submission details Hard copy by post accompanied by an sae, or by email attachment.

Liverpool University Press

4 Cambridge Street, Liverpool L69 7ZU
tel 0151-794 2233 *fax* 0151-794 2235
email robblo@liv.ac.uk
website www.liverpool-unipress.co.uk
Publisher Robin Bloxsidge

Academic and scholarly books in a range of disciplines. Special interests: art history, European and American literature, science fiction criticism, all fields of history, sociology. New series established include: *Liverpool Latin American Studies*, and *Studies in Social and Political Thought*. Founded 1899.

Loki Books

38 Chalcot Crescent, London NW1 8YD
tel 020-7722 6718
email all@lokibooks.u-net.com
website www.lokibooks.com
Contact Ann White

Specialist publishers of translations from modern Hebrew.

Luath Press

543/2 Castlehill, The Royal Mile, Edinburgh EH1 2ND
tel 0131-225 4326 *fax* 0131-225 4324
email gavin.macdougall@luath.co.uk
website www.luath.co.uk
Contact Gavin MacDougall

Committed to publishing well-written work worth reading. More than 200 books in print, including fiction and poetry.

Submission details Send hard copy by post, plus anything else of relevance.

Ludovic Press

Dunadd, Lewis Crescent, Kilbarchan PA10 2HB
tel (01505) 702906

Scottish pamphlet publisher.

Marion Boyars

24 Lacy Road, London SW15 1NL
tel 020-8788 9522 *fax* 020-8789 8122
email catheryn@marionboyars.com
website www.marionboyars.co.uk

A publishing house committed to the new, the unusual and the unexpected.

Mariscat

10 Bell Place, Stockbridge, Edinburgh EH3 5HT

tel 0131-343 1070
email hamish.whyte@btinternet.com
website www.scottish-pamphlet-poetry.com
Contact Hamish Whyte, Diana Hendry

Publisher of poetry pamphlets.
Submission details Send hard copy with sae.

Masque Publishing
PO Box 3257, Littlehampton BN16 9AF
email masque_pub@tiscali.co.uk
website myweb.tiscali.co.uk/masquepublishing
Contact Lisa Stewart

Publisher of poetry books and *Decanto*
magazine.

Matchbox
87 Thornton Road, Fallowfield,
Manchester M14 7NT
email matchbox@matchbox.org.uk
website www.matchbox.org.uk
Editor James Davies
Frequency/price Bi-monthly

Experimental poetry published in matchboxes.
One poet per issue along with a gift.

Maypole Editions Biennial Anthology
65 Mayfair Avenue, Ilford, Essex IG1 3DQ
Contact Barry Taylor

A small press platform for first-time poets who
might not otherwise get into print, and a
permanent showcase for those already
published who want to break into the
mainstream. Most editions come on CD, from
which hard copy (including full-colour cover)
can be printed without infringing copyright.

Menard Press
8 The Oaks, Woodside Avenue,
London N12 8AR
tel 020-8446 5571 *fax* 020-8445 2990
email menard@menardpress.co.uk
website www.menardpress.co.uk
Contact Anthony Rudolf

Has been publishing poetry (original and
translated) since 1969. Has also published
literary criticism and political studies.
Submission details No new submissions.

Mercier Press
Douglas Village, Cork, Ireland
email pr@mercierpress.ie
website www.mercierpress.ie

Publishes a wide range of books, including
poetry.

Mermaid Turbulence
Annaghmaconway, Clone, Leitrim, Ireland
website www.mermaidturbulence.com
Contact Mari-Aymone Djeribi

An independent publisher of books, artistbooks
and 'multiples'.

Mews Press
English Department,
Sheffield Hallam University,
Collegiate Crescent, Sheffield S10 2BP
email s.l.earnshaw@shu.ac.uk
website http://extra.shu.ac.uk/mews-press
Editor Dr Steven Earnshaw

Publishes work connected with the MA
Writing at Sheffield Hallam University. Each
year, in *Matter*, it features the work of students
alongside that of guest authors.

Mucusart
6 Chatsworth Road, Radcliffe,
Manchester M26 4NT
tel 0161-795 5235
email squire@hotmail.com
website www.mucusart.co.uk
Contact Paul Neads

Mucusart publishes small collections by
stranded writers.
Submission details Submit by post.

Mudfog
c/o Arts Development, The Stables,
Stewart Park, The Grove, Marton,
Middlesbrough, Tees Valley TS7 8AR
website www.mudfog.co.uk

A voluntary cooperative community press
dedicated to publication of new writers from
the Tees Valley area. Funded by ACE.
Published writers receive a fee and retain
copyright.
Submission details Send samples of 15-20
poems or 2-3 short stories with sae. Consult the
website for more details.

New Departures
PO Box 9819, London W11 2GQ
email www.connectotel.com/PoetryOlympics/
index.htm

Editor Michael Horovitz

Michael Horovitz founded New Departures publications and Live New Departures road shows while still a student in 1959. He also runs the Poetry Olympics.

New Island New Poetry

2 Brookside, Dundrum Road, Dublin 14
tel ++353 1 298 9937/298 3411
fax ++353 1 298 2783
email editor@newisland.ie
website www.newisland.ie
Editor Deirdre Nolan

New Island New Poetry has grown out of New Island's vibrant poetry list – a list which, over the last few years, has concentrated on publishing the finest new voices in Irish poetry. It took its spirit from Dermot Bolger's legendary Raven Arts Press, and, indeed, Dermot Bolger remains New Island's executive poetry and drama editor.

Northern Sky Press

PO Box 21548, Stirling FK8 1YY
tel (07981) 173819
email northernsky@hush.com
website www.northernskypress.co.uk

A radical, independent publisher producing politics and poetry pamphlets.

Object Permanence

email undigest@hotmail.com
website www.objectpermanence.co.uk
Editor Pater Manson

Once a magazine, now a small publisher based in Glasgow.

O'Brien Press

12 Terenure Road East, Dublin 6, Ireland
tel ++353 1 492 3333
email books@obrien.ie
website www.obrien.ie

Ireland's leading general publisher of both adult and children's books, with some poetry.

Odyssey Poets

Coleridge Cottage, Nether Stowey,
Somerset TA5 1NQ
tel (01278) 732662
email pqr.rev@virgin.net
Contact Tilla Brading, Derrick Woolf

A small press that will be relaunched in 2007, publishing innovative work and a regular review magazine.

Oleander Press

16 Orchard Street, Cambridge CB1 1JT
tel (01223) 357768
email editor@oleanderpress.com
website www.oleanderpress.com
Contact Dr Jeremy Toner, Mrs Jane Doyle

A small press founded more than 40 years ago. Typically publishes 1 poetry title each year.

Submission details No unsolicited manuscripts. Please send letter and sample in the first instance.

Onlywomen Press Ltd

40 St Lawrence Terrace, London W10 5ST
tel 020-8354 0796 *fax* 020-8960 2817
email onlywomenpress@btconnect.com
website www.onlywomenpress.com
Managing Director Lilian Mohin

Lesbian feminist theory, fiction and cultural criticism. Founded 1974.

The Oscars Press

BM Oscars, London WC1N 3XX
email pdaniels@easynet.co.uk
website http://easyweb.easynet.co.uk/pdaniels/oscars.html
Contact Peter Daniels

Publishes top-quality poetry anthologies by lesbians, gay men, and women from both sides of the Atlantic.

The Other Press

19 Marriott Road, London N4 3QN
tel 020-7272 9023
Contact Frances Presley

A very small press that publishes experimental work, usually by women.

Submission details Submit a short sample of work on A4 paper, enclosing sae.

Oversteps Books

Froude Road, Salcombe,
South Devon TQ8 8LH
tel (01548) 843713 *fax* (01548) 844384
email anne@oversteps.fsnet.co.uk
Contact Anne Born

Publishes good, modern poets ready for a first collection who have appeared in magazines and won prizes.

Submission details No unsolicited submissions.

Parthian Books

The Old Surgery, Napier Street, Aberteifi, Wales SA43 1ED
tel (01239) 612059 *fax* (01239) 612059
email parthianbooks@yahoo.co.uk
website www.parthianbooks.co.uk

An independent publisher, publishing innovative fiction, drama and poetry in Wales for 10 years. It aims to promote new talent and bring exciting new authors to as wide an audience as possible.

Partners

289 Elmwood Avenue, Feltham, Middlesex TW13 7QB
email partners_writing_group@hotmail.com
Editor Ian Deal

Magazine publisher. Titles include: *A Bard Hair Day*, *ImageNation* and *The Poet Tree*.

Paula Brown Publishing

26 Uplands Road, Drayton, Portsmouth PO6 1HS
tel (07796) 530826
website www.thepeoplespoet.com/paulabrownpublishing
Editor Paula Brown

Publishes at least 6 poetry collections each year – the Spring, Summer, Autumn and Winter single author collections, the Christmas Special edition, and the annual anthology. Occasionally undertakes separate funded community projects.

Peace & Freedom Press

17 Farrow Road, Whaplode Drove, Spalding, Lincs PE12 0TS
email p_rance@yahoo.co.uk
website http://uk.geocities.com/p_rance/pandf.htm
Contact Paul Rance

A small press founded in 1985. In 1995 it began to publish paperback anthologies of poetry, among other things.

Peepal Tree Press

17 King's Avenue, Leeds LS6 1QS
tel 0113-245 1703
email contact@peepaltreepress.com
website www.peepaltreepress.com

Publishes the very best in Caribbean, Black British and South Asian literature, fiction, poetry and academic books.

Peer Poetry

26 Arlington House, Bath Street, Bath BA1 1QN
tel (01225) 445298
email peerpoetry@msn.com
website www.publish-your-poetry.co.uk
Contact Paul Amphlett

A not-for-profit enterprise interested in all forms of well-written poetry, including the haiku genre. 3 winners voted for by readers and contributing poets will have a book of their poetry published, but not marketed.

Submission details Submit 3 poems by email, to determine whether they can be entered for the competition (no charge).

Pennine Pens

32 Windsor Road, Hebden Bridge, West Yorkshire HX7 8LF
tel (01422) 843724
email info@penninepens.co.uk
website www.penninepens.co.uk
Contact Elaine Connell

A small publisher working from its home office in Hebden Bridge in the Yorkshire Pennines.

Perdika Press

16b St Andrew's Road, Enfield, Middlesex EN1 3UB
email editions@perdikapress.com
website www.perdikapress.com

Publishes original and translated works by contemporary poets.

Peterloo Poets

The Old Chapel, Sand Lane, Calstock, Cornwall PL18 9QX
tel (01822) 833473 *fax* (01822) 833989
email info@peterloopoets.com
website www.peterloopoets.com
Publishing Director Harry Chambers *Trustees*

Brian Perman, Hannah Elliott, Rose Taw
Honorary President Michael Longley
Poetry. Founded 1976.

Photon Press
37 The Meadows, Berwick-upon-Tweed,
Northumberland TD15 1NY
tel (01289) 306523
email photon.press@virgin.net
website www.photonpress.co.uk
Contact John Light

Small independent publishing house. Founded
1986. No uninvited submissions.

Pigasus Press
13 Hazely Combe, Arreton,
Isle of Wight PO30 3AJ
tel (01983) 865668
email mail@pigasuspress.co.uk
website www.pigasuspress.co.uk

Publisher of genre poetry.

Pighog Press
PO Box 145, Brighton BN1 6YU
email info@pighog.co.uk
website www.pighog.co.uk

A small press committed to the publication of
unique voices.

Piper's Ash
Church Road, Christian Malford,
Chippenham, Wiltshire SN15 4BW
tel (01249) 720563
email pipersash@supamasu.com
website www.supamasu.com
Contact A Tyson

Small press publisher set up to discover new
authors, writers and poets with talent and
potential.
Submission details Telephone first, or email
proposal.

Piscean Press
6 Guernsey Street, Portland, Dorset DT5 1JR
tel (01305) 823709
email pisceanpressport@aol.com
Editor Frank Alcock

Publishes the true poet who can be equal to the
rigour of value judgements and sensitive to the
power of every word.

Submission details Submissions should be
typed on A4, loose in a wallet file, and
accompanied by a 50-word CV.

The Poetry Business
The Studio, Byram Arcade, Westgate,
Huddersfield, West Yorkshire HD1 1N
tel (01484) 434840 *fax* (01484) 426566
email editor@poetrybusiness.co.uk
website www.poetrybusiness.co.uk
Editor Peter Sansom

Publishes books and pamphlets under the
Smith/Doorstop imprint; also a poetry journal,
The North. Runs an annual book and pamphlet
competition.
Submission details Send a sample manuscript
of 20-25 poems accompanied by an sae. No
email submissions.

Poetry Salzburg
email editor@poetrysalzburg.com
website www.poetrysalzburg.com
Contact Dr Wolfgang Görtschacher

In 1971, James Hogg founded the University of
Salzburg Press, publishing books of literary
criticism in the fields of Jacobean Drama,
Romantic Studies, Elizabethan & Jacobean
Studies, and Poetic Drama & Poetic Theory. In
the early 1980s he started to publish collections
of poetry. Relaunched in 1999 as Poetry
Salzburg, the company now publishes 6-8
books per year: poetry, literary criticism,
anthologies, annotated bibliographies,
translations and plays. Publishes first
collections by new poets, as well as volumes of
Selected and Collected Poems by established
poets.

Polygon – see Birlinn Ltd

Poor Tom's Press
89a Winchester Avenue, Leicester LE3 1AY
tel 0116-289 5400

A poetry pamphlet publisher.

Protean Publications
4 Milton Road, Bentley Heath,
West Midlands B93 8AA
email versifierlester@yahoo.co.uk
website www.indigogroup.co.uk/llpp/
protean.html

Contact Paul Lester

Founded in 1980. Has published around 60 titles, including works by Roy Fisher, Les Roadhouse, and Adrian de Redman.

PS Avalon Press

PO Box 1865, Glastonbury BA6 8YR
tel (01458) 833864
email info@psavalon.com
website www.psavalon.com
Contact Will Parfitt

Publishes books of poetry with a psychospiritual content; contemplative and inspirational poetry with a dark, challenging edge.

   Submission details Up to 100 lines should be sent in the body of an email (not as an attachment), or via post accompanied by an sae.

Rack Press

The Rack, Kinnerton, Presteigne, Powys, Wales LD8 2PF
tel (01547) 560411 *mobile* (07817) 424560
email rackpress@nicholasmurray.co.uk
website www.nicholasmurray.co.uk/RackPress.html

Welsh poetry pamphlet imprint. Relaunched in January 2006; publishes 3 short poetry pamphlets a year.

Ragged Raven Press

1 Lodge Farm, Snitterfield, Warwickshire CV37 0LR
tel (01789) 730358
email raggedravenpress@aol.com
website www.raggedraven.co.uk
Contact Janet Murch, Bob Mee

Small press publishing 1-2 individual collections a year and an anthology linked to an annual competition. Also publishes *Iota*, a quarterly poetry magazine.

The Rialto

PO Box 309, Aylsham, Norwich NR11 6LN
website www.therialto.co.uk
Editor Michael Mackmin

Began in 1964 and has been publishing a magazine since then. Now also publishing first collections and pamphlets.

Submission details Send 6 poems and an sae or IRC. Response time is about 3 months.

The Rockingham Press

11 Musley Lane, Ware, Herts SG12 7EN
tel (01920) 467868 *fax* (01920) 467868
email david@rockpress.freeserve.co.uk
website www.rockingham-press.co.uk
Contact David Perman

David Perman set up the Rockingham Press in 1991, to champion new and neglected poets and also Middle Eastern poetry in translation. Since then it has published, on average each year, 5 paperback collections (always including a first collection) and 1-2 pamphlets.

Submission details Unable to accept submissions at present.

Rough Winds

56 Lady Somerset Road, London NW5 1TU
tel 020-7485 7703 *fax* 020-7485 1525
email info@roughwinds.co.uk
website www.roughwinds.co.uk

Aims to promote poetry in an exciting and original way that brings out the heart of the meaning in a clear and enjoyable manner. Rough Winds' primary interest lies with audio cassettes; however, from time to time poetry pamphlets and posters are published.

Route Books

PO Box 167, Pontefract, Yorkshire WF8 4WW
tel 0845-158 1565
email info@route-online.com
website www.route-online.com
Contact Ian Daley

Publisher of contemporary fiction and performance poetry.

Submission details By audio CD; consult www.id-publishing.com for details.

SAF Publishing

149 Wakeman Road, London NW10 5BH
tel 020-8969 6099 *fax* 020-8354 3132
email info@safpublishing.com
website www.safpublishing.com

Poetry and rock music book publisher.

Sahitya Press

1 Donnington Road, Sheffield S2 2RF
email debjani@chatterjee.freeserve.co.uk
website http://sahityapress.mysite.wanadoo-members.co.uk

Contact Debjani Chatterjee

An independent community writing and publishing press based in Sheffield. Run by 2 friends who were also founder-members of the Bengali Women's Support Group: Indian-born Debjani Chatterjee, and Bangladeshi-born Safuran Ara.

Salmon Publishing

Knockeven, Cliffs of Moher, Co Clare, Ireland
tel ++353 (0)65 708 1941
email info@salmonpoetry.com
website www.salmonpoetry.com

Taking its name from the Salmon of Knowledge in Celtic mythology, Salmon was established in 1981 with the publication of *The Salmon*, a journal of poetry and prose, as an alternative voice in Irish literature. Since then more than 200 volumes of poetry have been produced, and Salmon has become one of the most important publishers in the Irish literary world. By specialising in the promotion of new poets, Salmon has enriched Irish literary publishing and now has the most representative list of women poets in Ireland.

Salt Publishing

PO Box 937, Great Wilbraham,
Cambridge CB1 5JX
tel (01223) 882220 *fax* (01223) 882260
website www.saltpublishing.com
Publishing Director Christopher Hamilton-Emery

Publishes ground-breaking poetry, literary criticism, essays and biography for an international market. The management team, drawn from blue-chip companies, has successfully consolidated the operations of the Australian-born business in the UK. Salt is a class leader in the implementation of new publishing technologies and standards. Sales revenues from the rapidly expanding catalogue are growing at 40% per year. Stocks of award-winning titles are held with major distributors in the UK, USA and Australia, and sold in bookstores around the world.

Salty Press

Mains of Airlie, Kirriemuir, Angus
website www.scottish-pamphlet-poetry.com

A Scottish pamphlet publisher.

Saqi Books

26 Westbourne Grove, London W2 5RH
tel 020-7221 9347
website www.saqibooks.com

Founded in 1984 to bridge the divide between Middle Eastern and Western cultures. Since then Saqi has expanded its network to include writers from the Balkans, Afghanistan, Pakistan and France as well as from the UK.

The Seer Press

PO Box 29313, Glasgow G20 2AE
email admin@theseerpress.com
website www.theseerpress.com

A small pamphlet press publishing contemporary Scottish poetry. Aims to provide a viable outlet for the poetry pamphlet as a grassroots alternative to the publishing industry.

Selkirk Lapwing Press

Lower Kirklands, The Glebe, Selkirk TD7 5AB
email selkirklapwing@freeuk.com
website www.selkirklapwingpress.co.uk
Editor Robert Leach

A not-for-profit outfit, interested in poetry produced in the region either side of Hadrian's Wall – Cumbria, Dumfries and Galloway, Scottish Borders and Northumberland, plus perhaps Lothian, Tyne and Wear and County Durham.

Submission details Submit by post accompanied by sae, or by email. See website for details.

Seren

57 Nolton Street, Bridgend CF31 3AE
tel (01656) 663018 *fax* (01656) 649226
email general@seren-books.com
website www.seren-books.com
Publisher Mick Felton

Poetry, fiction, drama, history, film, literary criticism, biography, art – mostly with relevance to Wales. Has published poetry for 25 years. Founded 1981.

Submission details Hard copy with sae.

Shearsman Books

58 Velwell Road, Exeter, Devon EX4 4LD
tel (01392) 434511

email editor@shearsman.com
website www.shearsman.com
Contact Tony Frazer

Publisher devoted to contemporary poetry in Engish and in translation. Interested mainly in work that shows knowledge of the Modernist tradition.

Submission details Postal submissions must be accompanied by sae. If work is sent by email, no attachments other than PDFs will be opened.

Shepheard-Walwyn Publishers Ltd

Suite 604, The Chandlery,
50 Westminster Bridge, London SE1 7QY
tel 020-7721 7666
email books@shepheard-walwyn.co.uk
website www.shepheard-walwyn.co.uk
Managing Director Anthony Werner

An independent publisher that has been publishing books for over 30 years.

Shoestring Press

19 Devonshire Avenue, Beeston,
Nottingham NG9 1BS
tel 0115-925 1827
website www.shoestringpress.co.uk
Contact John Lucas (Publisher/Editor)

Publishes work by good contemporary poets, in full collection and pamphlet form. Also publishes poetry in translation, especially from the Greek, and very occasionally works in prose.

Submission details No more than 6 poems should be submitted, and only after a letter of enquiry.

Sixties Press

89 Connaught Road, Sutton, Surrey SM1 3PJ
tel 020-8286 0419
email sixtiespress@blueyonder.co.uk
website www.sixtiespress.co.uk or
www.barrytebb.co.uk or www.criticalobs.co.uk
Editor Barry Tebb

A writers' cooperative, which began as a literary press but increasingly concentrates on work by survivors of mental-health disorders.

Submission details Poet pays for individual collection, but not for inclusion in an anthology.

Skoob Books

Woodhill Farm, Willow Marsh Lane, Yoxford, Suffolk IP17 3JR
email skoobrussellsquare@hotmail.com
website www.skoob.com
Contact M Lovell

Former bookshop that publishes some poetry.

Smaller Sky Books

1st Floor, Llwyn Eilian,
Rhosgadfan Gwynedd LL54 7HE
mobile (07050) 632277
email editor@smallersky.com
website www.smallersky.com

An independent paperback publishing house, specialising in poetry and fiction. Committed to a supportive and nurturing relationship with authors, offering strong editorial support. **Smallersky.com** also offers a showcase of new writing.

Smith/Doorstop Books

tel (01484) 434840 *fax* (01484) 426566
website www.poetrybusiness.co.uk/
smithdoorstop.aspx
Contact Janet Fisher

A small independent publisher of contemporary poetry, publishing books and pamphlets.

Smokestack Books

PO Box 408, Middlesbrough TS5 6WA
tel (01642) 813997
email info@smokestack-books.co.uk
website www.smokestack-books.co.uk
Contact Andy Croft

Champions poets who are unfashionable, unconventional, radical or left-field, and who work a long way from the centres of cultural authority. Is interested in the world as well as the word, and believes that poetry is a part of and not apart from society.

Submission details See submission guidelines on the website.

Snapshot Press

PO Box 132, Waterloo, Liverpool L22 8WZ
email info@snapshotpress.co.uk
Editor www.snapshotpress.co.uk
Contact John Barlow

Publishers of haiku, tanka and other short poetry.

Spike

c/o 96 Bold Street, Liverpool L1 4HY
tel 0151-709 3688
Contact Dave Ward

Publishes first collections from Merseyside and the North West.

Submission details No unsolicited manuscripts.

Steve Savage Publishers

The Old Truman Brewery, 91 Brick Lane, London E1 6QL or 6 Hillview, Edinburgh EH4 2AB
tel 020-7770 6083
email mail@savagepublishers.com
website www.savagepublishers.com

Publishes books on Scottish history, literature, languages and folklore, as well poetry, guidebooks, humorous titles, and new and classic writing from Scotland and elsewhere.

Stride Publications

4B Tremayne Close, Devoran, Cornwall TR3 6QE
email editor@stridebooks.co.uk
website www.stridebooks.co.uk
Managing Editor Rupert M Loydell

Poetry, prose poetry, contemporary music and visual arts, and interviews. Inhabits the divide between the avant-garde and the traditional, the secular and the sacred, the mysterious and the everyday, the modern and the postmodern. Committed to innovative poetry and fiction by both known and unknown authors. Founded 1980.

Submission details No submissions are currently being sought.

the tall-lighthouse

STARK Gallery, 384 Lee High Road, London SE12 8RW
tel 020-8297 8279
email info@tall-lighthouse.co.uk
website www.tall-lighthouse.co.uk
Contact LK Robinson

An independent publisher, producing full collections and pamphlets and organising poetry readings, events and workshops in London and around the UK.

Submission details Email at submissions@tall-lighthouse.co.uk for guidelines.

Templar Poetry

Box No 7082, Bakewell DE45 9AF
tel (01629) 582500
email info@templarpoetry.co.uk
website www.templarpoetry.co.uk
Managing Editor Alex Macmillan

An independent publishing house based in Derbyshire, publishing new poetry and committed to promoting emerging poets.

Submission details Submit via the annual Pamphlet and Collection Competition, and by commission only. No unsolicited manuscripts will be considered.

Terra Firma Press

11 Sinclair Drive, Glasgow G42 9PR
Editor A Murray

A Scottish pamphlet publisher. All pamphlets £3 each (£5 for 2) inclusive of postage within the UK.

Submission details No submissions currently being sought.

Two Rivers Press

35-39 London Street, Reading, Berkshire RG1 4PS
tel 0118-966 2345
email enquiries@tworiverspress.com
website www.tworiverspress.com

A cooperative, with a growing reputation for bold design and illustration combined with distinctive new writing. The press is developing a strong line in illustrated poetry and prose from local writers, exemplified by *The Waterlog*, a journal of poetry, prose and visual arts featuring a range of writers from the well known (Peter Redgrove, Mario Petrucci, etc.) to the previously unknown.

Vane Women Press

19a Vane Terrace, Darlington DL3 7AT
website www.vanewomen.co.uk
Contact Dorothy Long

A writers' collective from the North of England; runs a press and workshops.

Vennel Press

8 Richmond Road, Staines, Middlesex TW18 2AB

email vennel@hotmail.com
website www.indigogroup.co.uk/llpp/
vennel.html
Contact Leona Medlin

A small press founded by Leona Medlin and Richard Price in 1990. Publishes modern Scottish poetry, poetry associated with 'The Poetry Workshop' (London), and modernist poetry in translation.

Waterways Publishing
PO Box 43771, Suite 13, London W14 8ZY
tel 0845-430 9517
email editor@waterways-publishing.com
website www.waterways-publishing.com
Editor Stuart Strong

Launched in 2001. Publishes outstanding poetry with a focus on writers who read well in public.

Submission details Submit 6 poems by email in the first instance. Editor will respond if interested.

The Waywiser Press
The Cottage, 14 Lyncroft Gardens, Ewell, Surrey KT17 1UR
tel 020-8393 7055 *fax* 020-8393 7055
email waywiserpress@aol.com
website www.waywiser-press.com
Editor Philip Hoy

A small independent company, with its main office in Surrey and a subsidiary in Baltimore. Founded in late 2001; started publishing in 2002. The press specialises in the publication of modern poetry in English, and is keen to promote the work of new as well as established authors. However, from time to time it also issues books belonging to other literary genres – fiction, memoir, criticism, history.

Wendy Webb Books
9 Walnut Close, Norwich NR8 6YN
email tipsforwriters@yahoo.co.uk
Contact Wendy Webb

Publishes traditional and new forms. Anthologies with form rules.

West House Books
40 Crescent Road, Sheffield S7 1HN
tel 0114-258 6035
email info@westhousebooks.co.uk
website www.westhousebooks.co.uk
Contact Alan Halsey

Publishers of poetry and poetry-related work, mainly contemporary and in the modernist tradition.

White Leaf Press
PO Box 734, Aylesbury HP20 9AL
email editor@whiteleafpress.co.uk
website www.whiteleafpress.co.uk
Contact Stephen Brown

An independent press dedicated to publishing exciting new work by poets and writers who aim to stretch boundaries and challenge preconceptions.

Submission details Send 10-12 poems initially by post or email, with a short biographical note. State which poems have already been published and where, if possible. For electronic submissions, work should be included in the body of the email (no attachments). Send to editor@whiteleafpress.co.uk with 'submissions' in the subject line.

Wild Honey Press
16a Ballyman Road, Bray, County Wicklow, Ireland
email poetry@wildhoneypress.com
website www.wildhoneypress.com

Publishes poetry books and CDs featuring Irish and international poets.

Wild Women Press
10 The Common, Windermere, Cumbria LA23 1JH
website www.wildwomenpress.com
Contact Vik Bennett

A not-for-profit press and poets' collective with a DIY ethic and a mission to celebrate life creatively.

Submission details Please view website for up-to-date news on submissions. Announcements are made on the site. At present only accepting online submissions.

Wolfhound Press
68 Mountjoy Square, Dublin 1, Republic of Ireland
tel (01) 874 0354

Publisher of Irish poetry.

Worple Press
2 Havelock Road, Tonbridge, Kent TN9 1JE
tel (01732) 367466 *fax* (01732) 352057

email TheWorpleCo@aol.com
website www.worplepress.co.uk
Co-director Peter Carpenter

Publishes mainly collections of poetry, but also produces arts titles. Showcases new writing and welcomes diversity of format and approach (anthologies, translations, interviews, dictionaries) and has an international outlook.

Wrecking Ball Press

email editor@wreckingballpress.com
website www.wreckingballpress.com
Editor Shane Rhodes

A magazine produced with a real passion for poetry.

Zum Zum Books

Goshem, Bunlight, Drumnadrochit, Inverness-shire IV63 6XH
tel (01456) 459368
email oramneil@yahoo.co.uk
website www.warp-experience.com
Contact Neil Oram

Publisher of erotic/philosophic poetry.

A view from the lighthouse...

Les Robinson, Director of poetry organisation and publisher, tall-lighthouse, provides sound advice to poets about finding an audience for their work.

It's an oft-heard statement that, without any persistent presence within the public eye, and seemingly being left behind by other emergent forms, poetry is dead; an antiquated form of artistic expression that is best left to fester with other relics of the 20th century. A cursory glance at the shelves of a high-street bookshop would appear to support this statement: work your way past the bestsellers and autobiographies and you'll find, hidden at the rear, a meagre poetry section comprising anthologies of love poems, long dead scribes and Pam Ayres collections.

Yet take a walk around the basement of the Poetry Café in Covent Garden, and you'll see a wall bustling with posters promoting events and readings throughout the capital. In any one evening in London – and, indeed, across the country – there is a diverse range of events showcasing the talents of both established and upcoming poets. Organisations such as Apples & Snakes and Penned in the Margins frequently manage to pack large theatre spaces with poetry in performance, and regular events such as Express Excess and Farrago Poetry Slam consistently engage audiences with an eclectic assortment of live verse.

It is not only in performance that there is such a wealth of options. Take a trip to the newly reopened Poetry Library and it is impossible not to be overwhelmed by the vast amounts of contemporary poetry committed to the page by the numerous small publishers. Whether it be the lovingly designed volumes from Donut and Pighog Press or the exhaustive range presented by Flipped Eye, it would seem that poetry is enjoying a period of rude health through the efforts of these small presses.

Tall-lighthouse is one of the many organisations attempting to sustain and promote the growth of contemporary poetry. We began in 2000 with a scissors-and-staples approach to publishing, initially working as the outlet for a creative writing group that regularly convened above a now sadly deceased pub in Greenwich. In an attempt to create a platform for contemporary poetry in the backwaters of South-East London, we organised readings at the STARK gallery in Lee Green; these soon began to attract poets from further afield, with big names such as Ken Smith, Michael Donaghy and John Hegley sharing the bill with local poets. We also began facilitating creative writing classes, and, working alongside our local council and community groups, took our poets into schools and organisations across the borough to lead poetry workshops.

Whilst continuing to publish poetry from our increasing roster of poets in our hastily assembled attic at home, we began regular events in central London at the Poetry Café, as well as moving out across South-East England with readings in Brighton and Exeter. Now, after seven years working to promote and publish poetry, we operate from a dedicated office space above the STARK Gallery, where we held our first series of readings.

First and foremost, we see ourselves as publishers, with an increasing catalogue of poetry books as our primary focus. However, we believe that to sustain a successful poetry business it's important to embrace every facet of the form – whether by introducing new audiences to poetry through our school work, or by maintaining a presence on the performance scene via our regular readings across the south of England. Despite a perceived dichotomy between the printed and the spoken word, we believe we have proved that the two can complement each other; as a small press without national distribution, events are often the main outlet for our books. The chapbook, a mainstay of small publishers such as ourselves, originated in the small self-published titles peddled by ballad-writers as they travelled and performed throughout 16th and 17th-century Britain, and this is a tradition that is in its own way still alive: around 80 per cent of our sales come from readings.

Sales are of course important, and the most significant and daunting challenge facing a small poetry press is finding audiences. Even the best poetry in the world can be rendered worthless if it sits dormant, gathering dust in a publisher's office. Without the clout of larger publishers, small presses have to create new ways of presenting their work to the book-buying public, be that through placing an emphasis on an Internet presence – as witnessed by Salt Publishing's advanced online sales model, and Shearsman's recent foray into the brave new world of e-books – or through our own attempt to find new audiences via young poets with our pilot project, a series of books showcasing the best new poets aged under 30. Whilst first and foremost acting as a platform for exciting new poets who would otherwise find it hard to find a publisher at this early stage of their careers, it has been extremely encouraging for us as publishers to see new and large audiences stirred by poetry from writers such as Adam O'Riordan and Helen Mort, both of whom prove that contemporary poetry is very much alive and well.

As a poet seeking to get your work in print, the old adage of using two ears and one mouth in proportion is pertinent when looking for a publisher. Merely carpet-bombing every small press in the country with unsolicited manuscripts will rarely lead to success. Before submitting anything it is vital to know who you are submitting to, and it's a good idea try to get into magazines first – this is a must in terms of knowing which poems 'work' for editors and those which don't. Once successful at that level, you can move on to seek publication of a volume of your work.

It is vitally important to be aware of what is going on, and poets should read as much contemporary poetry as possible; it's frustrating that many budding poets baulk at the idea of actually buying a poetry book (who would, therefore, buy theirs?), and most rejected manuscripts are evidently products of writers oblivious to the burgeoning scene around them. Most poetry nights employ an open-mic policy, and this still remains one of the most effective ways of keeping in touch with other writers' work and of showcasing your own efforts – indeed, the majority of our published poets, including Aoife Mannix, Pierre Ringwald, and Heather Taylor, made themselves known to us through such events. It was also through a reading that we met and subsequently published Brendan Cleary.

Once your research is complete and you have selected a publisher you respect, it's vital to keep the submission *brief*. Submit the six pieces that are most representative of your work and be careful with titles, as well as first and last lines, as these can often make or break a good submission. Finally, before submitting, get someone else to look at the work, at least to weed out the typos!

With so many poetry magazines and small presses in operation, it is highly likely there will be one out there that is suitable for your work. Good luck.

Tall-lighthouse is an independent poetry business dedicated to creating the appreciation of poetry. It publishes pamphlets, chapbooks, anthologies and full collections of poetry; it also organises poetry readings and events in and around London, South East and South West England, as well as facilitating writing workshops in conjunction with Arts, Education, Library and Community Services. See **www.tall-lighthouse.co.uk**.

Making a living as a poet

How do you reconcile the writing of poetry with the need to pay a mortgage and feed yourself? Especially as we are no longer content to starve in a garret – and why should we be? – to make our art? Poet **Michael Symmons Roberts** lays out the options open to poets as they strive for a decent lifestyle that also allows them to practise their craft.

The composer Jean Sibelius once moaned that "it is difficult to keep company with artists. You have to choose businessmen if you want to converse, because artists only talk about money". This rings true for many poets, and with good reason. Businessmen generally know where the money is coming from. Poets can be lauded by critics and admired by readers, but still struggle to make ends meet. Ends can be made to meet by poets in various ways, but most of them have little to do with the writing of poems.

Option one is to give up the day job, to go fully freelance as a poet. This is the purist's path, the route of no compromise. It is also virtually impossible. How many poets in the UK make a living solely from the writing and publishing of their poems? A handful at most. Giving readings can help, but many are not well paid, and they are better seen as a way of meeting readers than a way of earning a living. Short bursts of writing time can be funded by grants and awards. The Society of Authors' Gregory Awards for UK poets aged under 30 are a huge encouragement to poets as they begin to develop their work. There are other grants and awards – from the Arts Council and similar bodies – but they are not replacement salaries. They may allow you to take time out from a day job to write some poems, but they won't substitute for your salary in the long term. In the last few years, more fixed-tenure residencies and placements have been offered to poets: these usually involve some teaching or lecturing, and can provide considerable writing time. For poets with a track record, there are opportunities to teach short courses in libraries or schools, or with specialist organisations like the Arvon Foundation. However, even the hardest-working poet would struggle to keep the wolf from the door on a freelance mixture of writing poems, teaching courses, giving readings, and receiving grants. And the round of travel and form-filling could be a distraction from the writing of the poems themselves. You could find yourself living 'as a poet', but writing fewer poems than you did when you had a day job.

Option two is to give up the day job, and to go fully freelance as a *writer* – not just as a poet. This freelance life could include all of option one, but also writing in more lucrative forms such as journalism, fiction, script writing. The advantage of this is that you stand a chance of earning a living, but only if you make a success of these other forms of writing, and you will only do that if you genuinely enjoy them. As with option one, there is a danger of the poems being edged out of the picture by the more pressing deadlines and financial imperatives of the other writing. This is fine – and can be very rewarding – if you love writing fiction, journalism or scripts, but it can be just another form of day job if you don't.

Option three is to give up half the day job. This has become a better option in recent years, as employment legislation has begun to enhance and protect the status of part-time work. The advantage of this is that it gives a taste of freelance life, and a clear time in the week to focus on poetry, whilst maintaining a bedrock of income and security. Whether it works depends on the day job, and on the employer. There may be a price to pay in terms of career development in the day job, as many employers – wrongly – still regard part-time staff as under-motivated or lacking focus. But that price may be worth paying for the gains in time and mental space.

Option four is don't give up the day job. All kinds of day jobs have been tried and tested by poets over the years. Traditional favourites have included arts administration, broadcasting, teaching creative writing, teaching English in a school or university, and working in publishing or in libraries. How well any combination works depends on the poet and the job. For some poets, it's a perfect long-term solution, especially in education where (despite long hours in term-time) holidays are extensive and often free for writing. The frustration with so-called 'creative' jobs, or jobs close to writing, is that they frequently draw on the same energies that make the poems. You may be dealing with poetry or poets every day, but if you stop writing poems yourself, that may be scant compensation. Many poets have written (and still do) productively and well whilst holding down jobs completely unconnected with the arts or writing. When Ezra Pound famously attempted to 'liberate' TS Eliot from his day job at a bank in London, setting up a fund to allow the great poet to write full-time, Eliot was embarrassed and worried. He wasn't at all sure that the insecurity of the freelance life would benefit his writing. And of course, you don't have to be liberated from day jobs, even apparently un-creative day jobs, to fire the imagination. Wallace Stevens trained as a lawyer and pursued a career in insurance, ending up as Vice-President of the firm. On his way to work, this be-suited bureaucrat wrote some of the most expansive and groundbreaking poetry of the 20th century.

So how can a poet make a living? There is no single answer. What helps one will hinder another. Most poets have tried various options in their writing lives; it's a balancing act between putting bread on the table and securing time to write. And there is another gamble too: by becoming a full-time poet – even if you can make ends meet – you risk writing poems that don't need writing. Poems (unlike fiction) don't respond to you sitting at the desk at 9am daily, expecting them to show up. After all, poetry was never meant to function as a job, which is why poets end up talking about money.

Michael Symmons Roberts is the author of four collections of poetry, and won the Whitbread Prize for Poetry for his most recent book, *Corpus* (Jonathan Cape). His novel, *Patrick's Alphabet* (Jonathan Cape), was published in 2006.

Pamphlet power, poet power

Pamphlet publishing is becoming increasingly popular for two reasons. The first is that you can do it yourself; the second is that it avoids many of the financial issues involved in book publishing. **Hazel Cameron** explains where to look for help and inspiration, and gives some handy tips to the prospective pamphleteer.

From Jonathan Swift in the 1730s to Seamus Heaney, Philip Larkin and Liz Lochhead in modern times, poets have published their work in pamphlet form. Now the millennium has seen a revival in poetry pamphlets. New technology and access to desktop publishing methods have helped poets use their creativity and ingenuity to reach their readers, gaining independence from commerce and subsidy. The poetry pamphlet is flourishing and finding its way to new readers through quite different channels from the usual high-street bookshop. Instead, independent bookshops, local retailers, pamphlet fairs and the Internet can all accommodate the pamphlet and help poets reach their audience. If people write poetry and are serious about it, they should make it available to the public, who can then decide what they want to read. The pamphlet offers poets an opportunity to find their readership – something that has become almost impossible through the established methods of commercial publication.

In 2001, Tessa Ransford, founder of the Scottish Poetry Library, set up the Callum Macdonald Memorial Award in memory of her late husband Callum Macdonald, literary publisher and founder of Macdonald Publishers and Printers. The award recognises publishing skill and effort, and validates the practice of poetry publication in pamphlet form. It is supported by the Michael Marks Charitable Trust and many individuals, and is administered by the National Library of Scotland. Since its inception it has not only grown in itself, peaking with 53 entries in 2005, but has encouraged the confidence and development of pamphlet poetry.

Tessa also set up the pamphlet website **www.scottish-pamphlet-poetry.com**, which allows poets and publishers of pamphlets with a Scottish connection to list and sell their pamphlets on the Web. It helps pamphlet poetry to reach a wider audience, and many of the buyers are from abroad – from individuals, to English departments within overseas universities.

In 2004 the Edinburgh International Book Festival began taking a stand of independently published pamphlets for sale under the Scottish Pamphlet Poetry (SPP) umbrella. Sales increase annually, and last year more than 30 independent publishers were represented among the 200 pamphlets sold. This was a surprising achievement, and shows that the public enjoy the opportunity to discover and decide for themselves what they want to read in terms of poetry.

Pamphlet publishers were further encouraged in 2005 by the launch of *Sphinx* magazine, a magazine set up by the small press HappenStance specifically to review poetry pamphlets. Then in March 2006 the StAnza International Poetry Festival focused for the first time on the category of pamphlet poetry among its other international attractions. It held a successful pamphlet fair during the festival, allowing publishers to sell and display their pamphlets as well as giving poets and publishers the chance to meet and mix. The pamphlet fair is becoming a popular way of distributing poetry; it seems likely that 'market style' fairs will be seen on a regular basis at literary festivals.

There are many benefits to publishing in pamphlet form, as well as a few pitfalls. Generally, if you publish the pamphlet yourself, you can have full control over the contents, layout and cover. However, having your work checked and edited by an independent person before going to print is recommended. Unless you have experience in the printing industry, it is advisable to speak to and probably use a professional printer to produce your final work.

There are a growing number of small presses that produce poetry pamphlets on behalf of poets. Often they will approach a poet whose work they have seen published in poetry magazines, or heard at readings, but many are still happy to be approached by poets with a view to publication. This removes the production and some of the marketing from the poet, yet allows them to remain involved in the content and design of the pamphlet.

With the growing interest in poetry readings and performances, a pamphlet is an excellent way of having your work for sale if you do not have a book. It seems that the public are less likely to buy a book of poetry than to buy a pamphlet; often, they may purchase one to give as a gift or instead of a card. When it comes to distribution, this is usually cheaper and easier to do with pamphlets than with books. Local library shops and other small retailers are more likely to take a few for display on a sale-or-return basis.

If you decide to try the independent approach, please take into consideration the following points:

• It still takes time to produce a pamphlet – usually twice as long as you imagine; design especially is important and should not be rushed. Give yourself sufficient time to make the best of your work.

• Do not start with too many copies: 100 is a good first run.

• Look at other pamphlets; there are lots around. Collaborative projects can take longer, but can be more fun and very satisfying.

• Try to design an attractive cover and have a good title. Take care too with the quality of paper used and the size and style of font (typeface).

• Include a contact number or address in the pamphlet. An ISBN is not essential, but is helpful to shops and festivals – and *always* show a publication date.

• Send your pamphlet to local newspapers and poetry magazines for review.

• Arrange your own readings, or collaborate with others in order to publicise your work.

The best thing about producing a pamphlet yourself is that it is fun. So enjoy it.

Hazel B Cameron is a poet who has published a number of pamphlets. Her work can currently be found on the *Lippy Bissoms* pamphlet, which can be purchased from the Scottish pamphlet website, **www.scottish-pamphlet-poetry.com**.

An education in everything

Carol Ann Duffy, Sylvia Plath and the Arvon Foundation were instrumental in shaping the life of poet, **Colette Bryce**. Here, she tells us about her journey to becoming a poet.

Being a sorry excuse for a degree student, I was overcome with guilt every time I skulked into the English department to beg an extension on an essay deadline or to daydream my way through another seminar on a novel I had only half read. One of the last flowers of the welfare state, there I was squandering my big chance at an education. My lowest point was writing an essay, in the wee small hours, fuelled on ProPlus and cigarettes, on Tennyson's *Maud* which I hadn't read. I actually passed, which only goes to show that university lecturers have their own problems.

Then two things happened. Firstly, a tutor, Marion Lomax (now the poet Robyn Bolam) had organised a poetry event and appealed to us to attend. "Where's the harm," I said to my friends, sure it would be only a short hop to the pub afterwards; besides, a living poet was quite an exotic concept. The poet turned out to be Carol Ann Duffy and we thought she was rather good. Surprisingly, her poems seemed relevant to our lives. But for me, who secretly wanted to write, the knowledge that a young woman could work as a poet – that this was somehow possible – was a revelation, and a door very quietly opened somewhere in my mind.

The second thing was the appearance on the syllabus of the poetry of Sylvia Plath, closely followed by that of Philip Larkin, both of whom, in near opposite ways, seemed to wake me up with a jolt.

After finishing my degree I revisited the department for some reason and spotted a brochure for the Arvon Foundation's writing courses pinned to the noticeboard. I found myself extremely interested. I was aware, by then, that I had a huge need to write ... but a great fear of it too. I examined the brochure for a long time, and then stole it. That was the first move in my writing life.

But I had no money for an Arvon course. The Foundation offered part-bursaries but still I needed a couple of hundred pounds. I asked my landlord for an extension on the rent (I was an expert at securing extensions by then) and he agreed. I booked a week off work, which was stacking supermarket shelves on the night shift. I chose a beginners' course that was to be tutored by the only living poet I had ever met – the very same Carol Ann Duffy – along with the poet and crime novelist John Harvey. And off I went to Yorkshire with no idea what to expect.

I was very nervous. The other students seemed older and wiser and some had even had poems published in magazines. There was nothing for it but to come clean to the tutors. "I'm a beginner," I told them, "literally. Where do I begin?" And they set me on a path of contemporary reading that opened my eyes to poetry as a vital, relevant art form, full of possibilities. That changed everything: I haven't stopped reading, or writing, since.

I gave up the nocturnal shelf-stacking and took up daylight bookselling, ending up in Waterstone's on Hampstead High Street for a number of years. These were the good old days of bookselling: independents could still make a living; Bernard Stone was in Covent Garden; and Waterstone's was owned by Dan Dare and employed people with a passion for books and with capacious brains to memorise stock (and the legendary overstocks).

There were no computers, *imagine*. We would hand-write stock lists; phone through orders for hundreds of ISBNs, straight-faced; spend hours chasing the most obscure title for a customer; and squint at microfiche hieroglyphics to see if there just might be an American edition.

We prided ourselves on our sections. There seemed to be nothing the art buyer, the brilliant Mike Payne, didn't know about his subject, or the fiction buyer about hers. With the blessing of the manager and a seemingly limitless budget, I set about constructing my dream poetry section, a situation unthinkable today. Everything I had ever read or wanted to read was there. Everything I should have read and would one day get around to reading was there. All the classics. All the key translations. The Europeans. The Americans. When I discovered a new poet from the States (for example when Sharon Olds' *The Father* was published here) I would import their entire American backlist and pile them high on the table. And they sold.

Receiving poetry deliveries felt like Christmas. Michael Horovitz would appear at the desk bearing quantities of *Grandchildren of Albion*. I had a network of regular poetry readers who would drop in for a chat and to check out what was new. The New-Gen poets were making a splash. Bloodaxe was publishing wonderful anthologies and we stocked them all in generous quantities. Customers would wander in with a half-remembered poem in their heads, could I tell them who wrote it? (Yeats, nearly always.) I was developing a serious poetry habit and the considerable staff discount was keeping me in supplies. I was reading poetry on the bus, on the tube, in the staffroom, on the roof, and behind the till in the twilight zone of the late shift, when only the odd drunk or Bronco John would venture into the store.

Meanwhile, I was writing at night and learning. I would meet up once-weekly in Whitechapel with my friend and fellow poetry nut Kate Clanchy, then a schoolteacher, and swap poems and feedback over a glass of red. I attended a few more courses, and many readings around town, at bookshops and cafés. On days off I would write at a booth in the Poetry Library on the South Bank. This was my kind of education; one thing leading organically to another, a journey of discoveries. And the education was not only in poetry. Poetry, being about everything, is an education in everything.

In 1995, I had my first poems published in a new poets anthology, and I applied for and received an Eric Gregory award from the Society of Authors. It was a good year for me all round because I also fell in love. I was 25. But I was nowhere near ready to publish a collection. In a strange way, being published was beside the point. I had a sense, and still do, that poetry is a life's work and there should be no big rush to publish. Even five years later, when my first book came out, it felt very soon – but that's another story.

My advice? Read; it's as simple as that. And only those who need to will heed it.

Colette Bryce was born in Derry in 1970. Her first collection was *The Heel of Bernadette* (Picador), which won the Aldeburgh Poetry Festival Prize for Best First Collection; her second, *The Full Indian Rope Trick* was published by Picador in 2004.

There was this girl, you see ...

Roddy Lumsden writes about his early years as a poet.

When I was ten, I wanted to be an archaeologist; by age 12 I had changed my future career to vet. Both professions were entirely unsuitable, being hard work – something that never was my destiny. By 17, I had fallen back on the one thing that had brought me effortless returns as a child. I announced to my school-friends that I intended to be a poet; indeed, I already was one. I don't recall this bold declaration, but years later, one of those friends reminded me of how they had laughed. He was proud, though, that I had stuck to my task and achieved my dream.

As a poetry tutor, I see patterns in the writing lives of my students. It is common to find young women in their mid- to late 20s who, a few years into a career, return to poetry, having written in their teens. Frequently, too, people take up or return to poetry in their early 40s; these poets can take encouragement from poets such as Annie Freud and John Stammers who have received acclaim despite taking to poetry relatively late.

I always have a sneaking preference for those who are drawn early to the pleasures of matchmaking words and make their way up the steep steps of the craft. I empathise with poets who have boxes of juvenilia, jotters stuffed with odes to the self, private world musings and paeans to sexual frustration. I like to think of Clare Pollard at 16, preparing her manuscript for Bloodaxe, or Ahren Warner – a brilliant young poet, still only 20 – poring over every word in *Poetry Review* at 13.

There was this girl, you see, also a 13-year-old, who came on holiday to the seaside town where I grew up. I had just turned 15 and sat in the teenage disco with my arm around her. By the end of the week she preferred Paddy, who lived a few doors down from me. I wasn't too anguished, but I did, for some reason, write a remorseful poem about it. I hadn't written a poem since I was 11 or so, and that had been a comic piece about elephants, complete with a coloured pencil drawing. This was different; this was the deep stuff.

About a year and a half later, I began to write copiously: dreamy stuff, surreal stuff and formal stuff. At this point in my life, my artistic landmarks were Robert Hughes' book on modern art, *The Shock of the New*, the plays of Pinter, and two dog-eared poetry collections. George Macbeth's Longman anthology *Poetry 1900-1965* (school issue) introduced me to Plath, Gunn, Larkin and especially Eliot. Edward Lucie Smith's *British Poetry Since 1945* actually contained some poets younger than my parents, and I was particularly taken with WS Graham.

I went off to University in Edinburgh, where I studied ethnology. Interest in my course soon took a back seat to poetry when I discovered what seemed like miles of poetry books in the University library. Then one day I realised that was just the British stuff! American and Canadian poetry fascinated me. I spent my college years with a huge bag of library books on the handlebar of my bike. These were the years when I found, as you must, kindred spirits, mentors and influences.

My early 20s saw me fall under the spell of a succession of poets: the Canadians Alden Nowlan and Michael Ondaatje were favourites, as were the Irish poets Paul Durcan and Paul Muldoon. As for mentors, I was lucky. Liz Lochhead and Anne Stevenson were successive writers-in-residence: both helped me greatly and taught me important, sometimes conflicting lessons. Their workshops introduced me to my peers. The poet and folklorist Hamish Henderson also read my poems and gave encouragement, as did Robert Crawford who became the first person to publish me (outside of student magazines). He took a poem for the journal *Verse*. It was only a few lines long, but the pages around it contained work by modern gods of poetry – John Ashbery, Les Murray and the like.

As for kindred spirits, there were two important ones, still close friends. My schoolmate Mark Ayton, now a translator, confessed to me that he wrote poetry and we spent an afternoon at his house swapping poems: it no longer seemed like an odd thing to be doing (I don't come from a particularly bookish family). At University, I made friends with Andy Jackson (who, as AB Jackson, won the Forward Prize for Best First Collection a couple of years ago). Together, we started *Fox*, a student poetry magazine and later shared a flat, happily grilling each other's poems late into the night fuelled by Marlboros and toast. Andy seemed like the real thing to me – he would shave his head and disappear for days in his box room, emerging with the latest version of his epic about Christ in the wilderness.

Come 1990, when I was 24, I decided to have my first stab at an Eric Gregory award (the annual prizes for poets under 30). Six months later, the late Roy Jenkins handed me a cheque for £7000 and the poetry editor at Faber was asking to see a manuscript. The whole business freaked me out – I had never thought of my poetry as having a life beyond our smoky flat above the cinema. As instructed, I used some prize money on a trip abroad. In the Strand bookstore in Manhattan (where just a few weeks ago I bumped into my erstwhile hero Muldoon!), I picked up the *Collected Poems* of fellow Scot Edwin Morgan. I lay on my bed in a cheap hotel and held up this brick of a book, testing its weight. I decided I was not up to the task of becoming a poet. I wrote next to nothing for three years. And then there was this girl ...

Roddy Lumsden's *Mischief Night: New & Selected Poems* is published by Bloodaxe. His fifth collection *Third Wish Wasted* is due in Autumn 2008. He works as a poetry tutor and editor and also compiles puzzles, quizzes and trivia.

A poet's life

Annie Freud writes about her introduction to poetry and the influences that have guided her career.

How did I get into poetry? It's more a question of how poetry got into me. A few years ago I saw Anne Carson read from *Glass, Irony and God* at Poetry International. She made me sit up and take notice. I was electrified by her grief. Here was something grand, disturbing, like a horse rearing up on its hind legs in protest. Hearing her read was like being accosted by a sort of Ancient Mariner, and feeling her dread hand on my shoulder. It made a difference that I was there with my cousin (twice-removed), Wolf, who had sought my friendship after his wife died, and with whom I often went to readings. He was unusual in many ways, tremendously adaptable, open and adventurous. At his funeral, I read the first of Rilke's *Duino Elegies*.

I had written some film scripts which were adaptations of some short stories by EM Forster for television. The best one was *The Obelisk*. I sent it everywhere. I went to script-writing classes. I bought books about script-writing and pored over their contradictory sets of rules: I read Aristotle's *Poetics*; I read *Ecclesiastes*. I read other scripts. I tried and tried and got nowhere.

Something else had got me going. I had attended a seminar given by Dennis Brown (at that time, Professor of Modern Literature at the University of Hertfordshire) at a conference entitled 'Psychoanalysis and the Public Sphere – Thinking Under Fire'. "I'm not really interested in psychoanalysis," he said. "What interests me is why people write poetry." He read us *Adultery* by Carol Ann Duffy. It blew me away. He spoke about poetry as an enhancement of life and an enlargement of our sensibility. After that, something changed for me; I was in a state of wonder, like being in the presence of a continuous resonant silence – my stout Cortez stage!

In 1999, I enrolled for Michael Donaghy's class at City University. I had never heard of him before. At the time, I was mostly unaware of contemporary poetry. He was an incredibly inspiring and entertaining teacher – funny, gorgeous and passionate. It was as if a living, breathing, laughing Mercutio had arrived amongst us in modern dress. I saw him recite his poems many times. His voice was incredible. He had a marvellous way of using his hands when he was performing. Seeing him recite *Black Ice and Rain* was utterly compelling. Suddenly I had a whole new bunch of friends, forever branching out in different directions: new places to go to, new poems to listen to, new things to talk about, new places to drink and talk. Aha, we'd say, there's a poem in there! when one of our gang had seen someone doing something a bit strange on the underground. The point of it all was to raise our game, become our own 'best' critics and write fantastic poems.

I joined John Stammers' Group and that was the start of writing poems seriously. I found that my poems often changed beyond recognition when I worked on them. Their subject matter went through many mutations. Very occasionally I'd be lucky and I'd be on the bus and get a poem almost in one shot.

I discovered the pleasure of close reading in a group and finding poets I'd not read before: Berryman, Tonks, Celan, Ashbery, Tanstromer, Pessoa, Selima Hill and Reading; rediscovering poets I'd once loved and had since neglected: Cavafy, DH Lawrence, Frost,

Ogden Nash, Marvell, Stevie Smith, Rilke; and delighting in the works of poets whose work I'd dismissed through prejudice or laziness: Dickinson, Tennyson, Christina Rossetti, Meredith and Whitman. Sometimes I'd find that poems I'd loved when I was young became exasperating.

I began to get invitations to read my poems in public. I got such a kick out of it that for quite a long time I didn't really think about trying to get published. Later on, when John showed some of my poems to Don Paterson, he was immediately enthusiastic and soon afterwards I began preparing my first full collection for Picador. The editorial process was totally absorbing.

For some years, my main activity had been embroidery and tapestry. I covered knitwear, often second-hand, with flowers, butterflies, beetles and rabbits; I embroidered a pixelated stag on the back of an Armani suit for Graham Norton; I embroidered a waistcoat for Jon Snow with a design inspired by one of Gainsborough's portraits. I embroidered an image on a cardigan of a crouching dog taken from a mosaic in Pompeii. When I started to be serious about writing poems, the embroidery had to take a back seat. But somehow it continued to bleed into my poems.

Being interested in visual art, painting especially, is a useful stimulus for writing. It helps me to be ambitious for my poems and to hope that they can become art. There is a small portrait that I particularly love of a young girl by Lucas Cranach the Elder in the National Gallery in London. It shows her richly but simply dressed and wearing an elaborate headdress. The expression on her face fascinates me; she seems to be trying to make sense of something she has just seen or heard. Maybe she is just waiting for the painter to tell her that she can have a rest. It's not like looking at a painting of someone and wondering about the skill it took to make it. It's like being with her, or being her. I often think about her when I'm writing.

It's not easy to say who my influences are as I don't consciously try to emulate the contemporary poets I most admire: August Kleinzahler, Les Murray, Paul Muldoon, Hugo Williams. I read and reread *The Love Song of J Alfred Prufrock* and Keats's odes and sonnets in the hope that this might make me write something that feels as profound. I think that influence is largely a subliminal thing. It's haphazard. But something you have to keep an eye open for. You come into contact with things that affect you deeply and stay with you forever. As a child, I used to love Lear's poem, *The Yonghy-Bonghy-Bo*: its desolate landscape, the early pumpkins, the little heap of stones, his few possessions, the place names, his passion for the Lady Jingly Jones and his escape on the turtle's back when she turns him down and the way the whole thing sloshes backwards and forwards like waves breaking on the sea shore.

Annie Freud has published two volumes of poetry: *A Voids Officer Achieves the Tree Pose* (Donut Press, 2006) and *The Best Man That Ever Was* (Picador, 2007).

New to English: getting published in the UK

Choman Hardi has made a remarkable journey, from Kurdish refugee to successful poet. She writes about that journey, and the people and organisations who helped her en route.

I came to England in 1993 as a refugee from Iraqi Kurdistan. Two years later I started writing poetry in Kurdish. Until then I had been writing short stories and although I knew many Kurdish and Persian poems by heart I had not been able to write any myself. At 22 I published my first collection of poetry in Kurdish through a small diaspora publisher in Denmark. Suddenly it was all so clear, I wanted to write poetry and for a long time I deserted fiction altogether.

I began translating some of my poems into English in 1998 just after the publication of my second poetry book in Kurdish. Without realising it, I was becoming part of a large group of writers who came to English from another poetic tradition: poets who are forever unsatisfied with the translation of their work into English, who feel that English does not fit their poems, it restricts them, alienates them, and makes them seem ambitious. Needless to say I didn't like my poems in translation, they just didn't settle well in this precise and understated tradition.

In the same year I was invited by Jennifer Langer (who later founded Exiled Writers Ink! See page 179) to read my poems to a British audience for the first time. Thinking about the evening on the bus from Oxford to London, I wondered if this would be the beginning of becoming a British poet – but I soon ruled this out in my mind. I believed that writing in your mother tongue makes you a foreign poet even if you live all of your life in the UK and write about British things. It seemed impossible to me at the time that a writer like me could become an insider in the British literary scene.

In 1999 I finished my PPP degree, moved back to London where I started an MA in philosophy and got divorced from my Kurdish husband. I processed my Kurdish divorce in English language and wrote many poems which I have never published. These poems did what they were supposed to do – they moved me over from one tradition to the next, from one language to the next. I wrote in English because I needed some form of distancing from what I was writing about, because I found it easier to write about a personal and painful subject in a foreign language. But soon I realised that I even enjoyed writing in English and it gave me a new perspective and more freedom.

I have always said that I owe a lot to Jennifer Langer who, from the beginning, involved me in Exiled Writers Ink! This organisation was unique because it aimed to help refugee writers, some of whom were well-established writers in their own languages and who lived in Britain and were isolated and invisible. When I went there I met many writers from the Middle East, Eastern Europe and other parts of the world who were in the same boat as me. It was decided to have regular events in the Poetry Café (see page 107) on the first Monday of every month to give the poets an outlet and some exposure. I went to these readings and got involved in the committee without having had any previous experience of this kind of work. Soon we were like a community and it was always great to read, chat, compare notes and have a laugh. Over the years, representatives from different organisations came to listen to us and other possibilities opened themselves up.

I am also grateful to Apples and Snakes (see page 172) and the British Council (see page 176) who even before I had a publication record had faith in my work and involved me in their projects. Soon, I was doing many readings and attending conferences all over the UK. I became well-established as a poet in the reading circles. Some of the organisations and associations that invited me were ticking their Cultural Diversity boxes; as a result I sometimes read to three or four people in large empty venues. It was obvious that the events were not well marketed and nor well thought out. At times I felt frustrated by the numerous occasions when such things happened and because most of the time I was not paid or paid very little. Still I tried never to drop standards. I did my best in every reading and stayed positive and worked hard. I also got on a few mailing lists and went to readings, familiarised myself with the poets who were out there and went and read their work.

Exiled Writers Ink! was a great outlet for us. Through this channel we managed to secure some funding, organise joint conferences, publish anthologies, give and receive poetry workshops and later publish a literary magazine, all of which were essential for our development as writers. But getting published remained a distant possibility until Geraldine Collinge, the director of Apples and Snakes, selected me as one of four young poets from the organisation, under the supervision of mentors, to take part in Poetry International in 2002 (the other writers were Daljit Nagra, Zena Edwards and Fatima Kelleher).

I was very lucky to have the opportunity to work with Moniza Alvi during this project. She was brilliant in her feedback, generous with her time and extremely supportive. The final event was a great success and the four of us enjoyed being on the huge stage, reading to a large crowd of poetry lovers. Unknown to me, Neil Astley was in the audience and after the event Moniza introduced me to him. He encouraged me to send him some poems and two months later he told that he would publish my first book, on the condition that I produce some new work. Neil nominated me for the Jerwood-Arvon Young Poet's Scheme during which I worked with George Szirtes (another brilliant mentor and person) and *Life for US* was published two years later.

I have been really lucky in having had the support of so many great people. My first book was well received and although it was not shortlisted for any prizes or reviewed in the national press it was reprinted less than a year and a half later. This, and the experience of poets who are in a similar situation, shows that many different kinds of poetry are being produced in Britain, and that the British audience is very much interested in the new British poets – although the decisions of judges and selectors do not necessarily reflect this diversity. But I am an optimist and I believe that the fact that people like me can get published and be popular is a great success in itself.

Choman Hardi is a poet and painter who was born and raised in Sulaimaniya, Kurdistan. She lived in Iran and Turkey before arriving in England in 1993. Her collections of poetry (in Kurdish) are *Return with No Memory* (Denmark, 1996) and *Light of the Shadows* (Sweden, 1998), and *Life for Us* (Bloodaxe Books, 2004) in English.

A brief overview: poetry in a matchbox

There is a veritable mountain of poetry magazines published every year. Magazine editor **James Byrne** takes us through some history, and provides useful guidelines for submitting material to magazines.

Tracking the number of poetry magazines in the UK is an impossible task. The Poetry Library website (**www.poetrylibrary.org.uk**) puts the list at 182, while freely acknowledging that there are "obviously more" in circulation. The figure is more likely to be over 250.

Since its inception in 1964, the Poetry Store Collection (a UCL library initiative) has acquired more than 7000 titles. It also concedes that this figure does not account for every poetry publication available today. One of the reasons for this is that, while some poetry magazines might suddenly disappear, replacements steadily arrive. As this article is being written, a new publication from Manchester called *Matchbox* – a magazine that quite literally fits the size of a matchbox – is being prepared, along with countless others.

Old journals too are being pulled back from extinction. The exciting left-wing experimental magazine *Fragmente*, which fell away in the 1990s, is due for re-issue. But perhaps a more quirky example is *St Botolph's Review*, which has finally produced its second offering some 50 years after Sylvia Plath and Ted Hughes first met during its auspicious launch in Cambridge.

When I moved to London as an aspiring young poet, the Poetry Library, with its bulging stock of poetry magazines, was a crucial find. It has been difficult this past year seeing it wrapped under tarpaulin as part of the Royal Festival Hall's extensive renovations. However, almost as if to compensate for this, the PL now provides a digital library of poetry magazines (**www.poetrymagazines.org.uk**) which offers some delightful archive material and the digitisation of more than 30 poetry magazines. Each issue reads as closely as possible to original print formatting and celebrates a diversity of poetry that has the potential to reach new audiences. An "independent and free-standing" website, **poetrymagazines** already has a strong cast list, including many of the leading poetry journals in Britain. There are some real gems to be found, from *Poetry Review*'s inaugural issue in 1912, to the final editorial of the much-missed *Thumbscrew*. An eventual aim of the PL is to digitise its entire collection of magazines – a massive task, but one that would increase the readership of contemporary poetry and make the poet's job far easier in choosing where to submit their own writing.

Another important project for the preservation of poetry journals is provisionally entitled *The Little Magazine's Compendium*, due for publication in the autumn as this *Yearbook* goes to press. It documents thousands of poetry magazines from 1914 to 2000, and tells us where more than 5000 poets sent their work. Here we can find where poetry giants like Ezra Pound, TS Eliot and John Berryman first began to publish their poems as relative unknowns. Excitingly, we can also discover developing trends of writing and exactly where groups of writers made allegiances to particular schools or movements, such as Imagism and Surrealism.

Many of the magazines featured had short print runs or short lives and are now extremely rare. The *Compendium* lists the key libraries where these publications can still be found as well as mapping the birthplaces of magazines across the British Isles. Nearly ten years in the making, it's a book not just for the literary anorak or historian, but for poets of all abilities.

Perhaps you are a reader who is relatively new to poetry but with ambitions to publish. As editor of *The Wolf* I'll finish by offering a few simple do's and don'ts regarding the presentation of your work.

Firstly – and this has been hammered home by poetry editors for years now – read up on the journals before you lick that stamp. There will be poetry magazines which may not suit your style of writing, however original your submission may be. Indeed, certain poetry magazines publish only love poems; others (like *Mslexia*) will only accept work from female poets. What use would your epic poem on Norse mythology be to a poetry publication that tends only to publish cyberpunk poems?

For those about to send off work to poetry magazines for the first time, you should of course possess a current copy of *Poetry Writers' Yearbook*! – and you may also benefit from *Light's List*, now in its 21st year of publication. It's cheap at £4 and includes names, addresses, prices, page counts and the frequency of more than 1500 UK, US, Canadian, Australian, European, African and Asian small press magazines publishing creative writing in English.

However, most serious poetry magazines will have their own website. Skim through internal guidelines regarding submission. In many cases you will be required to send a short biography or covering letter. Know who it is you are addressing: finding out the editor's name shows good table manners. If you are sending poems via the Web, make sure that attachments can be opened and that you write a subject title in the email. Countless submissions come into *The Wolf*'s email account with 'no subject'; sadly many of these, if unrecognised, get deleted without ever having been read. For postal submissions you should send a stamped-addressed envelope. Furthermore, always write your name and contact details at the end of each poem. If you are sending a long poem you may wish to staple pages together: an editor going through 1000 poems for an issue might get the odd one jumbled up, and it would be terrible for the poem that you've slaved over to be misplaced or even attributed to someone else!

There are a host of other small measures I could suggest, but my last pinch of advice is to aim high and to keep writing better poems. If you think your own poetry good enough to be published, perhaps work out a sliding scale of exactly where you'd like to see yourself in print. Start at the top and work your way through. Inevitably rejection will come along, but it should be rationalised. If your poetry is rich and original it will be published eventually. Certain journals, particularly those which claim to be inundated with reams of submissions, might take an eternity to reply. I remember once having to wait a whole year only to be rejected by a magazine! After smouldering for days, I took comfort in learning that Ted Hughes was repeatedly refused by Faber in his early career, before *The Hawk in the Rain* appeared: a book that fast-tracked him to becoming a leading poet of the 20th century.

James Byrne is Editor of *The Wolf* poetry magazine. He is also currently editing *Priora* – an anthology of poetry and photography to be published by Phaidon in 2007. He has recently worked for the Poetry Translation Centre at the School of Oriental and African Studies, and is finishing a second collection of poems.

Magazines

The list below is a snapshot of the poetry magazine world as of summer 2007. However, by the time you read this it is likely that some of the magazines will no longer be in existence, and that brand new ones will have emerged. The magazines in this list range from photocopied, stapled sheets of densely typed A4 to perfect-bound, immaculately designed, high-quality glossy publications. What they all have in common, though, are relentless enthusiasm and an unbridled love of poetry. As ever, before you send work off, carry out some research to establish that your poetry is suitable, and always include an sae with submissions.

UK AND IRELAND

10th Muse
33 Hartington Road, Southampton SO14 0EW
email andyj@noplace.screaming.net
Editor Andrew Jordan
Frequency/price Occasional. £3.50 (£6 for 2 issues)

Publishes mainly poems written by poets who read poetry. The collision of archaic and modern elements can often create good poetry.

Submission details Submit no more than 6 poems or 2000 words of prose. Sae or IRC essential. Write name and address on each sheet. No multiple submissions or previously published work. Payment by complimentary copy.

14 Magazine
PO Box 253, Northwood, Middlesex HA6 2ZF
email mike_loveday@hotmail.com
website www.fourteenmagazine.com
Editor Rudy Gordon
Frequency/price 2 p.a. £2.95 plus 35p postage. £6 for 2 issues

Rhymed, unrhymed, traditional, unconventional; all styles accepted, but must have 14 lines only.

Submission details Up to 6 poems, typed, accompanied by sae. Poems may have already been published (provided poet has obtained permission).

AABYE
email geraldengland@yahoo.com
website www.geraldengland.org.uk
Editor Gerald England
Frequency/price £4.50

Eclectic collection of poetry from the traditional to the avant-garde, from haiku to long poems, including translations. Has ceased publication, but copies still available.

Abraxas
57 Eastbourne Road, St Austell, Cornwall PL25 4SU
Editor Paul Newman

Publishes contemporary poetry, with a special emphasis on the lyric mode.

Acorn
Bowes Pub, Fleet Street, Dublin 2, Ireland
email dubwriter@indigo.ie
website www.dublinwriters.org
Frequency/price £3.75

Magazine from Dublin Writers' Workshop.
Submission details Poems and short fiction of any style are considered, in English or French.

Active in Airtime
24 Regent Road, Brightlingsea, Essex
website www.areopagus.org.uk
Editor Julian Barritt
Frequency/price Quarterly. Subscription: UK £10; Europe £12.50; USA $17; Rest of World £15

A special-interest, quarterly, A5 publication for Christian writers, run voluntarily by a team based in various parts of the UK and USA. Publishes subscribers' fiction, poetry and articles.

Aereings Publications
Dean Head Farm, Scotland Lane, Leeds LS18 5HU
Editor Lesley Quayle, Linda Marshall
Frequency/price £4.50 per issue. Annual UK subscription £11

Aesthetica Magazine
PO Box 371, York YO23 1WL
tel (01904) 527560

email submissions@aestheticamagazine.com (submissions), info@aestheticamagazine.com (queries)
website www.aestheticamagazine.com
Editor Cherie Frederico, Bruce Corrie (Poetry Editor)
Frequency/price Bi-monthly. £4.50

A contemporary cultural arts publication that believes in creative expression. Prefers work to reflect issues of contemporary times and to make the reader feel, change or see a new perspective. No gratuitous use of bad language; read a copy before submitting.
   Submission details Submit 3-5 poems, via email only. Payment of complimentary copy. See website for guidelines.

Agenda

The Wheelwrights, Fletching Street, Mayfield, East Sussex TN20 6TL
tel/fax (01435) 873703
email editor@agendapoetry.co.uk
website www.agendapoetry.co.uk
Editor Patricia McCarthy
Frequency/price Quarterly. £28 p.a. (£35 libraries, institutions and overseas); £22 OAPs/students

Poetry and criticism. Young poets (and artists), aged 16 to 38, invited to submit work for online Broadsheets Workshop, details online.
   Submission details Study the journal before submitting MSS with an sae, or by email. Include email address and a brief biography.

Ambit

17 Priory Gardens, London N6 5QY
tel 020-8340 3566
website www.ambitmagazine.co.uk
Editor Martin Bax, Kate Pemberton *Poetry Editors* Henry Graham, Carol-Ann Duffy *Prose Editors* JG Ballard, Geoff Nicholson *Art Editor* Mike Foreman
Frequency/price Quarterly. £7.50 inc. p&p (£28 p.a. UK, £29/€52 Europe, £29/$56 rest of world; £40 p.a., £40/€70 p.a., £40/$73 p.a. institutions)

Poetry, short fiction, art, poetry reviews. New and established writers and artists. Payment: by arrangement. Illustrations: line, half-tone, colour. Founded 1959.

An Guth

Cruard, Isle Ornsay, Isle of Skye IV43 8QS
tel (01471) 833376
email anguth@btinternet.com
Editor Rody Gorman
Frequency/price Annual. £7

Poetry in Scottish or Irish Gaelic.
   Submission details Send poems to above address.

Angel Exhaust

35 Stewart's Way, Mannden, Nr Bishop's Stortford, Hertfordshire CM23 1OR
email aduncan@pinko.org
Editor Andrew Duncan, Charles Bainbridge

Recently relaunched poetry magazine.

Anon

67 Learmouth Grove, Edinburgh EH4 1BL
website www.blanko.org.uk/anon
Editor Mike Stocks (www.mikestocks.com)
Frequency/price As and when. £12 subscription, £4 per issue

A magazine to which poems are submitted anonymously and assessed blind, using procedures similar to those used by poetry competitions. Poems that are accepted for publication are published under the names of their authors. Payment is 1 free copy.
   Submission details Refer to website for submission guidelines.

Aquarius

Flat 4, 116 Sutherland Avenue, London W9 2QP
Editor Eddie Linden
Frequency/price Irregular

An irregularly published but influential magazine.

Areopagus

48 Cornwood Road, Plympton, Plymouth, Devon PL7 1AL
email editor@areopagus.org.uk
website www.areopagus.org.uk
Editor Julian Barritt

A magazine of Christian poetry, articles and fiction. Ask for details of subscription and submissions.

Areté

8 New College Lane, Oxford OX1 3BN
tel (01865) 289193 *fax* (01865) 289194
email craig.raine@new.ox.ac.uk
website www.aretemagazine.com
Editor Craig Raine
Frequency/price 3 issues p.a.

Fiction, poetry, reportage and reviews.
  Submission details Hard copy only. No international reply coupons. Unsolicited manuscripts should be accompanied by an sae.

Atlantean – see Atlantean on page 10.

Awen

38 Pierrot Steps, 71 Kursaal Way,
Southend-on-Sea, Essex SS1 2UY
email atlanteanpublishing@hotmail.com
website www.geocities.com/dj_tyrer/awen.html
Editor DJ Tyrer
Frequency/price Bi-monthly. Free with sae

Open to all styles of poem up to about 50 lines in length. New, unpublished and experienced poets are equally welcome. Payment is 1 complimentary copy.
  Submission details Unsolicited submissions with sae or in the body of an email are welcome.

Bad Poetry Quarterly

PO Box 6319, London E11 2EP
Editor Gordon Smith

Always on the lookout for new poems, poets and illustrations.

Banipal: Magazine of Modern Arab Literature

PO Box 22300, London W13 8ZQ
tel 020-8568 9747
email editor@banipal.co.uk
website www.banipal.co.uk
Editor Margaret Obank
Frequency/price 3 issues p.a. 1 year, £20; 2 years, £30. Rest of Europe, £20/£30. Rest of world, £30/£50

An independent literary magazine publishing contemporary authors and poets from all over the Arab world in English translation. Founded in 1998 by Margaret Obank and Iraqi author Samuel Shimon, the 3 issues a year present established and new authors – most for the first time – through poems, short stories or excerpts of novels. They also feature extensive author interviews, profiles and a series on authors writing about their literary influences. In 7 years of publication *Banipal* has presented works from more than 300 different authors.
  Submission details Submit hard copy only. See website for full guidelines.

Bard

38 Pierrot Steps, 71 Kursaal Way,
Southend-on-Sea SS1 2UY
email atlanteanpublishing@hotmail.com
website www.geocities.com/dj_tyrer/bard.html
Editor DJ Tyrer
Frequency/price Monthly. Free for sae

Open to all styles of poetry up to 20 lines (longer poems should be sent to *Monomyth*). New, unpublished and experienced poets welcome.
  Submission details Unsolicited submissions with sae or in the body of an email.

A Bard Hair Day

289 Elmwood Avenue, Feltham,
Middlesex TW13 7QB
email partners_writing_group@hotmail.com
Editor Ian Deal

A magazine with no rules.

Beat Scene

27 Court Leet, Binley Woods,
Coventry CV3 2Q
tel (02476) 543604
email kev@beatscene.freeserve.co.uk
website www.beatscene.net
Editor Kevin Ring

Celebrates the work of the Beat Generation, writers, artists, poets, photographers.

The Black Rose

56 Marlescroft Way, Loughton,
Essex IG10 3NA
email blackrose@coolvamp.btinternet.co.uk
website www.expage.com/blackrosepoetry
Editor Bonita Hall

Publishes all styles of poetry; new poets welcome.

Blithe Spirit

12 Eliot Vale, Blackheath, London SE3 0UW
website www.haikusoc.ndo.co.uk/journal.html
Editor Graham High

Frequency/price Quarterly

The journal of the British Haiku Society. Each issue is normally 64 pages and contains original poems, a diversity of statements about the writing and appreciation of haiku and related forms, book reviews, letters to the editor, and announcements of the winners of major awards, including the Museum of Haiku Literature Award (£50) for the haiku voted best in the previous issue.

Submission details Submissions from members only. Send sae or IRC if you want a reply. Each issue reflects the season just ended – e.g. March contains winter haiku.

Borderlines

Nant y Brithyll, Llangnyw, Welshpool, Powys SY21 0JS
tel (01938) 810263
Editor Kevin Bamford, Angie Quinn
Frequency/price 2 issues p.a. UK £2.50, £5 annual subscription. Europe, £3, £6 annual subscription. Outside EU, £3.50, £7 annual subscription

Publishes any style or subject. Payment of 1 complimentary copy.

Submission details Submit up to 6 poems, 32 lines maximum preferable, accompanied by sae. Name and address on each poem.

Brittle Star

PO Box 56108, London E17 0AY
email magazine@brittlestar.org.uk
website www.brittlestar.org.uk
Editor Jacqueline Gabbitas, Louisa Hooper, David Floyd, Martin Parker
Frequency/price 3 issues p.a. £3

Focuses on unpublished, original work by new writers, but is not looking for a particular style or subject matter. Read a copy of *Brittle Star* before submitting.

Submission details Submit 1-4 poems by post. Include covering letter and sae. Submissions by email should be sent as a Word or RTF attachment with a covering letter. Do not send work in the main body of the email.

BuzzWords

Calvers Farm, Thelveton, Diss, Norfolk IP21 4NG

website www.buzzwordsmagazine.co.uk
Editor Zoe King
Submission details No more than 6 poems, on any theme and in any style; each should be no longer than 40 lines. All postal submissions must be accompanied by an sae. Email submissions should be via Word or RTF attachments, and should contain the words 'BuzzWords Submission' and either 'Poetry' or 'Fiction' in the subject line. Send to submissions@buzzwordsmagazine.co.uk.

Cadenza

Broadlea House, Heron Way, Hickling, Norfolk NR12 0YQ
website www.cadenza-magazine.co.uk
Editor William Connelly
Frequency/price 2 issues p.a. £15.50, 4 issues

Aims to publish modern, vibrant short stories, articles, poetry and interviews. A5, perfect bound with a glossy cover and around 80-90 pages of content.

Submission details Poems should be a maximum of 40 lines in length. Will accept previously published poems.

Calabash

Centreprise, 136-138 Kingsland High Street, London E8 2NS
tel 020-7249 6572
email literature@centreprisetrust.org.uk
Editor Sharon Duggal

For writers of African and Asian descent.

Candelabrum

1 Chatsworth Court, Outram Road, Southsea PO5 1RA
tel 023-927 53696 (urgent enquiries only)
email darklantern@btinternet.com
Editor ML McCarthy
Frequency/price 2 issues p.a. £3 (US $6), subscriptions £6 annually, due in February

A 40-page, saddle-stitched, formalist magazine. Metrical and rhymed poetry preferred, although good-quality free verse is not excluded. 5/7/5 haiku considered. No room for long poems.

Submission details Submit 3-6 poems, typed on separate sheets with author's name and address on each sheet. Enclose an sae. No email submissions, but willing to reply by email.

The Cannon's Mouth
22 Margaret Grove, Harborne,
Birmingham B17 9JH
email greg@cannonpoets.co.uk
website www.cannonpoets.co.uk
Editor Greg Cox
Frequency/price Quarterly. £2. 4 issues, £8

The Quarterly Journal of Cannon Poets, who have been meeting every month for 21 years at the Midlands Arts Centre, Cannon Hill Park, Birmingham, UK.

Submission details Although *The Cannon's Mouth* is essentially for the benefit of Cannon Poets members and associate members, original poetry articles, reviews and artwork are welcomed from anyone. The standard of poetry published may vary, as the aim is to encourage and improve writing. Submissions by post (must be accompanied by an sae).

Cannon's Mouth
22 Margaret Grove, Harborne,
Birmingham B17 9JH
tel 0121-426 6413
email greg@connonpoets.co.uk
website www.cannonpoets.co.uk
Editor Grey Cox
Frequency/price Quarterly

Publishes current writing from Britain and overseas, as well as short articles and reviews.

Carillon
19 Godric Drive, Brinsworth, Rotherham,
South Yorkshire S60 5AN
email editor@carillonmag.org.uk
website www.carillonmag.org.uk
Editor Graham Rippon
Frequency/price 3 issues p.a. £3.20. Annual subscription, £9

Founded in June 2001, aiming to produce an eclectic poetry and prose magazine which gives a forum to talented writers of all shades of publication experience.

Submission details Maximum 40 lines to above address, with sae. Overseas subscriptions may be emailed to submits@carillonmag.org.uk.

Cauldron
10 Glyn Road, Wallasey, Wirral CH44 1AB
tel 0151-200940

email terence.grogan50@ntlworld.com
website www.thenewcauldron.co.uk
Editor Terence Grogan
Frequency/price Quarterly

A prose and poetry publication for which all genres of poetry are considered. Poems must be no more than 30 lines, in any style and on any subject. Poet receives £2 per published poem.

Submission details Submission in the form of hard copy direct to editor, or via email attachment.

Chanticleer Magazine
6/1 Jamaica Mews, Edinburgh EH3 6HN
email mohard@livermore8304.freeserve.co.uk
Editor Richard Livermore
Frequency/price Varies, but usually every 3 months. £3

Any type or style of poetry considered. A magazine of poetry and ideas – not necessarily in that order.

Submission details Send poems or prose.

Chapman
4 Broughton Place, Edinburgh EH1 3RX
tel 0131-557 2207
email chapman-pub@blueyonder.co.uk
website www.chapman-pub.co.uk
Editor Joy Hendry
Frequency/price 3 p.a. £24 p.a.

Poetry, short stories, reviews, criticism, articles on Scottish culture. Illustrations: line, half-tone, cartoons. Payment: £8 per page; illustrations by negotiation. Founded 1969.

Submission details If submitting, bear in mind that the longer you do not hear back, the further along your manuscript has got (in general). Do not try to second-guess editorial policy. Anything stereotypically 'Scottish' will almost certainly be returned.

Chillout
PO Box 3268, Brighton BN1 4FL
Editor Guy Oliver
Frequency/price 4 issues p.a. £1.50. Annual subscription £6 inc. p&p

Prose and poetry on the themes of ghosts, horror, mystery, crime, murder and the supernatural. £25 prize for best poem in each issue as voted by subscribers.

Submission details Direct submissions discouraged. Send sae with 2 x 2nd-class stamps for copy of the magazine and writers' guidelines.

Chroma

PO Box 44655, London N16 0WQ
email queerchroma@yahoo.co.uk
website www.chromajournal.co.uk
Editor Shaun Levin
Frequency/price 2 issues p.a. £4.95

Poetry and short fiction by lesbian, gay, bisexual and transgendered writers. Each issue has a theme. Welcomes work that is risky and lyrical.

Submission details Check the theme for each issue and submit 3 poems to the Poetry Editor.

Clough Words

Dean Clough Writers, Dean Clough, Halifax HX3 5AZ
Editor Andy J Campbell, Alan Littlewood

A free magazine, but send an sae.

The Coffee House

Charnwood Arts, Loughborough Library, 31 Granby Street, Loughborough, Leicestershire LE11 3DU
email info@charnwood-arts.org.uk
website www.charnwoodarts.com
Editor Deborah Tyler-Bennett
Frequency/price 2 issues p.a. £2.50 (£4.50 for 2, £8.50 for 4)

Publishes poetry and short stories. Quality is the most important factor, regardless of type or genre.

Submission details Submit 2-6 poems by post only.

Competitions Bulletin

17 Greenhow Avenue, West Kirby, Wirral CH48 5EL
email carolebaldock@hotmail.com
Editor Carole Baldock

Lists details of all current UK writing competitions.

Countryside Tales

Park Publications UK, 14 The Park, Stow on the Wold, Cheltenham, Gloucestershire GL54 1DX

tel (01451) 831053
email parkpub14@hotmail.com
website www.parkpublications.co.uk
Editor David Howarth
Frequency/price Quarterly. £3.50 per issue. Back issues £2 each

Publishes poems with a rural or countryside theme in any style.

Submission details Maximum 40 lines. All work should be sent as hard copy. No email submissions. £10 for the best poem. Free copy to other published poets.

Critical Quarterly

School of English, University of Exeter, Queen's Building, The Queen's Drive, Exeter EX4 4QH
tel (01359) 242375 *fax* (01359) 242880
website www.blackwellpublishing.com
Editor Colin MacCabe
Frequency/price Quarterly £26 p.a.

Fiction, poems, literary criticism. Length: 2000-5000 words. Payment: by arrangement. Founded 1959.

Submission details Study magazine before submitting.

Curlew

Hare Cottage, Kettlesing, Harrogate HG3 2LB
Editor PJ Precious
Frequency/price 2 issues p.a. £2

Anything considered. Payment of complimentary copy.

Submission details Sumission must be accompanied by sae.

Current Accounts

16-18 Mill Lane, Horwich, Bolton BL6 6AT
tel (01204) 669858
email bswscribe@aol.com
website http://hometown.aol.co.uk/bswscribe/myhomepage/writing.html
Editor Rod Riesco
Frequency/price 2 issues p.a. £3

Publishes any form or subject matter. Prefers poems that avoid cliches, abstract ponderings and sentimentality. Shorter pieces preferred because of limited space.

Submission details Submissions by post or email (in body of message). Sae required for postal submissions. Send maximum of 6 poems, unpublished.

Cutting Teeth

15 Granville Street, Glasgow G3 7EE
email info@cuttingteeth.org
website www.cuttingteeth.org
Contact Lynne Mackenzie
Frequency/price 2 issues p.a. UK £8; Europe £12; Outside Europe £15

A biannual small-press publication committed to promoting new Scottish writing.

Submission details Do not send more than 6 poems; each poem on a separate page. State your name and email address clearly on each submission. By post only.

Cyphers

3 Selskar Terrace, Ranelagh, Dublin 6, Republic of Ireland
tel (01) 4978 866 *fax* (01) 4978 866
Frequency/price €18/$30 for 3 issues

Poems, fiction, reviews, translations. Payment: €15 per page. Founded 1975.

Dandelion Arts Magazine

24 Frosty Hollow, East Hunsbury, Northants NN4 0SY
tel (01604) 701730
Editor Jacqueline Gonzalez-Marina
Frequency/price £17 p.a. (£30 Europe, $90 USA/ rest of world)

An international publication that is sent to subscribers worldwide. A modern magazine with poetry, articles, stories, art information and illustrations. Non-profit-making.

Submission details It is essential to become a subscriber when expecting to be published. Guidelines available from the editor.

The Dark Horse

c/o 3b Blantyre Mill Road, Bothwell, South Lanarkshire G71 8DD
website www.star.ac.uk/darkhorse.html
Editor Gerry Cambridge

An international literary magazine committed to British and American poetry; published in Scotland.

Dark Horizons

British Fantasy Society, 201 Reddish Road, South Reddish, Stockport SK5 7HR

website www.britishfantasysociety.org.uk
Contact Marie O'Regan

The journal of the British Fantasy Society; welcomes poetry submissions on any subject in the fantasy genre.

Submission details Although space for poetry is limited, *Dark Horizons* is keen to include poems dealing with any aspect of 'fantasy' – interpretation is up to the poet. The maximum number of lines is 50, and any style will be considered (except haiku).

The David Jones Journal

The David Jones Society, 22 Gower Road, Sketty, Swansea SA2 9BY
tel (01792) 206144 *fax* (01792) 470385
email anne.price-owen@sihe.ac.uk
website www.sihe.ac.uk/davidjones
Editor Anne Price-Owen
Frequency/price 1 issue p.a. £7.50

Publishes articles related to the poet/painter, David Jones (1895-1974) or in the spirit of his work – poetry, related criticism, religion, visual arts, 20th-century art, reviews, books, criticism. Poet receives 2 copies of journal in which his/ her work is featured.

Submission details Submit by post to editor, accompanied by an sae.

The Dawntreader

Indigo Dreams Press, The Manacles, Predannack, The Lizard, Cornwall TR12 7AU
email dawntreader@indigodreams.plus.com
website www.indigodreamspress.co.uk
Frequency/price 6 issues p.a. £3.50

Specialises in the landscape; myth and legend, nature, spirituality, pre-history, environment, ecology and the mystic.

Submission details Poetry in all forms to 36 lines inc. verse breaks (no more than 3 poems per submission).

Day by Day

Woolacombe House, 141 Woolacombe Road, London SE3 8QP
tel 020-8856 6249
Editor Patrick Richards
Frequency/price Monthly. £1.40

Articles and news on non-violence and social justice. Reviews of art, books, films, plays, musicals and opera. Cricket reports. Payment: prose, £2 per 1000 words.; poems, by arrangement. No illustrations required. Founded 1963.

Submission details Short poems and very occasional short stories in keeping with editorial viewpoint. MSS must be accompanied by an sae.

Decanto

Masque Publishing, PO Box 3257, Littlehampton BN16 9AF
email masque_pub@tiscali.co.uk/ masquepublishing
website http://myweb.tiscali.co.uk/ masquepublishing
Editor Lisa Stewart
Frequency/price 6 issues p.a.

All styles of poetry considered – not just contemporary.

Submission details Submit up to 6 poems by post or email.

Denise Smith

127 Milton Road West,
7 Duddingston House Courtyard, Edinburgh EH15 1JG
tel 0131-661 1156
Editor Denise Smith
Frequency/price 1 issue p.a. £4.50 per copy

Publishes all styles of poetry. Payment is 1 free copy of magazine.

Devil

247 Gray's Inn Road, London WC1X 8JR
tel 020-8994 7767
email steve@thedevilmag.co.uk
website www.thedevilmag.co.uk
Frequency/price Biannual. £6.99 per issue; £18 for 3 issues (UK only)

A journal of fiction, poetry and political essays.

Dial 174

21 Mill Road, Watlington, Norfolk PE33 0HH
email Tallyho-pro1@tiscali.co.uk
Editor Joseph Hemmings
Frequency/price £14 p.a. inc. p&p. Europe £16 inc. p&p. Rest of world £18 inc. p&p. £3.50 for a sample copy

Originally a poetry magazine, but now publishes 60 diversified pages plus a regular 24-page poetry anthology with every issue. Experienced and new poets welcome.

Dream Catcher

4 Church Street, Market Rasen, Lincolnshire LN8 3ET
tel (01673) 844325
email paulsutherland@hotmail.com
website www.poetrymagazines.org
Editor Paul Sutherland
Frequency/price 2 issues p.a. £6.50

Seeks to publish the very best in contemporary poetry in English in any style, including translations, from around the world. Long poems are welcomed, as is work from unknown writers.

Submission details Send 5-6 poems (fewer if long poems) by post in UK. Email submissions are accepted from overseas authors.

Dreams That Money Can Buy

35 Mitchell Hey, College Bank, Rochdale, Lancs OL12 6UL
tel (01706) 648040 *fax* (01706) 648040
email editorial@ dreamsthatmoneycanbuy.co.uk
website www.dreamsthatmoneycanbuy.co.uk
Contact Poetry Editor

A quarterly journal that explores the possibilities of contemporary art, poetry, prose and political satire.

E-Sheaf Magazine

Montgomery House,
Sheffield Hallam University, Sheffield, Yorkshire S24 3TJ
tel (01142) 255555
email www.shu.ac.uk
Contact Gary Kaye

Sheffield Hallam University's celebrated literary webzine provides a showcase for both student and local writers.

Earth Love

PO Box 11219, Paisley PA1 2WH
tel 0141-581 9806
email earth.love@ntlworld.com
website homepage.ntlworld.com/earth.love/ earthlove.htm
Editor Tracy Patrick

All submissions should be on a nature theme,

which can be protest or celebratory. The magazine was set up as a forum whereby poets can express their views about our relationship with the environment; all proceeds go directly to conservation charities.

Submission details Send poems with sae. Must be previously unpublished. No email submissions – will not respond via email.

Eastern Rainbow

17 Farrow Road, Whaplode, Spalding, Lincolnshire PE12 0TS
email p-rance@yahoo.co.uk
website http://uk.geocities.com/p-rance/pandf.htm
Editor Paul Rance
Frequency/price 1 issue p.a. £1.75 inc. p&p (6 issues £10)

Publishes poetry reflecting 21st-century culture. Poet receives sample copy.

Submission details Send up to 6 poems, maximum length 32 lines.

Eclipse Poetry Magazine

Everyman Press, 53 West Vale, Neston, South Wirral L64 9SE
Editor Elizabeth Royd
Frequency/price 6 issues, £18

Edinburgh Review

22a Buccleugh Place, Edinburgh EH8 9LN
tel 0131-651 1415 *fax* 0131-651 1415
website www.edinburghreview.org.uk
Editor Brian McCabe
Frequency/price 3 p.a. £17 p.a. (£34 institutions)

Fiction, poetry, clearly written articles on Scottish and international cultural and philosophical ideas. Payment: by arrangement. Founded 1969.

Egg Box Magazine

25 Brian Avenue, Norwich NR1 ZPH
tel (01603) 470191
email mail@eggboxpublishing.com
website www.eggboxpublishing.com
Editor Alexander Gordon Smith, Nathan Hamilton
Submission details Submissions should be accompanied by a brief biography. No email submissions.

Eildon Tree

SBC Library Headquarters, St Mary's Mill, Selkirk TD7 5DG
tel (01750) 724901 Mon-Thu
website www.eildontree.org.uk
Editor Julian Colton, Tom Murray

The *Eildon Tree* magazine was launched in 1999 as a showcase for writing and writers from the Scottish Borders. It now attracts submissions from all over Scotland and beyond. The magazine is published by Scottish Borders Council with support from the Scottish Arts Council. It also instigates initiatives such as CDs, events and creative writing competitions – fast becoming Scotland's leading literary magazine.

Submission details Send a maximum of 5 poems accompanied by an sae, to The Editorial Committee.

English: The Journal of the English Association

The English Association,
University of Leicester, University Road, Leicester LE1 7RH
tel (01162) 523982/2300
email engassoc@le.ac.uk
website www.le.ac.uk./engassoc
Frequency/price 3 issues p.a. Annual subscription £45

A journal aimed at teachers of English in universities and colleges of higher education, with articles on all aspects of literature and critical theory, a reviews section, and original poetry.

Envoi

Meirion House, Glan yr afon, Tanygrisiau, Blaenau Ffestiniog, Gwynedd LL41 3SU
tel (01766) 832112
website www.envoipoetry.com
Editor Jan Fortune-Wood
Frequency/price 3 p.a. £15 p.a.

New poetry, including sequences, collaborative works and translations; reviews; articles on modern poets and poetic style; poetry competitions; adjudicator's reports. Sample copy: £5. Payment: complimentary copy. Founded 1957.

The Ephemera: A Quarterly Magazine of Ideas and the Arts

c/o London Printing Company,
14-15 Station Parade, Whitchurch Lane,
Middlesex HA8 6RW
email enquiries@theephemera.org
website www.theephemera.org
Frequency/price Quarterly

A journal dedicated to undermining those widespread opinions which tacitly hold that literary magazines, particularly little literary magazines, are somehow lesser than their wider-circulating cousins, that their writing is somewhat worse, that their opinions are somehow parochial, that they publish the otherwise unpublishable, that their mission is one of charity, and that, despite their best intentions, they perpetuate the blight of bad writing.

   Submission details Send work by mail and, preferably, by post. Enclose an sae if you want your work to be returned.

Eratica

126 Furze Croft, Furze Hill, Hove BN3 1PF
tel (01273) 202876
email drjenner@ntlworld.com
Editor Dr Simon Jenner, Alan Morrison, Dr David Pollard
Frequency/price Annual. £9

Publishes all styles of quality poetry that shows the intelligent avoidance of mainstream blandishment. Creative oddballs – not the ineptly odd!

   Submission details Telephone and read your poem, or send 6 poems accompanied by sae.

European Judaism

Leo Baeck College, 80 East End Road,
London N3 2SY
tel 020-8349 5600 *fax* 020-8349 5619
email european.judaism@lbc.ac.uk
website www.berghanbooksonline.com/journals/ej/index
Editor Dr Jonathan Magonet *Poetry Editor* Ruth Fainlight
Frequency/price 2 issues p.a. Annual subscription £30

Poems should be short and have some relevance to matters of Jewish interest. Poet receives a copy of the magazine.

   Submission details Submit 3-4 poems, accompanied by sae.

Eve's Back

c/o The Pankhurst Centre,
60-62 Nelson Street, Manchester M13 9WP
email evesback@yahoo.com
Frequency/price 6 issues p.a. £1.50. Annual subscription £11

Women-only magazine (A4-sized, 32 pages), which features mainly articles, reviews and listings, but also some poetry and short fiction. Women are invited to get involved in the production, or to simply send in stuff they've written.

Exile

1 Armstrong Close, Hundon,
Suffolk CO10 8HD
email exile@2from.com
Editor John Marr

A poetry magazine for new poets. Welcomes new poetry in English on any subject.

   Submission details Maximum of 30-40 lines per poem, accompanied by sae.

Exiled Ink!

31 Hallswelle Road, London NW11 0DH
tel 020-8458 1910
email jennifer@exiledwriters.fsnet.co.uk
website www.exiledwriters.co.uk
Editor Jennifer Langer
Frequency/price 2 issues p.a. £3, or £3.50 inc. p&p. £7 for 1 year; £13 for 2 years

Poetry, short stories, literature by exiled writers only, worldwide. Articles, essays by exiled writers and others (semi-academic) on issues of literature and cultures of exile. Reviews of books by exiled writers about exiled literature and culture. Worldwide events to do with exile.

   Submission details Submit by email or by post.

Federation Magazine: The Magazine of The Federation of Worker Writers & Community Publishers

The FWWCP, Burslem School of Art,
Queen Street, Burslem, Stoke-on-Trent,
ST6 3EJ
email fwwcp@cwcom.net
website http://www.fwwcp.mcmail.com

Editor Nick Pollard
Frequency/price Quarterly. £1.50

The magazine of the Federation of Worker Writers & Community Publishers, which aims to further working-class writing and community publishing and to make writing and publishing accessible to all. Each issue is accompanied by a Federation Broadsheet featuring poetry and prose by members of the Federation.

Fern Publications

24 Frosty Hollow, East Hunsbury, Northants NN4 0SY
tel (01604) 701730
Contact Jacqueline Gonzalez-Marina

£17 p.a. (£30 Europe, $90 USA/rest of world)

2 magazines: *Dandelion Arts Magazine* and *The Student Magazine* (for people of all ages). International publications – sent all over the world.
  Submission details Submit a maximum of 4 pieces. To submit, you must be a magazine subscriber.

Fire Magazine

Field Cottage, Old White Hill, Tackley, Kidlington, Oxon OX5 3AB
Editor Jeremy Hilton
Frequency/price 1 issue p.a. £5; 2-issue subscription £7; 3-issue subscription £9

Promotes unpublished, unknown, and unfashionable writers, including young writers and those just starting out, alongside work solicited from more established writers.
  Submission details Submissions by post only, accompanied by an sae.

The Firing Squad

25 Griffiths Road, West Bromwich B71 2EH
email ppatch66@hotmail.com
website www.purplepatchpoetry.co.uk
Editor Geoff Stevens
Frequency/price 3 issues p.a. £1.80

Publishes all kinds of poetry, but prefers 40 lines maximum. If it rhymes, the rhyme should not intrude excessively.
  Submission details Submit at least 2 poems with sae or IRC.

First Offense

Syringa, Stodmarsh, Canterbury, Kent CT3 4BA
email tim@firstoffense.co.uk
website www.firstoffense.co.uk
Editor Tim Fletcher
Frequency/price 1-2 issues p.a.

A magazine for contemporary poetry which is not traditional, but is received by most ground-breaking poets. Contemporary language and experimental poetry and articles. Prints 300 copies.
  Submission details Manuscripts must be typed. No previously published poems and no reply without sae.

Flaming Arrows

Sligo VEC, Riverside, Sligo, Ireland
tel ++353 7 1914 7304 *fax* ++353 7 1914 3093
Editor Leo Regan
Frequency/price €7.50 inc. p&p

Publishes coherent, lucid, direct and strong expression grounded in the senses. Contemplative, metaphysical, mystical, spiritual themes expressed in a distinctive, original and mature voice. Work must sustain close and repeated reading, revealing itself through concentration and focus. Where is the sacred in the personal life, and how is it sustained?
  Submission details Send printed copy with letter and IRC. Payment is 1 complimentary copy.

Focus

13 Egremont Drive, Sheriff Hill, Gateshead NE9 5SE
email focus.editor@blueyonder.co.uk
website www.avnet.co.uk/home/amaranth/ BSFA/focus1.html
Editor Simon Morden
Frequency/price 2 issues p.a. Annual subscription £21 (UK; £26 overseas). Free to members of the British Science Fiction Association

The British Science Fiction Association's magazine for writers. Fiction, poetry, interviews, letters and articles.

Fortnight – An Independent Review of Politics and the Arts

11 University Road, Belfast BT7 1NA
tel 028-9023 2353 *fax* 028-9023 2650

email editor@fortnight.org
website www.fortnight.org
Editor Rudie Goldsmith
Frequency/price Monthly. £2.50

Current affairs analysis, reportage, opinion pieces, cultural criticism, book reviews, poems. Illustrations: line, half-tone, cartoons. Payment: by arrangement. Founded 1970.

Fras

Fras Publications, Roselea, Bridge of Tilt, Blair Atholl PH18 5SX
Editor John Herdman, Walter Perrie
Frequency/price Occasional (approximately 6-monthly). £4

Serious poetry, fiction and literary articles.
   Submission details Send a maximum of 10 poems with sae.

The Frogmore Papers

42 Morehall Avenue, Folkestone, Kent CT19 4EF
tel (07751) 251689
website www.frogmorepress.co.uk
Editor Jeremy Page
Frequency/price 2 issues p.a. £3.50. Annual subscription £7; £12 for 2-year subscription

Open to most varieties of poetry although the very traditional and very experimental are unlikely to find favour. No limits on length.
   Submission details Send a maximum of 6 poems, accompanied by sae.

From the Horse's Mouth

25 Wyecliffe Street, Ossett, Wakefield, West Yorkshire WF5 9ER
tel (01924) 315324
email blackhorsepoets@hotmail.com; paulncazz@blueyonder.co.uk
Editor Peter Bedford
Frequency/price Quarterly. Free

Publishes all styles and genres of poetry. No payment to poet.
   Submission details Submissions by email or post to the editor.

Gabriel: A Christian Poetry Magazine

27 Headingley Court, North Grange Road, Leeds LS6 2QU
Editor Thelma Laycock
Frequency/price Annual (in spring). £5 inc. p&p

Poetry on a Christian theme.

Submission details Submit between November and January each year. Each poem should be on an A4 sheet with name and city underneath poem.

Gairm

29 Waterloo Street, Glasgow G2 6BZ
tel 0141-221 1971
Editor Derick Thomson
Frequency/price Quarterly. Annual UK subscription £9; £11 overseas

An all-Gaelic magazine featuring short stories, poetry and song. Includes articles on historical and contemporary topics, politics, travel features and reviews.

Garbaj

38 Pierrot Steps, 71 Kursaal Way, Southend-on-Sea, Essex SS1 2UY
email atlanteanpublishing@hotmail.com
website www.geocities.com/dj_tyrer/garbaj.html
Editor DJ Tyrer
Frequency/price Quarterly. Free with sae

Publishes anything satirical, silly or subversive and, sometimes, serious. From 4-liners and limericks to sagas. Payment is 1 complimentary copy.
   Submission details Unsolicited submissions with sae, or in the body of an email.

Global Tapestry

Spring Bank, Longsight Road, Copster Green, Blackburn BB1 9EU
tel (01254) 249128
Editor Dave Cunliffe
Frequency/price Irregular. £3

All types of poetry considered. Post-Beat, innovative, trail-blazing, high-energy, bohemian tradition preferred.
   Submission details Submit 6 poems by post, accompanied by sae. Long poems considered.

Green Queen

BM Box 5700, London WC1N 3XX
Editor K Bell, E Wallace
Frequency/price 2 issues p.a. 80p per issue, plus postage

Publishes lesbian and gay poetry, or poems on green issues.
   Submission details Poems up to 40 lines in length. Submissions by post or email.

Haiku Scotland

2 Elizabeth Gardens, Stoneyburn,
West Lothian EH47 8BP
email haiku.scotland@btinternet.com
Editor Frazer Henderson
Frequency/price Quarterly

Original haiku, senryu, epigrams, aphorisms
and all short poetry forms. Work by established
and unpublished poets considered.

Handshake

5 Cross Farm, Station Road North, Fearnhead,
Warrington, Cheshire WA2 0QG
Editor John Francis Haines
Frequency/price Irregular. Send sae/IRC/stamps/
trade/nice letter

Specialises in short genre poems of all styles.
Most issues have only a single side of poetry, so
there is always a backlog: contributors must be
prepared for long waits between acceptance
and publication. See a sample copy of magazine
before submitting. All rights are returned to
author on publication. The other side of the
zine is occupied by news and information
useful to writers of genre poetry. Print run is
currently 80.
  Submission details Send up to 3 short genre
poems at a time, camera-ready; must be
previously unpublished. Send return postage.

Harlequin

PO Box 23392, Edinburgh EH8 7YZ
website www.harlequinmagazine.co.uk
Editor Jim Sinclair
Frequency/price Varies. £3

Publishes high-quality poetry and artwork of
beauty, mysticism and wisdom.
  Submission details Submit only inspired
material accompanied by sae.

HQ Poetry Magazine

(The Haiku Quarterly)
39 Exmouth Street, Swindon SN1 3PU
tel (01793) 523927
Editor Kevin Bailey
Frequency/price 3-4 p.a. £2.80 (4 issues £10 p.a.,
£13 non-UK)

International in scope, publishes both
experimental and traditional work. About one-
third of the content is devoted to haikuesque
and imagistic poetry. Plus review section and
articles. Payment: complimentary copies.
Founded 1990.
  Submission details No submission guidelines –
any amount, any time, but has to be very good
to be accepted.

ImageNation

289 Elmwood Avenue, Feltham,
Middlesex TW13 7QB
email partners_writing_group@hotmail.com
Editor Ian Deal

A magazine of poetry and art.

Inclement

White Rose House, 8 Newmarket Road,
Fordham, Ely, Cambs CB7 5LL
email inclement-poetry-
magazine@hotmail.com
Editor Michelle Foster
Frequency/price Quarterly. £4 (1 year, £15; 2
years, £26, inc p&p)

An independent magazine, funded solely by
subscriptions. Subscription is not a condition
for publication.
  Submission details All forms and lengths of
poetry considered. Now accepts work by email
as well as by post. Decision within 1 month of
submission.

Ink Sweat & Tears

Oak Lodge, Darrow Green Road, Denton,
Harleston, Norfolk IP20 0AY
tel (01986) 788666
email charles@legaltechnology.com
website www.ink-sweat-and-tears.com
Editor Charles Christian

Interlude Magazine

Limehouse Town Hall, 646 Commercial Road,
London E14 7HA
email submissions@interludemagazine.co.uk
website www.interludemagazine.co.uk
Editor Francesca Ricci, Helen Nodding, Becky
Philp
Frequency/price £3.50 plus 50p

An arts magazine that includes writings, poetry
and visual work.

The Interpreter's House

19 The Paddox, Squitchey Lane,
Oxford OX2 7PN

website www.interpretershouse.org.uk
Editor Merryn Williams
Frequency/price 3 issues p.a. £12 annual subscription

Publishes poems and short stories.

Iota

1 Lodge Farm, Snitterfield,
Warwickshire CV37 0LR
tel (01789) 730358
email iotapoetry@aol.com
website www.iotapoetry.co.uk
Editor Bob Mee, Janet Murch
Frequency/price Quarterly
  Submission details Send up to 6 poems by post with sae, or online in body of email – not as an attachment.

Irish Pages: A Journal of Contemporary Writing

The Linen Hall Library,
17 Donegall Square North, Belfast BT1 5GB
tel 028-9043 4800
email irishpages@yahoo.co.uk
website www.irishpages.org
Editor Chris Agee
Frequency/price Biannual. £10/€14

Poetry, short fiction, essays, creative non-fiction, memoir, essay reviews, nature writing, translated work, literary journalism, and other autobiographical, historical and scientific writing of literary distinction. Publishes in equal measure writing from Ireland and abroad. Payment: only pays for certain commissions and occasional serial rights. Founded 2002.

island

8 Craiglea Drive, Edinburgh EH10 5PA
email jaj@essencepress.co.uk
website www.essencepress.co.uk
Editor Julie Johnstone
Frequency/price 2 issues p.a. £6/$12. Annual subscription £10/$20

A bi-annual literary magazine providing a distinctive space for new writing inspired by nature and exploring our place within the natural world.
  Submission details Unsolicited submissions are welcome, although for most projects poets

and writers are now normally approached directly by the editor. Send no more than 5 poems accompanied by an sae.

The Journal

18 Oxford Grove, Ilfracombe,
Devon EX34 9HQ
tel (01271) 862708
email smithsssj@aol.com
website http://members.aol.com/smithsssj/index.html
Editor Sam Smith
Frequency/price 3 issues p.a. £2.50

Publishes work written with thought about what it is saying and how it is being said.
  Submission details Submit with sae or, if by email, in body of email; no attachments. Payment, complimentary copy.

Keystone

53 Arcadia Court, 45 Old Castle Street,
London E1 7NY
email tom_chivers@hotmail.com
website www.pennedinthemargins.co.uk/keystone/
Editor Tom Chivers
Frequency/price Irregular. 3-issue subscription £9

Staunchly eclectic, aims to publish work by young and unknown writers alongside that of better-known names. Accepts poetry, prose, reviews, essays and translations.

Khrizma

website www.khrizma.co.uk

Publishers of *Khrizmamagazine* (small press). Opportunities for poets, who should consult the website; this provides details of themed editions.

Krax

c/o 63 Dixon Lane, Leeds LS12 4RR
Editor Andy Robson
Frequency/price Annual. £3.50 ($7 US)

Light-hearted, amusing or whimsical poetry. Purely descriptive scenes are also accepted. No haiku or smutty limericks.
  Submission details Post hard copy, clearly written or typed. The author's name and address should be on the same sheet as the work.

La Reata

48 Bridge Lane, Temple Fortune,
London NW11 OE6
email panchromatic@msn.com
Editor Ariel Beller
Frequency/price Variable. £3 per issue

Publishes experimental and classical forms. No
political poems. Payment is a free copy.

Submission details Submit 5 poems by post
accompanied by sae. Submissions may be by
email but there is no guarantee of a reply.

Lallans

Blackford Lodge, Blackford,
Perthshire PH4 1QP
tel (01764) 682315
email mail@lallans.co.uk
website www.lallans.co.uk
Editor John Law
Frequency/price £6.50 per issue

Publishes poetry written only in the Scots
language. Payment to poet of £10 per published
poem.

Lamport Court

63 Lamport Court, Manchester M1 7EG
email lamportcourtsubmissions@gmail.com
website http://lamportcourt.blogspot.com
Editor Neil Campbell

A magazine of new fiction and poetry,
published in January, May and September.

Lapidus Magazine

BM Lapidus, London WC1N 3XX
tel 0845-602 2215
email info@lapidus.org.uk
website www.lapidus.org.uk
Editor Sheelagh Gallagher *Poetry Editor* Miriam
Halahmy
Frequency/price Quarterly. £2

Poetry, prose and articles on the use of poetry
in the therapeutic environment.

Submission details Email for guidelines.

Laughout

PO Box 3268, Brighton BN1 4AU
Editor Neil Barnett
Frequency/price 4 issues p.a. £1.50

All forms of poetry accepted with a humorous
theme or content. £25 cash prize to best poem
in each issue, as voted by subscribers.

Submission details Direct submissions
discouraged. Send an sae with 2 x 2nd-class
stamps for free copy and writers' guidelines.

Leeds Poetry Weekly

89 Connaught Road, Sutton, Surrey SM1 3PJ
website barrytebb.mysite.freeserve.com
Editor Barry Tebb

A magazine notorious for its editor's attacks on
the poetry establishment.

Liar Republic

7/8 Trinity Chare, Quayside,
Newcastle upon Tyne NE1 3DF
email psummers@liarincltd.fsnet.co.uk
Editor Ian Dowson, Paul Summers
Frequency/price £3.50

Essays and poetry presented in an interesting
and eye-catching format. For people who are
interested in literature pushed to the limits.

The Liberal

PO Box 42749, London N2 0XX
email editor@theliberal.co.uk
website www.theliberal.co.uk
Editor Ben Ramm
Frequency/price 6 issues, £17

Politics, culture and poetry.

Liminal Pleasures

100 Via Monastero, Cessapalombo, MC62020,
Italy
email editors@liminalpleasures.net
website www.liminalpleasures.net
Editor Andrew Nightingale
Frequency/price £3.50/€5

A biannual print-based poetry magazine.
Poems may be on any subject.

Submission details Send no more than 6
poems at a time. Submissions must be made by
email. Poems may be included in the body of
the email or in a Word, RTF, PDF or HTML
attachment.

Linkway

The Shieling, The Links, Burry Port,
Carmarthenshire SA16 0HU
tel (01554) 834486
Editor Fay C Davies
Frequency/price Quarterly. £3.60 inc p&p (1

year, £14.00; EU £4.00 or £17; others £5.00 or £20.00)

A general-interest magazine for all the family, publishing poetry, stories, articles, puzzles and other items. Poetry can be on any subject and in any style.

Submission details Send 4-6 poems, up to 42 lines in length. The poet's name and address should be on the back of his/her work. Send biographical details and a small photo. Submissions must be accompanied by an sae.

The Liver Bards

Flat 5, 28 Ullet Road, Liverpool, Merseyside L8 3SR
email thebrodiepress@hotmail.com

Brings together new and imaginative writing from the Merseyside area. Draws on talent that previously hasn't been given a platform, and covers topics as wide-ranging as trombones in Beijing and travels in Pakistan to central heating and local architecture.

The London Magazine: A Review of Literature and the Arts

Submissions The Editor, 70 Wargrave Avenue, London N15 6UB
tel 020-8400 5882 *fax* 020-8994 1713
email editorial@thelondonmagazine.net
Administration 32 Addison Grove, London W4 1ER
email admin@thelondonmagazine.net
website www.thelondonmagazine.net
Editor Sebastian Barker *Publisher* Christopher Arkell
Frequency/price Bi-monthly. £6.95 (£33 p.a.)

Poems, stories (2000-5000 words), memoirs, critical articles, features on art, photography, theatre, music, architecture, etc. Also publishes long poems. Payment: by arrangement. First published in 1732.

Submission details Send up to 6 poems, accompanied by a brief covering letter. Sae absolutely essential (3 IRCs from abroad). Submissions by email are not accepted except when agreed with the editor.

London Review of Books

28 Little Russell Street, London WC1A 2HN
tel 020-7209 1101 *fax* 020-7209 1102
email edit@lrb.co.uk
Editor Mary-Kay Wilmers
Frequency/price Fortnightly. £2.99

Features, essays, poems. Payment: by arrangement.

Submission details Submit by email or by post, accompanied by sae.

Lookout

PO Box 3268, Brighton BN1 4AU
Editor Philip Markham
Frequency/price 4 issues p.a. £1.50. Annual subscription £6 inc. p&p

Publishes all forms of poetry on any topic, theme or subject. Prize of £25 for best poem in each issue, as voted by subscribers.

Submission details Direct submissions not encouraged. Send name, address and sae with 2 x 2nd-class stamps for copy of magazine and writers' guidelines.

Magma

43 Keslake Road, London NW6 6DH
email magmapoetry@ntlworld.com
website www.magmapoetry.com
Editor David Boll
Frequency/price 3 issues p.a. £4.95. Annual subscription £14.50 (for 3), inc. postage

Contemporary poetry. Payment of free copy and more at discount.

Submission details Submissions by post or by email to: contributions@magmapoetry.com.

The Magpie's Nest

176 Stoney Lane, Sparkhill, Birmingham B12 8AN
email magpies-nest@tiscali.co.uk
Editor Bal Saini
Frequency/price Quarterly. £2

Poems and short stories on any subject.

Submission details Submit 3-5 poems, each no longer than 40 lines. Short stories; no longer than 2000 words.

Mango Season

Caribbean Women Writers Alliance, Caribbean Centre, Goldsmiths College, University of London, London SE14 6NW
tel 020-7919 7430
Editor Joan Anim-Addo
Frequency/price 3 times p.a. Annual

subscription: individuals £21 (UK and Europe), £26 (Rest of the world); institutions £48 (UK and Europe), £65 (Rest of the world).

The journal of the Caribbean Women Writers Alliance. Interviews, poetry, short stories, translations, criticism and articles on the visual arts, criticism, reviews, and events listings.

Manifold

99 Vera Avenue, London N21 1RP
tel 020-8360 3202
email @_manifold-poetry.co.uk
website www. manifold-poetry.co.uk
Contact Vera Rich
Frequency/price 4 issues p.a. Annual subscription: UK £12; Europe £14; other £15

More than 40 pages of poems, book and exhibition reviews.

Submission details Welcomes well-crafted poems in any known or innovative style, and on a wide range of subjects, accompanied by an sae. The basic requirement is that the work must succeed as poetry. Considers poems in all variants of English; major European languages (French, German, Italian, Latin, Spanish), usually untranslated; also parallel-text translations from other languages.

Markings

77 High Street, Kirkcudbright DG6 4JW
tel (01557) 331557
email markings@btinternet.com
Editor John Hudson
Frequency/price £5 p.a.
Submission details Submissions by post should be clearly typed on A4, name and address on each sheet, sae must be included. Submissions by email should be sent in the body of the text if the piece is short, or as an RTF attachment for longer pieces.

Metre

4 Wyndham Avenue, Bray, County Wicklow, Ireland
Editor David Wheatley

Themed magazine.

Modern Poetry in Translation

MPT, The Queen's College, Oxford OX1 4AW
tel (01865) 244701

email editors@mptmagazine.com
website www.mptmagazine.com
Editor David and Helen Constantine
Frequency/price 2 issues p.a. £11

All lively translations into English of poems in any language will be considered. Also original work – poems, essays on the magazine's particular themes, which are announced issue by issue.

Submission details Send hard copy with return postage. Email submissions only with prior agreement.

Monas Hieroglyphica

649 London Road, Hadleigh, Benfleet, Essex SS7 2EB
email visionarytongue@email.com
website http://myweb.tiscali.co.uk/ jamiespracklen/visiontongue/
Editor Jamie Spracklen
Frequency/price 2 issues p.a. £2.50/$5

Publishes dark fantasy fiction and insightful, purposeful verse. Payment: free copies.
Submission details See website for details.

Monkey Kettle

PO Box 5780, Milton Keynes MK10 1AX
email monkeykettle@hotmail.com
website www.monkeykettle.co.uk
Editor Matthew Michael Taylor
Frequency/price 3 issues p.a.

A poetry and creative-writing magazine. 40 pages, A5.
Submission details Submit 5-10 poems at a time.

Monomyth

38 Pierrot Steps, 71 Kursaal Way, Southend-on-Sea, Essex SS21 2UY
email atlanteanpublishing@hotmail.com
website www.geocities.com/dj-tyrer/ monomyth.html
Editor DJ Tyrer
Frequency/price Quarterly. £1.95

Publishes longer poems over 50 lines in length, or linked sets of shorter poems. Also publishes articles and news relating to poetry.
Submission details Unsolicited submissions with sae or in the body of emails are welcomed.

Moonstone

CH, Unit 2, Commercial Courtyard, Settle BD24 9RG

email talithaclare@btinternet.com
Editor Talitha Clare, Robin Brooks
Frequency/price 4 issues p.a. £2. Annual subscription £7

A magazine produced in the style of a pamphlet, specialising in pantheistic and ecological poetry.

Moving Worlds: A Journal of Transcultural Writings

The School of English, University of Leeds, Leeds LS2 9JT
email mworlds@leeds.ac.uk
Editor Shirley Chew
Frequency/price £12.50 single issues; £25/£10 individual subscriptions

Biannual international literary magazine, publishing creative work as well as criticism, literary as well as visual texts, scholarly and more personal writing, in English and in translation into English. Open to experimentation and representing work of different kinds from different cultural traditions, it re-appraises acknowledged achievements and promotes fresh talent. With a focus on the postcolonial and transcultural, special issues include: Naipaul; Postcolonial Ireland; Caribbean; Postcolonial Cities: Africa; Performing Arts and South Asian Literature; Food; Bicentennary of the Parliamentary Abolition of the British Slave Act.

Mslexia

PO Box 656, Newcastle upon Tyne NE99 1PZ
tel 0191-261 6656 *fax* 0191-261 6636
email postbag@mslexia.demon.co.uk
website www.mslexia.co.uk
Editor Daneet Steffens
Frequency/price 4 p.a. £21.75 p.a.

Magazine for women writers, which combines features and advice about writing with new fiction and poetry by women. Payment: by negotiation. Founded 1998.
  Submission details Considers unsolicited material. Length: up to 3000 words (short stories), articles/features by negotiation, up to 4 poems of no more than 40 lines each in any style which must relate to current themes (or adhere to poetry competition rules).

Naked Punch

email l.marsili@nakedpunch.com
website www.nakedpunch.com
Editor Lorenzo Marsili

Founded by a cultural collective, *Naked Punch* offers the voice of today's most outspoken critics, philosophers, and artists.

Neon Highway

37 Grinshil Close, Liverpool L8 8LD
email poetshideout@yahoo.com
website www.neonhighway.co.uk
Editor Alice Lenkiewcz, Jane Marsh
Frequency/price 1 issue p.a. £5.75

Publishes new and established writers, artists and poets. Looking for visionary, experimental work of a high standard.
  Submission details The magazine operates on a commission/subscription basis. The editor commissions poets. Unsolicited material is not accepted.

The Neoteric

43 The Village, Powick, Worcestershire WR2 4QT
Editor Geoffrey Mills
Frequency/price 2 issues p.a. £3. Annual subscription £5

A biannual literary publication intended to identify and disseminate the work of new writers. It is a small press magazine containing quality poetry, short fiction, reviews and essays submitted by writers from the Midlands, England and beyond.

Never Bury Poetry

Bracken Clock, Troutbeck Close, Hawhshaw, Bury BL8 4LJ
tel (01204) 884080
email n.b.poetry@zen.co.uk
website www.nbpoetry.care4free.net/
Editor Jean Tarry
Frequency/price Quarterly. £2.50 (£9.50 for 4 issues) inc. p&p

Each issue is based around a theme. Submissions should demonstrate innovative work, showing lateral thinking around the theme. Humorous poetry is welcomed, as is clever poetry that plays with words in a natural, unaffected way. A prosaic style, inversions and obvious rhymes are least likely to win favour.

Submission details Send no more than 5 poems of a maximum of 40 lines each.

New London Writers

c/o 38 Groom Place, London SW1X 7BA
tel 0171-249 8717 *fax* 0171-259 5369
email newlonrite@aol.com
Editor Alice Wickham
Frequency/price Subscription £11.80 ($26.50) per 6 issues

New Welsh Review

PO Box 170, Aberystwyth,
Ceredigion SY23 1WZ
tel (01970) 628410
email admin@newwelshreview.com
website www.newwelshreview.com
Editor Francesca Rhydderch
Frequency/price Quarterly. £5.40. Annual subscription £20

All styles of poetry considered.

Submission details Send hard copy with sae for return.

The New Writer

PO Box 60, Cranbrook, Kent TN17 2ZR
tel (01580) 212626
email admin@thenewwriter.com
website www.thenewwriter.com
Editor Suzanne Ruthven
Frequency/price Bimonthly. £4.50

Publishes previously unpublished poems. The guest poetry editor, Catherine Smith, prefers poems which show a good use of language, and offer challenging imagery.

Submission details No more than 3 poems should be submitted at any one time. Submissions should be typed, single-spaced, on 1 side of white A4 paper, accompanied by an sae.

New Writing Scotland

ASLS, c/o Dept of Scottish Literature,
7 University Gardens, University of Glasgow,
Glasgow G12 8QH
tel/fax 0141-330 5309
email office@asls.org.uk
website www.asls.org.uk

Editor Duncan Jones
Frequency/price Annual. £6.95

Accepts previously unpublished short fiction and poetry from writers resident in Scotland, or Scots by birth or upbringing. There are no limits to the type or style of submissions, which may be in English, Scots or Gaelic. Payment of £20 per printed page.

Submission details Submit no more than 6 poems. Author's name and details should not appear on the submission but should be included in a covering letter. Poems should be typed and submitted on single-sided A4 sheets.

Nightingale

32 Queens Road, Barnetby-le-Wold,
North Lincolnshire DN38 6JH
email joe.warner@btinternet.com
Editor Joe Warner
Frequency/price 50p plus postage

A monthly magazine for short poetry (18 lines or fewer) and short fiction (800 words maximum), produced in the UK but with authors and subscribers around the world.

Nomad

Survivors Press, 30 Cranworth Street,
Glasgow G12 8AG
tel 0141-357 6838 *fax* 0141-357 6939
email sps@gisp.net
Editor Gerry Loose

Poetry and creative writing by survivors of the mental health system, of abuse or addictions.

Norfolk Poets and Writers – Tips

9 Walnut Close, Taverham, Norwich NR8 6YN
email tipsforwriters@yahoo.co.uk
Editor Wendy Webb
Frequency/price 6 issues p.a., variable. £2. Annual subscription £12

Themed challenges and competitions; new forms – Davidian, Magi, Echotain, Andropian, Triptych, Fresco, Incubus.

Submission details See copy of magazine before submitting; free sample copy available.

North

The Poetry Business, The Studio,
Byram Arcade, Westgate,
Huddersfield HD1 1ND

tel (01484) 434840
email edit@poetrybusiness.co.uk
Editor www.poetrybusiness.co.uk
Frequency/price Biannual. Annual subscription £12

A forum for poetry and critical prose.

Northwords

PO Box 5706, Inverness IV1 9AF
tel (01463) 231758
email rhoda8@btopenworld.com

A literary magazine in newsprint format. Free at a wide range of stockists across Scotland. Poetry and fiction may be send to the PO Box. 'Home Delivery' costs £5 for 3 issues (Spring, Summer, Autumn).

Obsessed with Pipework

Flarestack Publishing, 8 Abbot's Way, Pilton, Somerset BA4 4BN
tel (01749) 890019
email cannula.dementia@virgin.net
website www.flarestack.co.uk
Editor Charles Johnson (see www.poetrypf.co.uk)
Frequency/price Quarterly: January, April, July, October. £3.50

Does not publish the predictable or the rhyme-led. Must be work that says something about the predicament of being human in the 21st century, and in original language.
   Submission details Send a maximum of 6 poems. If emailing, send poems in the body of a message. If posting, must be accompanied by sae big enough to send work back.

Open Wide Magazine

40 Wingfield Road, Lakenheath, Brandon, Suffolk IP27 9HR
tel (07790) 962317
email contact@openwidemagazine.co.uk
website www.openwidemagazine.co.uk
Contact James Quinton (Managing Editor), Elizabeth Roberts (Editor)
Frequency/price Biannual. £4

Paperback publication of punchy poetry and short fiction, contemporary music, art, film, culture reviews and interviews.
   Submission details See website for guidelines.

Orbis

17 Greenhow Avenue, West Kirby, Wirral CH48 5EL

tel 0151-625 1446
email carolebaldock@hotmail.com
Editor Carole Baldock
Frequency/price Quarterly £4 (£5/€10/$11 overseas) £15 p.a. (£20/€30/$36 overseas)

Poetry, prose (1000 words), news, reviews, views, letters. Payment: £50 for featured writer. £50 Readers' Award: for piece(s) receiving the most votes (4 winners submitted to Forward Poetry Prize, Single Poem Category); £50 split between 4 (or more) runners-up. Founded 1968.
   Submission details Up to 4 poems by post; via email, overseas only, up to 2 in body (no attachments). Enclose sae/2 x IRCs with all correspondence.

The Orphan Leaf Review

26 Grove Park Terrace, Bristol BS16 2BN
email orphanleaf@jpwallis.co.uk
website www.orphanleaf.co.uk
Editor James Paul Wallis
Frequency/price 3 issues p.a. £4

All styles and genres accepted. Each issue follows a theme; see website for details. Mostly English, but other languages also featured. 'Single lines' also published – works of 70 characters in length.
   Submission details Submit by email. Contributions printed as 'orphan leaves'. See website for details.

Other Poetry

29 Western Hill, Durham DH1 4RL
website www.otherpoetry.com
Editor Michael Standen (Managing), Crista Ermiya, Peter Bennet, JR Burns, Peter Armstrong (Consulting)
Frequency/price 3 p.a. £4.50 £13/$30 p.a.

Payment: £10 per poem. Founded in 1979.
   Submission details Submit up to 4 poems with sae.

Outposts Poetry Quarterly

22 Whitewell Road, Frome, Somerset BA11 4EL
tel (01373) 466653 *fax* (01373) 466657
email rjhippopress@aol.com
Editor Roland John *Founder* Howard Sergeant MBE

Frequency/price Quarterly. £4 £14 p.a.

Poems, essays and critical articles on poets and their work. Payment: by arrangement. Founded 1943.

Painted, Spoken

24 Sirdar Road, Wood Green,
London N22 6RG
website www.hydroho.net
Editor Richard Price
Frequency/price Irregular. Free

A little magazine with a print run of around 100 copies appearing very irregularly. For a copy, send sae (A5) with 2 x 1st-class stamps to cover the postage.
   Submission details Not currently open to submissions.

Panda Poetry

46 First Avenue, Clase, Swansea,
West Glamorgan SA6 7LL
tel (01792) 414837
email esmond.j@ntlworld.com
website http://pandawales.tripod.com
Editor Esmond Jones
Frequency/price Quarterly. £3. Annual subscription £10 (Overseas: $5/$15)
   Submission details Submit either by post or email.

Parameter

PO Box 220, Wythenshawe,
Manchester M23 0WE
email editor@parametermagazine.org
website www.parametermagazine.org
Editor Tom Jenks
Frequency/price 2/3 issues p.a. £3.75.

Focus of magazine is mainly on poetry, but prose pieces, including essays and reviews, are also welcome. No restrictions in terms of style or content; just good work. Payment of complimentary copy.
   Submission details Submit a maximum of 6 previously unpublished poems, maximum length 40 lines (prose pieces maximum 2000 words). Email submissions welcome.

Park Publications

14 The Park, Stow on the Wold, Cheltenham, Gloucestershire GL54 1DX

tel (01451) 831053
email parkpub14@hotmail.com
website www.parkpublications.co.uk
Editor David Howard
Frequency/price 4 issues p.a. £3.50 (£2 back copy)

Publishes work with a rural or countryside theme. All poems accepted appear in the quarterly magazine, *Countryside Tales*, which also features articles and short fiction. £10 for best poem in each issue. Free complimentary copy to others.
   Submission details Poems in any style, up to 40 lines in length. Submit typed work on single A4 sheets by post.

The PBS Bulletin

Fourth Floor, 2 Tavistock Place,
London WC1H 9RA
email info@poetrybooks.co.uk
website www.poetrybooks.co.uk
Editor Chris Holifield
Frequency/price Quarterly. Free to members

A quarterly publication from the Poetry Book Society, offering a definitive review of new poetry books published in the UK.

Peer Poetry International

6 Arlington House, Bath Street, Bath, Somerset BA1 1QN
tel (01225) 445298
email peerpoetry@msn.co.uk
website www.publish-your-poetry.co.uk
Editor Paul Amphlett

PEF Poetry Combination Module

PEF Productions,
Poetry Combination Module, 196 High Road,
London N22 8HH
email page84direct@yahoo.co.uk
website www.geocities.com/andyfloydplease
Editor Mr Page 84
Frequency/price Late spring, early autumn, mid-winter. Free on request. Also printable from the Internet

Poetry, anti-poetry, artwork and aphorism.
   Submission details Submit by post or email. 20-word bio may be published on webfile. Poet receives 3 copies of magazine.

Penniless Press

100 Waterloo Road, Ashton, Preston PR2 1EP
tel (01772) 736421

Editor Alan Dent
Frequency/price Quarterly

Publishes poetry, stories, essays, criticism and reviews. Payment is 1 free copy.

Pennine Ink

The Gallery, Mid Pennine Arts, Yorke Street, Burnley, Lancs BB11 1HD
email sheridansdandl@yahoo.co.uk
Editor Laura Sheridan
Frequency/price 1 issue p.a. £3

Publishes poetry and prose of all kinds.
Submission details Submit by post or email. Poems should be up to 40 lines in length.

Pennine Platform

Frizingley Hall, Frizinghall Road, Bradford BD9 4LD
tel (01274) 541015
website www.pennineplatform.co.uk
Editor Nicholas Bielby
Frequency/price 2 issues p.a., May and November. £4.50 (£8.50 annual subscription) inc. p&p

Publishes original poetry only. Concrete poems, haiku and prose poems are discouraged. Metrical poetry is welcomed and intelligent (even intellectual) poetry is preferred. Sequences are considered. All poems submitted receive constructive comment.
Submission details Send A4 hard copy by post, printed black for scanning.

Phoenix New Life Poetry

Sea-Dragon, 12 Place Road, Fowey, Cornwall PL23 1DR
tel (01726) 833343
email unialli@tiscali.co.uk
website www.universalalliance.org.uk
Editor David Allen Stringer
Frequency/price 4 issues p.a. £3.50/6.25 euros/ $7.50 or free as email attachment

All writing styles and genres are considered. Poetry on themes of peace, freedom, social and political justice, social comment, spiritual, psychic and religious experiences, nature, classical myths, legends, etc. No romantic themes.
Submission details Submissions by email as word attachment or by post with sae or IRC.

Planet: The Welsh Internationalist

PO Box 44, Aberystwyth, Ceredigion, Wales SY23 3ZZ
tel (01970) 611255 *fax* (01970) 611197
email planet.enquiries@planetmagazine.org.uk
website www.planetmagazine.org.uk
Editor Helle Michelsen
Frequency/price 6 issues p.a. £3.75. Annual subscription £18

Publishes a wide range of styles and subject matter. Pays a minimum of £30 per poem.
Submission details Submit 6-8 poems typed in double spacing, either by post or by email. Enclose sae with postal submissions.

PN Review

(formerly Poetry Nation)
Carcanet Press Ltd, 4th Floor, Alliance House, 30 Cross Street, Manchester M2 7AQ
tel 0161-834 8730 *fax* 0161-832 0084
email info@carcanet.co.uk
website www.pnreview.co.uk
Editor Michael Schmidt
Frequency/price 6 p.a. £6.99 £36 p.a.

Poems, essays, reviews, translations. Payment: by arrangement. Founded 1973.
Submission details Submissions by post only.

Poems in the Waiting Room

PO Box 488, Richmond TW9 4SW
email pitwr@blueyonder.co.uk
website www.pitwr.pwp.blueyonder.co.uk
Editor Michael Lee
Frequency/price 4 issues p.a. Free

Any poetic form with content and sentiment suitable for patients to read while waiting for medical consultation when they may be in heightened or anxious mental state.
Submission details Short poems are preferred and they should be accessible. Submit by email or send typescript by post.

Poet in the Round

18 Blackbridge Lane, Horsham, West Sussex RH12 1RP
Editor Olivia Manning-Daniels
Frequency/price £4.50 (£6 overseas). 4 issues, £17 (£23 overseas)

Glossy, illustrated magazine.

The Poet Tree

289 Elmwood Avenue, Feltham,
Middlesex TW13 7QB
email partners_writing_group@hotmail.com
Editor Ian Deal

A general poetry magazine.

Poetic Hours

43 Willow Road, Carlton,
Nottingham NG4 3BH
email erranpublishing@hotmail.com
website www.poetichours.homestead.com
Editor Nick Clark
Frequency/price 2 issues p.a., spring and
autumn. £3.75
   Submission details By email ideally; 3-4
poems in the body of the text or by post to the
editor. A4 length maximum, any subject. No
gothic, political or extremist.

Poetic Licence

70 Aveling Close, Purley, Surrey CR8 4DW
tel 020-8645 9956
email licence@poetsanon.org.uk
website www.poetsanon.org.uk
Contact Peter Evans (Editorial Coordinator)
Frequency/price 3 issues p.a. £3.50 per issue; £10
subscription of 3

New poetry.
   Submission details By post with sae, or by
email, posted in the body of the email. No
more than 6 poems to be submitted for any
issue.

Poetry and Audience

c/o School of English, University of Leeds,
Leeds LS2 9JT
email panda@leeds.ac.uk
Editor Kamille Stone Stanton
Frequency/price 2 issues p.a. £3
   Submission details Submissions are invited
from new and established poets. Please include
sae or IRC.

The Poetry Church Magazine

Feather Books, PO Box 438, Shrewsbury,
Shropshire SY3 0WN
tel (01743) 872177
email john@waddysweb.freeuk.com
website www.waddysweb.freeuk.com

Editor Rev John Waddington-Feather
Frequency/price Quarterly. £3.50

Subject matter covers a wide range: from
prisoners' to university academics' verse.
Publishes Christian poems not more than 30
lines in length. Any style; free verse or rhyme.
Also publishes prayers in verse.

Poetry Cornwall

11a Penryn Street, Redruth, Kernow TR15 2SP
tel (01209) 218209
email poetrycornwall@yahoo.com
website poetrycornwall.freeservers.com
Editor Les Merton
Frequency/price 3 issues p.a. £3.50. Annual
subscription £10

Publishes all types of poetry, plus poems in
original language of poet with English
translation. Articles on poetry up to 1000
words considered.
   Submission details Submit only 3 poems at a
time. No multiple submission. Submissions
must be accompanied by sae or IRC. Look at a
copy before submitting.

Poetry Ealing

Questors Theatre, Mattock Lane,
Ealing W5 5BQ
tel 020-8567 7234 or 020-8567 0011
email nala.ques@virgin.net or
pitshanger.poets@virgin.net
website pitshangerpoets.co.uk
Frequency/price 1-2 issues p.a. £3

Poetry Ealing started as a community venture to
encourage writers who live, work and play in
Ealing. Now includes the winners of an annual
competition and is open to a wide range of
contributors, though preference will be given to
writers from West London.

Poetry Express: Quarterly from Survivors' Poetry

Studio 11, Bickerton House,
25-27 Bickerton Road, London N19 5JT
tel 020-7281 4654
website www.survivorspoetry.com
Editor Alan Morrison
Frequency/price Free, but donations welcome

A magazine promoting the poetry of survivors

of mental illness. Published by Survivors' Poetry, the national literature and performance organisation that enables survivors to participate in writing or performance training workshops, as well as publishing and performances nationwide.

Poetry Fanzine

Unit 3, 5 Durham Yard, London E2 6QF
tel 020-7729 3724
email words@poetryfanzine.org
website www.poetryfanzine.org
Editor Martin McGrath, Jason Skowronek
Frequency/price £6.50

Publishes all sorts of poetry.

Poetry Ireland Review/Éigse Éireann

2 Prouds Lane, off St Stephens Green, Dublin 2, Republic of Ireland
tel (01) 478 9974 *fax* (01) 478 0205
email poetry@iol.ie
Editor Peter Sirr
Frequency/price Quarterly. €7.99 €30.50/$52 p.a.

Poetry. Features and articles by arrangement. Payment: €32 per contribution or 1 year's subscription; €51 reviews. Founded 1981.

Poetry London

1a Jewel Road, London E17 4QU
tel 020-8521 0776
email admin@poetrylondon.co.uk
website www.poetrylondon.co.uk
Poetry Editor Maurice Riordan *Reviews Editor* Scott Verner
Frequency/price 3 issues p.a. £5

Publishes the best, most exciting poetry being written now. Welcomes work from unpublished as well as established poets.
    Submission details Send a maximum of 6 poems to: Maurice Riordan, 6 Daniels Road, London SE15 3LR, accompanied by sae or IRC.

Poetry Nottingham

11 Orkney Close, Stenson Fields, Derby DE24 3LW
Editor Adrian Buckner
Frequency/price 3 p.a. £4 £12 p.a. (£20 overseas)

Poems; reviews; articles. 60pp perfect bound. Publishes work that is philosophical and

discursive as well as the finely wrought lyric. Payment: complimentary copy and occasional payment for articles. Founded 1946.
    Submission details Send up to 6 poems. Response within 2 months.

Poetry Now

Remus House, Woodston, Peterborough PE2 9JX
tel (01733) 898105
email info@forwardpress.co.uk
website www.forwardpress.co.uk
Editor Heather Killingray
Frequency/price Quarterly. Annual subscription £12

Poetry features, articles, listings, featured poet.

Poetry Quarterly Review

Odyssey Publications, Coleridge Cottage, Nether Stowey, Somerset TA5 1NQ
Editor Derrick Woolf
Frequency/price Quarterly. £1.75. Annual subscription £6

Mostly reviews and criticism.

Poetry Review

22 Betterton Street, London WC2H 9BX
tel 020-7420 9883 *fax* 020-7240 4818
email poetryreview@poetrysociety.org.uk
website www.poetrysociety.org.uk
Editor Fiona Sampson
Frequency/price Quarterly £30 p.a. (£40 institutions, schools and libraries)

Poems, features and reviews; also cartoons. Payment: £50 per poem.
    Submission details Send no more than 6 poems with sae. Preliminary study of magazine essential.

Poetry Scotland

Kings Bookshop, 91-93 Main Street, Callander FK17 8BQ
website www.poetryscotland.co.uk
Editor Sally Evans *Webmaster* Colin Will
Frequency/price 5/6 issues per year

A wide variety of poetry styles. Occasional payment for longer or commissioned work.
    Submission details Standard postal submissions with sae. Submission advice on website.

Poetry Wales
57 Nolton Street, Bridgend CF31 3AE
tel (01656) 663018
email poetrywales@seren-books.com
website www.seren-books.com,
www.poetrywales.co.uk
Frequency/price Quarterly £5 £20 p.a.; 2-year
private subscription £36; annual institutional
subscription £30 (rates for abroad available on
request)

Poetry, criticism and commentary from Wales
and around the world. "Challenging, original –
an honest magazine." Payment: by
arrangement. Founded 1965.

poetrymonthly.com
39 Cavendish Road, Long Eaton,
Nottingham NG10 4HY
tel 0115-946 1267
email poetrymonthly@btinternet.com
website www.poetrymonthly.com
Editor Martin Holroyd
Frequency/price Monthly. £4

Now a print and online magazine, publishing
imaginative, well-crafted work.
   Submission details Submit by post with sae,
or by email.

The Poet's Letter
tel (07931) 357109
email editor@poetsletter.com
website www.poetsletter.com
Frequency/price £2.75

Poetry, politics, literature, philosophy, books,
children's literature, book reviews, arts, theatre
and music with specific specialist areas of
poetry, politics and philosophy.

Premonitions
Pigasus Press, 13 Hazely Combe, Arreton,
Isle of Wight PO30 3AJ
tel (01983) 865668
email mail@pigasuspress.co.uk
website www.pigasuspress.co.uk
Frequency/price £4.50

Science fiction, fantasy, horror, genre poetry
and fantastic artwork.

Presence
90d Fishergate Hill, Preston PR1 8JD
email martin.lucas2@btinternet.com
website http://haiku-
presence.mysite.orange.co.uk

Editor Martin Lucas
Frequency/price 3 issues p.a. £4.50

Haiku, haiku-related poetry and essays on
topics of haiku interest.
   Submission details See website for examples
and submission details, or to order a sample
copy.

Pretext
School of Literature and Creative Writing,
University of East Anglia, Norwich,
Norfolk NR4 7TJ
tel (01603) 592783 *fax* (01603) 507728
website www.inpressbooks.co.uk/penandinc/

An international literary magazine that features
the best and most exciting new fiction, poetry
and essays from around the world.
   Submission details Submissions by post only,
printed in a plain legible font with your name
on each page. Faxes and emails are not
accepted. Include a covering letter and a
biography of no more than 70 words. Covering
letters for poetry submissions must list the titles
of all the poems. Enclose sae (or IRCs if you are
outside the UK). Indicate (and enclose
sufficient postage) if you would like your work
returned. Payment of £50 and 1 contributor's
copy of publication.

Pulsar
Ligden Publishers, 34 Lineacre, Grange Park,
Swindon SN5 6DA
tel (01793) 875941
email pulsar.ed@btinternet.com
website www.pulsarpoetry.com
Editor David Pike
Frequency/price Biannual (every March and
September). £4 per edition; $9 US. Annual
subscription £8 ($18 US)

Publishes inspirational, hard-hitting work that
has a message and a meaning. No racist or
abusive material or deeply religious work.
Study the FAQ page of website before
submitting. Successful poets receive a free copy
of the magazine.
   Submission details Submission by email,
sending no more than 3 poems. By post, no
more than 6 poems accompanied by sae or
IRC. Poems must be unpublished and not

submitted to another publisher for consideration. Email file attachments will not be read.

Purple Patch
25 Griffiths Road, West Bromwich B71 2EH
email geoff@purplepatchpoetry.co.uk
website www.purplepatchpoetry.co.uk
Editor Geoff Stevens
Frequency/price £2. 3 issues £5

Well-produced and well-established magazine, founded by Geoff Stevens and Olive Hyett in 1976 and still very much alive in 2007.

Submission details Open to submissions of poetry (with sae for reply) at any time on any subject, and from all writers, whether they subscribe or not.

Pussy Poetry
6 Rookery Close, Keddington Park, Louth, Lincolnshire LN11 0GF

A magazine of women's poetry.

Quantum Leap
York House, 15 Argyle Terrace, Rothesay, Isle of Bute, Scotland PA20 0BD
Editor Alan Carter
Frequency/price Quarterly

Welcomes both beginners and old-hands, and pays for all poems published.

Submission details Send sae or 2 x IRCs for guidelines. Maximum 6 poems accompanied by sae or 2 x IRCs.

Quarry
45 Richard Avenue, Wivenhoe, Colchester, Essex CO7 9JQ
Editor DJ Weston
Frequency/price 3 issues p.a.; 70p, $2, 1 euro per issue

Poetry of all kinds. Submissions and subscriptions to DJ Weston at the above address.

Quarterly Tadeeb International
14 North View Street, Keighley, West Yorkshire BD20 6AD
tel (01535) 607505
email tadeebuk@hotmail.co.uk
website www.tadeeb.com

Editor Helen Goodway (English Section Editor), Dr Debjani Chatterjee (Associate Editor), Hameed Qaiser (Urdu Section Editor)
Frequency/price £7. £25 p.a. (UK; enquire for rates for the rest of the world)

A dual-language literary and cultural journal devoted not only to established writers of English and Urdu (and other South Asian languages), but also to embracing new, high-quality writing in those languages by previously unpublished writers, particularly the young. It is committed to fostering the art of translation and aims to include translated work to be situated in both the Urdu and English sections. The magazine is proud to be associated with the Ilkley Literature Festival in organising the annual Ilkley Litfest Mushaira, to which all contributors are welcome.

The Quiet Feather
St Mary's Cottage, Church Street, Dalton-in-Furness, Cumbria LA15 8BA
tel (07901) 522454
email editors@thequietfeather.co.uk
website www.thequietfeather.co.uk
Editor Taissa Csaky, Dominic Hall, Tom Benson, Tim Major
Frequency/price Quarterly. £2.50

Adventurous and intelligent poetry. Entertaining poetry. Fresh and lively poetry. Dark and frightening poetry. Payment 1 free copy.

Submission details Submit poems of 100 lines or fewer. By email or post, but email submission preferred. See website for further details.

The Radiator
Flat 10, 21 Greenheys Road, Liverpool L8 0SX
email scottthurston@btinternet.com
Editor Scott Thurston
Frequency/price Annual. £2 single issue; £5 3 issues

Currently publishes only commissioned essays on poetry and poetics by innovative writers, to act as a resource and incitement to its readers. Is prepared to consider proposals, presented in no more than 200 words in the body of an email sent to the above address.

Rain Dog

PO Box 68, Manchester M19 2XD
email rd_poetry@yahoo.com
website www.panshinepress.co.uk
Editor Jan Whalen, Suzanne Batty
Frequency/price 2 issues p.a. £3.50. Annual subscription £6

Publishes strong, original voices with something worth saying. Submissions welcomed from new and experienced writers and especially interested in poetry from women.
Submission details Send up to 5 poems with an sae, or email.

Rainbow Poetry News

14 Lewes Crescent, Brighton BN2 1FH
tel (01273) 687053
Editor Hugh Hellicar
Frequency/price Quarterly. £1.50 (postage free)

Preference is given to short poems, under 25 lines, by poets who are members of the Rainbow Poetry Movement. Place poems, nature and love poems preferred.
Submission details Send 2 poems and biographical details by post.

Raw Edge Magazine

PO Box 4867, Birmingham B3 3HD
Editor Dave Reeves
Frequency/price 2 issues p.a.

For West Midlands poets only. All styles considered. 16,000 copies distributed per issue. Also publishes a selection of information of interest to readers, including details of opportunities and live events in the region.
Submission details Only writers with a connection to the West Midlands region considered. Send up to 6 poems with A4 sae.

Reach

Indigo Dreams Press at The Manacles, Predannack, The Lizard, Cornwall TR12 7AU
website www.indigodreamspress.co.uk
Editor Ronnie Goodyer
Frequency/price Monthly. £3.50

All welcome, whether established or new to poetry. Join the family-feel that is unique to this publication. 68 pages for just 3.50 per month. Subscribe for as many as you wish and submit your poetry during that period.
Submission details No house style, no age barrier.

The Reader

19 Abercromby Square, Liverpool L69 7ZG
tel 0151-794 2830
email readers@liverpool.ac.uk
website www.thereader.co.uk
Editor Philip Davis
Frequency/price Quarterly. £6

Publishes new poetry as well as short fiction and essays. Payment by prior arrangement only.
Submission details Postal submissions only; must include sae.

The Reater

Wrecking Ball Press, 24 Cavendish Square, Hull, East Yorkshire HU3 1SS
tel (01482) 210226
website www.wreckingballpress.com
Editor Shane Rhodes
Frequency/price 2 issues p.a. Price varies

Publishes well-crafted poetry in a well-designed magazine with excellently illustrated covers. Spearheads lesser-known writers.
Submission details Maximum of 6 poems. If possible all submissions should be on a disk as well as hard copy.

Red Banner: a magazine of socialist ideas

PO Box 6857, Dublin 6, Ireland
email red_banner@yahoo.com
website www.redbannermagazine.com
Frequency/price Quarterly

Red Lamp

6 Madras Road, Cambridge CB1 3PX
tel (07736) 129694
email evans.baj@yahoo.com
website www.geocities.com/redlamp
Editor Brad Evans
Frequency/price £2.50

Publishes left-wing poetry. Payment of complimentary copy.
Submission details Read submission guidelines on website.

The Red Wheelbarrow

c/o The Poetry House, School of English,
University of St Andrews, St Andrews,
Fife KY16 9AL
email redwheelbarrow@st-andrews.ac.uk
website www.st-andrews.ac.uk/academic/
english/redwheelbarrow/
Frequency/price Biannual. £3

Accepts poetry submissions loosely
surrounding a theme for each issue; check the
website for further information. Also publishes
essays, interviews, and reviews on
contemporary poetry.
  Submission details Available on the website
or can be obtained by post. Submissions by
post: must be accompanied by sae or an email
address to which a response may be sent (the
latter is preferred). Submitted poems will not
be returned. No email submissions.

Retort

7 Downside Court, Nutfield Road, Merstham,
Surrey RH1 3YY
Editor John Lemmon
Frequency/price Quarterly. Annual subscription
£19

The Rialto

PO Box 309, Aylsham, Norwich NR11 6LN
email mail@therialto.co.uk
website www.therialto.co.uk
Editor Michael Mackmin
Frequency/price 3 issues p.a.

Started in 1984 aiming to publish work by new
poets alongside that of established poets. A 64-
page A4 magazine, described by Carol Ann
Duffy as "simply the best". Has also published
a small number of first collections, 3 of which
have won major prizes.
  Submission details Read the magazine before
submitting. Send no more than 6 poems, plus
sae or IRC with sufficient postage to cover
return costs. For book publication, please write
to the editor before sending poems. Please
note, it will be at least 12 weeks before you hear
about your work.

A Riot of Emotions

Dark Diamonds Publications, PO Box HK 31,
Leeds, West Yorks LS11 9XN

Editor Andrew Cocker
Art/poetry fanzine with small press and music
reviews.

Roisin Dubh Free Poetry Zine

3 Irvine Road, Newmilns, Ayrshire KA15 9JB
Editor Michael Mackmin

Roundyhouse

c/o 3 Crown Street, Port Talbot SA13 1BG
tel (01639) 886186
Editor Editorial board: Byron Beynon, Phil
Carradice, Sally R Jones, Brian Smith, Alex
Trowbridge-Matthews
Frequency/price 3 issues p.a. £3.50. Annual
subscription £9

No limit on subject matter or style, but
preferably accessible. Poet receives a free copy
of the issue containing his/her work.
  Submission details No more than 6 poems
should be submitted, accompanied by sae if
return required. Poems should be up to 50
lines; longer poems are less likely to be
accepted.

Route

PO Box 167, Pontefract,
West Yorkshire WF8 4WW
tel (01977) 797695
email info@route-online.com
website www.route-online.com,
www.id-publishing.com
Contact Ian Daley, Isabel Galan

Contemporary fiction (novels and short
stories) and performance poetry, with a
commitment to new writing. Imprint of ID
Publishing.
  Submission details Unsolicited work
discouraged. Visit the website for current
guidelines. Ring or write for a free catalogue.

Rubies in the Darkness

The Red Lantern Retreat, 41 Grantham Road,
Manor Park, London E12 5LZ
Editor Peter Geoffrey Paul Thompson
Frequency/price 2 issues p.a. £5. Annual
subscription £10

Traditional, lyrical, spiritual as well as work in
broad sympathy with the 18th/19th century
Romantic school (e.g. Shelley, Keats Blake,
etc.). Rhythm and rhyme are favoured.

Submission details Send typed poems by post only. Must include covering letter and sae. Only considers poetry by subscribers.

Sable

Saks Media, PO Box 33504, London E9 7YE
Frequency/price Quarterly. £6. Annual subscription £20

Literary magazine for writers of colour. Offers professional development for writers through its courses and workshops.

Saccade

93 Green Lane, Dronfield, Sheffield S18 6FG
Editor Robert Gill

Bizarre and fantastic fiction, non-fiction, poetry, artwork (any style), horror, SF, fantasy.

Salopoet

5 Squires Close, Madeley, Telford,
Shropshire TF7 5RU
tel (01952) 587487
email rogerhoult@blueyonder.co.uk
Editor Roger Hoult
Frequency/price Quarterly. £3.50 inc. p&p

The magazine of the Salopian Society, founded in 1976. Publishes poetry written by members of the society. *Snippetts* sent with copies of the magazine, contains information of interest to poets generally. Runs an annual open poetry competition (1st prize, £200; total prize money, £500), closing date 31st August. Membership of the Society is £12.50 per year (UK), £15 (EU) and £20 elsewhere.

Saw

4 Masefield Avenue, Barnstaple,
Devon EX31 1QJ
email sawpoems@btinternet.com
website www.indigogroup.co.uk/llpp/saw.html
Editor Colin Shaddick
Frequency/price 2 issues p.a. £4. 3 issues, £10; 6 issues, £18

Publishes poetry with an edge.

Submission details A maximum of 80 lines per poem, including title and stanza breaks. Email submissions can be sent either as an attachment, or in the body of the email using Microsoft Word if possible. If submitting by post, send an sae.

Scintilla

Little Wentwood Farm, Llantrisant,
Usk NP5 1ND
website www.cf.ac.uk/encap/scintilla
Editor Anne Cluysenaar
Frequency/price Annual. £9.50

An annual journal devoted to literature written, and inspired, by the Breconshire writers Henry and Thomas Vaughan. Each volume includes poetry, prose fiction, drama, and essays, which explore themes relevant to the Vaughans, in modern (if not necessarily fashionable) terms. *Scintilla* is published by the Usk Valley Vaughan Association (UVVA), founded in the tercentenary year of Henry Vaughan's death, 23 April 1695, with financial support from the Arts Council of Wales and Cardiff University. The UVVA exists to explore, celebrate, and question the works and lives of Henry Vaughan, poet and doctor, and his twin brother, the famous alchemist Thomas Vaughan, while encouraging the work of modern writers and artists.

Scots Magazine

DC Thomson & Co Ltd, 2 Albert Square,
Dundee DD1 9QJ
tel (01382) 223131
email mail@scotsmagazine.com
website www.scotsmagazine.com
Frequency/price Monthly. £1.60

Articles on all subjects of Scottish interest. Scottish short stories and poetry.

The Scottish Review of Books

The Sunday Herald, 9/10 St Andrew Square,
Edinburgh EH2 2AF
email media.office@scottisharts.org.uk
Editor Alan Taylor

A quality literary magazine, supported by the Scottish Arts Council and aimed at promoting Scottish literature. Published by Argyll and Birlinn Publishing, it includes articles from leading literary commentators, reviews of recently published books, and poetry.

Scrawl

Questing Beast Distribution, PO Box 1,
Blaenau Ffestiniog LL41 3AX
Editor Lucy Neville
Frequency/price Quarterly. £3. Annual subscription £12

Seam

PO Box 1051, Sawston, Cambridge CB22 3WT
email seam.magazine@googlemail.com
website www.seampoetry.co.uk
Editor Anne Berkeley, Frank Dullaghan
(Consulting Editor)
Frequency/price 2 issues p.a. (March,
September) £4.50 single copy

21st-century poetry by established and
emerging writers. Publishes both formal and
free verse, placing value on expert handling of
language. Will occasionally accept longer
poems, but page length is restricted to 32 lines
(inclusive of stanza beaks) plus title.

   Submission details Submit 5-6 poems with
name and address on each. Enclose sae or email
address for response. Email submissions are
not accepted.

Second Light

9 Greendale Close, London SE22 8TG
tel 020-8299 0088
email dyliswood@tiscali.co.uk
Editor Dylis Wood (and guest editors)
Frequency/price 2 issues p.a. £4 to non-
members

Second Light is the voice of the Second Light
Network of women poets. Membership is by
invitation only. It publishes well-honed,
exciting poems dealing with all subjects in all
styles, including formal.

Sentinel Poetry Quarterly

60 Titmuss Avenue, Thamesmead,
London SE28 8DJ
tel (07940) 249812
email info@sentinelpoetry.org.uk
website www.sentinelpoetry.org.uk/
quarterlymagazine/
Editor Nnorom Azuonye
Frequency/price Quarterly. £3.95 (UK) or £4.95
(overseas)

A 60-page journal of poems, essays and
interviews from the Sentinel Poetry Movement.
Payment of complimentary copy.

   Submission details Send up to 6 poems (40
lines maximum per poem, includes stanza
breaks), any style or theme. Poems must be
previously unpublished. Poems posted on

Internet discussion boards as part of the
writing process are not deemed to have been
previously published.

Seshat

PO Box 9313, London E17 8XL
Editor Terence Duquesne (and others)

Cross-cultural perspectives in poetry and
philosophy.

The Seventh Quarry – Swansea Poetry Magazine

Dan-y-bryn, 74 Cwm Level Road, Brynhyfryd,
Swansea SA5 9DY
Editor Peter Thabit Jones
Frequency/price 2 issues p.a. £7 ($10)

Serious, quality poems (formal or informal).
   Submission details Submit no more than 6
poems (no very long poems) accompanied by
sae or IRC. Payment, complimentary copy.

Shearsman

58 Velwell Road, Exeter EX4 4LD
tel (01392) 434511
email editor@shearsman.com
website www.shearsman.com
Editor Tony Frazer
Frequency/price Biannual. £7.50

Publishes work in the Modernist tradition. No
mainstream British poetry. Payment: 2 copies
of magazine.

   Submission details Postal submissions must
be accompanied by sae. If by email, no
attachments other than PDFs.

Sheffield Thursday

School of Cultural Studies,
Sheffield Hallam University,
Collegiate Crescent, Camous, Sheffield S10 2BP
Editor EA Markham

Sheffield Thursday is published biannually by
PAVIC at SHU, and features a high national
standard of poetry, short stories and reviews,
with regular competitions. Editorial and
production associates include Margaret
Drabble, Mimi Khalvati, Sharon Kivland, Mel
McClellan and Sudeep Sen (Asia).

   Submission details Submissions accompanied
by an sae or equivalent are welcomed.

The Shop: A Magazine of Poetry

Skeagh, Schull, Co Cork, Republic of Ireland
email hilary.theshop@theshop-poetry-
magazine.ie

website www.theshop-poetry-magazine.ie
Editor John Wakeman, Hilary Wakeman
Frequency/price 3 p.a. £7/€8.50

Poems on any subject in any form and occasional essays on poetry, especially Irish poetry. No submissions by email. Illustrations welcome. Length: 2000–3000 words (essays); any (poems). Payment: by arrangement. Founded 1999.

Smiths Knoll

Goldings, Goldings Lane, Leiston,
Suffolk IP16 4EB
tel (01728) 830631
email michael.laskey@ukonline.co.uk
Editor Joanne Cutts, Michael Laskey
Frequency/price 3 issues p.a. £5. Annual subscription £14

Publishes poetry that is well-made and linguistically alive.
    Submission details Submit up to 6 poems by post, accompanied by sae.

Smoke

The Windows Project, First Floor,
Liver House, 96 Bold Street, Liverpool L1 4HY
tel (01517) 093688
website www.windowsproject.demon.co.uk
Editor Dave Calder/Dave Ward
Frequency/price 2 issues p.a. 80p plus p&p (£4 for 5 issues) made payable to 'Windows Project'

New ideas, new ways of using language. Poems with something to say. *Smoke* can introduce you to new writing, poetry and graphics from some of the most established names, alongside new work from Mersyside, as well as from all over the country and around the world.
    Submission details Send 6 poems with sae.

Snapshots

Snapshot Press, PO Box 132, Waterloo,
Liverpool L22 8WZ
email info@snapshotpress.co.uk
website www.snapshotpress.co.uk
Contact John Barlow
Frequency/price 3 issues p.a. £5.50. Annual subscription £11

A magazine of haiku.

South Poetry Magazine

PO Box 3744, Cookham, Maidenhead SL6 9UY
email south@southpoetry.org
website www.southpoetry.org

Editor Run by management team with different poem selectors for each issue
Frequency/price Twice-yearly (April and October). £5.60 inc. UK postage

Previously unpublished poems in English in any style, but study the magazine before submitting. No translations. Articles on poetry of about 800 words, particularly if related to the southern counties of England. Book reviews. Complimentary copy to successful poets. Poetry reading event to launch each issue.
    Submission details Maximum 3 poems per submission – 2 copies of each poem. Poet's name/address or other identifying details must not appear on the manuscript, as poems are selected anonymously. Use the submission form, available (with full guidelines) on the website, or separate covering letter giving name/address/list of poems. Submit work at any time, but selection process does not begin until after the deadline for each issue (30th November and 31st May). Decision takes about 8 weeks from then. No fax, email or multiple submissions.

Spanner

14 Hopton Road, Hereford HR1 1BE
email meeq03@dial.pipex.com
website www.shadoof.net/spanner/
Editor Allen Fisher

A samizdat magazine which focuses on particular authors or subjects in each issue.

Sphinx

HappenStance, 21 Hatton Green, Glenrothes,
Fife KY7 4SD
email nell@happenstancepress.com
website www.happenstancepress.com/Sphinx.htm
Editor Helena Nelson

A magazine which promotes, celebrates and evaluates poetry in chapbook form. It introduces the people behind the poetry imprints and tells the stories of the publishers and the poets through features and interviews.
    Submission details No unsolicited poems accepted, but ideas for features welcome.

Splizz

4 St Mary's Rise, Burry Port,
Carmarthenshire SA16 0SH

email splizzmag@yahoo.co.uk
website www.myspace.com/splizz
Editor Amanda Morgan
Frequency/price Quarterly: March, June,
September, December. £2

All styles of poetry are considered, provided the
work is not racist or homophobic.

Stand Magazine

School of English, University of Leeds,
Leeds LS2 9JT
tel 0113-343 4794
email stand@leeds.ac.uk
website www.standmagazine.org
Managing Editor Jon Glover
Frequency/price Quarterly £6.50 plus p&p £25
p.a.

Poetry, short stories, translations, literary
criticism. Send sae/IRCs for return. Payment:
£20 per 1000 words (prose); £20 per poem.
Founded 1952.

Staple

114–116 St Stephen's Road,
Nottingham NG2 4JS
Editor Wayne Burrows
Frequency/price 3 p.a. £15 p.a. (£25 overseas)

Contemporary poetry, short fiction, articles
and reviews. Payment: £5 per poem, £10
fiction/articles. Founded 1982.
    Submission details Send up to 6 poems by
post.

The Stinging Fly

PO Box 6016, Dublin 8, Ireland
email stingingfly@gmail.com
website www.stingingfly.org
Editor Declan Meade
Frequency/price 3 issues p.a. €7/£5

Publishes poetry and fiction by Irish and
international writers, and is particularly
interested in promoting new writers. Each issue
has a 'Featured Poet' section, showcasing the
work of a poet yet to publish his or her first
collection.
    Submission details Full guidelines on the
website. Submissions read January-March each
year.

Submit

3 Bristol Place Edinburgh EH1 1EY
tel 0131-220 4538

email submitmagazine@yahoo.co.uk
website www.theforest.org.uk/

A magazine of prose and poetry available from
the Forest Café and bookshops.

Tandem

13 Stephenson Road, Barbourne,
Worcester WR1 3EB
email tandem@mitt.demon.co.uk
website www.progression.co.uk/tandem
Editor Michael J Woods
Frequency/price 3 issues p.a. Annual
subscription £12

New fiction and poetry.

Tangled Hair (Tanka Journal)

Snapshot Press, PO Box 132, Waterloo,
Liverpool L22 8WZ
email info@snapshotpress.co.uk
website www.snapshotpress.co.uk
Frequency/price 3 issues p.a. £5.50. Annual
subscription £11

A magazine of tanka.

Tears in the Fence

38 Hod View, Stourpaine, Blandford Forum,
Dorset DT11 8TN
tel (01258) 456803 *fax* (01258) 454026
email david@davidcaddy.wanadoo.co.uk
website www.myspace.com/tearsinthefence
Editor David Caddy
Frequency/price 3 issues p.a. £15 or £6 for single
copies

Internationally renowned literary journal of
contemporary writing. Appreciates a wide
range of poetry, fiction and critical essays that
is socially and politically aware. Enjoys what is
spontaneous, strong and direct, alongside
writing which prompts close and divergent
readings and takes the art form forward.
    Submission details Submit by post with short
biography and sae.

The Text

The Word Hoard, Unit 25,
The Gatehouse Centre, Albert Street,
Lockwood, Huddersfield HD1 3QD
tel (01484) 426626
email hoard@200.co.uk
website www.wordhoard.co.uk

Editor Keith Jafrate
Frequency/price 2 issues p.a. £2.50

Publishes radical and experimental poetry in any form.

Submission details No short poems – only long poems or long poem series considered. See website for submission guidelines. Must include sae/IRC. Email submissions accepted.

The Ugly Tree Poetry Magazine

Mucusart Publications, 6 Chiffon Way,
Trinity Riverside, Manchester M3 6AB
email paul@mucusart.co.uk
website www.mucusart.co.uk/theuglytree.htm
Editor Paul Neads
Frequency/price 3 issues p.a. (Feb, Jun, Oct); £3.50/£10

Poetry for page and performance; reviews and interviews. For full information, including samples, submission guidelines and how to subscribe, consult the website.

The Third Half Literary Magazine

16 Fane Close, Stamford,
Lincolnshire PE9 1HG
tel (01780) 754193
Editor Kevin Troop

Publishes new and established writers. 4 writers appear in each issue with a mini-collection from each. Authors can buy their books at a reduced price.

Submission details Send new material only. Up to 8 typed poems with letter and sae.

TLS (The Times Literary Supplement)

Times House, 1 Pennington Street,
London E98 1BS
tel 020-7782 5000 *fax* 020-7782 4966
website www.thetls.co.uk
Editor Peter Stothard
Frequency/price Weekly. £2.40

Will consider poems for publication, literary discoveries and articles on literary and cultural affairs. Payment: by arrangement.

Tolling Elves

649 Fulham Road, London SW6 5PU
email tevans21@hotmail.com
website www.onedit.net/tollingelves
Contact Thomas Evans

Tremblestone

Stowford House, 43 Seymour Avenue,
St Judes, Plymouth, Devon PL4 8RB
website www.tremblestone.co.uk
Editor Kenny Knight
Frequency/price Annual subscription £4. 3 issues £10; 6 issues £18

A magazine with an international outlook. Has published contemporary poetry from across a broad spectrum of alternative poetries ever since the first issue was launched in November 1999. Perfect bound. 80-96 pages of poetry, including book and magazine reviews.

Submission details Send 5-6 poems with sae or IRCs.

Triumph Herald

Remus House, Coltsfoot Drive, Woodston,
Peterborough, Cambs PE2 9JX
tel (01733) 890099
Contact Chris Walton

Christian writers' magazine with poetry, stories and articles written by subscribers.

The Ugly Tree

Mucusart Publications, 6 Chiffon Way,
Trinity, Manchester M3 6AB
email paul@mucusart.co.uk
website www.mucusart.co.uk/theuglytree.htm
Editor Paul Neads
Frequency/price 3 issues p.a. (Feb, June, Oct). £3.50. Annual subscription £10

Poetry for performance and the page; poetry, reviews and interviews. Features an eclectic mix of wisdom from around the globe, while retaining its roots with regular contributions from both new and established North West poets. Particularly interested in the translation of performance poetry to the page, although this is not the magazine's prime mover.

Submission details Unsolicited submissions always welcome and no barrier as to style, form or content. Send no more than 5 poems by email (no postal submissions, email only – main body or attachment). See website for full details.

Understanding

127 Milton Road West,
7 Duddingston House Courtyard,
Edinburgh EH18

Editor D Smith
Frequency/price 1 issue p.a. £4.50

Publishes all styles of poetry.
  Submission details Submit 5-6 poems.

The Unruly Sun

17 Bay View Terrace, Swansea SA1 4LT
email sales@unrulysun.co.uk
Editor Geoff Sawers
Frequency/price Irregular. £1.50

Poetry magazine based at Reading's Rising Sun
Arts Centre. A modest little booklet, aiming to
present the best in contemporary poetry from
the fringes.

Urthona Magazine

19 Mulberry Close, Cambridge CB4 2AS
tel (01223) 316019
email urthonamag@onetel.com
website www.urthona.com
Editor Ratnagarbha
Frequency/price 2 issues p.a. £3.95

Publishes anything imaginative, alive and
down-to-earth. Vacuous, spiritual uplift,
buddhas, etc. not wanted.
  Submission details Submissions must be
accompanied by an sae.

Various Artists

24 Northwick Road, Bristol BS7 0UG
email tonylj@firewater.fsworld.co.uk
Editor Tony Lewis-Jones

Velvet

PO Box 19, Cambridge CB4 2WZ
email editor@velvet-mag.co.uk
website www.velvet-mag.co.uk
Frequency/price Quarterly. £3. Annual
subscription £11

A magazine aimed at lesbian women. A bit
more 'intellectual' and issue-based than what's
currently on the market, with a bit of fun and
humour as well, and some political articles
dealing with lesbian-specific issues, along with
book and film reviews and a poetry section.
Quarterly, glossy, and full colour.

Vigil

2 Rougeront Terrace, Axminster,
Devon EX13 5JP

tel (0129) 733959
Editor John Howard-Greaves
Frequency/price 2 issues p.a. £2.25, inc. postage
(£1.95 cover price)

Publishes poetry and prose of emotional force
or intensity, colour, imagery and appeal to the
senses.
  Submission details Up to 6 poems of 40 lines
maximum.

Voice & Verse

Robooth Publications, Robooth,
7 Pincott Place, London SE4 2ER
tel 020-7277 8831
email robooth@gofornet.co.uk
Editor Ruth Booth
Frequency/price Quarterly. £3

Wasafiri

1-11 Hawley Crescent, Camden Town,
London NW1 8NP
tel 020-7556 6110
email wasafiri@open.ac.uk
website www.wasafiri.org
Editor Susheila Nasta
Frequency/price 3 issues p.a. £7. Annual
subscription £21

A literary magazine primarily concerned with
new and postcolonial writers, with an emphasis
on the diversity and range of black and
diasporic writers worldwide. It aims to create a
definitive forum for the voices of new writers,
and to open up lively spaces for serious critical
discussion not available elsewhere. Britain's
only international magazine for Black British,
African, Asian and Caribbean literatures.

Weyfarers

1 Mountside, Guildford, Surrey GU2 4DJ
tel (01252) 702450 *fax* (01252) 703650
email admin@weyfarers.com
website www.weyfarers.com
Editor Martin Jones, Stella Stocker, Jeffrey
Wheatley
Frequency/price 3 issues p.a.

An international publication with poetry in
English, or in English translation, from many
parts of the world. Modern and traditional
work published from both new and established
poets. Reviews of books and magazines.

Submitted work should not have been published or currently submitted elsewhere. Copyright remains with the authors. Payment of a copy of magazine to poets whose work is accepted.

Submission details Manuscripts should be typed with name and address on each poem on separate sheets. Include sae or IRC for the return of unaccepted work.

The Wolf

Fagnal Lane, Winchmore Hill,
Amersham HP7 0PG
email s@thewolfpoetry.org.uk
website www.thewolfpoetry.org.uk
Editor James Byrne
Frequency/price 3 issues p.a. £3. Annual subscription £10

Founded in April 2002 by James Byrne and Nicholas Cobic, with a clear emphasis on publishing emerging new poets alongside more established writers. Includes interviews with leading contemporary poets. The poets, however, come purely through submissions.

Submission details Email and postal submissions are both welcome. Send no more than 5 poems, on any style or theme, but originality is a prerequisite. Reviews and essays on any poetry subject are also welcome. Submissions cannot be returned.

Writers' Forum

Writers International Ltd, PO Box 3229,
Bournemouth BH1 1NZ
tel (01202) 589828
email editorial@writers-forum.com
website www.writers-forum.com
Editor John Jenkins
Frequency/price Monthly. £3.50

Magazine publishing the winners of the Writers' Forum poetry competition.

Submission details Poems should be a maximum of 40 lines on any subject or style. The deadline is the 15th of every month. There is a first prize of £100 and a Chambers Dictionary. Entry fee, £5 per poem and £7 for 2.

Writing Magazine

PO Box 168, Wellington Street, Leeds LS1 1RF
tel (01132) 388333

email derek.hudson@writersnews.co.uk
website www.writersnews.co.uk/main/wm.asp
Editor Derek Hudson
Frequency/price 6 issues p.a. £14.95

Advice on how to break into the writing business, with articles on writing fiction, magazine articles, poetry, short stories, writing for children, screenwriting and other genres. Includes author interviews around the globe.

X-Magazine

Flipped Eye Publishing Ltd, PO Box 43771,
London W14 8ZY
email submissions @x-bout.com
website www.flippedeye.net/xmag
Editor Stazja McFadyen, NA Parkes
Frequency/price Quarterly. £4. Annual subscription £15

Publishes poetry and prose of high quality.
Submission details See website for details. Email submission only.

Young Writer

Glebe House, Weobley,
Herefordshire HR4 8SD
tel (01544) 318901 *fax* (01544) 318901
email editor@youngwriter.org
website www.youngwriter.org
Editor Clare Pollard
Frequency/price 3 p.a. £3.75 (£10 p.a.)

Specialist magazine for young writers under 18 years old: ideas for them and writing by them. Includes interviews by children with famous writers, fiction and non-fiction pieces, poetry; also explores words and grammar, issues related to writing (e.g. dyslexia), plus competitions with prizes. Length: 750 or 1500 words (features), up to 400 words (news), 750 words (short stories – unless specified otherwise in a competition), poetry of any length. Illustrations: colour – drawings by children, snapshots to accompany features. Payment: most children's material is published without payment; £25-£100 (features); £15 (cover cartoon). Free inspection copy. Founded 1995.

Submission details Send by email or, if by post, preferably typed.

OVERSEAS

Chimera

19 Le Bout du Pont, 22570 Plelauff, Brittany, France

email robert@chimeramagazine.co.uk
website www.chimeramagazine.co.uk
Editor Robert Cole
Frequency/price Annual. £7 inc p&p

Publishes unconventional, experimental work alongside the traditional and, as the title suggests, fantastic or grotesque product(s) of the imagination. Longer poems up to 2 pages.

Submission details Submit by post from the UK and by email from elsewhere (as an attachment). If submitting by post, please include sufficient IRCs to cover return if required.

The Fiddlehead

Campus House, 11 Garland Court, University of New Brunswick, Fredericton NB E3B 5A3, Canada
tel (506) 453-3501 *fax* (506) 453-5069
email fiddlehd@unb.ca
website http://www.lib.unb.ca/Texts/Fiddlehead/
Editor Kathryn Taglia
Frequency/price 4 issues $30 (CAD) $36 (US)

Open to good writing in English from all over the world; looks for freshness and surprise. Response can take 1-6 months.

Submission details With the exception of the annual contest (see below), no deadlines for submissions. Typed, double-spaced, spell-checked. No more than 4000 words for fiction, and no more than 10 poems per submission (3-5 preferred). No fax or email submissions. Include sae, and Canadian postage, IRC or cash. Pays $20 per published page, plus complimentary copy.

Annual contest

Closes on December 15th; $1000 for best poem, $500 each for 2 x Honourable Mentions. Submit up to 3 poems of no more than 100 lines each. No name and address on MSS; include a cover page with the title(s) of the submission plus genre, name, address, email and phone number. Entry fee, $30 (CAD) for Canadian entries, $36 (US) for US and overseas. See website for more details.

The Louisville Review

c/o Fleur-de-Lis Press, 851 South 4th Street, Louisville, KY 40203, USA

tel 502 585 9911 ext. 2777 *fax* 502 585 7158
website www.louisvillereview.org

Paper Wasp

14 Fig Tree Pocket Road, Chapel Hill, QLD 4069, Australia
email ksamuelowicz@optusnet.co.au
Editor Katherine Samuelowicz
Frequency/price Quarterly – summer, autumn, winter and spring issues; $20 for 4 issues inclusive of p&p (overseas, US$26; cash only)

An international journal publishing haiku, senryu, renga, tanka and haibun. Acknowledges a range of forms and styles, from one-liners to the conventional 5-7-5 form, and variations. Individual issues available to order at $6 in Australia, and US$8 (cash only) elsewhere. All overseas orders sent by airmail.

Submission details Submit by email or by post to the above address.

Poetry

444 North Michigan Avenue, Suite 1850, Chicago, IL 60625, USA
tel 312 799 8015 *fax* 312 787 6650
email valeriejohnson@poetrymagazine.org
Contact Valerie Johnson (Editorial & Marketing Assistant)

Poetry Canada

2431 Cyprus Avenue, Burlington, Ontario, L7P 1G5, Canada
email tracy@innersurf.com
website www.poetrycanada.com
Editor Tracy Repchuk

Poetry Kanto

tel 081-045 7867205
email alan@kanto-gakuin.ac.jp
website http://home.kanto-gakuin.ac.jp/~kg061001/
Editor Alan Botsford

Poetry Monash

1/20 Nandina Street, Forest Hill, Vic 3131, Australia
email mcguiganl@hotkey.net.au
Editor Lorraine McGuigan
Frequency/price Biannual. 3 issues $21
Submission details Submissions of 1 page preferred, for reasons of space.

Poetry Salzburg Review

email psr@poetrysalzburg.com
website www.poetrysalzburg.com/psr
Contact Dr Wolfgang Gortschacher, *UK*
Contact David Miller, 99 Mitre Road, London
SE1 8PT

Founded in 2001 as a biannual magazine,
Poetry Salzburg Review publishes poems (also
long poems), translations, interviews, artwork,
essays on poetics and review-essays focusing on
recently published collections of poetry.
Supports no particular school of writing. Aims
to be as eclectic as possible, while maintaining
high quality, through seeking out a wide range
of different types of writing. Prints emerging
writers alongside the most recent work of
established writers. "A fascinating mixture of
styles, poets, generations, etc., which is an
exemplary lesson in non-partisan attention to
quality." (Glyn Pursglove, Critic)

Poets' Podium

2-3265 Front Road, Hawkesbury,
Ontario K6A 2R2, Canada
Editor Ken Elliott
Frequency/price Subscription $15 (1 year), $23
(2 years); $29 (3 years). Back issues $3 each

Quarterly not-for-profit newsletter designed for
poetry lovers of all ages. Aims to encourage the
reading and writing of poetry. Comments and
contributions of poetry welcome.

Submission details Submissions should be
made by regular mail – no email submissions.
A postal coupon should be included.

Polestar Writer's Journal

PO Box 196, Drayton North, QLD 4350,
Australia
email polestarwj@hotmail.com
Frequency/price Biannual (June, December).
$20 (12 months), $35 (24 months)

Submission details Short stories to 2000
words, open theme. Poems preferably to 18
lines, open theme. Allow at least 6 weeks for a
response; enclose sae for reply – submissions
will not be returned. Contributors receive a
complimentary copy of the Journal.

Pratibha India

IP Staff Bungalow, 31 Shamnath Marg,
Delhi – 110 054 (India)

email siteshaloke@hotmail.com
Editor Aruna Sitesh

Quarterly journal publishing literary writings
and translated poetry by Indian poets writing
in their own regional languages.

Rock Pebbles

Naranpur, Post-Kodandapur, Via-Devidwar,
Dist-Jaipur, Orissa, India 755007
tel 943 744 9490 , 986 101 2630
email rockpebbles2007@rediffmail.com
Editor Uday Majhi
Frequency/price Annual subscription 100
rupees, US$12, £10; life subscription 1000
rupees, US$120, £100

A biannual literary magazine (June and
December). Publishes poems, short stories,
literacy essays, travelogues, artwork, book
reviews, etc. First among the purely literary
magazines in India.

Studio

727 Peel Street, Albury, NSW, 2660, Australia
email studio00@bigpond.net.au
Frequency/price Annual subscription $60AUD

Quarterly journal of Christians' writing.
Publishes poetry and prose of literary merit,
offering a venue for previously published, new
and aspiring writers. Seeks to develop a sense of
community among subscribers across the
globe, including universities and libraries.

Submission details Submit no more than 3
poems, by post or by email. Allow up to 3
weeks for response. Payment is made by
complimentary copy of the edition in which
accepted work is published; additional copies
are available at special author rates.

Tampa Review

c/o The University of Tampa Press,
401 West Kennedy Boulevard, Tampa,
FL 33606, USA
tel 813 253-6266 *fax* 813 258-7593
email utpress@ut.edu
website http://tampareview.ut.edu
Editor Don Morrill, Martha Serpas

Submission details Submissions can be
directed to either editor, or to 'The Poetry
Editor'. Only considers submissions
postmarked from 1st September to 31st

December, annually. Pays $10 per printed page upon publication. Does not accept simultaneous submissions, or submissions sent by email. Further guidelines are available via the website.

The New Orphic Review

New Orphic Publishers, 706 Mill Street, Nelson, British Columbia, VIL 4S5, Canada
tel 250 354 0494 *fax* 250 352 0743
website www3.telus.net/neworphicpublishers-hekkanen
Contact Ernest Hekkanen (Editor-in-Chief), Margrith Schraner (Associate Editor)

Frequency/price 2 issues p.a. (Spring, Fall)

Established in 1998, with a circulation of 300. A completely independent magazine that does not rely on government grants or subsidies from institutions.

Submission details Poetry up to 30 lines. In the best Orphic tradition, submissions should try to get to the essence of things. Considers a wide variety of approaches, but shies away from leggy, neo-beat poetry. There are fewer poems in *The New Orphic Review* than there is fiction. A Featured Poet section is included in nearly every issue.

E-poetry and e-zines

The Internet provides poets with an exciting new outlet for their poetry. **Kostas Hrisos**, founder and editor of poetry e-zine, *Interpoetry*, provides a useful and practical guide to the fast-growing world of the poetry e-zine and e-poetry.

Fiction and poetry are very difficult to write. But it's even more difficult, especially with poetry, to get them published. Poetry has little commercial appeal and publishing is a cut-throat business. The expense of print publication is prohibitive and that of distribution exorbitant. But poetry belongs to the people, and despite these problems, is flourishing – though it may be marginal to the interests of the general reader. Although a somewhat minority art, an astonishing number of people do write poetry and an even more astonishing number read it. Thanks in no small part to the Internet .

As the Internet expands its reach, a rapidly growing legion of international online journals (e-zines) is appearing. They build on the reputation of the established ones, which have demonstrated that they can be just as well edited – and just as creatively and inventively formatted – as anything in print. An e-zine can be put up online at an insignificant cost; distribution is global and immediate; and it is all available – latest issue and, unlike with books, back issues and archives – 24/7. This thriving arena of journals, resource portals and hybrids of writing, news and art offers everyone the opportunity to publish, and allows for easy communication and ready access to a vast pool of material.

The Internet opens endless possibilities for contemporary/visual poetry to create works that synthesise both arts and media. There are many types of 'digital poetry' – also referred to as e-poetry or electronic poetry – that take advantage of and harness the flexibility of digital media/multimedia, and which use the Internet's interactive nature to enhance and expand poetic and artistic techniques. The Internet provides a doorway to a wide diversity of styles of digital poetry – defined as 'approaches to poetry that all have in common the use of computers'.

Digital poetry creates a combination/montage of visual and verbal signs of contemporary poetics and aesthetics. It interacts with the reader and exploits the graphic form of the letter, the word or the text; it uses visual images (animations, drawings, photos, numbers, or other graphic elements) as compositional components of the poem through formal interrelationship and semantic interpenetration.

Writing is a lonely activity. The Internet publishes aspiring authors and greatly assists the amateur and the new poet. It also promotes many established poets, through posting their work, their books and web page links, and creates a connected web of writers that helps to promote poetry locally and globally. The web has no countries – it is international.

Hypertext, listservs (email-based mailing-list applications), blogs (websites that provide commentary or news on a particular subject.) and other forms of network communication create communities of collaborative writing and publications. Poetical wikis are designed to allow multiple authors to add, remove and edit content. Poets (and authors) have only begun to exploit the Internet's possibilities – the more ambitious among them experiment with multimedia, sound, animation and video. Flash, Applets and other programs interact with the user to create a poem (here quality is questionable but the results are fun). Cursors reveal, conceal or wipe out text and background images. Shape-shifting poems and 3D poems enable you to transform at a click of a mouse button, or to generate text, kinetic poetry, code poetry and sound poetry.

By encouraging these rich ways of mixing different kind of signs, the user/reader is now obliged to adopt an intelligent approach to reading a poem, and not just engage in a mechanical interaction.

In general, publishing poetry through these channels is no different from submitting to conventional magazines. They offer many amateurs their only chance of seeing their work published. Submitting to poetry ezines is quick and free – usually an attachment to an email – and sometimes you can use a library's or a college's computers to send the email.

Quality varies. There are excellent, reputable literary e-zines/journals out there that take email submissions for their online site and also produce a print journal. They are well moderated (edited) and have excellent articles, bulletin boards, workshops and forums, where poems and writing matters are discussed and encouraged. There are also long-established small presses with Internet presence.

Never underestimate the user's/reader's intelligence. They know enough to appreciate e-zines for good quality. New poets know they can join a few well-established poetry forums, for good workshops that offer legitimate, constructive critique from a variety of other poets and readers. This way they can determine if their poetry holds universal appeal. If they constantly receive excellent reviews and feedback, then they will want to submit for publications to reputable literary and poetry e-zines and print press.

This way, new and established authors learn to create better poems and they increase their web presence and thus their reputation and credibility.

There is a downside: the Internet does not yet have the reputation of printed work. The work could be plagiarised. It does not pay anything. However, there are many reputable e-zines that will pay for good material and any work can be plagiarised out of a print journal.

Does digital poetry work? If you are asking, then you are interested. And if you are interested, you have to boldly go out there and use it. Even better: create it yourself and put it out there.

You might decide that you'd like to run a poetry e-zine, like **interpoetry.com**, which provides a platform where all kinds of creative innovations can be published, and a space where new creative writers and artists can be seen next to more successful, established ones. An artist/photographer is selected for the issue's cover. Then you will have to decide if you are going to be a one-man-band – the web designer, the webmaster, the editor, the promoter and the public relations person – or share the responsibility. Either way, it takes dedication, effort and time. You must decide on the scope and the content of the e-zine, design it, build it with HTML, Dreamweaver or any other program at home and then upload it/update it.

The easiest part is to buy and register a website site (domain name). If you are lucky, you might even find a domain name with 'poetry' in it that is free; just search for 'domain names' with any search engine. Then, the same company may offer you 'website hosting', where you publish your website. Prices vary. If you plan to publish your own work, then you have everything you need. If you are planning to publish other people's work, then you become an editor – and that is where quality and reputation make a significant difference. Content is the most important feature of an e-zine. It is the editor's responsibility to ensure the quality of the materials published that will attract visitors, engage better contributors, and build the e-zine's reputation.

Once all this is completed, you need an FTP (File Transfer Protocol) program to upload and manage the site to the host server. How often? It is entirely up to you. **interpoetry.com** receives a number of submissions/contributions for each issue, from poets all over the word. Its reputation is built on its design, and equally on its content, with contributions by Alamgir Hashmi, Anne Stevenson, Elizabeth Smither, John Hegley, Lee Harwood, Linda France, Patrick Pritchett, Pedro Serrano, to mention but a few.

I upload to the e-zine the materials that the editorial team selects, from the number submitted, mostly by email, as soon as I can. This way the site attracts visitors daily and they can observe the process of the issue being developed. Please take a look and do submit/contribute.

The real impact of e-poetry lies in the future, when handheld A4 computers (just like the eframes for images/video now) will be available and will not only display text, but enable it to be interactive too. Publishing processes, the role of the author and the possibilities of literary education will change drastically. Authors, poets and artists will collaborate directly to create a holistic eproduct for a holistic experience.

Kostas Hrisos is founder, editor and webmaster of poetry e-zine, *Interpoetry*. kostas.hrisos@interpoetry.com
www.interpoetry.com

E-magazines

There has been an explosion of poetry e-magazines, and many of the sites are classy, exquisitely designed productions. The list below, comprising poetry e-mags from both the United Kingdom and around the world (mostly US, of course), is by no means comprehensive – that would be almost impossible – but it does demonstrate the breadth of choice that exists, and the kind of quality to which many e-magazines can aspire.

2 River View
www.2river.org

Poetry, podcasts and commentary.

3AM Magazine
www.3ammagazine.com

Poetry, fiction, music, criticism, etc.

3rd Muse
www.3rdmuse.com

Published monthly online, as well as quarterly in a print edition.

42opus
www.42opus.com

An online magazine of the literary arts.

63 channels
www.63channels.com/

Poetry, interviews, featured poet.

Abalone Moon
www.abalonemoon.com

An eclectic and thematic journal of contemporary poetry and art.

ABCTales
www.abctales.com

Poems and short stories, tips and advice.

Able Muse
www.ablemuse.com

Poetry writing, poetry critique, online workshop forums, art, photography.

Adagio Verse Quarterly
www.geocities.com/adagioversequarterly

Stylish poetry and art e-zine.

Adirondack Review
www.adirondackreview.homestead.com/

Reviews, features and poetry.

Agniezka's Dowry
http://asgp.org/agnieszka.html

Webzine from A Small Garlic Press.

Aileron
http://unblinkingeye.com/Poetry/Aileron/aileron.html

Literary magazine edited by Ed Buffaloe. *"Combines graphics with words to make a visual/verbal/intellectual feast."*

Alba
www.ravennapress.com/alba

A journal of short poetry.

Alice Blue Review
www.alicebluereview.org

Twice yearly, nicely put together magazine of poetry and prose.

A Little Poetry
www.alittlepoetry.com/

E-zine that includes a place for poets to store their own pages.

Alsop Review
www.alsopreview.com/index2.html

Literary showcase – several associated magazines.

Amaze
www.amaze-cinquain.com

Dedicated to developing, promoting, and publishing cinquains.

Ancient Heart Magazine
www.ancientheartmagazine.co.uk

E-zine published by Lionheart Press, Bristol.

Another Sun
www.anothersun.co.uk

A 21st-century e-zine for poetry and the arts from London.

Apple Valley Review
www.applevalleyreview.com

Poetry, short fiction, and essays.

Archipelago
www.archipelago.org

Poetry and fiction.

The Argotist Online
www.argotistonline.co.uk

Non-mainstream poetry, essays and interviews.

Ariga
http://ariga.com/visions/poetry

Poetry from dozens of contributors from around the world.

Ascent Aspirations
www.ascentaspirations.ca/

Poetry and fiction with a dark edge.

aucklandpoetry.com
http://aucklandpoetry.blogspot.com/

Publishes poetry by a different local featured poet each month, as well as maintaining a live poetry gig guide, news, and links section.

The Aurora Review
www.theaurorareview.com

Eclectic literary and cultural magazine dedicated to promotion of music, literature, and visual arts.

Barnwood Magazine
www.bsu.edu/classes/koontz/barnwood/mag/mag.html

The best new poetry, served online by The Barnwood Press.

The Beat
www.the-beat.co.uk

Short stories, flash fiction, poetry, and art.

Beltway
www.washingtonart.com/beltway/contents.html

Poetry quarterly.

Big Bridge
www.bigbridge.org

Webzine featuring poetry, fiction, non-fiction, essays, journalism, and art of all kinds.

Big Toe Review
www.bigtoereview.com

Flash fiction and poetry.

Big Ugly Review
www.biguglyreview.com

Flash fiction, short stories, poetry and non-fiction accepted.

Birmingham Words
www.birminghamwords.org

Online community for readers and writers.

The Blackbird
www.blackbird.vcu.edu/v5n2/index.htm

An online journal of literature and the arts.

Blaze Vox
www.blazevox.org

Post-avant poetries and fiction.

Blood Lotus
www.bloodlotus.org

A young, online literary journal.

BMP Press
http://nzpoetsonline.homestead.com

New Zealand online mag encouraging local as well as international submissions.

Born Magazine
www.bornmagazine.org

An experimental venue marrying literary arts and interactive media.

Boxcar Poetry Review
www.boxcarpoetry.com

Poetry, artwork, photography, interviews, and reviews.

Buzzwords
www.buzzwords.ndo.co.uk

Poetry, fiction and reviews from all over the world.

Cadillac Cicatrix
www.cadillaccicatrix.com

Began as a one-time publication by students of The Jack Kerouac School of Disembodied Poetics at Naropa University. It evolved into the title under which NorthernPros.com publishes its semi-annual journal of literature and art.

Caught in the Net
www.poetrykit.org/pkl/CITN/caughtin.htm

An email poetry magazine.

Centrifugal Forces
www.centrifugalforces.co.uk

E-zine for mobile phone users.

Cezannes Carrot
www.cezannescarrot.org

Literary journal featuring prose, poetry, and visual art that embodies spiritual, transformational, visionary, and contemplative themes.

Clickable Poems
www.clickablepoems.com

Conte
www.conteonline.net

An online journal of narrative writing, both prose and poetry.

Contemporary Poetry Review
www.cprw.com

Devoted to poetry criticism.

Contemporary Rhyme
www.contemporaryrhyme.com

E-journal that seeks to highlight current achievements in poetry.

Contrary magazine
www.contrarymagazine.com

Publishes commentary, fiction, poetry, and work that declines to conform to single categories.

The Cortland Review
www.cortlandreview.com

An online literary quarterly in RealAudio with monthly features and interviews.

Creature Magazine
www.creaturemag.com

Innovative site and magazine.

Crimson Feet
http://magazine.crimsonfeet.org

Bi-monthly e-zine.

CrossConnect
http://ccat.sas.upenn.edu/xconnect

A literary review; fiction and poetry.

Crossing Borders
www.crossingborders-africanwriting.org/magazine

Short stories and poetry from writers from across Africa.

Dead Drunk in Dublin
www.deaddrunkdublin.com

Poems; stories; manifestos.

The Del Sol Review
http://webdelsol.com/Del_Sol_Review

Poetry, prose poetry, creative non-fiction, short stories, and flash fiction.

The Diagram
http://thediagram.com

An electronic journal of text and art.

Dirt Press
www.dirtpress.com

A journal of contemporary arts and letters with the occasional printed anthology.

dotlit
www.dotlit.qut.edu.au

Australian literary and creative writing journal.

Dragon Fire
www.dfire.org

Magazine from Drexel University, Philadelphia.

The Drunken Boat
www.thedrunkenboat.com

Online international poetry journal featuring poetry in translation and interviews with poets.

Ducky Mag
www.duckymag.com/DV

Published online twice per year.

Eclectica
www.eclectica.org

Quarterly poetry e-zine.

Electronic Acorn
http://acorn.dublinwriters.org

Ireland's first online literary quarterly.

Erbacce
www.erbacce.com

Print and online journal edited by Alan Corkish and Andrew Taylor.

Facets Magazine
www.facets-magazine.com

Original, unpublished poetry, fiction, and creative non-fiction.

Failbetter.com
www.failbetter.com

Stanford University-based literary e-zine.

The Fairfield Review
www.fairfieldreview.org

Online literary magazine.

FlashPoint
www.flashpointmag.com

Poetry, essays, fiction, graphics.

Foliate Oak
www.uamont.edu/foliateoak

Poetry and short story mag. Plus annual printed anthology.

Food_and_Car_Poems
www.geocities.com/food_and_car_poems

A journal accepting non-emotive poetry of specific forms.

Four Volts
http://fourvolts.co.uk

A UK e-zine that publishes work from emerging and semi-professional authors, with a focus on the unusual, original, and dark.

Freebase Accordion
www.petermanson.com

Eclectic and engaging poetry e-zine.

Frigg Magazine
www.friggmagazine.com

A magazine of fiction and poetry.

Gentle Chaos Magazine
http://gentlechaos.chaoticdreams.net

Ginosko Literary Journal
http://ginoskoliteraryjournal.com

Short-run print magazine in San Francisco area posted as an e-mag.

Gorelets: Unpleasant Poetry
www.gorelets.com

Poetry with a horror theme.

Great Works
www.greatworks.org.uk

Innovative writing: modernist, postmodernist, archaic, poetry and prose.

Green Interger Review
www.greeninteger.com

A magazine of innovative poetry.

Hamilton Stone Review
www.hamiltonstone.org

Excellent magazine.

Hawkwind
www.hawkwindcreations.com

Literary e-zine out of San Antonio, Texas.

Hearsay
http://pages.prodigy.net/lilliankennedyesq

Poetry written by lawyers.

Heron's Nest (The)
www.theheronsnest.com

Haiku journal.

HOW2
www.asu.edu/pipercwcenter/how2journal

Essays; reflections, letters, journals, paragraphs, graphics; in-progress drafts, research, translations, alphabets, cross-overs.

Ink and Ashes
www.inkandashes.com

Poetry, creative non-fiction, essays and visual art.

Ink, Sweat & Tears
www.ink-sweat-and-tears.com

A poetry and prose webzine with a particular interest in prose poetry (including free verse and haibun) and e-poetry (including hypertext & Flash).

Interactions Online Jersey
www.interactionspoetry.com

Poetry and art from the Island of Jersey.

Interpoetry
www.interpoetry.com

Monthly webzine of poetry, art and photography from all over the world.

Jack
www.jackmagazine.com

Jack Magazine is an offshoot of Beat Generation News.

Jacket
www.jacketmagazine.com

Stylish Australian e-zine edited by the leading Australian poet, John Tranter.

Joined Up Writing
www.joinedupwriting.org

A journal of poetry and prose by members of online writing workshops and groups.

Kaleidowhirl
http://home.alltel.net/ellablue

A quarterly journal of poetry and flash fiction by emerging and established writers.

The King's English
www.thekingsenglish.org

Book reviews, poetry, novella-length fiction and long personal essays.

Kritya
www.kritya.in

Poetry magazine from India.

Laika Poetry Review
http://laikapoetryreview.blogspot.com

Blog-based magazine.

La Petite Zine
www.lapetitezine.org

Magazine of poetry, essays, flash-fiction and drama.

Le Marginal
www.themarginal.com

French-Canadian literary mag.

Litter Magazine
www.leafepress.com/litter

Organic magazine updated regularly.

The Little Magazine
www.littlemag.com

Web version of South Asia's only professionally produced print magazine – devoted to essays, fiction, poetry, art and criticism.

Light Quarterly
www.lightquarterly.com

A quarterly of light and occasional verse, squibs, satire, puns, and wordplay.

Limelight
www.thepoem.co.uk

Contemporary British and Irish poetry.

Lively Arts
www.lively-arts.com

General cultural zine.

Living Poets Society
http://livingpoetssociety.com/

Features poetry contests with cash prizes.

Lowdown
www.lowdown.co.zm

Zambia's online poetry magazine.

Lunarosity
www.zianet.com/lunarosity

A bi-monthly publication

Lynx: Poetry from Bath
www.dgdclynx.plus.com

Magazine containing critical articles on poetry.

Lynx
www.ahapoetry.com/ahalynx/203HMPG.html

Haiku, haibuns, ghazals and poetry sequences.

Madelaine
www.madelaine.dome2.com

Online magazine with a food theme.

The MAG
www.muse-apprentice-guild.com

Poetry reviews, book reviews, writing contests.

Malleable Jangle
www.malleablejangle.netfirms.com

Australian-based, monthly online poetry journal with an international outlook.

Man in the Moon
www.maninthemoon.co.uk/

Children's poetry site

Masthead
www.masthead.net.au

Australian literary e-zine.

The Melic Review
www.melicreview.com

Poetry and fiction.

Memorious
www.memorious.org

New verse and poetics.

Miranda Literary Magazine
http://mirandamagazine.com

Developed by a group of creative artists and writers to promote and focus on the best writing, art, and ideas of our time.

Mississippi Review
www.mississippireview.com

Themed issues.

Monsoon Magazine
www.monsoonmag.com

Art, autobiographical sketches, essays, fiction, interviews, photography, poetry, reviews, and translations.

Moria
www.moriapoetry.com

Experimental and innovative styles of poetry.

The Morpo Review
www.morpo.com

Quarterly electronic publication of poetry and fiction.

Motleys
www.motleys.bravehost.com

Quarterly literary e-zine with a comic slant.

Mudlark
www.etext.org/Poetry/Mudlark

An electronic journal of poetry and poetics.

MUGround
www.mallasch.com/mug

E-zine and poetry community.

Murmurs of a Nobody
www.murmursofanobody.co.uk

A site that discusses the trials and tribulations of modern life through poetry.

The Muse Apprentice Guild
www.muse-apprentice-guild.com

Poetry, fiction, hyper-literary fiction, articles, essays, reviews, interviews, and works in progress.

Muses Review
www.musesreview.org

Online journal of literature and arts from San Jose, California.

Neon Highway
www.neonhighway.co.uk

Features work by poets and artists.

Nidus
www.pitt.edu/~nidus

Journal of contemporary art and literature.

Noö Journal
www.noojournal.com

Quarterly magazine of politics, prose, poetry and pictures.

Nthposition
www.nthposition.com

Political, innovative and just plain weird poetry.

Overland Express
www.overlandexpress.org

Online literary journal of poetry, prose, hypertext.

The Page
http://thepage.name

Aims to gather links to the most interesting new poems and writing about poetry and ideas.

Panic! Brixton Poetry
http://homepages.which.net/
~panic.brixtonpoetry

Online magazine of poetry and art dedicated to the people of Brixton, South London.

Pave Journal
www.pavejournal.org

A multimedia literary and art journal promoting creative content, active discussion, and a forum for unheard creative minds.

The Penniless Press
www.pennilesspress.com

An online magazine publishing new and avant garde poetry, ideas, literature, criticism, art, non-fiction, reviews and essays.

Perigee
www.perigee-art.com

Quarterly publication of the arts.

Perihelion
http://webdelsol.com/Perihelion

Literary theory articles and poetry.

Picolata Review
http://picolatareview.blogspot.com

Blog-based mag.

Pif Magazine
www.pifmagazine.com

One of the oldest, continually published literary zines online; original works of fiction, poetry, creative non-fiction, essays, and book reviews.

Pocket Full of Poesy
http://pocketfullofpoesy.blogspot.com

Blog-mag poems in English from anywhere in the world.

The Poem
www.thepoem.co.uk

Contemporary British and Irish poetry.

Poems Niederngasse
www.niederngasse.com

Four magazines, English, Italian, German and Spanish plus a print published 'best of'.

Poetix
www.poetix.net/

Site dedicated to the poetry scene in South California.

Poetry Daily
www.poems.com

An anthology of contemporary poetry offering new poems from books, magazines and journals currently in print.

Poetry Kit Magazine
www.poetrykit.org

Poetry Kit's own on-site magazine.

Poetry London
www.poetrylondon.co.uk

One of Britain's leading poetry magazines, featuring original poems, and reviews, and sponsoring an annual contest for unpublished poems.

poetry pf
www.poetrypf.co.uk

A showcase for modern poets.

PoetrSz
www.poetrysz.net

Demystifying mental illness with work from all over the world.

Poetry Victims
www.geocities.com/poetryvictims

An online email poetry newsletter sent daily to interested poets and poetry lovers.

The Poet's Canvas
www.poetscanvas.org

Original, unpublished poetry.

Pores
www.pores.bbk.ac.uk

An avant gardist journal of poetics research from the Contemporary Poetics Research Centre (CPRC), Birkbeck College.

Qualm
www.qualm.co.uk

Small uncompromising showcase for contemporary poetry in English.

Quid Magazine
http://jacketmagazine.com/20/quid.html

Poetry e-zine from Cambridge.

Quill & Parchment
http://quillandparchment.com

A website for "writers and poets, readers and romanticists, gourmet cooks, photographers, painters and lovers".

Ramble Underground
www.rambleunderground.org

Quarterly journal of fiction, poetry, art, and photography.

Raving Dove
www.ravingdove.org

Poetry, non-fiction essays, fiction, photography, and art.

Readings
www.bbk.ac.uk/readings

A web-journal from the CPRC Birkbeck and the British Electronic Poetry Centre (BEPC).

Red Ink
www.incwriters.com

A PDF publication publishing series of poems by eight poets per issue, as well as fiction.

The Richmond Review
www.richmondreview.co.uk/

The UK's first literary magazine to be published exclusively on the World Wide Web. Contains poetry, short stories and reviews.

The Roundtable Review
www.roundtablereview.co.uk

Online arts journal devoted to "poetry, art, fiction, theatre and ideas".

The Salt River Review
www.poetserv.org

Online magazine featuring poetry, fiction and creative non-fiction, also in translation.

Scorched Earth Publishing
http://scorchedearthpublishing.com

Prose and poetry.

Segue
www.mid.muohio.edu/segue

Online literary journal of Miami University-Middletown.

Sentinel Poetry Online
www.sentinelpoetry.org.uk

Monthly magazine featuring poems, interviews, essays, competitions and links to great poetry sites.

Shadow Train
http://shadowtrain.com

A monthly collection of poems, translations, articles and other writings.

Shampoo Poetry
www.shampoopoetry.com

Online magazine that features original poetry and shampoo photography.

Shit Creek Review
http://theshitcreekreview.blogspot.com

Original poetry, mostly witty, traditional or free verse. Also original short fiction and literary criticism.

Signals Magazine
www.signalsmagazine.co.uk

Poetry, comment and reviews.

Simply Haiku
http://simplyhaiku.com

Showcase for the Japanese short form poetry written in the English language.

Siren
www.sirenlit.com

Online literary and art journal

Slope
www.slope.org

Online journal of original poetry.

Small Spiral Notebook
www.smallspiralnotebook.com

Online and in-print versions.

Snakeskin
http://homepages.nildram.co.uk/~simmers/

Monthly poetry webzine.

SNR
www.snreview.org

A literary journal of prose and poetry, founded in 1999.

Sol Magazine
www.sol-magazine.org

Juried competitions, interviews with poets, poetry website reviews, answers to readers' questions, and explanation of poetic terms.

Sound Eye
http://www.soundeye.org/

Magazine focusing on the innovative tendency in Irish poetry as well as a full range of supporting materials, including review and survey articles, bibliographies, and news of relevant readings, festivals and conferences.

Southern Ocean Review
http://www.book.co.nz/

An international online literary and arts magazine based in New Zealand.

Spoken War
www.spokenwar.com

Poetry, spoken word, writing, performance poetry, slam, real audio, photos.

Spokes
www.simegen.com/writers/spokes

An international poetry e-zine that welcomes poetry, short fictional prose and images of all kinds.

Stellar Showcase Journal
www.stellarshowcasejournal.com

Promotes and aids poets, writers and readers by providing information and resources that cater to their unique needs.

Stirring : A Literary Collection
www.sundress.net/stirring

Monthly, online literary collection which prides itself in collecting the best of the Web's burgeoning writers for publication.

Stride Magazine
www.stridemagazine.co.uk

Once a print magazine and now reincarnated as a webzine.

Stupid Poetry
http://whyfronts.tripod.com/stupidpoetry

Comic verse website.

Stylus Poetry Journal
www.styluspoetryjournal.com

Bi-monthly Australian e-zine that features contemporary poetry, haiku and its related forms, articles, reviews and interviews.

Switchback
www.swback.com

A publication of the Master of Fine Arts in Writing Program of the University of San Francisco.

Tallulah
http://members.lycos.co.uk/anitasethi21

Originally founded as part of the Cambridge University Creative Writing Society, Tallulah is now an online creative arts magazine publishing poetry, short prose, photography and artwork.

Textualities
www.textualities.net

A wide range of features on books and writing.

Three Candles Journal
www.threecandles.org

A literary arts journal.

Thylazine
www.thylazine.org

Australian-based mag.

Toad in Mud
www.toadinmud.co.uk

Online journal of new writing also offering critical and commentary services.

Triplopia
www.triplopia.org

Poetry, prose, and aesthetic discussions, as well as book, film, music and art reviews, and digital photography and artwork.

Tryst
www.tryst3.com

Journal dedicated to the promotion of poetry, art and artists.

Turbine
www.vuw.ac.nz/turbine/

Annually published New Zealand online literary journal.

Vallum Contemporary Poetry
www.vallummag.com

A biannual journal featuring poetry by emerging and established writers from Canada, the US and abroad.

Valparaslo Poetry Review
www.valpo.edu/english/vpr/v6n2.html

Poems, interviews, and essays by new, emerging, or well-known poets.

The Verse Marauder
www.theversemarauder.com

Online poetry magazine publishing poetry in or translated into English.

Ward 6 Review
www.ward6review.com

US-based monthly online literary magazine striving to be a premiere destination for international literature on the Internet.

West47
http://www.galwayartscentre.ie/west47/west47-12/index.html

Magazine of the Galway Arts Centre, now entirely online.

Western Writer's Centre, Ireland
www.twwc.ie/

Taking story and poetry submissions.

White Leaf Review
http://whiteleafpress.co.uk/2.html

New poems and reviews of poetry books and pamphlets.

Woodwork
www.woodwork.indiegroup.com

Perth, Australia e-zine interested in receiving submissions from language poets and anything fresh from anyone with a creative bent.

Wow
www.wordsontheweb.net/

Galway's online literary magazine.

Words-Myth
www.words-myth.com

Interational journal of poetry in the English Language.

World Haiku Review
www.worldhaikureview.org

The magazine of the World Haiku Club.

Writers Hood
www.writershood.com

A multi-genre monthly online magazine that caters to beginning writers.

Ygdrasil: A Journal of the Poetic Arts
www.etext.org/Poetry/Ygdrasil

A journal of the poetic arts.

Zafusy
www.zafusy.com

A contemporary poetry journal.

Poetry podcasts

Association of Poetry Podcasting
website http://poetrypodcasting.org

Provides an outlet for poetry podcasters. (USA)

Audiolingo
website http://audiolingo.org

A 'gumbo' of mashups, poetry, words and music. (USA)

Black Country Podcasting
website www.blackcountrypodcasting.com

Music, poetry, short stories, interviews with people from around the Black Country area of England. (UK)

Bodies at Rest
website www.bodiesatrestonline.com

A 'haven of peace', hosted by the poetess, Celestial Dancer. (USA)

Cloudy Day Art
website www.cloudydayart.com

A weekly podcast featuring poetry, interviews with poets and commentary on the world of poetry. (USA)

ESC Magazine's Coffee House to Go
website http://coffeehousetogo.blogspot.com

A monthly podcast for writers and the small press community, featuring readings of poetry, short fiction, interviews and reviews. (USA)

The Everyday Muse
website www.prosodyetc.com/edm/index.htm

One author confronts his muse, writing a poem a day for a year. Each week the poem is presented along with his thoughts on the creative process. (USA)

The Friction Fiction Show
website http://frictionfiction.libsyn.com

A guide to what's 'live in Web 2.0'; music, fiction, poetry and art. (USA)

German Poems
website http://german-poems.podspot.de/rss

Classical German poetry by Goethe, Schiller, Heine etc. (Ger)

Griffin Poetry Prize Poetry Readings
website www.griffinpoetryprize.com/podcast/rss.xml

Samples of the work of the poets who have been shortlisted for the Canadian Griffin Award, in text, audio and video formats. (Can)

Gypsy Art Show
website http://belinda_subraman.podomatic.com

Interviews with singer/songwriters, musicians, poets and artists of many genres and samples of their work. (USA)

Homegrown Podcast
website http://homegrownpodcast.co.uk

Independent music, poetry and prose. (UK)

IndieFeed: Performance Poetry
website www.indiefeedpp.libsyn.com

A community-oriented micro-media broadcast network. (USA)

Latin Poetry Podcast
website http://itech.dickinson.edu/blog

Fascinating ancient poetry from the Dickenson College blog in the USA.

Mefeedia
website http://mefeedia.com/tags/poetry

More than 2000 videoblogs and podcasts about poetry. (USA)

Muddy Bank
website www.2river.org/blog

Podcasts of poets reading their own work. (USA)

Mystic Babylon
website http://mysticbabylon.podomatic.com

Poetry from the Haight and San Francisco area. (USA)

The Northzine Podcast
website http://northzine.net

A poetry podcast from north-east Scotland. (UK)

Podcast.com

website www.podcast.com

Poetry for podcasters. (USA)

Podcast.net

website www.podcast.net/cat/130

A directory of podcasts about books and poetry. (USA)

Podcast Directory

website www.podcastdirectory.com/format/ Poetry

A directory of readings and lectures by poets and critics. (USA)

Podlounge

website www.podlounge.com.au

Australian directory with some poetry podcasts listed. (Aus)

Poetcast

website www.poets.org/page.php/prmID/344

The official podcast of the Academy of American Poets. (USA)

The Poetic Voice

website www.thepoeticvoice.com

Poetry X Radio

website http://poetryx.com

A weekly podcast featuring news, interviews, reviews, blues and poetry. (USA)

Ratapallax Podcast

website www.ratapallax.com

Free podcast featuring some of the best poets, writers, translators and performers in international literature. New updates every week. (USA)

Slam Idol

website http://slamidolpodcast.com

A poetry slam contest with voting.(USA)

Surrealwords.com

website http://odeo.com/tag/poetry

Spoken-word poetry selections. (USA)

VI Radio

website www.vocalizedink.org

Streaming radio from Vocalized Ink, including original content and many podcasts from the Association of Poetry Podcasts. (USA)

White House Poets

website http://druidpaddy.blogmatrix.com

An edited version of the White House Poetry Revival recorded at the White House Pub in Limerick, Ireland. Open floor followed by guest poet. Regularly updated. (Ire)

Poetry broadcast and audio

Many people prefer to hear poetry read aloud, rather than reading it on a page. There are an increasing number of sources for this, whether on radio or on websites where you can listen to poets from the present and the past reading their work. Of particular note is the UK's Poetry Archive, a superb online collection of poets reading their work.

American Oral

website www.nd.edu/~ameroral

Work appears as text, as well as orally in the voice of the author.

An Audio Anthology

website www.theatlantic.com/unbound/poetry/antholog/aaindx.htm

For subscribers to *Atlantic Monthly*. Features current and past *Atlantic Monthly* authors reading in RealAudio. (USA)

Archive of the Now

website www.archiveofthenow.com/

An online and print repository of recordings, printed texts and manuscripts, focusing on innovative contemporary poetry being written or performed in Britain. (UK)

Art of Words

website www.SolarRadio.com (and Sky Channel 0129; UK and Ireland only)

A monthly mixture of cutting-edge lyrical soul, jazz, world music, interviews, literature, poetry, community figures and lively debate. Airs the last Monday of the month at 2am GMT and is broadcast simultaneously on Sky Channel 0129. (UK)

Atlantic Unbound's Soundings

website http://www.theatlantic.com/unbound/poetry/soundings

Classic poems read by contemporary poets from *Atlantic Monthly*.

Audia Book Radio

website www.audiobookradio.net

An Internet radio station dedicated to the spoken word.

BBC

website www.bbc.co.uk/arts/books

BBC poetry pages carry a range of online poetry sites, from audio featuring poets past and present to DIY poetry.

BBC Poetry Out Loud

website www.bbc.co.uk/arts/poetry/outload/index.shtml

Well-known poets, such as Sylvia Plath and Benjamin Zephaniah, read their own work.

BBC Radio Berkshire

website www.bbc.co.uk/berkshire/stage/poets/poetprofiles.shtml

Work from 31 Berkshire poets, compiled by Paul Walter. (UK)

The Book of Voices

website http://voices.e-poets.net/

E-poets' new media library of poetry in spoken word, performance, and text. A portal into aural poetry culture gathered from some of the more interesting voices of our day, with readings from the USA, Canada, Australia, and Europe.

Bradford Spoken Word Radio

website www.live365.com/stations/306906?play

The iRadio station for the poets of West Yorkshire.

Conjunctions

website www.conjunctions.com/av.htm

Produced at Bard College, recordings of around 20 poets, from Leslie Scalapino to Antonin Artaud.

The Cortland Review

website www.cortlandreview.com/audio.php

Contains links to Cortland authors and to other audio-poetry sites.

Electronic Poetry Center

website http://wings.buffalo.edu/epc/sound/links.html

A listing of poetry audio links. (USA)

Fooling with Words

website http://www.pbs.org/wnet/foolingwithwords/main_video.html

PBS series with Bill Moyers covering the 1998 Geraldine R Dodge Poetry Festival. Several contemporary poets reading their poems and interview segments in RealAudio and Quicktime.

Granta
website www.granta.com/audio

Interviews, readings, and more audio content. (USA)

Harper Audio
website http://town.hall.org/radio/

Recordings of popular and important 20th-century poets such as Pound and Eliot.

Internet Poetry Archive
website www.ibiblio.org/ipa

Readings by Czeslaw Milosz, Seamus Heaney, Richard Wilbur and others. (USA)

Knopf Poetry Center
website www.randomhouse.com/knopf/poetry/index.pperl

Knopf Publishing Group poets read selections of their poems.

Lannan Audio Archives
website www.lannan.org/lf/audio/lannan-archives

Contains several hundred hours of programs; many are once-in-a-lifetime events featuring a wide-ranging group of writers, poets, social and cultural activists and thinkers.

Laurable
website http://laurable.com

Very useful directory of audio links featuring 475 poets and 2500 poetry links.

Leisure Talk
website www.magespell.com/ltrn

Interviews with writers and poets. (USA)

Library of Congress Webcasts
website www.connectlive.com/events/libraryofcongress

Archive cybercasts including the Favourite Poem project national reading.

Listening Booth
website www.poets.org/page.php/prmID/361

Beginning with John Berryman's historic first reading of *The Dream Songs* on Halloween night, 1963, the Academy of American Poets has presented and recorded over 700 poetry readings, lectures, and symposia, making its Poetry Audio Archive one the world's richest aural records of poetry.

Mehfil-e-Mushaira
website http://mushaira.org/

Audio clips of Urdu poetry in poets' own voices. (India)

PBS Newshour with Jim Lehrer
website www.pbs.org/newshour/topic/entertainment

Pulitzer Prize winners, Poet Laureates, Favourite Poems, timely poems, selected by Robert Pinsky and others.

Penn Sound
website www.writing.upenn.edu/pennsound/x/authors.html

The University of Pennsylvania modern poets sound archive. (USA)

The Poetry Archive
website www.poetryarchive.org

The world's premier and ever-expanding online collection of historic and modern recordings of poets reading their own work. (UK)

Poetry Foundation
website www.poetryfoundation.org/features/audio.html

The audio archive of the Poetry Foundation. (USA)

Poetry Please
website www.bbc.co.uk/radio4/arts/poetryplease.shtml

Britain's longest-running poetry radio programme.

Readings in Contemporary Poetry
website www.diacenter.org/prg/poetry/audio.html

Heaney, Glück, Creeley and many more reading their work.

UBUWEB
website www.ubu.com

Largely experimental poetry including some Beat.

Wired for Books

website wiredforbooks.org/poetry/

Readings and interviews from Ohio University – of such poets as Robert Creeley, Allen Ginsberg and Robert Pinsky.

The Writer's Almanac

website writersalmanac.publicradio.org

A daily programme of poetry and history hosted by Garrison Keillor, that can be heard each day on public radio stations throughout the USA. Each day's programme is about five minutes long. (USA)

Performance poetry: more ear than eye?

Performance poetry venues are springing up the length and breadth of the country, with plenty of opportunities for virgin performers to take advantage of an Open Mic Evening and share their poetry with an unsuspecting world. There is more, however, to performance poetry than just standing in front of an audience and spouting your work. To make performance poetry really work takes technique and considerable restraint, as explained by a master of the art, **Mario Petrucci**.

'Poetry on the page' and 'performance poetry' are kissing cousins rather than differentiable species. A child muttering the line of verse s/he traces with a finger; even poetry metred out in the head while composing – these, too, are 'performative' acts. We're all (to some extent or other) performance poets. And yet, performance poetry – in spite of its remarkable variety – is often instantly recognisable as a genre. What, then, are its hallmarks? Below, I provide a 'pros/cons' paraphrase of some of the more polarised answers to that, selected (and, I admit, somewhat caricaturised) to be provocative. Whether you're gearing up for your first Open Mic slot, launching a book at a poetry festival, or adding a punchy audio clip to your multimedia website, you'll be entering into negotiation with yourself (consciously or otherwise) regarding where you stand among the extremes in this list. I hope you'll contest them vigorously, while allowing yourself to be challenged.

They're so refreshing; not dry or academic.
There's such physical involvement with the words!
An object lesson in vocal range and dynamism.
The rhythmic motifs really sustain it.
Wow! Such stage presence.
It's a natural extension of poetry's long oral tradition.
It's all about grass roots, difference, individuality.
They're essentially subversive, anti-establishment.
It's bang on! The future!
The key is access: anyone can relate to this stuff.

Half of them haven't even heard of modernism.
I wish they'd bloody well stand still.
Why that silly voice?
All rhythm – no content.
Where's the poetry?
Pap for the masses. It won't last.
They all sound much the same.
Failed stand-ups, stage-junkies, wannabe celebs.
It's the end. The whimper.
Not one of them has even heard of modernism.

I'll leave that with you.

Now for some pragmatics and specifics: a few tips and insights regarding poetry performance. The following notes are far from exhaustive, but they're gleaned from performance workshops across a wide range of interests and styles. I'm sure they cover many of the more salient, recurring concerns.

Breath, pace, nerves

You probably won't engage an audience powerfully if you're not prepared, relaxed, breathing. So, develop a simple backstage relaxation ritual. Breathe slowly, right into the pit of your stomach. Sigh. Say a loud doctor's "Ahhh!!" or hum a tune, deeply, changing the notes. Free up the lips, tongue, face. Shake the joints out – especially knees/shoulders/neck/jaw. Wear comfy clothes (shoes in particular). Do some gentle stretches. Hydrate fully. Go onstage beforehand; get a feel for what it's like up there. Most hosts are happy to change something that's genuinely bothering you (being snow-blinded by spotlights is my bugbear).

In the reading itself, speak in a measured way. Slow down till it feels *far* too slow, and it might be about right. Trust those hard-won words – not your stage 'image' or style – to carry you through. Picture words as tiny, unsinkable boats. If you get the shakes, or begin to stall – pause. Are your breaths snatched, shallow? You may be tightening up *because you're forgetting to breathe*. Starving the brain of oxygen deepens anxiety and confusion. Take a solid breath; start again. Become aware of a column of air moving freely through your body. Take good breaths between, as well as during, poems (we often forget). Occupy that wonderful space on stage and hold it. Ask yourself: "Am I enjoying this?" Even if the answer is a resounding *no*, try to find in yourself some shard of a *yes*. Focus on that. It helps you connect with your text, lifting your voice into those subtle variations of pace, tone and emphasis that avoid a flat delivery. As for nerves, they're natural; accept them, then move on. That awful sensation of trembling on the brink is just your body preparing itself for a 'yes' – for flight.

'The position of readiness'

This is a natural, breathing, postural stillness adopted on stage: it keeps the speaking voice central to what's happening, with the body balanced, relaxed and in support. If you're at the mercy of habitual gestures or distorted posture (what I call 'body-noise') then you simply don't have that potent tool of stillness in your performance toolbox. Body-noise can be anything from pacing the stage, audibly playing with the loose change in your pocket, to a slight cocking of the head or constant re-adjusting of specs. By reducing your body-noise, you amplify the effect of any gesture you *do* choose to make. I generally keep such gestures to a minimum because, in the ongoing dialogue between stillness and animation that a poetry performance (and, for that matter, a person) is, I tend to favour the ear over the eye. Ultimately, I suspect that performance poetry tends to work best when the emphasis is on the poetry. Of course, some occasions demand (or tolerate) the opposite, and I'd certainly defend the possibility of a poetry employing the entire body for its delivery; having said that, I rarely gain much from the insistent movements some performers deploy as stock-in-trade. These can descend into predictable mannerism, a kind of running commentary that distracts from the words. If you want to explore this issue further, video yourself performing, or just read to a mirror; but I'd prefer that you address this by collaborating with other writers. If you can, work with people who don't share your propensities or house style. Ask for constructive feedback regarding what you do with voice/body that distracts them from the text. Paradoxically, the detachment achieved in presenting together a *shared* (i.e. co-authored) piece can actually help you towards being more quietly distinctive, more 'yourself', in what you do.

Poems: breath projectiles?

Listen out for it at readings: that faintly precious, slightly mesmerised, dreamy-sweet intonation many poets audibly 'put on' whenever they slip from introduction into poem: like a decaf cappuccino with too much froth. Then there are those performers who go overboard the other way – driving the text too hard in an instinctive attempt to make the poem arrive impressively, moment to moment, as sonic explosions from stage to ear. Alas, too much caffeine! These two extremes invoke that eternal debate between the merits of an 'internalised delivery', which draws the audience into the world of the poem (along Stanislavsky's lines), and an externalised technique or presentation of a 'mask' (as per Brecht, say). Charles Olson offers a third way. In his essay 'Projective Verse', he suggests that poetry proceeds from:

the HEAD, by way of the EAR, to the SYLLABLE
the HEART, by way of the BREATH, to the LINE

Even if you don't agree with that, his idea at least reminds us that words are objects, a series of sonic elements channelled through head and heart, to be sounded in relationship and tension. For Olson, the poet must go "down through the workings of his own throat to that place where breath comes from, where breath has its beginnings, where drama has to come from". You may feel that a stylised delivery (or mask) is a large part of the drama of your performance; but even where a piece is composed entirely for live distribution, Olson's contract between head and heart, between content and delivery, is struck syllable by syllable, line by line. To this, let me add a thought of my own. Whenever we read a poem in a voice that isn't our usual (I hesitate to say 'natural') voice, shouldn't that be done to meet a distinct need in the poem? The greater the departure from your usual voice, the greater and more insistent that need.

The set; the time

The best readings often have a kind of geometry to them. Just as individual poems possess shape and form, so does a reading. Frequently, that shape reveals a variety of pace, tone and content. There are subtle recurrences. There is, in a sense, the larger poem (that 'whole' of the performance set) of which the particular poems are parts. Allowing that larger poem to happen is mostly a case of trusting your instincts, of being alert to the creative possibilities of performance beyond the unit of the single poem. So, choose your poems, and their order, with love and care.

Finally, a word about time. Sorry guys, but 17 poems (plus intros, anecdotes, impromptu observations, dramatic pauses to sip from wineglass) will somewhat exceed the ten minutes you were allotted on stage. And another thing: time running out is not a cue simply to read *faster*. I know we all overrun from time to time. Occasionally, the audience will not mind. Being enthused by your own work, and wanting others to share that enthusiasm, is spot on. But going on for half an hour when you're booked for ten minutes is – bluntly – rude. Invest in a working watch, take a king-sized egg timer on stage, whatever you need. Please, be one of those who face their audience (as I must now) with the thought, if not the words: 'There's so much more I wanted to get across, to share with you. Alas, I'm out of time. Enough said.'

(For more on voice and collaborative performance ('ShadoWork'), see: **http://mario-petrucci.port5.com**.)

Mario Petrucci is an ecologist, physicist, voice trainer, songwriter and poetic innovator. Recent residencies at the Imperial War Museum and BBC Radio 3 have confirmed his reputation as one of the country's leading exponents of public/site-specific poetry. Publications include: *Fearnought: poems for Southwell Workhouse* (National Trust, 2006), a unique meeting of poetry, history and photography; and *Catullus* (Perdika Press, 2006), a ribald, but unusual, take on the famous Roman poet. Four times a winner of the London Writers Competition, Petrucci was awarded the *Daily Telegraph*/Arvon Prize for *Heavy Water: a poem for Chernobyl* (Enitharmon, 2004), now the subject of a remarkable new film by Seventh Art commemorating the 20th anniversary of the disaster (**www.heavy-water.co.uk**).

Poetry venues

Cabarets, spoken-word club nights, music and poetry evenings – there are a wealth of venues where a poet may stand in front of a microphone and perform his or her poetry. It is a fast-moving world, however, and venues move or change all the time. Look out for venues with open-mic opportunities where novices can climb up on stage alongside more experienced performers. It is advisable, of course, to confirm that the event is actually taking place before turning up.

LONDON

African Writers
Poetry Café, 22 Betterton Street,
London WC2H 9BX
tel 020-7420 9888
website www.poetrysociety.org.uk

Bimonthly evening of African writing hosted by Nii Parkes.

Ambit Writers
The Bountiful Cow, 51 Eagle Street,
London WC1R 4AP

Second Tuesday of each month. Featured artists with floor spots available after the interval.

Apples & Snakes
Battersea Arts Centre, Lavender Hill,
London SW11 5TN
tel 020-7924 3410
email apples@snakes.demon.co.uk
website www.applesandsnakes.org

Fortnightly on the second and and last Friday of each month, 9pm. This is the place to check out the up-and-comers and polished performers.

Aromapoetry
Poetry Café, Betterton Street,
London WC2H 9BX
tel 020-7420 9888
website www.x-bout.com/aroma

Every other Sunday hosted by Nii Parkes, from 4.30-6.30pm. Poetry and prose, open mic (6 min each). Very relaxed atmosphere. Always has a fine range of readers. A good place to read for the first time.

Brixtongue
Brixton Art Gallery, 35 Brixton Station Road,
London SW9

tel (07986) 357156
email brixart@brixtonartgallery.co.uk
website www.brixtonartgallery.co.uk

Second Saturday of the month, 8pm. A monthly blend of poetry, music and humour with MC John Rogers and resident Reggae sound system Zinc Fence. Interested acts and for more info, call.

Calder Events
Calder Bookshop, 51 The Cut,
London SE1 8LF
tel 020-7620 2900
email info@calderpublications.com
website www.calderpublications.com

Thursdays, at 6.30 pm, featuring high-calibre readings by the author or by actors with expert lecturers.

CB1 Café
32 Mill Road, Cambridge CB1 2AD

Provides a platform for local poets; also attracts widely known poets. Tuesdays, 8.00-9.45pm.

The Cellar
Poetry Café, 22 Betterton Street,
London WC2H 9BX
tel 020-7420 9888
website www.poetrysociety.org.uk

Saturday evening event celebrating what is currently brilliant about the poetry scene; brings together written and performance poetry and nurtures new talent. Host Niall O'Sullivan.

Coffee-house Poetry at the Troubadour
265 Old Brompton Road, Earls Court, London
tel 020-8354 0660
email CoffPoetry@aol.com
website www.troubadour.co.uk

A year-round programme of poetry readings at the famous café in London.

Dutchpot

Bush Hall, 310 Uxbridge Road, London W12
tel 020-8222 6933
email notes@bushhallmusic.co.uk

Last Friday of the month hosted by Noel
Mckoy, at 8 pm. An acoustic night where
singers, songwriters, musicians, and poets
perform their original material (of all genres)
in a chilled cafe vibe.

Exiled Writers Ink

Poetry Café, 22 Betterton Street, London WC2
tel 020-7420 9888
website www.poetrysociety.org.uk

Usually first Monday of the month, at 7.30pm.
A blend of featured performers and floorspots
of writers exiled from their homelands.

Express Excess

The Enterprise, 2 Haverstock Hill,
London NW3 2BL
tel 020-7485 2659

A mix of comedy, poetry and storytelling every
Wednesday at The Enterprise.

The Foundry

94-96 Great Eastern Road, London EC2A 3JL
email poetry@foundry.tv
website www.foundry.tv

Sundays, 7pm.

FourCast

Poetry Café, 22 Betterton Street,
London WC2H 9BX
tel 020-7420 9888
website www.poetrysociety.org.uk

Monthly readings hosted by Roddy Lumsden,
with 4 guest readers.

Fourth Friday: Poetry & Acoustic Music at the Poetry Cafe

Poetry Café, Betterton Street,
London WC2H 9BX
tel 020-8299 2767
email info@fourthfriday.co.uk
website freespace.virgin.net/mp3.city
Contact Hylda Sims, Liz Simcock

A poetry and music event at the Poetry Café, at
the headquarters of the Poetry Society in
London's Covent Garden. At 8pm on the
fourth Friday of (almost) every month, poets,
singers, songwriters and musicians will be
featured – known and not so known.

Irish Poetry Night

Hammersmith & Fulham Irish Centre,
Blacks Road, Hammersmith, London W6
tel 020-8563 8232
email irish.centre@lbhf.gov.uk
Contact Niall McDevitt

A bimonthly gathering.

The Klinker

107a Culford Road, London N1
email eggpress@eggstore.demon.co.uk
Contact Paul Hill

Thursdays, and the last Friday of the month, at
8.30pm. Poetry performance event.

Piccadilly Poets

tel (01908) 340 379
email piccadillypoets@yahoo.co.uk
website http://dspace.dial.pipex.com/town/
park/yaw74/Piccadilly.htm
Contact Leo Aylen

A whole range of poetry events.

poetry@brick lane

coffee@brick lane, 154 Brick Lane,
London E1 6RU
tel 020-7247 4654

Every 4 weeks on a Thursday; hosted by Ian
Joynson. 7 pm. Free event open to all genres of
poetry, prose and music.

The Poetry Café

22 Betterton Street, London WC2H 9BX
tel 020-7420 9880
email poetrycafe@poetrysociety.org.uk
Contact Jess York

In the afternoon, people sit and write; in the
evening they may stay to listen to poets
perform or read in the basement to a small but
informed audience. Sometimes the café is full
of exiled writers well known in their own
countries but glad of an audience here; at other
times people are crowding out of the door to
get a seat for a famous poet who has been
caught on their way through London. With

each event the café mood changes, while the place itself, the delicious vegetarian food we offer and the classic dishes like marmite toast and Portuguese custard tarts, remain constant. At the moment there is a series of poets resident in the café who put on new and interesting events, as well as offering their services for poetry surgeries to look at anyone's work who cares to approach them. Customers say: "Lovely staff, peaceful, friendly, aesthetically pleasing," and *The Guardian* included the café in its guide this summer to the "most funky, stylish and interesting cafés".

Poetry Society Stanzas

22 Betterton Street, London WC2H 9BX
tel 020-7420 9880
email membership@poetrysociety.org.uk
website www.poetrysociety.org.uk/

Poetry Society Stanzas are an opportunity to meet other Poetry Society members. Any Poetry Society member is welcome to volunteer their contact details in order to form a local Stanza. A section of *Poetry News* is dedicated to publicising all Stanza locations and contact details around the UK.

Poetry@TheRoom

The Room, 33 Holcombe Road, Tottenham, London N17 9AS
tel 020-8808 9318
email info-theroom@fsmail.net
website www.the-room.org.uk

An Arts Council-funded London poetry event that takes place at 7.30pm on the first Wednesday of every month. Presents a diverse selection of talented poets of all different styles, both new and established, in a salon-type atmosphere. £5 and free wine.

Poetry Unplugged

Poetry Café, 22 Betterton Street, London WC2
tel 020-7420 9888
website www.poetrysociety.org.uk

Tuesdays, hosted by Niall O'Sullivan, at 7.30pm. Presents a wide range of material.

The Poet's Letter

Poetry Café, 22 Betterton Street, London WC2H 9BX

tel 020-7420 9888
website www.poetrysociety.org.uk

Monthly readings hosted by Munayem Mayenin, with a distinguished stable of poets. Second Monday of month.

Pure Poetry

The Horseshoe, Clerkenwell Close, London EC1
tel 020-7687 6742

Mondays, 8.30pm.

Shangwe

Poetry Café, 22 Betterton Street, London WC2
tel 020-7420 9888
email nicole@shangwe.com
website www.shangwe.com

Shangwe showcases and promotes fresh emerging artists in a supportive atmosphere. Hosted by Nicole Moore, a published poet and creative writig tutor, each event features three poets, followed by questions from the audience. Open mic performers are welcome and often perform here for the first time. "Shangwe has a great atmosphere which is uplifting and inspiring" (Poetry Cafe regular) Last Thursday of every month.

Shortfuse

Camden Head, Camden Walk, Islington, London N1
tel 020-8536 0652
email shortfuse@morethanwords.co.uk

A mix of performance comedy, stand-up poetry and music. Thursdays, 8.30pm.

The South Bank Centre

The South Bank Centre, Royal Festival Hall, London SE1 8XX
tel 020-7921 0904
email mcolthorpe@rfh.org.uk
website www.rfh.org.uk
Contact Martin Colthorpe

The South Bank Centre has an uninterrupted commitment to presenting poetry. It is home to the Poetry Library; hosts Poetry International, a biennial festival of world poetry; and is constantly looking for opportunities to introduce poetry to new audiences.

Survivors Poetry

Poetry Café, 22 Betterton Street, London WC2
tel 020-7420 9888
website www.poetrysociety.org.uk

Monthly open mic for survivors on the second
Thursday of the month.

Tall Lighthouse

Poetry Café, Betterton Street, London WC2H
tel 020-8299 2767
website http://www.poetrysociety.org.uk/
content/cafe/events/
Contact The Manager

Last Wednesday of the month, with Tall
Lighthouse, featuring the finest contemporary
poetry in the intimate surroundings of the
Poetry Cafe with a unique mix of voices and
regular open mic slots. The event features a
diverse range of poets from outright
performance to poetry normally only seen on
the page with some of the UK's best poets
headlining.

Torriano World Poetry

99 Torriano Avenue, Kentish Town,
London NW5 2RX
tel 020-7281 2867
email philhenrypoole@yahoo.co.uk
Organiser Phil Poole

Meets every Friday.

Vic's Cabaret Corner

The Windmill, Blenheim Gardens,
Brixton Hill, London SW2
email viclambrusco@hotmail.com
website www.urban75.org/brixton/features/
poets.html

Every second Thursday, 9pm.

Voice Box

Level 5, Royal Festival Hall, London SE1 8XX
tel (08703) 804300

A performance space for readings at the South
Bank Centre.

SOUTH EAST ENGLAND

The Marlborough Theatre

Prince's Street, Brighton, East Sussex
tel (01273) 695294

email paul@stopalltheclocks.co.uk
website www.stopalltheclocks.co.uk
Contact Paul Stones

The only venue run by poets in Brighton, the
Marlborough has a regular programme of
spoken-word events and is the centre of the
fringe literature festival. Under the
management of Brighton's foremost
promoters, it has garnered a reputation as the
best and most accesible venue for poetry in the
city.

Sallis Benney Theatre

University of Brighton, 58-64 Grand Parade,
Brighton, East Sussex BN2 2JY
tel (01273) 643010
email c.l.matthews@bton.ac.uk
website www.bton.ac.uk

The University of Brighton theatre; puts on
alternative touring plays, spoken-word and
musical events.

Speakeasy

The Quaker Centre, 1 Oakley Gardens,
Downhead Park, Milton Keynes,
Buckinghamshire MK15 9BH
tel (01908) 663860
email speakeasy@writerbrock.co.uk
website www.mkweb.co.uk/speakeasy
Contact Martin Brocklebank

Provides a meeting place and encouragement
for writers in the Milton Keynes area. Attracts
poets, aspiring and published novelists, and
writers of short stories, articles and comedy.
Regular guest evenings provide an opening for
nationally recognised writers, while its poetry
forum and critique group enable members to
refine and develop their work. The Speakeasy
open poetry competitions are now an
established part of the annual competition
calendar, and attract entries from around the
world.

SOUTH WEST ENGLAND

Buzzwords

The Beehive, Montpellier Villas, Cheltenham
tel (07855) 308122
email cheltpoetry@yahoo.co.uk
website http://www.angelfire.com/poetry/
buzzwords/index.html

Cheltenham's poetry café, running the first Sunday of every month. Each event starts with writing time: exercises, themes and tips to get you going, followed by a guest poet. Starts 7pm if wishing to write, otherwise 8pm. There are also open mic slots available on a first come, first served basis.

Café Frug

Chapel House, Chapel Street, Penzance, Cornwall TR18 4AQ

Every second Thursday, 8pm.

Can Openers

The Poetry Can, Unit 11, Kuumba Project, Hepburn Road, Bristol BS2 8UD
tel (01179) 426976
email info@poetrycan.demon.co.uk
website www.poetrycan.demon.co.uk/canopeners.htm

Events run by the poetry organisation, The Poetry Can, in Bristol and Bath.
   Bristol: Second Thursday of the month. Held at the YHA, Narrow Quay. Starting time 8pm. For more information contact Lucy Hudson on (01179) 245764 or lucy@poetrycan.demon.co.uk.
   Bath: Third Thursday of the month. Held at the Windows Arts Centre, St James Memorial Hall, Lower Borough Walls. Starting time 8pm. For more information contact Richard Carder on (01225) 313531.

The Garden Café

16 Stony Street, Frome, Somerset
tel (01373) 454178
email jazz@nunneyjazzcafe.org

Regular poetry events.

The Language Club

Plymouth Arts Centre, Looe Street, The Barbican, Plymouth
tel (01752) 206114

Final Saturday of each month, except August and December, at 7.30pm.

Perceptive Perspective

Hanger Farm Arts Centre, Aikman Lane, Totton, Southampton SO40 8FT
tel (02380) 667274
email hstanden@totton.ac.uk
website www.hangerfarm.totton.ac.uk
Contact Hannah Standen

An event bringing together local professional poets and London-based performance artists to present poetry to a wide audience of all ages. Also provides a forum for all members of the community to read their poetry, in a professional theatre environment.

Poems, Portcullis and Potation

The Portcullis, Clifton, Sion Hill, Bristol BS8 4LD
tel 0117-973 8955

Second Thursday of the month; 7.30 for 8.00pm.

Salisbury Poetry Café

Salisbury Arts Centre, Bedwin Street, Salisbury Wiltshire SP1 3UT

Last Thursday of every month at 8pm. The programme includes a different guest poet every month, and an open mic.

Scavel An Gow

3 Penlee Villas, Playing Place, Truro, Cornwall TR3 6EY
tel (01872) 865176
email paul@a39LM.freeserve.co.uk
Contact Paul Farmer

A group of leading Cornish writers dedicated to the creation of new work for live performance. The stories range around the world, but are often strongly rooted in the Cornish communities that inspire them. Scavel An Gow shows are unique, weaving words and music together to explore new areas in the field of live performance, in a warm and informal environment. Shows take place in village halls and venues throughout Cornwall and beyond.

Shaftesbury Poetry Group

The Upstairs Parlour, Bell Street Café, Bell Street, Shaftesbury, Dorset
tel (01747) 853703
Contact Krissy Elliot-Foster

First Wednesday of the month, 8-10pm.

Uncut Poets

Black Box, Media Centre, Exeter Phoenix, Gandy Street, Exeter

mobile (07879) 888319
Contact James Bell

Thursdays, 7.30pm. Call to book an open mic slot.

EAST ANGLIA

The Fitzwilliam Museum
Trumpington Street, Cambridge CB2 1RB
tel (01223) 332900
email fitzmuseum-enquiries@lists.cam.ac.uk
website www.fitzmuseum.cam.ac.uk

Holds occasional poetry events.

The Tea House
5 Wright's Court, Elm Hill, Norwich, Norfolk
email Sara@thepoetrycubicle.org.uk
website http://www.thepoetrycubicle.org.uk

Monthly series of live poetry and music events, with Norfolk's most innovative and talented poets and musicians.

Ten Bells
74-78 St Benedicts Street, City Centre, Norwich NR2
tel (01603) 667833

Open mic meets on the last Sunday of the month at the Ten Bells pub in St Benedicts Street, at 8.30pm.

MIDLANDS

Catweazle Club
East Oxford Community Centre,
corner of Cowley Road & Princes' Street,
Oxford
email mother@catweazleclub.org

Oxford's well-established performing arts club. Thursdays, 8pm.

City Voices
City Bar, 2-3 King Street,
Wolverhampton WV1 1ST
tel (01902) 552061

Regular showcase for local writers, poets, comedians, storytellers and musicians.

Hammer and Tongue Poetry Slam
The Zodiac, 190 Cowley Road, Oxford
tel (01865) 200550

email poetry@hammerandtongue.org
website www.hammerandtongue.org
Contact Steve Larkin

Hammer and Tongue is a monthly open poetry slam and showcase that has built up a lively, dynamic performance poetry scene in Oxford. First Tuesday of every month with open poetry slam and some of the best UK and international performers as guest artists.

Liquid Cafe Bar
City Arcade, Coventry,
West Midlands CV1 3HX

A poetry night every third Tuesday.

Mac
Cannon Hill Park, Birmingham,
West Midlands B12 9QH
tel 0121-440 3838
email info@macarts.co.uk
website www.macarts.co.uk

Mac, the most visited arts centre in the Midlands, offers a huge range of literature events for adults and children. From poetry readings, meet-the-author, courses and workshops, music, literature, and theatre with a strong basis in literature – there is something for everybody!

Purple Patch Poetry Evenings
Barlow Theatre, Langley Nr Oldbury,
West Midlands
website www.poetrywednesbury.co.uk

Guest poets, open mic and music.

Research Centre in Modern and Contemporary Poetry
Oxford Brookes University, Oxford OX3 0BP
email rbuxton@brookes.ac.uk
website http://ah.brookes.ac.uk/index.php/
english/poetry
Contact Dr Rachel Buxton

Hosts an annual programme of events whose ambition is to involve academics alongside poets in the discussion of central themes and ideas relating to British, Irish, American and postcolonial poetries in English across the 20th and into the 21st centuries.

Spiel Unlimited
20 Coxwell Street, Cirencester, Glos GL7 2BH
tel (01285) 640470

email spiel@scarum.freeserve.co.uk,
spiel@arbury.freeserve.co.uk

NORTH WEST ENGLAND

Cafe Caprice, Clitheroe
6-8 Moor Lane, Clitheroe, Lancaster BB7 1BE
tel (01200) 422034
email cafecaprice@talk21.com

Poetry readings organised by the Clitheroe
Bookshop.

The Citadel
Waterloo Street, St Helen's WA10 1PX
tel (01744) 735436
website www.citadel.org.uk

A once-a-month event where *you* can perform
your own songs, your own poems, your own
comedy routine.

Clitheroe Books Open Floor Poetry Readings
New Inn, Parson Lane, Clitheroe,
Lancashire BB7 2JN
tel (01200) 444242
email joharbooks@aol.com
website www.roundstonebooks.co.uk
Contact Jo Harding

Hosts open-floor poetry readings at the New
Inn on the last Thursday of each month,
starting at 7.30pm. Admission free.

Come Strut Your Stuff
The Egg Café, Top Floor,
16-18 Newington Buildings, Liverpool L1 3ED
tel 0151-280 5453
email info@comestrutyourstuff.co.uk

Popular, long-running poetry and acoustic
music event that takes place once a month in
the intimate and friendly atmosphere of
Liverpool's Egg Café.

Dead Good Poets Society
Everyman Bistro, Third Room, Hope Street,
Liverpool L1 9BH
tel 0151-708 9545
website www.deadgoodpoetssociety.co.uk/
evening.html

Provides monthly Open Floor events and
monthly Guest Nights. Currently these take
place on the first Wednesday of the month
(Open Floor) and the third Wednesday of the
month (Guest Night).

The Masque
90 Seel Street, Liverpool L1 4BH
tel 0151-708 8708
website www.masquevenue.co.uk

Regular poetry events.

Speakeasy
The Green Room,
54-56 Whitworth Street West,
Manchester M1 5WW
tel 0161-236 1261

Open mic nights with guests.

STAMPS
3 Coronation Road, Crosby, Merseyside
tel 0151-525 0417
email brian@seftonarts.freeserve.co.uk
Contact Brian Wake

This special venue for poetry readings and
music has been active for more than 5 years. It
has welcomed guests such as Adrian Henri,
Henry Graham, Levi Tafari, Pete Morgan, Pete
Finch, Richard Hill, Janine Pinion, and David
Bateman. Its open mic slot has helped to
introduce a whole number of new writers to
local audiences, and is valued by a younger
generation of writers anxious to air their work
in a friendly but competitive atmosphere.

Wirrall Ode Show
Stork Hotel, Price Street, Birkenhead
tel 0151-638 3648
email jasonrichards69@hotmail.com

Third Thursday each month – open floor 8.30-
11pm.

NORTH EAST ENGLAND

Colpitt Poets
website www.colpittspoetry.co.uk

Colpitts Poetry was founded in 1975 by 2 poets
and academic librarians, David Burnett and
Richard Caddel, and a lecturer at Durham
University, Diana Collecott. Since then, it has
mounted more than 360 live readings in

Durham, presenting an enormous range of poets, mainly from the UK but also from the USA, Europe and elsewhere, as well as a number of distinguished prose writers.

Exploding Alphabets

West Walls, Back Stowell Street, Newcastle upon Tyne
email explodingalphabets@hotmail.co.uk

Prefers no old work and delights in an open stage filled with experimental performance. Nights correspond to the number of the month, i.e. 10/10, 11/11, 12/12, etc.

The Hydrogen Jukebox

Darlington Arts Centre, Vane Terrace, Darlington D13 7AX
tel (01325) 486555
email jocolley@ntlworld.com
website www.hjbox.co.uk

Cabaret, poetry and music.

The Morden Tower

West Walls, Back Stowell Street, Newcastle upon Tyne
email conniepickard@btopenworld.com
website www.mordentower.com

One of the oldest poetry venues in England.

Poems at the Albert

40 Leymoor Road, Golcar, Huddersfield, West Yorkshire HD3 4SP
tel (01484) 305179
Contact John Bosley

Second Thursday of each month at 8pm.

The Shed

Brawby, Malton, North Yorkshire YO17 6PY
tel (01653) 668494
website www.theshed.co.uk
Contact Simon Thackray

Music and poetry venue created by Simon Thackray in 1992. The finest modern jazz, blues, folk, country, classical, world and improvised music, comedy, poetry and knitting are all performed in front of an old shed door in one of the smallest venues in the world, with an audience of just over 100 people around candlelit tables.

Spoken Word Antics

The Red Deer, 18 Pitt Street, Sheffield S1 4DD
tel 0114-272 2890

An open mic without the mic, reliant on the warmth of human technology. All forms of spoken word are welcome. Second Tuesday of the month (usually), 8.30pm.

Subtle Flame

Tiger Inn, Lairgate, Beverley, East Yorkshire
tel (01262) 601398
email mloz21@hotmail.com
Contact Sue Lozynskyj

Performers produce a varied and balanced programme of poems, stories and music.

The Writers' Café

Georgian Theatre, Green Dragon Yard, Stockton-on-Tees, Cleveland TS18 1AT
tel (01642) 674115

One of the biggest and best performance nights in the North East. The word is spreading, and the Writers' Café is growing fast along with a network of other great performance venues.

WEST OF SCOTLAND

Brel Bar

Ashton Lane, Glasgow G12 8SG
tel 0141-342 4966

Hosted by Viv Gee and starting at 3.00pm, a great place to hear the latest and best from Glasgow's writers. On the last Sunday of every month.

Reading the Leaves

Tchai Ovna House of Tea, 42 Otago Lane, Glasgow G12 8PB
email readingtheleaves@hotmail.com

Monthly readings on first Friday of every month, 8-10pm. An evening of poetry and creative writing, featuring writers from Glasgow and beyond.

Sammy Dow's

69 Nithsdale Road, Glasgow G41 2AJ
tel 0141-423 0107

On the first Monday of the month, when the South Side Writers' Group hosts its popular Words and Music events. The Mayfest poetry competition for performance poetry is also be held at this venue during May, in addition to the regular monthly event.

The Scotia Bar

112 Stockwell Street, Glasgow G1 4LW
tel 0141-552 8681

The best of Glasgow's poetry, literature and music scene. On the last Tuesday of the month at 8.00pm.

Speakeasy Cafe/Bar

Speakeasy Cafe/Bar, Glasgow Lesbian, Gay, Bisexual & Transpeople Centre,
11 Dixon Street, St Enoch, Glasgow G1 4AL
tel 0141-429 4672
email lgbtart@gglc.org.uk

A celebration of the spoken word and music with poets, writers, comedians, soap-box stars, folk singers, guitarists, opera singers, pop singers, authors, actors, drama queens, cellists. Third Wednesday of the month, from 7.30pm till late.

EAST OF SCOTLAND

Big Word Performance Poetry

The Tron Bar, 9 Hunter Square, Royal Mile, Edinburgh
tel 0131-229 3633
email jemrolls@bigword.fsnet.co.uk

Fortnightly cabaret 9.00-11.00pm.

Foakies

1 Infirmary Street, Edinburgh EH1 1LT
email tomf@miscorp.ed.ac.uk
Contact Tom Fairnie

20-minute spots featuring a singer-songwriter and then a poet, followed by a 40-minute spot featuring the main act, usually a singer-songwriter. First Tuesday of every month.

Shore Poets

The Canons' Gait, 232 Canongate, Edinburgh EH8 8DQ

Readings by mainly Scottish poets on the last Sunday of every month, 7.45pm.

Silencio

The Counting House, West Nicolson Street, Edinburgh EH8 9DD

mobile (07969) 163065
email silenciocabaret@yahoo.co.uk
Contact Jennifer Williams

Glamorous and decadent cabaret featuring poetry, experimental music, theatre, spoken word, visuals, comedy and more, with MC Penny Pornstar and DJ Daniel.

NORTH OF SCOTLAND

The Dead Good Poets, Aberdeen

22 Belmont Street, Aberdeen AB10 1JH
email koopoetry@btinternet.com

A reading-for-charity poetry group, which holds meetings on the last Thursday of every month at Books and Beans, 22 Belmont Street, Aberdeen. The meetings are informal, incorporating a guest reader and open mic. Experienced poets and beginners welcome. 6.30-8.30pm.

WALES

Last Thursday at the Dylan Thomas Centre

Somerset Place, Maritime Quarter, Swansea SA1 1RR
tel (01792) 463980
email dylanthomas.lit@swansea.gov.uk
website www.dylanthomas.org

Popular monthly live music and poetry night. Last Thursday of the month, 8pm.

IRELAND

Poets Anonymous

Harry's Bar, Nassau Street, Dublin 2
email nedluddtc@yahoo.com

A weekly poetry event which aims to provide a platform for up-and-coming poets to perform their work, to gain insight into the work of 1 featured poet each week, and to bring poetry to a wider audience. Wednesday evenings 7-30-9.30pm.

The poetry slam

Poetry slams are becoming an increasingly popular, if controversial, way for poets to expose their work to an audience. Who better than poetry-slam pioneer, **John Paul O'Neill**, to explain what a poetry slam is.

Love them or loathe them, poetry slams have become a major part of Britain's performance poetry scene over the last few years, attracting large audiences in every major city, much media attention and even a BBC Radio 4 national competition. In this article I am going to describe what a poetry slam is and give you a bit of UK slam background and history.

For the completely uninitiated, or the not entirely sure, the poetry slam is an open mic format originally invented in late 1980s Chicago by Marc Smith, as an egalitarian strike against the stuffy academic poetry scene of that city at the time. Olympic-style score-cards and judges not only caused the intended outrage, but also attracted large new audiences for poetry. The format became a huge success and was admired, shared and adapted by poets from all over America and the rest of the world who had visited the Chicago slam and the numerous slams that were subsequently set up. This led eventually to the formation of the US National Slam, the largest English spoken-word event in the world – and ultimately, to the poetry slam going global.

Back in 1993 an Australian troubadour and co-founder of the Austin International Poetry Festival, by the name of 'Thom the World Poet', performed at the Farrago poetry club I was running at Chats Palace Arts Centre in Hackney. He came with outlandish tales of these incredible events called poetry slams in America, where he was living, and claimed that they attracted audiences of over 300 people and massive media attention.

Piecing together what information I could about what constituted a slam, I organised and ran the UK's first poetry slam in February 1994, inviting every London-based poetry group, club and organisation I could to the first Farrago London Slam! Championships. We got a capacity audience in the Chats Palace Theatre, and a brilliant poetry event.

Following on from this success I set up the country's first regular slam club and later, in 1994, the UK Slam! Championships, which have been run by Farrago Poetry ever since. Other slams followed nationwide; Glen Carmichael went back to Bristol and set up the slam there after attending a Farrago show at the ICA. Thom then persuaded Marcus Moore to start a slam at the Glastonbury Festival and eventually set up the Cheltenham UK All Comers Slam. Many others were inspired to organise slams following UK tours by the Nuyorican Poets, from New York. There have been active slams all over Britain for well over a decade now.

For those of you wondering, slam is not a particular kind of poetry or a feat of daredevil improvisation on the spot; nor is it a form of rap (music), though hip hop poetry is welcome. Winners of Farrago slams have read and performed every kind of poetry. The dynamism and energy that characterise slams are not the preserve of the young poets who tend to make up the majority of the participants; slams have been won by septuagenarians and teenagers.

The key difference between a poetry slam and a standard open mic is that a slam is run mainly for the benefit of the audience, to grab their attention and get them listening to poetry. That is not to say that slams don't benefit the poet beyond giving an audience; it's just that mumbling indulgently for longer than is decent is not allowed in a slam – most have three-minute-per-poet time limits.

That three minutes can be a terrifyingly long time for the first-time or 'virgin' slammer, but can be over far too quickly for the more experienced open mic poet. The advantage is that most poets, even newcomers, can come up with a decent three-minute slot. If you are in the audience, watching and not enjoying or understanding a particular poet's work, another poet is coming along shortly and over the course of the night there are going to be a lot of good poets and many different kinds of poetry.

The toughest thing for anyone taking part is the judging and scoring that comes at the end of the three minutes! However, the people who go to slams do appreciate how hard it is, particularly for new and less experienced poets, to get up on stage and share often heartfelt poetry, and are very supportive! Former Nuyorican host and slam pioneer Bob Holman used to start his slams by demanding that the poets "check their egos in at the door". This might be easier said than done, but the prospect of instant feedback is at least encouraging poets to do their best work, something that definitely doesn't happen at the traditional open mic session.

Ultimately, of course, a poetry slam is a competition; the highest scoring poet is the winner at the end of the night. But at all decent poetry slams, the emphasis is on celebrating the poetry and the participation of all the poets. The judging should be part of the theatre of the event, with the audience on the side of the poets and the judges the villains when not scoring highly enough. Bob Holman's other famous pronouncement that "the best poet always loses" is really important: the judges at slams are most of the time chosen at random, and the scores they give subjective; they are not a definitive pronouncement on a poet's or a poem's worth.

Finally, the poets who complain that there is no place for judging or competition in poetry have obviously never received a rejection slip. Although the slam poetry form used by all UK events may be an interpretation of the US original, such poets know nothing of the tradition of bardic competition that has existed in these islands since long before the word even got written down! Slams are wonderful open forums for poetic expression, so please attend your local one – or better still, take along your poetry and take part!

John Paul O'Neill is one of Britain's leading new poetry performers and MCs, co-founder and coordinator of Farrago Poetry, one of London's foremost independent poetry organisations, and European slam poetry pioneer.

A poet's life

John Burnside

When I started writing poetry, I had no idea what I was doing. I was working in the computer industry, and poetry began for me out of a personal need, something I did to balance out my life – numbers and logic by day, words and the imagination by night (either by temperament, or because of time constraints, I usually found myself writing in the small hours). To begin with, I had no intention of publishing my efforts, I just wanted to see if I could write a poem that would satisfy me on my own rather generous terms. Later, though, as I got going, I started sending work out – and that was when the other questions, questions I had not anticipated, came to the fore.

At that point, the poetry I wrote, like the poetry I most admired, was rather unfashionable. I wrote about the world I saw around me and, since I lived at the edge of the suburbs, in a thin headland between town and woods (with the occasional sojourn in Gloucestershire farming country), I wrote a good deal about the sky, the weather, the land, trees, flora and fauna. It's definitely not a term I would use, but other people considered this 'nature poetry' and everybody knew, at the time, that nature poetry wasn't a serious pursuit. It's interesting to think how recently this view was held by intelligent people – and alarming to note that there are still those who think that if a bird flaps through a piece of verse, it's a piece of self-indulgent neo-romanticism, to be condemned as unworthy of enlightened critical attention.

Of course, the deeply unfashionable part is easy to admit: there is even cachet to be gained from being 'misunderstood'. The harder thing to admit is that my first efforts were nowhere near as good as they ought to have been. Sometimes, talking to younger poets, I recollect how many of my early poems I destroyed, more in sorrow than in anger or frustration, but there were many more that should have been cast into the fire. One tendency we have, starting out, is to read the current magazines, and the prize-winning poems, and all the rest, with the growing conviction that we could do better. Couple that with the aforementioned glow of being deeply unfashionable (and with the idea that everything that goes around comes around), and it is easy to settle into a groove of writing brilliant misunderstood poems that will, one day, find the audience they deserve (possibly in the unreal afterlife of posterity). I was working in isolation; I knew no other poets, or even poetry readers, and never went to a workshop, which meant that it was easy to sustain these romantic illusions for some time – until, that is, a (possibly inebriated) editor took some of my poems and I got to see them in print. That was when the romantic bubble burst, and I saw that I had been deceiving myself. I wasn't misunderstood, I was just incompetent.

Or perhaps just lazy. I hadn't taken my vocation seriously enough. In fact, I hadn't taken it seriously at all. All the time I had felt a misunderstood legend in my own living room, I had really just been a dilettante who didn't bother to do the work that any vocation – from poetry to mathematics to gardening – demands. I did not know my craft. I had a poor understanding of poetic traditions and, most important of all, I had no idea what it meant to make poetry. After that first set of publications, I stopped and examined what I was doing: how I made a poem, where and when I made it, and what I did to convince myself that it was finished. At the time, I wrote poetry after some vague model I had in my head from a desultory education in literature; I sat down with a sheet of paper, worked at it, revised, deliberated, stared out of the window. (I did a good deal of staring out of windows, in fact.) Yet this process was entirely unlike my self, unlike the way I operated in any other field. Outside (and sometimes inside) my workaday box, I was – and still am – an intuitive, spontaneous, wu-wei type. (Wu-wei is probably my one guiding principle: a principle that has been called "doing by not doing", though I would describe it as an unceasing vigilance aimed at allowing one's true nature to come forth, spontaneously [yes: it's a paradox].) Another angle on this might be to remember Robert Frost's view that the work of the poet is to avoid getting in the way of the poem.)

Now, over a period of weeks, I changed my working method. I began by destroying everything I wrote, no matter what I thought of it. I never sat down at a desk to write, and I stopped carrying my little notebook around or jotting down striking images that came to me as I went about my business. Whatever was not memorable enough to stay in my head was left by the wayside. I had read about a process that Osip Mandelstam called "writing on the lips"; a process that he had adopted; one that had served Dante, and many others; a process that keeps the poet in touch, both with the oral tradition from which s/he springs and with the song of the earth itself (the rhythm, one might say, of all that surrounds us: earth and sea and sky and living things). I adopted this same process ... and the results surprised me. I found myself writing poems I liked, I went outside my own expectations of poetry (for example, I began to write prose poems, and I didn't consider 'form' until it began to emerge in the poem itself). From that point onwards, I was on what I thought of as an unending journey, a lifelong discipline in making poems according to their own nature, without interference from 'me' (I say 'me', because by this I mean ego, the social self, the educated, deliberating, controlling person).

I hope it is obvious, however, that I am not advocating a freefall into self-expression here. Poetry is work – but it is work in the way that making a garden or being a parent is work: it is, in other words, work, not effort, the work of setting aside the preordained, the resigned, the easy, the conditioned, and allowing the real to emerge and live. The real, not the conditioned, response. A surrender, not a submission. The graceful, as opposed to the merely easy. This probably sounds mystical and, in some ways, it is, but the only advice I have for anybody starting out in this privileged discipline is that success is determined – not by the world, and not by one's own feeling of having expressed something, but by the poem itself. I would never advocate the garrety existence of the deeply misunderstood, unfashionable poet, but I would also say that nothing the world gives us – the published book, the award, the good review – is anything like the blessing of the poem itself, still warm and alive in the little grey cells and ready to be copied down on to the cool, white page. Marianne Moore, paraphrasing *The Baghavad Gita*, said: "If I do well I am blessed, whether anyone bless me or not." This is the true guide to success in poetry: the gut-feel, the intimation, the pure (and fleeting) blessing of the poem itself.

John Burnside has had a number of collections published, including the recent *Selected Poems* (Jonathan Cape). His memoir, *A Lie About My Father*, was published in 2006.

Getting seen
Poetry agents

Congratulations! If you are perusing this page you are, indeed, a rare bird – a poet in need of an agent! Most agents actively discourage submissions from poets: "No poetry" is written in bold capitals in many entries in *Writers' & Artists' Yearbook*. The list below includes a couple who would welcome submissions from poets, but mostly you are going to have to be very persuasive (or enjoy the surname Heaney) to be taken on by a mainstream literary agent. It is, of course, worth considering whether you do in fact require the services of an agent. Most poets do not.

A & B Personal Management Ltd
Suite 330, Linen Hall, 162-168 Regent Street, London W1B 5TD
tel 020-7434 4262 *fax* 020-7038 3699
email billellis@aandb.co.uk

Aitken Alexander Associates Ltd*
18–21 Cavaye Place, London SW10 9PT
tel 020-7373 8672 *fax* 020-7373 6002
email reception@aitkenalexander.co.uk
website www.aitkenalexander.co.uk

Caroline Davidson Literary Agency
5 Queen Anne's Gardens, London W4 1TU
tel 020-8995 5768 *fax* 020-8994 2770
email cdla@ukgateway.net
website www.cdla.co.uk

Handles novels and non-fiction of high quality, including reference works (12.5%). Send preliminary letter with CV and detailed, well thought-out book proposal/synopsis and/or first 50pp of novel. No email submissions. Large sae with return postage essential. No reading fee. Quick response.

Authors include Peter Barham, Nigel Barlow, Andrew Beatty, Andrew Dalby, Emma Donoghue, Chris Greenhalgh, Ed Husain, Tom Jaine, Huon Mallalieu, Simon Unwin, Caroline Williams. Founded 1988.

DGA Ltd
55 Monmouth Street, London WC2H 9DG
tel 020-7240 9992 *fax* 020-7395 6110
email assistant@davidgodwinassociates.co.uk
website www.davidgodwinassociates.co.uk
Directors David Godwin, Heather Godwin

Literary fiction and general non-fiction (home 15%, overseas 20%, film 15%). No reading fee; send sae for return of MSS. Founded 1995.

Robert Dudley Agency
8 Abbotstone Road, London SW15 1QR
tel 020-8788 0938 *mobile* (07879) 426574
fax 020-8780 3586
email rdudley@btinternet.com
Proprietor Robert Dudley

Fiction and non-fiction. Specialises in history, biography, sport, management, politics, militaria, current affairs (home 15%, overseas 20%; film/TV/radio 15–20%). No reading fee. Will suggest revision. All material sent at owner's risk. No MSS returned without sae.

Authors include Steve Biko, Simon Caulkin, Peter Collins, Ali Dizaei, Jim Drury, Paul Gannon, Chris Green, Tim Guest, Mungo Melvin, Brian Holden Reid, Tim Phillips, Heather Reynolds, Michael Scott, Rosy Thornton, Dan Wilson. Founded 2000.

Eddison Pearson Ltd
West Hill House, 6 Swains Lane,
London N6 6QS
tel 020-7700 7763 *fax* 020-7700 7866
email info@eddisonpearson.com
Contact Clare Pearson
Authors include Valerie Bloom, Sue Heap, Robert Muchamore, Ruth Symes.

Fox & Howard Literary Agency*
4 Bramerton Street, London SW3 5JX
tel 020-7352 8691 *fax* 020-7352 8691
Partners Chelsey Fox, Charlotte Howard

General non-fiction: biography, history and popular culture, reference, business, mind, body & spirit, health and fitness (home 15%, overseas 20%). No reading fee, but preliminary letter and synopsis with sae essential for response. Founded 1992.

Barrie James Literary Agency
(including New Authors Showcase)
Rivendell, Kingsgate Close, Torquay,
Devon TQ2 8QA
tel (01803) 326617
email mail@newauthors.org.uk
website www.newauthors.org.uk
Contact Barrie James

Internet site for new writers and poets to
display their work to publishers. No unsolicited
MSS. First contact: send sae or email. Founded
1997.

Lutyens & Rubinstein*
231 Westbourne Park Road, London W11 1EB
tel 020-7792 4855 *fax* 020-7792 4833
email susannah@lutyensrubinstein.co.uk
Directors Sarah Lutyens, Felicity Rubinstein
Submissions Susannah Godman

Fiction and non-fiction, commercial and
literary (home 15%, overseas 20%). Send
outline/2 sample chapters and sae. No reading
fee. Founded 1993.

Laura Morris Literary Agency
21 Highshore Road, London SE15 5AA
tel 020-7732 0153 *fax* 020-7732 9022
email laura.morris@btconnect.com
Director Laura Morris

Literary fiction, film studies, biography, media,
cookery, culture/art, humour (home 10%,
overseas 20%). No unsolicited MSS, no
children's books.

Authors include Peter Cowie, Christobel
Kent, Laurence Marks and Maurice Gran, the
Barbara Pym Estate, David Thomson, John
Travolta, Brian Turner, Janni Visman.
Founded 1998.

David O'Leary Literary Agency
10 Lansdowne Court, Lansdowne Rise,
London W11 2NR
tel/fax 020-7229 1623
email d.oleary@dsl.pipex.com

Popular and literary fiction and non-fiction.
Special interests: Ireland, history, popular
science (Fees: home 10%, overseas 20%,
performance rights 15%). No reading fee.
Write with sae, call or email before submitting
MSS.

Authors include Alexander Cordell, Donald
James, Nick Kochan, Jim Lusby, Derek
Malcolm, Daniel O'Brien, Ken Russell.
Founded 1988.

PFD (The Peters Fraser & Dunlop Group Ltd)*
Drury House, 34–43 Russell Street,
London WC2B 5HA
tel 020-7344 1000 *fax* 020-7836 9539
website www.pfd.co.uk
Joint Chairmen Maureen Vincent and St John
Donald, *Books* Caroline Dawnay, Simon
Trewin, Michael Sissons, Pat Kavanagh, Charles
Walker, Rosemary Scoular, Robert Kirby,
James Gill, Carol Macarthur, Anna Webber,
Children's books Rosemary Canter *Translation
rights* Jessica Craig, Jane Willis, *PFD New York*
Zoë Pagnamenta, Mark Reiter, Erin Edmison,
Film/TV/theatre agents Natasha Galloway,
Anthony Jones, Tim Corrie, Charles Walker, St
John Donald, Rose Cobbe, Jago Irwin, Hannah
Begbie, Lynda Mamy, Andrew Naylor, Alice
Dunne

Represents authors of fiction and non-fiction
(home 15%; USA/translation 20%), children's
writers, screenwriters, playwrights, directors,
documentary makers, technicians, presenters
and actors throughout the world. Has 85 years
of international experience in all media,
particularly film and TV. Outlines, sample
chapters and author biographies should be
addressed to the Books Dept. Material should
be submitted on an exclusive basis; or in any
event disclose if material is being submitted to
other agencies or publishers. Return postage
essential. No reading fee. Response to email
submissions cannot be guaranteed. See website
for submission guidelines. The film and script
department does not accept unsolicited
material.

PVA Management Ltd
Hallow Park, Worcester WR2 6PG
tel (01905) 640663 *fax* (01905) 641842
email md@pva.co.uk
website www.pva.co.uk
Managing Director Paul Vaughan

Full-length MSS. Non-fiction only (home 15%,
overseas 20%, performance rights 15%). Send

synopsis and sample chapters together with return postage.

Raft
9-10 Jew Street, Brighton BN1 1UT
tel (01273) 730070
email info@raftpr.com
website www.raftpr.com

Currently looking for authors of narrative non-fiction, history, politics, current affairs, music, self-help, poetry and business projects. Raft also has a significant track record in event management and tour booking which enables it to work creatively with talent from booking individual performances, and seasons through to whole tours whether spoken word, live music or drama.

Rogers, Coleridge & White Ltd*
20 Powis Mews, London W11 1JN
tel 020-7221 3717 *fax* 020-7229 9084
website www.rcwlitagency.com

Sheil Land Associates Ltd*
(incorporating Richard Scott Simon Ltd 1971 and Christy & Moore Ltd 1912)
52 Doughty Street, London WC1N 2LS
tel 020-7405 9351 *fax* 020-7831 2127
email info@sheilland.co.uk
Agents UK & US Sonia Land, Vivien Green, Ben Mason, *Film/theatre/TV* Sophie Janson, Emily Hayward, *Foreign* Gaia Banks

Quality literary and commercial fiction and non-fiction, including: politics, history, military history, gardening, thrillers, crime, romance, drama, biography, travel, cookery, humour, UK and foreign estates (home 15%, USA/translation 20%). Also theatre, film, radio and TV scripts. Welcomes approaches from new clients either to start or to develop their careers. Preliminary letter with sae essential. No reading fee. *Overseas associates* Georges Borchardt, Inc. (Richard Scott Simon). *US film and TV representation* CAA, APA and others.

Clients include Peter Ackroyd, Pam Ayres, Hugh Bicheno, Melvyn Bragg, Steven Carroll, David Cohen, Anna del Conte, Elizabeth

Corley, Seamus Deane, Robert Green, Bonnie Greer, Susan Hill, Richard Holmes, HRH The Prince of Wales, Mark Irving, Ian Johnstone, Simon Kernick, Richard Mabey, Michael Moorcock, Graham Rice, Steve Rider, Martin Riley, Diane Setterfield, Tom Sharpe, Martin Stephen, Jeffrey Tayler, Andrew Taylor, Rose Tremain, Barry Unsworth, Kevin Wells, Prof. Stanley Wells, John Wilsher, Paul Wilson, Chris Woodhead and the Estates of Catherine Cookson, Patrick O'Brian and Jean Rhys. Founded 1962.

The Susijn Agency Ltd
3rd Floor, 64 Great Titchfield Street, London W1W 7QH
tel 020-7580 6341 *fax* 020-7580 8626
email info@thesusijnagency.com
website www.thesusijnagency.com
Agents Laura Susijn, Nicola Barr

Specialises in world rights in English- and non-English-language literature: literary fiction and general non-fiction (home 15%, overseas 20%, theatre/film/TV/ radio 15%). Send synopsis and 2 sample chapters. No reading fee.

Authors include Peter Ackroyd, Bidisha, Uzma Aslam Khan, Robin Baker, Abdelkader Benali, Robert Craig, Tessa De Loo, Travis Elborough, Radhika Jha, Karen Mcleod, Jeffrey Moore, Karl Shaw, Paul Sussman, Dubravka Ugrešić, Alex Wheatle, Adam Zameenzad. Founded 1998.

Jonathan Williams Literary Agency
Rosney Mews, Upper Glenageary Road, Glenageary, Co. Dublin, Republic of Ireland
tel (01) 2803482 *fax* (01) 2803482
Director Jonathan Williams

General fiction and non-fiction, preferably by Irish authors (home 10%). Will suggest revision; no reading fee unless a very fast decision is required. Return postage appreciated (no British stamps – use IRCs). Sub-agents in Holland, Italy, France, Spain, Japan. Founded 1981.

Parapoetry

While you are waiting for that first slim volume to be published, how do you get close to the poetry world? **Julia Bird** calls herself a 'parapoet', working in many areas of poetry.

Sometimes, when I describe my job to people, I call myself a 'parapoet'. Before they get carried away with the idea of someone covered in camouflage paint delivering yomping quatrains about the glories of war, I explain that it's akin to 'paramedic', or 'paralegal'. While I do write myself, the living I make from poetry is not as a writer. As an administrator, I work alongside poets and support their writing and performance.

That first slim volume of our own: an untoppable writerly thrill. But while we're all waiting for that to happen, this parapoetry can strengthen our involvement with the art, while keeping us from bug-eyed obsession about publication prospects. Full-time career or weekend passion? It can be both.

So, where to start? Submitting your own work to poetry magazines is a recognised first step towards formal publication. But setting up your *own* magazine gives you additional poetry-related editorial, design, typesetting, sales and distribution experience. Poetry mags flutter in and out of existence all the time: visit **www.poetrylibrary.org.uk/magazines** or **www.poetrymagazines.org.uk** to find and plug the current gap in the market with your own tone, style and content. If the Photoshop & Quark / Letraset & Tippex approaches don't appeal, try a web or e-zine. Actual or virtual, launch each issue with a reading of featured poets and a knees-up for your existing and potential subscribers. While vanity publishing probably won't do much for either your poetic career or your mortal soul, self-publishing is a very different enterprise. Avoiding the photocopier and the clip-art, it doesn't cost that much to edit, set and print a decent-looking short-run poetry pamphlet. Sell it at readings; distribute it generously to other publishers and poetry advocates to promote yourself as a writer. Self-published pamphlets are currently also eligible for the Poetry Book Society's quarterly Pamphlet Choice scheme – see **www.poetrybooks.co.uk** for details.

If publishing your own work gives you a taste for the world of font, stock and end-papers, consider establishing your own small press, where you'll enjoy creative freedom over every aspect of book production and marketing. Publishing needn't involve whole books or pamphlets – for example, the Poetry Cubicle offers a platform for writers in Norwich by publishing one poem at a time (**www.thepoetrycubicle.org.uk**). Look at Lollipop (List of Little Press Publications – **www.indigogroup.co.uk/llpp/**) for more small-press inspiration.

Develop your own poetry performance skills. You don't have to be an actor or a stand-up comedian to hold a crowd, but audiences expect more than an unprepared set from a mumbler with a mic. Pick up hints from poets whose readings you rate (or don't!). Try out a couple of poems at open mic slots; get to know the event promoters and introduce them to your written and spoken work; and build up to performances where your name is on the bill. *Poetry London* and *Mslexia* magazines both have excellent (national) listings pages with ideas of where you might read.

Setting up your own events or series of readings calls for production and promotion skills – and a certain ringmasterly panache if you want to compere the events yourself. If you live in a place where there is lots of competition from existing poetry events, invent a way of presenting writers and readers that stands out in the listings pages. I've heard of poetry pub quizzes, poetry curry banquets, poetry cabarets – even speed-poetry, a literary equivalent of speed-dating (**www.20six.co.uk/shortfuse**). A few years ago, the Poetry Society commissioned a promoters' tool kit – there are still some good tips here: **www.newaudiences2.org.uk/downloads/poetrytoolkit.pdf**. But if there is one golden guarantee of a successful night, it's keeping it short. Attending to poetry demands an intense attention – and more than an hour and a half of it (including the interval) is exhausting. I have worked in poetry and literature development for the last ten years, involved with author tours, writers' residencies, literature festivals, poets' commissions and general organisational support. This last decade has seen a real clarification in the purpose of the individuals and organisations who work in the profession, so if your creative interest in poetry and literature is complemented by promotional, administrative and management skills, there is an increasing range of jobs open to you. Your first stop for advice, contacts, case studies, skill sharing and job adverts should be NALD – the National Association for Literature Development (**www.nald.org.uk**). A support and advocacy organisation, NALD is the professional body for all involved in developing writers, readers and literature audiences. The National Association of Writers in Education (**www.nawe.co.uk**) features the Literature Training Bulletin on its website, another excellent source of information about jobs, courses, training and conferences. Subscribe to the Arts Council's ArtsJobs e-mailing list (via **www.artscouncil.org.uk**) for a wealth of opportunities, especially part-time and short contract work.

You may have heard the grumble that the poetry world is impenetrable, too tightly controlled – some would say policed – and that the circles of publishing, reviewing, mentoring and prize-giving overlap way too closely. Perhaps that's a valid complaint – but in the last ten years I have seen small presses, magazines, new promoters and performers spring from nowhere to prominent positions in that world. You may want to be part of this establishment or you may want to knock the helmets off the poetry police, but enthused, imaginative people and groups of like-minded individuals can find a public platform for their ideas.

Life as a parapoet lets you experience ideas and writing you might not otherwise have encountered. If, after publishing your own magazine, setting up your own small press and running your own month-long haiku festival, you still yearn to see your own name in print, exposure to these good, bad and frankly bananas ideas will only have had a positive effect on your own writing and its promotion.

Julia Bird worked for the Poetry Book Society for eight years. She now works for the Poetry School and as a freelance live literature producer and promoter.

Win some, lose some ...

Gordon Kerr has just had his first experience of judging a poetry competition and passes on some tips to prospective poetry competition entrants.

Having just completed the judging of the first A&C Black *Poetry Writers' Yearbook* Poetry Competition, I feel eminently qualified to dispense advice to poetry competition entrants. But that's the only competition you've ever judged, I hear you say! And, of course, you are absolutely right. I was a poetry competition virgin until a thick brick (more of a breeze block, actually) of a parcel containing hundreds of entries to our competition was delivered by a grudging and slightly breathless postman a few weeks ago. "There's quite a lot," I had been told. I had, of course, failed to spot the relief in the voice at the other end of the line when I agreed to judge the competition.

Seriously, however, it was a fascinating exercise and I do not make light of people's enthusiasm – firstly for the writing of poetry in the face of the impossibility of ever getting published, and secondly, of course, for entering the competition set up by the publisher of this book. The quality was, on the whole, far better than I had expected and there were about a dozen top-notch poems that could grace any anthology or magazine.

However, it would be remiss of me not to take this opportunity to make a few practical points about the business of submitting poetry for competitions.

• Read the rules. Or, rather, read the rules *and* ahere to them. Most competitions will stipulate a line length and/or a style. No point entering your 3000-line epic about herring fishing off the Faroe Islands for a competition restricted to 30-line poems about Siamese cats (note to competition organisers – *never* set anything to do with cats; your postman will take a contract out on you!).

• Stick to the subject. Don't just find a poem of yours that you rather like and amend it to deal with the subject – that will rarely work. Think carefully about the subject and bring your own thoughts, images and language to it. The poem will be a much better piece of work and you will stand a better chance of doing well in the competition. If a subject is not something that gets your creative juices flowing, forget it and move on to another. There are plenty out there.

• Read previous winners' work (if available). There is no point entering a competition if you are not aware of the calibre of work that is being sought and which does well. Repeatedly in this book, writers exhort poets to read the work of other poets, to understand the world into which you are trying to place your work. And too many of us are not reading poetry being published in books, in magazines and on the Internet. This was very evident from many of the poems entered for our competition. A number of entrants had obviously not read any poetry since their schooldays, if then.

• Submit according to the rules. Faced with a pile of 500 poems to be judged before breakfast, a poetry judge is likely to be happy to consign any that breach the rules to the wastepaper basket. This is especially true where the rules stipulate that your work is presented in such a way that the judge can judge the poem anonymously.

• Beware of scams. There are unscrupulous people out there who are in it for the money – and there is quite a bit of money to be made from gullible poets desperate to see their work in print (see Johnathon Clifford on *Anthologisers* on page 126). There is nothing wrong with people charging for entry to competitions – it is necessary to cover administration and prizes and so on – but I would recommend that you check the quality of the work in previous competitions and make sure that firstly, you are not being ripped off and secondly, that you are happy for your work to be seen in that context. However, there are certainly enough good, honest poetry competitions for you to submit in the knowledge that it is all above board.

Some people suggest that poetry competitions are anathema to the poetry world, and that, somehow, poetry is above that kind of thing. However, poetry has through the ages been the subject of competitions. What is the Eisteddfod, after all, but a massive, ancient poetry slam? After all, in a world where poets are not exactly showered with riches, the major awards provide a valuable source of income with prizes that go into the thousands of pounds. Of course, these are, on the whole, shared amongst a small group of well-known, established and published poets. However, there are numerous prizes of several hundred pounds that are also available and are more often than not won by unpublished and often unsung poets. Have a go and you never know. As they used to say about the National Lottery – you've got to be in it to win it!

Gordon Kerr is a freelance writer, editor and poet.

Anthologisers

Johnathon Clifford coined the phrase 'vanity publishing' and since 1991 has campaigned unceasingly for truth and honesty in the vanity publishing world, becoming recognised as the leading authority on the subject. He tells us to beware of the anthologiser.

For many years there had been a gathering weight of complaint against various anthologisers, culminating in my exposé of *The International Library of Poetry* both in *The Observer* and *Sunday Telegraph*, and on BBC1's *Bookworm* on 3rd November 1996.

You should bear in mind that:

• If your work is accepted for inclusion in an anthology by one of the major publishers, you will usually receive a payment and a free copy of that anthology.

• If you are accepted by one of the Small Presses (who cannot afford a payment), you will still usually receive a free copy of the anthology.

There is nothing wrong with selling anthologies as long as those who are in that business do not try to give the impression that they accept work 'on merit'. Or that it is anything more than vanity publishing (the writer is, after all, paying the price of the anthology to see his or her work in print). Or that their anthologies are read by any other than the smallest of readerships.

Too often, claims made by some businesses in an attempt to persuade clients into buying copies of anthologies are not genuine. In those cases it simply becomes a dishonest attempt to hoodwink gullible members of the public.

Many companies who make a business of selling anthologies will tell you – or at least give you the impression – that your work has been accepted 'on merit' (whatever its poetic quality) and, more misleadingly, that it was chosen 'in competition with other entries'. Many will go to great lengths to tell you how fine the anthology is in which your poem is to appear and how widely it will be distributed, while impressing upon you that you can buy it at the stated price only as a pre-publication offer.

You must remember that the majority of these anthologies are read by very few people other than those who appear in them and their families, and are seldom stocked by book shops or libraries.

I have also received complaints from both parents and teachers that some of the anthologisers have been 'targeting school children'. The best example is a school in Nottinghamshire, where over 50 children submitted poems and *every one* had a poem accepted. Obviously once a child has had a poem accepted for inclusion in an anthology it is very hard for a parent to refuse to buy a copy – a very lucrative business indeed!

The internationally accepted definition of vanity publisher, which I wrote for the Committee of Advertising Practice at the Advertising Standards Authority in 1997 for their *Advice Note, Vanity Publishers,* is: "any company which charges a client to publish a book or offers to include short stories, poems or other literary or artistic material in an anthology and then invites those included in it to buy a copy of that anthology".

So how does it work?

(Extract from *Vanity Press & The Proper Poetry Publishers* by Johnathon Clifford)

"… I invite you (and every other poet I can contact) to submit poems for an anthology. I set the rules to state 'only 2 poems per person' and 'no longer than 30 lines'. I then accept one poem from every entrant, advising the poet in each instance that the poem is to appear in the anthology which may be purchased for (for argument's sake) £9.50. Effectively this means that each poet (if buying a copy of the anthology when invited to do so) has paid £9.50 to have one poem published! Better still, there is a strong chance that many poets included will buy copies for their friends and loved ones because they have been included – I invite them to do so. Go further – invite them to buy more than one copy with a once-and-only offer of a discounted, pre-publication price. 'The anthology will cost the general public £12,' I tell them as inducement.

Some months later I can send each poet a couple of pounds as 'royalties' and everyone is happy. Let us say that the anthology has cost me £3.75 a copy to produce, market and publicise. Each copy has sold for £9.50 and I have just sent each poet £2.35. That means that I have a profit level of £9.50 less £3.75, less £2.35 = £3.40 *per copy* sold. You will no doubt be aware from your own experience that the asking price for these anthologies is much higher, in some instances as much as £50 per copy.

It works as long as you have a large enough number of entrants and you're not too choosy what you accept as 'good enough to publish'.

Picking your subject areas must also be cleverly handled. If you were to publicise nationwide that you are to publish an anthology of poems by left-handed greengrocers about plums, you'd get precious few entries. Publicise that you want poems for an anthology entitled My Favourite Cat and you'd be inundated with well written poems (a few) and utterly bilious, icky-sicky, poetical tripe (an immense number) for years.

Finely organised, quite a substantial prize is offered for the best poem, though too often the 'best poem' has apparently been picked with a pin and has little or no poetic merit.

Thankfully, everyone in the past who tried it has found it fail in the end – you cannot be all things to all men. Sooner or later the good poets realised what was going on and dropped away and eventually the weak poets (who stood little chance of getting published elsewhere) got bored. Back in the late 50s early 60s, a company working this ploy, sharpened it a little by simply leaving out the poems from those (who'd been told they were 'in') who hadn't bought a copy of the anthology. It is alleged that some anthologisers have started that sharp practice again."

Johnathon Clifford is an expert on the world of vanity publishing. Find out more at: **www.vanitypublishing.info**. *Vanity Press & The Proper Poetry Publishers* by Johnathon Clifford (1994. ISBN 0 9522503 5 7)

Competitions and awards

There are literally hundreds of poetry competitions in this country alone. Prizes range from publication to hundreds or even thousands of pounds. Funding opportunities are also listed.

Aber Valley Arts Festival Annual Literature Competitions

Undercurrents – Aber Valley, 15 Graig y Fedw, Abertridwr, Caerffili CF83 4AQ
tel 029-2083 1668
email eryl893107392@aol.com
website www.academi.org
Prizes 1st prize, £50; 2nd prize, £30; 3rd prize, £15

Usually on a theme.
Submission details Maximum length, 60 lines.

Academi Cardiff International Poetry Competition 2008

Academi, Mount Stuart House,
Mount Stuart Square, Cardiff, Wales CF10 5FQ
tel 029-2047 2266 *fax* 029-2047 0691
email post@academi.org
website www.academi.org
CEO Peter Finch

Eight prizes awarded annually for unpublished poetry written in English and not a translation of another author's work (1st £5000; 2nd £500; 3rd £250; plus 5 prizes of £50). For submission details, contact Academi or send sae. Closing date, 1st February 2008.

Academi Poetry Competition

The Welsh Academy, Mount Stuart House,
Mount Stuart Square, Cardiff CF10 5YA
tel 029-2047 2266 *fax* 029-2049 2930
email post@acdemi.org
website www.academi.org
Contact Peter Finch
Prizes 1st prize, £5000; 2nd prize, £1000; 3rd prize, £700

An annual competition, offering one of the largest money prizes for a competition of its kind. Judged on poems of any style and on any subject.
Submission details Poems must be in English and can be submitted by writers of any nationality and from any country. They should be no more than 50 lines in length and typed, printed or clearly written on one side of the paper only. No covering letter or other material should be enclosed with an entry. Any number of poems may be submitted. See website for details and to obtain entry form. Entry fee, £5 per poem.

Arran Theatre and Arts Trust – The McLellan Award for Poetry

Corriegills Farm, Corriegills, Isle of Arran, Scotland KA27 8BL
email info@mclellanfestival.co.uk
website www.mclellanfestival.com
Prizes 1st prize, £1000, 2nd prize, £350, 3rd prize, £150

Competition for poems of not more than 40 lines in Scots or English, on any subject.
Submission details Send for a form, with sae, to address below, or enter online. Entry fee, £3 per poem Closing date, 31st July.

Arvon Foundation International Poetry Competition

The Arvon Foundation,
42a Buckingham Palace Road,
London SW1W 0RE
tel 020-7931 7611
email london@arvonfoundation.org
website www.arvonfoundation.org
Prizes £10,000

A prestigious biennial competition. Andrew Motion, Poet Laureate, was the first winner of the prize in 1980.
Submission details Entry fee, £7 for first poem; £5 thereafter. No line or word limit, no restrictions on theme. See website for entry form.

Asla Open Poetry Competition

Searle Publications Ltd, PO Box 52,
Welshpool, Powys SY21 8WQ
tel (01743) 260960
email asla@searlepublications.com
website www.searlepublications.com

Contact Lydia Searle
Prizes £250

Quarterly competitions on varying topics. See entry form at entries@searlepublications.com. Telephone for details: (01938) 554695.

The Authors' Foundation

The Society of Authors, 84 Drayton Gardens, London SW10 9SB
tel 020-7373 6642
email info@societyofauthors.org
website www.societyofauthors.org

Grants are available to novelists, poets and writers of non-fiction who are published authors working on their next book. The aim is to provide funding (in addition to a proper advance) for research, travel or other necessary expenditure. Closing dates, 30th April and 30th September. Send sae for an information sheet. Founded in 1984 to mark the centenary of the Society of Authors.

Award (Formerly the Haiku Award)

1 Lambolle Place, Belsize Park, London NW3 4PD
website www.into.demon.co.uk

Biannual competition for free-form and conventional haiku (5-7-5) and tanka (5-7-5-7-7).

Submission details Entry fee, £2 per haiku or tanka, or £10 for a set of 6. For more information and entry forms visit the website, or write to above address. Closing date, 31st March and 30th September annually.

Bardd Plant Cymru (Children's Poet Laureate)

Welsh Books Council, Castell Brychan, Aberystwyth, Ceredigion SY23 2JB
tel (01970) 624151 *fax* (01970) 625385
website www.cllc.org.uk

A venture established by Planed Plant, S4C, the Welsh Books Council and Urdd Gobaith Cymru, and recently the Academi to raise the profile of poetry among children, and to encourage them to compose and enjoy poetry.

BBC Wildlife Magazine Poet of the Year Awards

Origin Publishing Ltd, 14th Floor, Tower House, Fairfax Street, Bristol BS1 3BN
tel 0117-927 9009 *fax* 0117-934 9008
email sophiestafford@originpublishing.co.uk
website www.bbcwildlifemagazine.com
Contact Sophie Stafford
Prizes 1st prize, publication in *BBC Wildlife Magazine*, possible broadcast on BBC Radio 4's 'Poetry Please' programme and a wildlife weekend in the UK; runners-up, publication in *BBC Wildlife Magazine*, possible broadcast on BBC Radio 4's 'Poetry Please' programme, and poetry books

Poems must be about the natural world and/or our relationship with it (no domestic plants or animals, please). Don't feel you have to write about 'big issues' – start with your own 'lived experience' and call upon your senses to create fresh images.

Submission details Poems can take any form, in rhyme, free or blank verse but must be no longer than 50 lines. Names must not be on entries.

Bedford Open Poetry Competition

38 Verne Drive, Ampthill, Bedford MK45 2PS
email achisholm@britishlibary.net
website www.interpretershouse.org.uk
Contact Anne Chisholm
Prizes 1st prize, £300; 2 x 2nd prizes, £100 each; 3rd prize (Bedfordshire only), £50

Poems on any subject.

Submission details Submit poems up to 40 lines in length. Entry form from the above address or via the website.

Belmont Poetry Prize

Belmont Arts Centre, 5 Belmont, Shrewesbury SY1 1TE
tel (01743) 243755
email admin@belmontartscentre.org.uk
website www.belmontartscentre.org.uk
Contact Neil Rathmell
Prizes £500

The only national competition for poets writing for children. The final judging is based on votes cast by children in primary schools. The winner is announced on National Poetry Day.

Submission details Only open to poems written for children. Maximum of 40 lines in length. Entry fee £3.

Blinking Eye Publishing Competition

Blinking Eye Publishing, PO Box 549,
North Shields, Tyne & Wear NE30 2WT
tel 0191-257 3778
email Jeanne@millview77.freeserve.co.uk
website www.blinking-eye.co.uk
Contact Jeanne MacDonald
Prizes Publication of overall winner's collection
and 100 copies given to the winner. Entry into
anthology of commended poets

Annual competition for poets over 50 years of
age. Closing date, 7th August.
  Submission details Entry fee: £10 for 10
poems; £5 for 5 poems.

Bluechrome Award for Poetry

PO Box 109, Portishead, Bristol BS20 7ZJ
tel (07092) 273360
email submissions@bluechrome.co.uk
website www.bluechrome.co.uk
Contact Anthony Delgrado

Annual competition. See website for details.

The Bridport Prize

Details Bridport Arts Centre, South Street,
Bridport, Dorset DT6 3NR
tel (01308) 485064
email frances@bridportprize.org.uk
website www.bridportprize.org.uk
Contact Frances Everitt
Prizes 1st prize, £5000; 2nd prize, £1000; 3rd
prize, £500; 10 x runners-up prizes of £50

Annual prizes are awarded for poetry and short
stories. Winning stories are read by a leading
London literary agent, without obligation, and
an anthology of winning entries is published
each autumn.
  Submission details Entries should be in
English, original work, typed or clearly written,
and never published, read on radio/TV/stage.
Send sae for entry form or enter online.
Closing date, 30th June each year.

The Callum Macdonald Memorial Award

The Callum Macdonald Memorial Fund,
National Library of Scotland,
George IV Bridge Building,
Edinburgh EH1 1EW
website www.nls.uk
Contact The Administrator

Prizes The Callum Macdonald Quaich and a
cash prize of £500

This Award has been created to recognise
publishing skill and effort; to validate the
practice of poetry publication in pamphlet
form; and to encourage the preservation of
printed material of this kind in the national
collections. It has been created in memory of
Callum Macdonald MBE, Scottish literary
publisher and founder of Macdonald
Publishers and Printers.
  Submission details Publishers of Scottish
origin, living in Scotland, or engaged with
Scottish culture may submit up to 3 pamphlets,
which should not be less than 6 pages or more
than 30 in length. The original print run will
not exceed 300 copies. It is also acceptable for
pamphlets to be published by poets themselves.

Carillon Magazine Poetry Competitions

19 Godric Drive, Brinsworth, Rotherham,
South Yorkshire S60 5AN
website www.carillonmag.org.uk
Contact Graham Rippon
Prizes 1st prize, £80; 2nd prize, £40; 3
additional prizes of £20. Plus an annual
subscription to *Carillon*
  Submission details Poetry should be 15-20
lines. No email entries. No entry form required
– include a cover sheet with contact details and
titles of all entries. Entry fee, £3 first entry; £1
each additional entry. Theme for 2008 is
'Silence'; submissions from 1st May until the
deadline, 1st November.

Christopher Tower Poetry Competition

Christ Church, Oxford OX1 1DP
tel (01865) 286591
email info@towerpoetry.org.uk
website wwwtowerpoetry.org.uk
Contact Peter McDonald
Prizes 1st prize, £3000; 2nd prize, £1000, 3rd
prize, £500; Highly Commended prizes, £200
  Submission details Submissions must be no
longer than 48 lines on a set theme. 1 entry per
person. Email submissions are not accepted.

Cinnamon Press Poetry Collection Award

Meirion House, Glan yr afon, Tanygrisiau,
Blaenau Ffestiniog, Gwynedd LL41 3SU

email jan@cinnamonpress.com
website www.cinnamonpress.com
Prizes The winning author will have his/her poetry collection published with Cinnamon Press and receive a commissioning fee of £100. The runners-up and best short-listed poetry will be included in a winners' anthology and receive a complimentary copy (in addition to the copy sent to all entrants)

Submission details Entry fee, £16. Closing date, 30th June.

CLPE Prize for Poetry

CLPE (Centre for Literacy in Primary Education), Webber Street, London SE1 8QW
tel 020-7401 3382/3 *fax* 020-7928 4624
email info@clpe.co.uk
website www.clpe.co.uk
Contact Ann Lazim (ann@clpe.co.uk)

Annual prize presented in June, for a book of poetry for children or young people first published in the UK or Republic of Ireland during the previous year.

Submission details Send books to Ann Lazim at the above address.

The Duff Cooper Prize

Details Artemis Cooper, 54 St Maur Road, London SW6 4DP
tel 020-7736 3729 *fax* 020-7731 7638

An annual prize for a literary work in the field of biography, history, politics or poetry published in English or French and submitted by a recognised publisher during the previous 12 months. The prize of £4000 comes from a Trust Fund established by the friends and admirers of Duff Cooper, 1st Viscount Norwich (1890–1954) after his death.

Corneliu Popescu Prize for European Poetry Translation

Translation Prize, The Poetry Society, 22 Betterton Street, London WC2H 9BX
tel 020-7420 9880 *fax* 020-7240 4818
email competition@poetrysociety.org.uk
website www.poetrysociety.org.uk
Prizes £1500

Awarded every 2 years, and open to collections which feature poetry translated from a European language into English. It is named

after Corneliu M Popescu, translator of the work of one of Romania's leading poets, Mihai Eminescu, into English. Popescu was tragically killed in the violent earthquake of 4th March 1977, aged 19.

Costa Book Awards

(formerly the Whitbread Book Awards)
Details The Booksellers Association, Minster House, 272 Vauxhall Bridge Road, London SW1V 1BA
tel 020-7802 0801 *fax* 020-7802 0803
email naomi.gane@booksellers.org.uk
website www.costabookawards.co.uk
Contact Naomi Gane

The awards celebrate and promote the most enjoyable contemporary British writing. Judged in 2 stages and offering a total of £50,000 prize money, there are 5 categories: Novel, First Novel, Biography, Poetry and Children's. They are judged by a panel of 3 judges and the winner in each category receives £5000. 9 final judges then choose the Costa Book of the Year from the 5 category winners. The overall winner receives £25,000. Writers must be resident in Great Britain or Ireland for 3 or more years. Submissions must be received from publishers. Closing date: end of June.

Creating Reality Poetry Competition

8a Womersley Road, London N8 9AE
email mail@creatingreality.co.uk
website www.creatingreality.co.uk
Contact Milly Chapman
Prizes Poetry £1000, £250, £100; Haiku £150, £50, £25; Flash £300, £100, £50

A non-profit-making collective of writers and artists running competitions and providing small bursaries and services, drastically reduced in price for writers and artists.

Submission details See website for up-to-date information on all competitions, as guidelines, dates and prizes may vary from year to year.

Davidian Open Poetry Competition

Norfolk Poets and Writers, 9 Walnut Close, Norwich NR8 6YN
email tipsforwriters@yahoo.co.uk
Contact Wendy Webb

Annual competition to promote poetry in the Davidian form.

Submission details See entry form for length and theme. Entry fee, £2 (5 for £10). Closing date, 23rd April, annually.

Geoffrey Dearmer Prize

Poetry Society, 22 Betterton Street, London WC2H 9BX
tel 020-7420 9880
email poetryreview@poetrysociety.org.uk
website www.poetrysociety.org.uk

An annual prize, established in 1997, for a Poetry Review contributor who has not yet published a book.

The City of Derby Short Story and Poetry Competition

PO Pox 7065, Derby DE1 OAD
tel (01332) 725362
email info@cityofderbywriting
competition.org.uk
website www.cityofderbywriting
competition.org.uk

Competition for poetry on any theme.
Submission details Maximum of 40 lines.

Derwood Aldeburgh First Collection Prize

The Poetry Trust, The Cut, 9 New Cut, Hales, Suffolk IP19 8BY
tel (01986) 835950
email info@thepoetrytrust.org
website www.thepoetrytrust.org
Prizes £3000 plus a week of paid 'protected' writing time and a fee-paying invitation to read at the following year's Aldeburgh Festival

Funded by the Derwood Charitable Foundation, an annual competition for any first collection of at least 40 pages published in Britain, Northern Ireland or the Republic of Ireland since 1st August of the previous year.
Submission details Send 3 bound or proof copies with a note of the publication date by 31st July.

John Dryden Translation Competition

School of Literature and Creative Writing, University of East Anglia, Norwich NR4 7TJ
tel (01603) 593360
email transcomp@uea.ac.uk
website www.bcla.org
Contact Dr Jean Boase-Beier

Annual competition for translations (prose and drama as well as poetry) from any language into English.
Submission details Entry fee, £7 (single entry); £12 (2 entries); £16 (3 entries). Up to 25 pages translated into English.Closing date, mid-February.

Earlyworks High Fantasy Challenge

PO Box 258, Hastings TN34 9BB
email earlyworks@tiscali.co.uk
website www.earlyworkspress.co.uk
Contact K Green
Prizes Cash prizes and publication for top 30 entries

Genre poems and stories.
Submission details Closing date, 30th June. Entry fee, £2.50 per poem. Send sae for details, or email.

Envoi International Poetry Competition

Meirion House, Glan Yr Afon, Tanygrisiau, Blaenau Ffestiniog, Gwynedd LL41 3SU
tel (01766) 832112
Prizes 1st prize, £150; 2nd prize, £100; 3rd prize, £50, plus 3 annual subscriptions

Runs 3 times per year with the following deadlines: 20th February, 20th June, 20th October.
Submission details Work must be unpublished and not entered into other competitions. Poems must be 40 lines maximum length. Name and address on a separate sheet. Send sae. Entry fee, £3 per poem and 5 for £12.

Essex Poetry Festival Open Poetry Competition

website www.essex-poetry-festival
Prizes 1st prize, £500; 2nd prize, £200; 3rd prize, £100; 3 runner-up prizes of £10 book tokens. Winners and runners-up will be invited to read their winning poems at the festival. Winning poems will be published on the website
Submission details For further details, rules and entry form, visit website. Closing date, 31st August.

European Jewish Publication Society Grants

PO Box 19948, London N3 3ZL
tel 020-8346 1668

email cs@ejps.org.uk
website www.ejps.org.uk
Contact Dr Colin Schindler

A charity, which was founded in 1995 and has since assisted in the publication of many books of Jewish interest, including poetry.

Christopher Ewart-Biggs Memorial Prize

The Secretary, Memorial Prize, Flat 3, 149 Hamilton Terrace, London NW8 9QS

This prize of £5000 is awarded once every 2 years to the writer, of any nationality, whose work is judged to contribute most to:

• peace and understanding in Ireland;
• closer ties between the peoples of Britain and Ireland;
• cooperation between the partners of the European Union.

For further details, contact The Secretary.

The Geoffrey Faber Memorial Prize

An annual prize of £1000 is awarded in alternate years for a volume of verse and for a volume of prose fiction, first published originally in the UK during the 2 years preceding the year in which the award is given which is, in the opinion of the judges, of the greatest literary merit. Eligible writers must be not more than 40 years old at the date of publication of the book and a citizen of the UK and Colonies, of any other Commonwealth state or of the Republic of Ireland. The 3 judges are reviewers of poetry or fiction who are nominated each year by the literary editors of newspapers and magazines which regularly publish such reviews. Faber and Faber invite nominations from reviewers and literary editors. No submissions for the prize are to be made. Established in 1963 by Faber and Faber Ltd, as a memorial to the founder and first Chairman of the firm.

firstwriter.com Poetry Competitions

website www.firstwriter.com
Prizes Publication

Has at least 1 poetry competition running at all times.

Submission details Entry fee, £5.

Forward Prizes for Poetry

Details Forward Poetry Prize Administrator, Colman Getty Consultancy, 28 Windmill Street, London W1T 2JJ
tel 020-7631 2666 *fax* 020-7631 2699
email pr@colmangetty.co.uk

3 prizes are awarded annually:

• The Forward Prize for best collection published between 1st October and 30th September (£10,000);
• The Felix Dennis Prize for best first collection published between 1st October and 30th September (£5000); and
• The Forward Prize for best single poem in memory of Michael Donaghy, published but not as part of a collection between 1st May and 30th April (£1000).

Submission details All poems entered are also considered for inclusion in the *Forward Book of Poetry*, an annual anthology. Entries must be submitted by book publishers and editors of newspapers, periodicals and magazines in the UK and Eire. Entries from individual poets of their unpublished or self-published work will not be accepted. Established 1992. More information can be found at www.forwardartsfoundation.co.uk.

Foyle Young Poets of the Year Award

Poetry Society, 22 Betterton Street, London WC2H 9BX
tel 020-7420 9892
email fyp@poetrysociety.org.uk
website www.poetrysociety.org.uk
Prizes Include books, posters, membership of the Poetry Society, visits to schools by a leading poet and, for the 15 overall winners, a week-long residential course at the prestigious Arvon Centre in Lumb Bank, as well as publication in the annual anthology

Britain's most prestigious poetry prize for young writers between the ages of 11 and 17. The closing date each year is 31st July.

The Frogmore Poetry Prize

42 Morehall Avenue, Folkestone, Kent CT19 4EF
mobile (07751) 251689
website www.frogmorepress.co.uk
Prizes 200 guineas plus a subscription to *The Frogmore Papers*

The prize was founded in 1987; previous winners include Ann Alexander, Tobias Hill and Mario Petrucci. Unpublished poetry only.

Submission details 40 lines maximum. Name and address on a separate sheet. Entry fee, £2 per poem.

Griffin Poetry Prize

The Griffin Trust for Excellence in Poetry, 6610 Edwards Boulevard, Mississauga, Ontario L5T 2V6, Canada
tel 905-565 5993 *fax* 905-564 3645
website www.griffinpoetryprize.com

Two annual prizes of Can.$50,000 will be awarded for collections of poetry published in English during the preceding year. One prize will go to a living Canadian poet, the other to a living poet from any country. Collections of poetry translated into English from other languages are also eligible and will be assessed for their literary quality in English. Submissions only from publishers. Closing date: 31st December. Founded 2000.

Haiku Calendar Competition

Snapshot Press, PO Box 132, Waterloo, Liverpool L22 8WZ
email info@snapshotpress.co.uk
website www.snapshotpress.co.uk
Contact John Barlow
Prizes £360 total prize money

The Haiku Calendar Competition has been held annually since 1999. As a result of the contest, 52 haiku are published each year in *The Haiku Calendar*.

Submission details Collections should comprise 50-100 haiku. Poems may have been previously published in magazines, journals or anthologies, but must not have appeared in an individual collection. Any number of manuscripts may be entered, provided each is accompanied by the entry fee. Entry fee, £20 per manuscript.

Haiku Presence Award

90d Fishergate Hill, Preston PR1 8JD
website http://
haiku.presence.mysite.orange.co.uk
Contact Martin Lucas
Prizes 1st prize, £100; 4 x 2nd prizes, £25 each

An annual competition.

Submission details Send 2 copies of each haiku, adding name and address to 1 copy. For full details, see website or send an sae to the above address. Closing date, 31st October. Entry fee, £5 for up to 5 haiku; additional haiku £1 each.

Hastings International Poetry Competition

194 Downs Road, Hastings,
East Sussex TN34 2DZ
Contact Josephine Austin
Prizes 1st prize, £150; 2nd prize, £75; 3rd prize, £50; winners published in *First Time* Spring issue 2008
Submission details Entry fee, £2. Closing date, 21st October.

The Hawthornden Prize

The Administrator, 42a Hays Mews, Berkeley Square, London W1J 5QA

This prize of £10,000 is awarded annually to the author of what, in the opinion of the Committee, is the best work of imaginative literature published during the preceding calendar year by a British author. Books do not have to be specially submitted.

The Felicia Henmans Prize for Lyrical Poetry

The Sub-Dean, Faculty of Arts,
The University of Liverpool,
Foundation Building, Brownlow Hill,
Liverpool L69 7ZX
tel 0151-794 2458
email wilderc@liv.ac.uk
Contact The Sub-Dean

An annual prize open to past and present members and students of the University of Liverpool only. It is awarded for a lyrical poem, on any subject.

Submission details Only 1 poem may be submitted, either published or unpublished. The prize will not be awarded more than once to the same competitor. Poems, endorsed 'Henmans Prize', must be submitted by 1st May.

Ilkley Literature Festival Annual Poetry and Short Story Competition

Manor House, 2 Castle Hill, Ilkley LS29 9DT
website www.ilkleyliteraturefestival.org.uk/
competitions.html

Prizes Arvon Foundation Poetry Course
Submission details Poems of any length on any subject. See website for details.

Ilkley Literature Festival Children's and Young People's Poetry Competition
Manor House, 2 Castle Hill, Ilkley LS29 9DT
website www.ilkleyliteraturefestival.org.uk/competitions.html
Submission details A competition for schools and individual children. 3 age-groups – see website for details.

Indigo Dreams Press Poetry Awards
The Manacles, Predannack, The Lizard, Cornwall TR12 7AU
email ronnie.g@indigodreams.plus.com
website www.indigodreamspress.co.uk/competition.html
Contact ronnie.g@indigodreams.plus.com
Prizes 1st prize, £100; 2nd prize, £75; 3rd prize, £25

Any length, any style.
Submission details Entry fee, £3 per single poem; £5 per 3 poems; £9 per 5 poems.

The International Poetry Mart Ongoing Competition
51 Leeds Road, Mirfield,
West Yorkshire WF14 OBY
Prizes £300
Submission details Entry: £2 for the first poem, £1 for subsequent poems.

International Queer Writing Competition
Chroma Writing Competition, PO Box 44655, London N16 0WQ
website www.chromajournal.co.uk
Prizes 1st prize, £300; 2nd prize, £150; 3rd prize, £75 and publication in *Chroma*

A short story and poetry competition for lesbian, gay, bisexual and trans writers.
Submission details For poems of up to 50 lines. Entry fee, £5. Closing date, 10th September 2008.

Irish Times Poetry Now Award
Poetry Now Festival, The Arts Office,
Dun Laoghaire-Rathdown County Council,
Marine Road, Dun Laoghaire, County Dublin, Ireland

tel (003531) 2719532
email cbrown@dircoco.ie
website www.dircoco.ie/arts
Contact Carolyn Brown
Prizes €5000

The only award of its kind, recognising and rewarding work by Irish poets. It is given to the author of the best single volumes of poems published by an Irish poet, or by Irish publisher annually.
Submission details Volumes published in English by Irish presses or by Irish writers in the calendar year are eligible. Translations and anthologies are not eligible. Only single volumes (and not selected poems or collected poems) are eligible. Self-published collections, or editions of deceased poets, will not be accepted. Each press (but not individual poets) should submit 5 copies of each title eligible for the award, in book, proof or galley form.

JBWB Poetry Competition
87 Home Orchard, Yate,
South Gloucestershire BS37 5XH
tel (01454) 324717
email competitions@jbwb.co.uk
website www.jbwb.co.uk
Contact Jenny Hewitt, Doug Watts
Prizes 1st prize, 100; 2nd prize, £50; 3rd prize, £20

Popular quarterly competition that has been running for 8 years.
Submission details Poems no longer than 30 lines on any subject. See website for details.

Keats Shelley Prize
KSMA Competition Secretary,
School of English, The University,
St Andrews KY16 9AL
website www.keats-shelley.co.uk
Contact Sandra McDevitt

Sponsored by Barclays Bank plc, the Cowley Foundation and the School of English, University of St Andrews.
Submission details Maximum length, 50 lines. Entry fee of £5 for a single entry, plus a further £5 for each additional entry. Closing date, 30th June.

The Petra Kenney Poetry Competition
Details Morgan Kenney,
The Belmoredean Barn, Maplehurst Road,
West Grinstead RH13 6RN

email morgan@petrapoetrycompetition.co.uk
website www.petrapoetrycompetition.co.uk

This annual competition is for unpublished poems on any theme and in any style, and is open to everyone. Poems should be no more than 80 lines. Entry fee: £3 per poem. Prizes: 1st – £1000 plus publication in *Writing Magazine*, 2nd – £500, 3rd – £250 plus a Royal Brierley crystal vase; Highly Commended: 3 prizes of £125; Comic Verse – £250; Young Poets (age 14–18) £250 and £125. Closing date, 1st December each year. Founded 1995.

Kent & Sussex Poetry Society Open Poetry Competition

website www.kentandsussexpoetrysociety.org
Prizes 1st prize, £500; 2nd prize, £200; 3rd prize, £100; 4th prize, £50

Submission details 40 lines maximum, typed on A4. Name and address on separate sheet. Closing date, 31st January each year.

The Kilkenny International Swift Society Competition

website www.swiftsociety.com/competition/competition.html
Prizes 1st prize, €1000

For an an unpublished satirical poem, in the spirit and style of Swift, on a topic of current and relevant social/political interest. The competition is both a celebration of Swift as one of Ireland's greatest satirists and a move to promote political and social commentary through satire.

Killie Writing Competition

Details Killie Writing Competition, Kilmarnock College KA3 7AT
tel (01355) 302160
email enquiries@killie.co.uk
website www.killie.co.uk

Annual competition usually with 4 categories: 5–7 year-olds, 8–11 year-olds, 12–16 year-olds, adults. Free expessive writing (poetry or fiction) with no limit on subject, word count, style or format. See website for guidelines. Work submitted must have been previously unpublished. Various prizes with the overall best entry receiving £1000 and a trophy. Closing date: April. Founded 2000.

Leaf Books Short Poetry Competition

website www.leafbooks.co.uk
Prizes All selected poems will be featured in a Leaf Book. The overall winner will receive £200

Competition for short poems (16 lines or fewer) on any theme.

Submission details £2.50 per entry; cheques made payable to Leaf Books. Entry forms available on the website. Entry fee, £3. Closing date, 31st July.

Ledbury Poetry Festival Competition

Ledbury Poetry Festival, Church Street, Ledbury, Herefordshire HR8 1DH
tel (01531) 634156
email charle@poetry-festival.com
website www.poetry-festival.com
Contact Charles Bennett
Prizes Category 1 (18 and over) 1st prize, Ty Newydd writing course; 2nd prize, £250; 3rd prize, £150. Category 2 (11-17) 1st prize, £100; 2nd prize, £50; 3rd prize, £25. Category 3 (10 and under) 1st prize, £25 book token; 2nd prize, £15 book token; 3rd prize, £10 book token

See website for full details.

Linkway Magazine Open Writing Competition

Linkway Magazine, The Shieling, The Links, Burry Port, Carmarthenshire SA16 0HU
Contact FC Davies
Prizes vary

Quarterly competitions only – send sae to the above address for details.

Literary Review Grand Poetry Prize

44 Lexington Street, London W1F 0LW
tel 020-7437 9392 *fax* 020-7734 1844
website www.literaryreview.co.uk

Runs a competition each month for poems on a given subject which rhyme, scan and make sense and are no more than 24 lines. Monthly prizes of £300 and £150 are awarded. The Grand Prize of £5000 is awarded to the best of these each year. Closing date: September. Founded 1990.

Litfest Poetry Competition

PO Box 751, Lancaster LA1 9AJ
tel (01524) 62166

email all@litfest.org
website www.litfest.org
Contact Jonathan Bean

A biannual open competition, relaunching in 2008.
  Submission details Entry forms are available from the Litfest office. See website for details.

Local Poem Competition

United Press Ltd, Admail 3735,
London EC1B 1JB
tel (0870) 2406190
website www.unitedpress.co.uk
Contact The Competition Secretary

Annual poetry competition inviting entries 'on someone or something from the poet's home town'. Top prize of £1000 in cash.
  Submission details Send up to 3 poems, each of up to 20 lines and 160 words, by the closing date of 31st December.

Love and Out of Love

Gti Suite, Valleys Innovation Centre,
Navigation Park, Abercynon,
Rhondda Cynon Taff CF45 4SN
tel (01443) 483341 *fax* (01443) 654278
email leafbooks@yahoo.co.uk
website www.leafbooks.co.uk
Contact Cecile Morreau
Prizes 1st prize, £200 and publication; 2nd prize, £50 and publication

Entries accepted on any theme.
  Submission details Entry via form (available on website, or by post with a covering letter including name and contact details). Entry fee, £5 (cheques payable to 'Leaf'.

Manchester Cathedral Poetry Competition

The Religious Poetry Competition,
The Cathedral, Manchester M3 1SX
email albert.radcliffe@dsl.pipex.com
Contact Albert Radcliffe
Prizes 1st prize, £300; 2nd prize, £150; 3rd prize, £75

The poems submitted should be broadly religious; that is, spiritual in nature and, like all good religious poetry, should appeal to those who would not necessarily describe themselves

as such. 'Religious' thus includes poems that are Christian, as well as those from within other faith traditions. Those struggling to discover their own sense of the sacred are also invited to submit entries. Poems are welcome in any style or form and will be judged solely on their merits as poetry.
  Submission details Entry fee, £3. Closing date, 1st July.

McLellan Award for Poetry

email poetry@mclellanfestival.com
website www.mclellanfestival.com
Prizes 1st prize, £1000; 2nd prize, £350; 3rd prize £150

Awarded as part of the McLellan Festival on the Isle of Arran; celebrates the work of playwright, poet and short story writer Robert McLellan, who spent most of his working life on Arran writing exclusively in Scots, the living language of the communities he grew up in. The McLellan Award for Poetry invites entries in all varieties of Scots and in English. All the poems will be judged in 1 category, with no distinction being made on the basis of the language used. Poems may be on any subject and will be judged anonymously.
  Submission details Maximum length of 40 lines. See entry form on website.

Mere Literary Festival Poetry Competition

c/o Lawrences, Old Hollow, Mere,
Wiltshire BA12 6EG
tel (01747) 860475
email merewilts@aol.com
website www.merewilts.org.uk
Organiser Adrienne Howell
Prizes Cash prizes and local and junior categories. Shortlisted poems are showcased at a festival event in October

A biennial poetry competition in aid of charity, running in *odd* years.
  Submission details Maximum 40 lines on any theme. Entry forms available from 1st March (with sae), or can be downloaded from the website.

National Poetry Anthology

United Press Ltd, Admail 3735,
London EC1B 1JB

tel 0870-240 6190
website www.unitedpress.co.uk
Prizes 1st prize, £1000

The biggest free annual competition in the UK. Around 250 winners are selected every year, each one representing a different UK town. All winners are published in the National Poetry Anthology, and all receive a free copy of the book.

Submission details Send up to 3 poems on any subject, up to 20 lines and 160 words each, by the annual closing date of 30th June.

National Poetry Anthology Competition

United Press Ltd, Admail 3735,
London EC1B 1JB
tel 0870-240 6190
website www.unitedpress.co.uk
Prizes 1st prize £1000

Seeks aspiring poets for the UK's biggest free annual poetry competition. Around 250 winners are selected every year, each one representing a different UK town. All winners are published in the National Poetry Anthology, and all receive a free copy of the book.

Submission details Send up to 3 poems on any subject, of up to 20 lines/160 words each, by the annual closing date of 30th June, to the address given above.

National Poetry Competition

Competition Organiser, The Poetry Society,
22 Betterton Street, London WC2H 9BX
tel 020-7420 9895 *fax* 020-7240 4818
email marketing@poetrysociety.org.uk
website www.poetrysociety.org.uk
Prizes 1st prize, £5000; 2nd prize, £1000; 3rd prize, £500 – plus 10 commendations of £50. The opportunity to read at Ledbury Festival 2008

One of Britain's major annual open poetry competitions. Poems on any theme, up to 40 lines. All poems will be read by a team of poetry specialists before the final judging process.

Submission details For rules and entry form, send an sae. Entries also accepted via the website. Closing date, 31st October each year.

The New Writer Prose and Poetry Prizes

Details PO Box 60, Cranbrook, Kent TN17 2ZR
tel (01580) 212626 *fax* (01580) 212041
email admin@thenewwriter.com
website www.thenewwriter.com
Prizes Collection, 1st prize £300; 2nd prize, £200; 3rd prize, £100. Single, 1st prize, £100; 2nd prize, £75; 3rd prize £50

Short stories up to 4000 words, novellas, essays and articles; poets may submit either 1 or a collection of 6-10 previously unpublished poems. Total prize money £2000 as well as publication for the prize-winners in the *New Writer* magazine. Founded 1997.

Submission details Poems must be no more than 40 lines in length. In single-poem section they must be unpublished. In collection of poems section, work may be previously published and there is no limit as to length. Entry fees: £4 per poem; £10 for a collection of 6-10 poems. Closing date: 30 November each year.

New Writing Ventures

c/o Booktrust, Book House, 45 East Hill,
London SW18 2QZ
tel 020-8516 2972 *fax* 020-8516 2978
email tarryn@booktrust.org.uk
website www.newwritingpartnership.org.uk
Contact Tarryn McKay (Prizes Administrator)

An annual series of major national prizes and awards for emerging writers in poetry, fiction and creative non-fiction. Winners in each of the 3 categories receive £3000 and a year of creative mentoring from The Literary Consultancy. Runners-up receive £1000 each (2 runners-up per category).

Submission details £12.50 per entry; no limit to the number of entries. Closing date (annual competition): 31 May. For more details on entry criteria, and a downloadable entry form, visit the website; alternatively contact Tarryn McKay for an entry form by post.

The Nobel Prize in Literature

Awarding authority Swedish Academy,
Box 2118, S–10313 Stockholm, Sweden
tel (08) 555 12554 *fax* (08) 555 12549

email sekretariat@svenskaakademien.se
website www.svenskaakademien.se

This is one of the awards stipulated in the will of the late Alfred Nobel, the Swedish scientist who invented dynamite. No direct application for a prize will be taken into consideration. For authors writing in English it was bestowed upon Rudyard Kipling in 1907, W.B. Yeats in 1923, George Bernard Shaw in 1925, Sinclair Lewis in 1930, John Galsworthy in 1932, Eugene O'Neill in 1936, Pearl Buck in 1938, T.S. Eliot in 1948, William Faulkner in 1949, Bertrand Russell in 1950, Sir Winston Churchill in 1953, Ernest Hemingway in 1954, John Steinbeck in 1962, Samuel Beckett in 1969, Patrick White in 1973, Saul Bellow in 1976, William Golding in 1983, Wole Soyinka in 1986, Joseph Brodsky in 1987, Nadine Gordimer in 1991, Derek Walcott in 1992, Toni Morrison in 1993, Seamus Heaney in 1995, V.S. Naipaul in 2001 and Harold Pinter in 2005.

Northern Writers' Awards

2 School Lane, Whickham NE16 4SL
tel 0191-488 8580
email mail@newwriting.com
website www.newwritingnorth.com

Awards introduced to support writers, both new and established, who live and work in the North East region. There are now 4 different types of awards, from support for talented new writers to specific support for established writers who are working on new projects. This year, awards up to the value of £25,000 are being made.

Norwich Writers' Circle Open Poetry Competition

25 Wensum Valley Close, Norwich NR6 5DJ
tel (01508) 536912
email Shirley.Collin@mac.com,
jshackleton7@aol.com
website www.norwichwriters.org.uk
Contact Mrs Jean Shackleton
Prizes 1st prize, £200; 2nd prize, £100; 3rd prize, £50; Entrant's Address Norfolk or Suffolk, £25; Humorous poem, £15 (John Coleridge Prize); Minimalist Poem, £15 (Hilary Mellor Prize)

Annual competition with different adjudicators each year.

Submission details Poems should be a maximum of 40 lines in length. They should be typed on A4, with details of poet and titles of poems on a separate sheet. Closing date, second Tuesday in February.

Nottingham Open Poetry Competition

Jeremy Duffield, Chairman, 71 Saxton Avenue, Heanor, Derbyshire DE75 7PZ
tel (01773) 712282
email info@nottinghampoetrysociety.co.uk
website www.nottinghampoetrysociety.co.uk
Contact Viv Apple (*tel* 0115-914 5838; *email* viv.apple@ntlworld.com)
Prizes 1st prize, £300; 2nd prize, £150; 3rd prize, £75 plus 10 merit prizes of subscriptions to *Poetry Nottingham*

Submission details Entries should be in English, unpublished and not accepted or submitted for publication elsewhere. Poems must be no longer than 40 lines and each poem should be typed on a separate sheet of A4 paper. Poems are judged anonymously. On a separate piece of paper please state name and address and provide a list of poems submitted. Entry fee: £3 per poem; £10 for 4 poems.

The Royal Society of Literature Ondaatje Prize

Royal Society of Literature, Somerset House, Strand, London WC2R 1LA
tel 020-7845 4676 *fax* 020-7845 4679
email paulaj@rslit.org
website www.rslit.org
Contact Paula Johnson
Prizes £10,000

Endowed by Sir Christopher Ondaatje and awarded annually to a book of literary merit, fiction or non-fiction, best evoking spirit of place.

Submission details All entries must be published within the calendar year and should be submitted between 1st September and 1st December. The writer must be a citizen of the United Kingdom, Commonwealth or Ireland. Each UK publisher or imprint of a publisher may enter 1 book published or due to be published within the calendar year. An entry form must be completed.

Open Summer Competition

c/o Norfolk Poets & Writers, 9 Walnut Close, Norwich NR8 6YN
email tipsforwriters@yahoo.co.uk
Contact Wendy Webb

Open Davidian competition. Contact as above for more details.

Oxfambooks Poetry Calendar Competition

Oxfam Ireland, 9 Burgh Quay, Dublin 2, Ireland
website www.oxfamireland.org
Contact Sheila Powers
Prizes Winners will join poets Tony Curtis, Seamus Heaney, Jean O'Brien, Nessa O'Malley and Paul Perry on Oxfambooks Poetry Calendar

Competition for poems of up to 20 lines. Entry fee, €5.

Partners Writing Group Competitions

289 Elmwood Avenue, Feltham, Middlesex TW13 7QB
email partners_writing_group@hotmail.com
Contact Ian Deal
Prizes 1st prize, £300; 2nd prize, £100; 3rd prize, £50; 4th prize, entry fee refunded

An annual competition for poems of any style or length.
Submission details Names should not appear on poems, but on separate sheet. Send sae for full guidelines. Entry fee, £2.50 per poem. Closing date, 1st May.

Patrick Kavanagh Poetry Award

c/o Rosaleen Kearney,
Patrick Kavanah Society, Lacklum, Inniskeen, Co Monaghan
Prizes €2500

Annual competition, open to poets born in the island of Ireland, or of Irish nationality, or long-term resident in Ireland, who have not previously published an individual collection of poems.
Submission details Original, 20 poems. Individual poems no more than 40 lines,

unpublished. No return of manuscripts. Only Irish nationals eligible.

Peace & Freedom Press Competitions

17 Farrow Road, Whaplode Drove, Spalding, Lincolnshire PE12 0TS
email p-rance@yahoo.co.uk
website http://uk.geocities.com/p-rance/pandf.htm
Contact Paul Rance
Prizes 1st prize, £100; 5 runners-up, £10 each
Submission details Send sae for details.

Peterloo Poets Open Poetry Competition

2 Kelly Gardens, Calstock, Cornwall PL18 9SA
tel (01822) 833473
email info@peterloopoets.com
website www.peterloopoets.com
Prizes 1st prize, £1500; 2nd prize, £1000; 3rd prize, £500; 4th prize, £100; 10 prizes, £50 each

Annual competition. Closing date, 2nd March. Entry fee, £5 per poem. See website for entry form.

Pier Pressure Poetry Competition

Obligations Competition, Pier Pressure, c/o 17 Wilbury Crescent, Hove, Sussex BN3 6FL
website www.pierpressure.org
Prizes £100

Annual short story and poetry competitions.
Submission details See website or write to the address above.

Playground Poets

website www.playground-poets.com
Contact Coral Milburn-Curtis

A project designed to encourage youngsters to have fun writing poetry. Has been awarded a grant for publication of the anthologies; all profits from the printed books are donated to Save the Children. Playground Poets is drawing the attention of children all over the world – now on its 3rd anthology. For more details, visit the website.

Plough Prize

The Plough Arts Centre, 9-11 Fore Street, Torrington EX38 8HQ

tel (01805) 624624
email sarah.willans@theploughprize.co.uk
website www.theploughprize.co.uk
Contact Sarah Willans
Prizes 1st prize, £500; 2nd prize, £200; 3rd prize, £100

Open category for poems up to 40 lines in length. Short poem category for poems up to 10 lines in length. Poems should be original, unpublished and should not have won a prize in any other competition.
   Submission details Work should be typed, single-spaced on a single side of A4. Name, address, telephone number, email address and poem title(s) should be printed clearly on a separate sheet. Mark each poem 'O' or 'S' to indicate category. Entry fee, £4 per poem, £14 for 4 poems. Thereafter, £3.50 per poem. Free check-box critique for every poem sent with sae; full critiques available at £10 per poem (send a copy, marked 'Critique' and an sae or email address to which it can be sent). Closing date, 30th November, annually.

The Poetry Business Book and Pamphlet Competition

The Poetry Business, The Studio,
Byram Arcade, Westgate,
Huddersfield HD1 1ND
tel (01484) 434840 *fax* (01484) 426566
email edit@poetrybusiness.co.uk
website www.poetrybusiness.co.uk
Contact Anita Fenton

An annual competition.
   Submission details Submit a short manuscript (16-24pp). Contact the above address for rules and entry form, or visit the website. Closing date, 31st October.

Poetry Can Competition

Poetry Can, Unit 11, 20-22 Hepburn Road,
Bristol BS2 8UD
email info@poetrycan.co.uk
Prizes Publication, plus 500 copies of collection
   Submission details Closing date, 30th June. Entry fee, £15. Submit 10 poems.

Poetry London Competition

1a Jewel Road, London E17 4QU
tel 020-8521 0776

website www.poetrylondon.co.uk
Contact Maurice Riordan
Prizes 1st prize, £1000; 2nd prize, £500; 3rd prize, £200
   Submission details Entries must be in English, your own unaided work, not a translation of another poet, and unpublished. The maximum length is 80 lines. For *Poetry London* subscribers the entry fee is £3 per poem; for non-subscribers, £4.

Poetry on the Lake International Poetry Competition

c/o Gabriel Griffin, Poetry on the Lake,
Isola San Giulio, 28016 Orta NO, Italy
tel +39 347-8464227
email poetryonthelake@yahoo.co.uk
website www.poetryonthelake.org
Contact Gabriel Griffin

Annual poetry competition with 3 categories: Silver Wyvern – themed, max. 60 lines; Bill Winter – open theme, max. 10 lines; Formal Verse – open theme, max. 40 lines. Various prizes; results in July. Autumn awards and readings, with possible anthology publication with Italian translation facing for winning and selected entries. Line illustrations welcomed. Further details via the website.
   Submission details No entry form required. Send 2 copies of each poem (unpublished, unprized); one copy should be anonymous, the other marked with name and contact details. Closing date, 30th May.

Poet's Letter Beowulf Poetry Prize

tel (07931) 357109
email Editor@poetsletter.com
website www.poetsletter.com
Prizes 1st prize, £10,000; 12 x 2nd prizes, a one-year Poet in Residence with a bursary of at least £500; 12 x 3rd prizes, £100 each

Annual competition based on a theme.
   Submission details Maximum length, 60 lines. Entry fee, £10 for 1 poem; subsequent entries, £8 each.

Postcode Poetry Competition

108 Deepdale Road, Preston PR1 5AR
tel (07786) 570415 *fax* (01772) 200462

email philipmorris99@hotmail.com;
postcodee.poetry@hotmail.co.uk
website www.postcode-poetry.co.uk
Contact Philip Morris
Prizes Fame, fortune and food

A web-based poetry competition based around
UK postcode areas, open to all poets, with no
restrictions other than that of being a UK
resident.

   Submission details Entry guidelines and
details of entry fee can be found on the website.
Closing date: 31st August, each year.

Pulsar Poetry Competition

34 Lineacre, Grange Park, Swindon,
Wiltshire SN5 6DA
email pulsar.ed@btopenworld.com
website www.pulsarpoetry.com
Contact David Pike
Prizes 1st prize, £125; 2nd prize, £75; 3rd prize,
£50

For poems of not more than 40 lines, on any
subject.

   Submission details Entry fee, £2.50 first
poem, subsequent poems £1.50 each.
Minimum entry fee, £2.50.

Quantum Leap Open Poetry Competitions

York House, 15 Argyle Terrace, Rothesay,
Isle of Bute, Scotland PA20 0BD
Prizes £125 in prizes

Competition for poems not exceeding 36 lines.

   Submission details Entry fee, £3 per poem.
Closing date, 30th April and 31st October.
Essential to send sae or 2 x IRCs initially, for
rules.

Ragged Raven Press Poetry Competition

1 Lodge Farm, Snitterfield, Stratford-on-Avon,
Warks CV37 0LR
website www.raggedraven.co.uk
Prizes 1st prize, £300; 4 runners-up prizes of
£50. Selected entries published in anthology

For poems of any length and on any subject.

   Submission details Entry fee, £3 per poem,
£10 for 4 poems. Closing date, 31st October.
See website for details.

Susan Rands Memorial Poetry Prize

18 Chequers Lane, Prestwood,
Great Missenden,
Buckinghamshire HP16 9DW
tel (01494) 866318
email dwoods@hotmail.com
website www,christies.org
Contact David Woods
Prizes 1st prize, £50; 2nd prize, £40; 3rd prize,
£25 (all winners are published)

Open to all UK residents aged 16 years and
over. All monies are donated to cancer research
at Christie's Hospital. The competition was
founded in memory of Susan Rands, the British
record survivor of the terminal Mesothelioma
strain of cancer.

   Submission details Entrants may submit as
many poems as they wish, provided each is a
maximum length of 40 lines. Contact details
should be enclosed on a separate sheet of
paper, as entries are be judged anonymously.
Poems must be typed, and cannot be returned.
Enclose sae for results. Entry fee: £4 for 1
poem; £2 for each subsequent entry. Closing
date: 1st May, October 31st, annually.

The Rise Londonwide Youth Slam Championship

Poetry Society, 22 Betterton, Street,
London WC2H 9BX
tel 020-7420 9893
email jtaylor@poetrysociety.org.uk
website www.poetrysociety.org.uk/respect
Prizes All entrants win a year's membership of
the Poetry Society, plus books, CDs and the
chance to perform alongside professionals at
top London venues. Winners will spend a
weekend developing their acts with a
professional spoken-word artist, record their
track at a major London recording studio for a
compilation album, and showcase their work at
the Mayor's annual anti-racism festival, Rise,
before crowds of up to 100,000

Presented by the Mayor of London, in
association with the Poetry Society. Open to all
aged between 12 and 18. The top 12 who are
successful in both the quarter-finals and semi-
finals go on to form the Londonwide Slam
Championship showcase team, and will

represent the capital in the UK Slam Championship.

Tom Roder Memorial Prize for Poetry

Dept. of English Literature, The University, Sheffield S10 2TN
email s.vice@sheffield.ac.uk

Annual poetry prize awarded for a collection of 20-30 individual unpublished poems (around 24 pages). Closing date: 30th Sept.

The Rooney Prize for Irish Literature

Details JA Sherwin, Strathin, Templecarrig, Delgany, Co Wicklow, Republic of Ireland
tel (01) 287 4769 *fax* (01) 287 2595
email rooneyprize@ireland.com

An annual prize of €10,000 is awarded to encourage young Irish writing talent. To be eligible, individuals must be Irish, published and under 40 years of age. The prize is non-competitive and there is no application procedure or entry form. Founded in 1976 by Daniel M Rooney, Pittsburgh, Pennsylvania.

Rubies in the Darkness Poetry Competition

41 Grantham Road, Manor Park, London E12 5LZ
Contact Peter Geoffrey Paul Thompson
Prizes Publication in magazine and appearance on published Honours List. Also book prizes

Judged annually by poet and editor Peter Geoffrey Paul Thompson.

Submission details Poems of any length on any theme. Entry fee, £3 per poem. Closing date, 1st November.

Runciman Award

The Anglo-Hellenic League, 16-18 Paddington Street, London W1U 5AS
tel 020-7486 9410
email info@anglohellenicleague.org
website www.anglohellenicleague.org
Contact The Administrator
Prizes Prize money of £9000 to be distributed at the discretion of the judges

Award in honour of the late Sir Steven Runciman for work wholly or mainly about some aspect of Greece or the world of Hellenism, published in English in any country of the world in its first edition.

Submission details Closing date, mid-January every year.

The David St John Thomas Charitable Trust Competitions & Awards

The David St John Thomas Charitable Trust, PO Box 6055, Nairn IV12 4YB
tel (01667) 453351 *fax* (01667) 452365
email dsjtcharitynairn@fsmail.net
website www.dsjtcharitabletrust.co.uk
Contact Lorna Edwardson

A programme of writing competitions, some run with others, such as *Writing Magazine*, including a ghost story (1600–1800 words, 1st prize £1000) and poetry (up to 32 lines, total prize money £1000). Publication of winning entries is guaranteed. The Self-Publishing Awards are open to anyone who has self-published a book during the preceding calendar year, with a total award of £1000. For full details of these and other awards, including an annual writers' groups anthology, send a large sae or see website.

Salisbury House Poets Poetry Competition

Salisbury House Poets, Salisbury House, Bury Street West, Enfield, Middlesex N9 9LA
website www.chela.co.uk/poetry.php
Contact The Competition Secretary
Prizes 1st prize, £500; 2nd prize, £250; 3rd prize, £100

For poems in English not over 50 lines.

Submission details Closing date, 1st November.

Scintilla Open Poetry Competition

Little Wentwood Farm, Llantrisant, Usk, Mon NP15 1ND
email anne.cluysenaar@virgin.net
Contact Anne Cluysenaar
Prizes Prizes in each category, £200, £100, £50

Competition in 2 sections; short poems and long poems/sequences.

Submission details Entry fee, £3 for first short poem, then £2 per short poem. Long poems/sequences, £5 for first poem, then £4.

Scottish Arts Council Book of the Year

Scottish Arts Council, 12 Manor Place,
Edinburgh EH3 7DD
tel 0131-226 6051
website www.scottisharts.org.uk
Prizes £10,000

The biggest prize for Scottish writing.

Second Light Network Poetry Competition

9 Greendale Close, London SE22 8TG
tel 020-8299 0088
email dyliswood@tiscali.co.uk
Contact Dylis Wood
Prizes 1st prize, £250; 2nd prize, £100; 3rd prize, £50

An annual competition. Second Light Network is a network of older woman poets.

Submission details For women aged 30 years or over. Entry fee, £3 for 1 poem: £7 for 3 poems: £12 for 8 poems.

Snapshot Press Haiku Competitions

website www.snapshotpress.co.uk
Prizes £200/US$300 and publication of collection as a perfect-bound book

Established in 1998 and now an annual event, alternating between haiku and tanka. It provides a rare and equal opportunity for authors to have a collection published in a professional manner, regardless of reputation and publishing history.

Submission details Haiku may be free-form or 5–7–5 and must be the original work of the individual entrant. Entry fee, £20/US$30 per manuscript.

Somerset Maugham Awards

84 Drayton Gardens, London SW10 9SB
tel 020-7373 6642 *fax* 020-7373 5768
email info@societyofauthors.org
website www.societyofauthors.org
Contact Awards Secretary

Granted for a full-length published work of poetry, fiction, criticism, biography, history, philosophy, travel or belles-lettres by a British author under 35. No dramatic works.

Submission details Entry by publisher only. Apply to the Society for full details and an entry form.

Southport Writers' International Poetry Competition

Poetry Competition, 32 Dover Road,
Southport, Merseyside PR8 4TB
tel (01704) 560923
Contact Mrs Hilary Tinsley
Prizes 1st prize, £200; 2nd prize, £100; 3rd prize, £50; £25 Humour prize; £25 Local prize

Open to all subjects and forms.
Submission details 40 lines maximum. Enclose sealed envelope marked with poem titles and containing an sae. Entry fee, £3 per poem. Closing date, 30th April, annually.

Southwark Poets of the Year

Languages and Humanities Dept.,
Morley Cottage, 61 Westminster Bridge Road,
London SE1 7HT
tel 020-7928 1836
website www.southbanklondon.com
Contact Edward Anderson

To enter you must live, work or study in the borough, and poems must be inspired by some aspect of life in Southwark: its people, places or history.
Submission details Poems should be no longer than 50 lines.

Speakeasy – Milton Keynes Writers' Group Open Creative Writing Competition

website www.mkweb.co.uk/speakeasy
Prizes Poetry 1st Prize £100; 2nd Prize £50; 3rd Prize £25.

For poetry and short stories. Poetry maximum of 60 lines.
Submission details No names and addresses, drawings, clip art, or any other marks that will make the entry stand out from the other entries will be allowed. Entries must be accompanied by a signed entry form and the required entry fee. Each entry must have the number of lines printed on the top left hand corner of the first sheet. Entry fee, £3 (£10 for 4 poems). No maximum entries. Closing date, 31st October. Entry forms and further details available from the Speakeasy website.

Spice Box Open Poetry Competition

Aramby Publishing, 1 Alanbrooke, Broadway,
Knaphill, Surrey GU21 2RU

email thespicebox@aol.com

An ongoing poetry competition.

Submission details Closing date, 1st June annually.

Strokestown Poetry Prize

Strokestown Poetry Festival Office,
Strokestown, County Roscommon, Ireland
tel (003537) 1963 3759
email pbushe@eircom.net
website www.strokestownpoetryprize.com
Director Paddy Bush
Prizes €4000 (approximay £2500 sterling),
€2000 and €1000; in addition there are up to 7
commended poets who will be invited to read
at the Strokestown Festival for a reading fee
and travelling expenses totalling €450

Prestigious annual competition for an
unpublished poem.

Submission details For an unpublished poem
in English not exceeding 70 lines. Entry fee, €5
(£4 sterling or $5) per poem.

Dylan Thomas Literary Prize

The Dylan Thomas Centre, Ty Llen,
Somerset Place, Swansea SA1 1RR
tel (01792) 474051/463980
website www.dylanthomasprize.com

An award of £60,000 is given to the winner of
this prize, which was established to encourage,
promote and reward exciting new writing in
the English-speaking world and to celebrate the
poetry and prose of Dylan Thomas. Entrants
should be the author of a published book (in
English), under the age of 30, writing within
one of the following categories: poetry, novel,
collection of short stories by one author, play
that has been professionally performed, a
broadcast radio play, a professionally produced
screenplay that has resulted in a feature-length
film. Authors need to be nominated by their
publishers, or producers in the case of
performance art. Closing date: May.

Times Stephen Spender Prize for Poetry Translation

3 Old Wish Road, Eastbourne,
East Sussex BN21 4JX
tel (01323) 452294

email info@stephenspender.org
website www.stephen-spender.org
Contact Robina Pelham Burn
Prizes Open Category: 1st prize, £500; 2nd
prize, £250; 3rd prize, £100. 18 and Under: 1st
prize, £250; 2nd prize, £100; 3rd prize, £50. 14
and under, £100

An annual competition awarded for the
translation into English of a poem in any
language, modern or classical.

Submission details Submit with a
commentary of no more than 300 words (see
website or phone the number above for details
and entry form). Maximum length of 60 lines.
£3 entry fee for Open Category and free entry
for 18 and under. For British residents only.

Torbay Poetry Competition

The Mount, Higher Furzeham, Brixham,
Devon TQ5 8QY
tel (01803) 851098
email pwoxley@aol.com
website www.acumen-poetry.co.uk
Contact Patricia and William Oxley

Annual competition.

Submission details For submission form, send
sae to above address. Entry fee, £3. Closing
date, 15th August.

John Tripp Award for Spoken Poetry

Academi, Mount Stuart House,
Mount Stuart Square, Cardiff CF10 5FQ
tel 029-2047 2266 *fax* 029-2049 2930
email post@academi.org
website www.academi.org
Contact Peter Finch, Chief Executive

A competition for any form of spoken poetry
in the English language. There are 5 regional
heats around Wales, with the winners from
each heat going forward to a Grand Final.
Performers have 5 minutes to read their work
at each stage of the competition and are judged
on the content of their poetry and their
performance skills. Anyone either born or
currently living in Wales is eligible to enter, and
all works must be unpublished. Founded 1990.

TS Eliot Prize

Fourth Floor, 2 Tavistock Place,
London WC1H 9RA

tel 020-7833 9247 *fax* 020-7833 5990
email info@poetrybooks.co.uk
website www.poetrybooks.co.uk
Director Chris Holifield

Awarded annually for the best single collection of poetry published during the calendar year. Prize money increased for 2007 prize to £15,000, making it the richest UK poetry prize with £1000 given to each of the shortlisted poets. Added a school shadowing scheme to run from 5th November to 10th December 2007; details at www.poetrybookshoponline.com.

Submission details Submissions by publisher only, by sending 4 copies of each eligible title to the Poetry Book Society. Closing date, early August.

Understanding Poetry Competitions

127 Milton Road West,
7 Duddingston House Courtyard,
Edinburgh EH15 1JG
tel 0131-661156
Contact Denise Smith
Prizes £150

An annual competition.

Submission details Guidelines available on request. Entry fee, £2 to £5 per poem, depending on competition.

Ver Poets Open Competition

181 Sandbridge Road, St Albans AL1 4AH
tel (01727) 762601
email gillknibbs@yahoo.co.uk
website www.verpoets.org.uk
Contact Gillian Knibbs
Prizes 1st prize, £500; 2nd prize, £300; 3rd prize, £100

Poems on any theme, up to 30 lines in length. Winning and selected poems are published in an anthology.

Submission details Send 2 copies of each poem on separate sheets of paper. There should be no identification on poems. Name and address should be typed on accompanying A4 sheet. No translations and only unpublished work.

Wendy Webb Poetry Competitions

email wwbuk@yahoo.co.uk
Contact Wendy Webb

Various poetry competitions for poems on different themes and styles. Email for details.

Wells Festival of Literature International Poetry Competition

The Competitions' Organiser,
Chegworth House, Moor Lane, Draycott,
Cheddar BS27 3TD
website www.somersite.co.uk/wellsfest.htm
Prizes 1st prize, £500; 2nd prize, £200; 3rd prize, £100; Wyvern prize, £100

Submission details For poems of up to 40 lines. Poets may submit up to 5 poems. Entry fee, £4. Closing date, 31st July.

Wigtown Poetry Competition

Wigtown Book Town Company,
Freepost NAT5359, Wigtown,
Newton Stewart DG8 9BR
tel (01988) 402036
website www.wigtown-booktown.co.uk/poetrycomp
Prizes £2000, £1000, £500; Gaelic Prize, £1000

Aims to be Scotland's biggest poetry competition.

The Raymond Williams Community Publishing Prizes

The Literature Dept, Arts Council England,
14 Great Peter Street, London SW1P 3NQ
tel 020-7973 5325
website www.artscouncil.org.uk

This award commends published works of outstanding creative and imaginative quality that reflect the life, voices and experiences of the people of particular communities. The winning entry will be awarded £3000 and the runner-up £2000.

Winchester Writers' Conference Competitions

Faculty of Arts, University of Winchester,
Winchester, Hants SO22 4NR
tel (01962) 827238
email barbara.large@winchester.ac.uk
website www.writersconference.co.uk
Contact Barbara Large

Fifteen writing competitions are attached to this major international Festival of Writing, which takes place at the end of June. Each entry is adjudicated and 64 sponsored prizes are presented at the Writers' Awards Dinner. Categories are the First Three Pages of the Novel, Short Stories, Shorter Short Stories, Writing for Children, A Page of Prose, Lifewriting, Slim Volume, Small Edition, Poetry, Retirement, Writing Can be Murder, Local History, and Young Writers' Poetry Competition. Deadline for entries, 7th June 2008.

The Writers Bureau Poetry Competition

The Writers Bureau, Sevendale House, 7 Dale Street, Manchester M1 1JB
email studentservices@writersbureau.com
website www.writersbureau.com/competition
Prizes 1st prize, £1000; 2nd prize, £400; 3rd prize, £200; 4th prize, £100; 6th prize, £50 x 6
    Submission details Poems must not exceed 40 lines and must be typed. Entry forms can be downloaded from the website; it is also possible to enter online.

Writers' Week Poetry Competition

24 The Square, Listowel, Co Kerry, Ireland
tel 068-21074 *fax* 068-22893
email info@writersweek.ie
website www.writersweek.ie
Contact Eilish Wren, Maire Logue
Prizes Various

In its 36th year; has grown to become one of Ireland's leading literary festivals. Holds 3 poetry competitions – contact as above for details and submission guidelines.

Yorkshire Open Poetry Competition

32 Spey Bank, Acomb Park, York YO24 2UZ
Prizes 1st prize, £500; 2nd prize, £250; 3rd prize, £50
    Submission details For poems up to 80 lines. For details, send sae. Entry fee, £4 per poem (£14 for 4 poems). Closing date, 31st July.

Signed, sealed, delivered: self-publishing is nothing to be ashamed of

Poets are increasingly publishing, marketing and distributing their own books. Diminishing opportunities from mainstream publishers, and developments in design and print technology, make this a very viable way to bring your work to the public eye. **Gordon Kerr** has done just that, and shares his experiences.

It arrived in the post, carefully packed in bubblewrap, exotic American stamps decorating the white package. I opened it with trembling hands, carefully snipping the end with scissors. Reaching inside I gripped the corners of a small hardback book, and pulled it out. There it was. I already knew what it looked like, because I had designed it, learning Quark Xpress for just that purpose. But I was stunned, all the same. A book of my very own poetry. All those years – almost 40, in fact – of writing, on those pages.

These days, of course, you can publish your poetry in many different ways, but it is quite a feeling seeing your work published for the first time in the old-fashioned way, between the covers of a book. I had never tried to make my poetry public. It was between me and the page in front of me, almost a guilty secret I carried round with me – and I had resigned myself to it staying that way. However, for some reason I cannot recall, I sent a poem to an artist friend of mine who liked it and asked if I had any more. When I said I had hundreds, he suggested that we collaborate. He would respond to each poem with a line drawing, and we could publish and produce a limited-edition run of books. In fact, he said, he knew just the printer – a man called Walt, in Arizona, who produces exquisite chapbooks. 'Walt?' I thought. 'Arizona!' I thought. Now, how is that going to work? It actually worked very well. I selected the poems and got them to my artist friend. He spent a few months working on them and back came a pile of 50 illustrations. I designed the book and sent a disk off to Walt. Walt and I then became email buddies and a couple of months later, there I was, standing in my hallway, clutching a book with tears rolling down my face!

There is nothing to be ashamed of in self-publishing. Very few of the many thousands of people who write poetry actually get published, and, in fact, the opportunities to get picked up by a mainstream (let alone a small) publisher are becoming fewer. Why not do it yourself? You can produce a small run of books and sell them to friends and family to cover costs, or you can just give them away, if you feel so inclined. You can sell them through your website or blog. There are lots of ways to get rid of that pile of books in the corner. Don't expect to get them into your local branch of whatever high street bookseller is in your town, though.

What makes it all so easy, of course, is the new technology available. There are wonderful packages on the market with which you can lay out your work in whatever way you wish. If you have always liked that font – Trebuchet MS – well you can have it, without arguing with some spotty designer at a publishing house who looks at you as if you have about as much visual sense as a plank of wood. Printers will even do it for you, if you feel that a course in Adobe InDesign is beyond you. That brings an added cost, of course.

So what does it involve? You have to consider the following:

Keying in the text, and proofing it

You will probably do this yourself. But make sure another pair of eyes looks through it for embarrassing typos and spelling errors.

Layout/design

Quark Xpress and InDesign are just two of a number of computer programmes that will enable you to lay out your book in whatever way you want.

Cover design

Be adventurous and make your book as attractive as possible, especially if you are going to try to sell it to complete strangers. That particularly fetching photo of you wearing a fedora might not be the best idea!

ISBN

This is the identifying number on the back of every book sold. You may choose not to put an ISBN on your book if it is being sold privately, but without an ISBN the book cannot appear on Amazon, for example. ISBNs in the UK are supplied by the ISBN Agency (**www.isbn.nielsenbookdata.co.uk**) and cost £94 for a block of ten (they are not available singly).

Print

There are many options. You will undoubtedly have many local printers in your area. Check previous work by them for quality, and shop around to get the best price. There are also print-on-demand printers who can handle small runs very cost-effectively. A search on the Internet will provide you with lots of options.

Marketing/publicity

The local press is usually very sympathetic towards local authors. Also, if you were brought up somewhere else, don't forget the local paper there – or the local library, which will often take a copy of a local author's privately produced book.

Warehousing and distribution

This may, of course, be a corner of the bedroom and delivery by hand. However, if you print 300 books, they will take up a fair amount of space. Make sure you have it! There are companies who can do all this for you, of course, at a price. The Internet will again provide you with lots of options.

Not vanity publishing ...

Self-publishing is not vanity publishing. You control the process from beginning to end, and are not handing over a wad of cash to an anonymous publisher to produce unsatisfactory product in an uncaring and often fraudulent way. If you do wish to go down the vanity publishing route, it is essential to be careful: there are many unscrupulous publishers out there. Check them out as throughly as you can. Ensure that they do, in fact, provide the services they promise – or your book may forever be tainted. For good advice about vanity publishing, see the websites listed below:

www.zyworld.com/alanjulia/Alan/vanitypublish.htm (names and shames some websites it is worth avoiding)

www.poetrykit.org (the ever-useful poetry site with good advice)

http://en.wikipedia.org/wiki/Vanity_publishing (helpful entry)

www.societyofauthors.net (good article about vanity publishing)
www.cultural-alliance.org/pubs/selfpublishing.htm (American; deals with the basics)
www.sff.net/people/VictoriaStrauss/poetbeware.html (helpful advice)
www.publishers.org.uk (the Publishers Association)
www.anotherealm.com/prededitors/pubwarn.htm (really useful tips on how to spot a scam)

And my little book? It was called *You Can't Get to East Kilbride from Here*, and I'm afraid you can't get it, because it sold out. However, if you go to the library in my home town of East Kilbride you will find a copy nestling on the shelves. It was worth it just for that, alone.

Gordon Kerr is a freelance editor, writer and poet.

Poetry festivals

Festivals provide a good opportunity to see successful poets in action, and to learn from them. Many festivals also run workshops and/or seminars, which can be very helpful in taking your work forward.

Aber Valley Arts Festival

Undercurrents – Aber Valley, 15 Graig y Fedw, Abertridwr, Caerffili CF83 4AQ
tel 029-2083 1668
email eryl893107392@aol.com
website www.academi.org
Takes place October

Aldeburgh Poetry Festival

The Poetry Trust, The Cut, 9 New Cut, Halesworth, Suffolk IP19 8BY
tel (01986) 835950
email info@thepoetrytrust.org
website www.thepoetrytrust.org
Director Naomi Jaffa
Takes place First weekend in November

An annual festival of contemporary poetry with readings, workshops, talks, discussions, open mic, poetry quiz, masterclass and children's event. Features leading international and UK poets, including the winner of the Derwood Aldeburgh First Collection Prize. Contact Helen Mitchell for further details.

Ashbourne Festival

Ashbourne Arts, PO Box 5552, Ashbourne DE6 2ZR
tel (01335) 348707
email info@ashbournearts.com
website www.ashbournearts.co.uk
Takes place June

17 days of literary events, including poetry.

Aspects: A Celebration of Irish Writing

North Down Borough Council, North Down Heritage Centre, Town Hall, The Castle, Bangor, County Down BT20 4BT
tel (02891) 278032
email GlynisWatt@Northdown.gov.uk
website www.northdown.gov.uk
Contact Glynis Watt
Takes place September

Brings a wealth of Irish talent, covering all tastes and age ranges. Has included many established and emerging writers,

Bay Lit

Academi, Mount Stuart House, Mount Stuart Square, Cardiff CF10 5FQ
tel 029-2047 2266 *fax* 029-2049 2930
email post@academi.org
website www.academi.org
Contact Peter Finch, Chief Executive
Takes place Spring

A bilingual (Welsh and English) literature festival, held in Cardiff Bay. It is organised by Academi, the Welsh National Literature Promotion Agency and Society for Writers, and features an array of writers from Wales and beyond.

Beverley Literature Festival

Wordquake, Council Offices, Skirlaugh, East Riding of Yorkshire HU11 5HN
tel (01482) 392706 *mobile* (07870) 584889
email john@bevlit.org
website www.beverley-literature-festival.org
Contact John W Clarke
Takes place October

A festival of readings and discussions (which, along with readings, continue throughout the year) on contemporary and historic poetry; seeks to magnify the pleasure and understanding of poetry.

Brighton Festival

12a Pavilion Buildings, Castle Square, Brighton BN1 1EE
tel (01273) 700747 *fax* (01273) 707505
email info@brightonfestival.org.uk
website www.brightonfestival.org.uk
Takes place 10th May to 1st June 2008

An annual arts festival with an extensive national and international programme featuring theatre, dance, music, opera, literature, outdoor and family events. Programme published end of February.

Cambridgewordfest

6 St Edwards Passage, Cambridge CB2 3PJ
tel (01223) 503333
email cam.wordfest@btinternet.com
website www.cambridgewordfest.co.uk
Festival Director Cathy Moore
Takes place April

An annual literature festival held in the spring
in Cambridge and surrounding area. It aims to
provide a richly packed weekend of some of the
best in contemporary fiction, political debate,
workshops and events for children. It is a
festival for writers as well as readers.

Camelford Poetry Festival

The Indian King Arts Centre, Camelford,
Cornwall PL32 9PG
tel (01840) 212161
email indianking@btconnect.com
Contact Helen Jagger Wood
Takes place April

Formerly the Jon Silkin Memorial Poetry
Festival, as a tribute to the support the poet
gave to the Indian King Arts Centre. Geared to
writers of poetry, with plenty of workshops as
well as open mic readings, informal discussion,
and performances.

Canterbury Festival

Festival Office, Christ Church Gate,
The Precincts, Canterbury, Kent CT1 2EE
tel (01227) 452853 *fax* (01227) 781830
email info@canterburyfestival.co.uk
website www.canterburyfestival.co.uk
Takes place October

An annual general arts festival with a literature
programme. Programme published in July.

The Times Cheltenham Literature Festival

109-111 Bath Road, Cheltenham,
Glos. GL53 7LS
tel (01242) 227979 (box office), 237377
(brochure), 775861 (festival office)
email clair.greenaway@cheltenhamfestivals.com
website www.cheltenhamfestivals.com
Artistic Director Sarah Smyth
Takes place October

This annual festival is the largest of its kind in
Europe. Events include talks and lectures,
poetry readings, novelists in conversation,
exhibitions, discussions, workshops and a large
bookshop. *Book It!* is a festival for children
within the main festival with an extensive
programme of events. Brochures are available
in August.

Chester Literature Festival

Viscount House, River Lane, Saltney,
Chester CH4 8RH
tel (01244) 674020 *fax* (01244) 684060
email info@chesterlitfest.org.uk
website www.chesterlitfest.org.uk
Festival Administrator Katherine Seddon
Takes place October

An annual festival commencing the first
weekend in October. Events featuring
international, national and local writers and
poets are part of the programme, as well as a
literary lunch and festival dinner. There is a
poetry competition for school children, events
for children and workshops for adults. A
Cheshire Prize for Literature is awarded each
year; only residents of Cheshire are eligible.

City of London Festival

12–14 Mason's Avenue, London EC2V 5BB
tel 020-7796 4949 *fax* 020-7796 4959
email admin@colf.org
website www.colf.org
Takes place Last week of June and first 2 weeks
of July 2008

An annual multi-arts festival with a
programme predominantly of music.
Programme published in April.

Cley Little Festival of Poetry

Cley, Sheringham, Norfolk NR26 8HU
tel (01263) 821012
Contact Helen Birtwell
Takes place October

Founded by Elsa Martin; organised by the Cley
Poetry Circle. Set up more than 50 years ago,
the group and festival provide a welcome
platform for poetry in North Norfolk.

The Cúirt International Festival of Literature

Galway Arts Centre, 47 Dominick Street,
Galway, Republic of Ireland

tel (091) 565886 *fax* (091) 568642
email info@galwayartscentre.ie
website www.galwayartscentre.ie
Progamme Director Maura Kennedy
Takes place 22nd to 27th April 2008

An annual week-long festival to celebrate writing, bringing together national and international writers to promote literary discussion. Events include readings, performances, workshops, seminars, lectures, poetry slams and talks. The festival is renowned for its convivial atmosphere ('cúirt' means a 'bardic court or gathering').

Cuisle, Limerick City International Poetry festival

The Belltable Arts Centre, 69 O'Connell Street, Limerick, County Limerick, Ireland
tel (00353) 6131 9866
email info@belltable.ie
website www.limerickcity.ie
Takes place October

An annual poetry festival that celebrates poets and poetry.

DLR Poetry Now Festival

The Arts Office,
Dun Laoghaire Rathdown County Council,
Dun Laoghaire, Co Dublin, Ireland
tel (00353) 01 2719532
email cbrown@dlrcoco.ie
website www.dlrpoetrynow.ie,
www.dircoco.ie/arts
Contact Carolyn Brown
Takes place 3rd to 6th April 2008

Ireland's leading poetry festival. DLR Poetry Now brings poetry from around the world to the Pavilion Theatre, Dun Laoghaire Co Dublin each year. The festival hosts some of the best contemporary Irish and international poets. Since its inception, the curation and direction of DLR Poetry Now has been consistently innovative and exciting – a fact which is central to its continuing success. DLR Poetry Now is a Dun Laoghaire Rathdown County Council initiative.

Dublin Writers' Festival

c/o Dublin City Council, Arts Office, The Lab, Foley Street, Dublin 1, Republic of Ireland

tel (01) 2227847 *fax* (01) 8178985
website www.dublinwritersfestival.com
Takes place June

An annual festival with readings by major Irish and international poets and writers to celebrate the best in contemporary literature.

Dulwich Festival

0208 299 1011
email enquiries@dulwichfestival.co.uk
website www.dulwichfestival.co.uk
Contact Alison Lloyd
Takes place May

A community arts festival that features literary talks and readings, poetry, historical/architectural walks, theatre, music, art and family entertainment.

Durham Literature Festival

c/o Durham City Arts Ltd, 2 The Cottages, Fowlers Yard, Durham DH1 3RA
tel 0191-375 0763
email enquiries@durhamcityarts.org.uk
Festival Coordinator John McGagh
Takes place October

Edinburgh International Book Festival

5ᴀ Charlotte Square, Edinburgh EH2 4DR
tel 0131-718 5666 *fax* 0131-226 5335
email admin@edbookfest.co.uk
website www.edbookfest.co.uk
Director Catherine Lockerbie
Takes place August

Now established as Europe's largest book event for the public. In addition to a unique independent bookselling operation, more than 650 writers contribute to the programme of events. Programme details available in June.

Essex Poetry Festival

Cramphorn Theatre, Fairfield Road, Chelmsford, Essex CM1 1JG
email derek@essex-poetry-festival.co.uk
website www.essex-poetry-festival.co.uk
Contact Derek Adams
Takes place October

A lively and varied series of poetry events and workshops.

Farrago festival of the Spoken Word

Farrago Poetry, 108 High Street, West Wickham, Kent BR4 0ND

tel (07905) 078375
email farragopoetry@yahoo.co.uk
website http://London.e-poets.net/
Contact John O'Neill
Takes place May

A festival aimed at children and young people. A selection of poets perform their own work. There are also poetry workshops.

Folkestone Literary Festival
Church Street Studios, 11 Church Street, Folkestone, Kent CT20 1SE
tel (01303) 211300 *fax* (01303) 211883
email info@folkestonelitfest.com
website www.folkestonelitfest.co.uk
Takes place 2–10 Nov 2007

An annual festival with over 40 events, including a Children's Day.

The Guardian Hay Festival
Festival Office, The Drill Hall, 25 Lion Street, Hay-on-Wye HR3 5AD
tel (0870) 7872848 (admin)
website www.hayfestival.com
Takes place May/June

This annual festival aims to celebrate the best in writing and performance from around the world, to commission new work, and to promote and encourage young writers of excellence and potential. More than 400 events over 10 days, with leading guest writers. Programme published April.

Guildford Book Festival
c/o Tourist Information Office, 14 Tunsgate, Guildford GU1 3QT
tel (01483) 444334
email deputy@guildfordbookfestival.co.uk
website www.guildfordbookfestival.co.uk
Festival Director Glenis Pycraft
Takes place Last 2 weeks in October

An annual festival. Diverse, provocative and entertaining, held throughout the historic town. Author events, poetry, workshops for all age groups from 6 months onwards. Its aim is to further an interest and love of literature by involvement and entertainment. Founded 1990.

Hackney Word Festival
London Borough of Hackney, Hackney Town Hall, Mare Street, London E8 1EA

tel 020-7249 6572
email literature@centerprisetrust.org.uk
website http://www.hackney.gov.uk/discoverhackney
Takes place September

Brings acclaimed talents to venues and stages throughout Hackney. Also gives new talent a chance to shine, and to learn directly from the stars of the festival. Poetry workshops for all ages plus a poetry competition.

Huddersfield Literature Festival
University of Huddersfield, Queensgate, Huddersfield HD1 3DH
tel (08709) 905025
email enquiry@litfest.org.uk
website www.litfest.org.uk
Takes place March

Organised through the English Division at the University of Huddersfield ,and funded by the University of Huddersfield and Arts Council England, Yorkshire. Works closely with local organisations including The Media Centre, Kirklees Metropolitan Council, Huddersfield Art Gallery, Huddersfield Library and The Poetry Business.

The Humber Mouth
City Arts Unit, Central Library, Kingston upon Hull HU1 3TF
tel (01482) 616961
email Maggie.Hannan@hullcc.gov.uk
Contact Maggie Hannan
Takes place June

Hull's biggest festival, attracting major writers and artists to the city over a 16-day period.

King's Lynn Poetry Festival
19 Tuesday Market Place, Kings Lynn, Norfolk PE30 1JW
tel (01553) 691661
email tony.ellis@hawkins-solicitors.com
website www.lynnlitfests.com
Contact Tony Ellis
Takes place 26th to 28th September 2008

A 23-year-old festival featuring writers and poets from all over the world. There are 6 sessions, from Friday afternoon until Sunday at 5pm. The sessions consist of writers and poets reading from their works and holding discussions on a variety of associated subjects.

Lancaster Litfest

Litfest, PO Box 751, Lancaster LA1 9AJ
tel (01524) 62166
email all@litfest.org
website www.litfest.org
Contact Jonathan Bean

Annual literature festival in mid-November,
featuring contemporary poetry and prose. See
the website for details.

Latitude Festival

website www.latitudefestival.co.uk
Takes place July

Three-day performing arts festival in
Southwold, Suffolk.

Laugharne Arts Festival

c/o Corran Bookshop, King Street, Laugharne,
Carmarthenshire SA33 4RY
tel (01994) 427444
email janetremlett@btconnect.com
Contact Jane Tremlett
Takes place August

Events throughout the year, with main festival
in August. A programme that brings together
the local and the international in the unique
setting that was home and inspiration to Dylan
Thomas. A blend of poetry, art, drama, music,
film, literature, creative workshops, talk and
fun.

Ledbury Poetry Festival

tel 0845-458 1743
website www.poetry-festival.com
Takes place July 2008

Art, music and poetry.

Lewes Live Literature

PO Box 2766, Lewes, East Sussex BN7 2WF
tel (01273) 400560
email info@leweslivelit.co.uk
website www.lewesliveliterature.co.uk
Takes place October/November

Lewes Live Literature aims to create enjoyable,
interesting events in a sociable, artistic
environment. Working across traditional
artform boundaries, LLL festivals bring
together the spoken word, performance,
creative writing workshops, music, film and
visual art. The LLL year revolves around 2

main programmes of work: a variable spring
season covering activities from April to June
(including events as part of the Brighton
Festival), and the intensive 3-day Lewes Live
Literature Festival, which takes place at the end
of October/beginning of November.

Lichfield Festival

tel (01543) 412121
website www.lichfieldfestival.org
Takes place July

Annual celebration of literature, drama and art.

Lincoln Book Festival

c/o City of Lincoln Council, DDES, City Hall,
Beaumont Fee, Lincoln, Lincolnshire LN1 1DF
tel (01522) 873844
email arts@lincoln.gov.uk
website www.lincolnbookfestival.co.uk
Contact Sara Bullimore
Takes place May

A celebration of books and all that they inspire.
The programme includes poetry competitions
and events.

Lincolnshire Literature Development Programme

Community Services,
Lincolnshire County Council, County Offices,
Lincoln LN1 1YL
tel (01522) 553235 *fax* (01522) 552811
email chris.kirkwood@lincolnshire.gov.uk
Arts Officer Chris Kirkwood
Takes place Throughout the year

A series of varied literary events. Annual
festivals, tours, publications in Lincolnshire.

Lit.Com

King Edward Street, Grimsby,
North East Lincolnshire DN31 3LU
tel (01472) 323382
email charlotte.bowen@nelincs.gov.uk
website www.nelincs.gov.uk/leisure/arts
Contact Charlotte Bowen
Takes place October

A celebration of both literature and comedy,
including book and poetry readings, writing
workshops, open mic and the best in up-and-
coming stand up.

Litfest

26 Sun Street, Lancaster LA1 1EW
tel (01524) 62166

email all@litfest.org
website www.litfest.org
Takes place November

One of the country's oldest literature festivals, held in Lancaster.

Live Poetry at The Cut
The Cut Arts Centre, 9 New Cut, Halesworth, Suffolk IP19 8BY
tel (01986) 835950
website http://www.thepoetrytrust.org/html/cut_poetry.htm
Contact Charlotte Du Cann
Takes place July

Small poetry festival.

Liverpool Poetry in the City Festival
website www.poetryinthecity.co.uk
Takes place March

A festival that aims to celebrate the variety of poetic voices in the city, and to create opportunities for involvement in poetry.

Lowdham Book Festival
c/o The Bookcase, 50 Main Street, Lowdham NG14 7BE
email info@fiveleaves.co.uk
website www.lowdhambookfestival.co.uk
Contact Janet Streeter, Ross Bradshaw
Takes place June

An annual 10-day festival of literature events for adults and children, with a daily programme of high-profile national writers. The last day always features dozens of free events and a large book fair.

Ludlow Festival
Ludlow Festival Box Office, Castle Square, Ludlow, Shropshire SY8 1AY
email admin@ludlowfestival.co.uk
website www.ludlowfestival.co.uk
Takes place June/July

Manchester Literature Festival
Third Floor, 24 Lever Street, Manchester M1 1DZ
tel 0161-236 5725
email admin@
manchesterliteraturefestival.co.uk
website www.manchesterliteraturefestival.co.uk
Takes place September/October

The successor to the Manchester Poetry Festival, presenting quality live literature in an annual festival.

Mere Literary Festival
Lawrence's, Old Hollow, Mere, Warminster, Wiltshire BA1Z 6EG
tel (01747) 860475
email howellatmere@aol.com
website http://hometown.aol.co.uk/merewitts/MLFHome.html
Contact Adrienne Howell
Takes place October

Middlesex University Literary Festival
Middlesex University, Bramley Road, London N14 6YZ
tel 020-8411 5000
Contact Sarah Wardle
Takes place March

Cross-genre university literary festival, open free to the wider community, organised by third-year undergraduate writing students, under the supervision of a member of staff.

National Eisteddfod of Wales
40 Parc Ty Glas, Llanisien, Cardiff CF14 5DU
tel 029-2076 3777 *fax* 029-2076 3737
email elfed@eisteddfod.org.uk
website www.eisteddfod.org.uk
Chief Executive Elfed Roberts
Takes place August

Wales's largest cultural festival, based on 800 years of tradition. Activities include competitions in all aspects of the arts, fringe performances and majestic ceremonies. In addition to activities held in the main pavilion, it houses over 300 trade stands along with a literary pavilion, a music studio, a movement and dance theatre, outdoor performance stages and a purpose-built theatre. The event is set in a different location each year, and will take place on the outskirts of Mold in 2007 and in Cardiff in 2008.

Off the Shelf Literature Festival
Central Library, Surrey Street, Sheffield S1 1XZ
tel 0114-273 4400 *fax* 0114-273 4716
email offtheshelf@sheffield.gov.uk
website www.offtheshelf.org.uk

Contact Maria de Souza, Su Walker, Lesley Webster
Takes place October/November

The festival comprises a wide range of events for adults and children, including author visits, writing workshops, storytelling, competitions and exhibitions. Programme available in September.

Oundle Festival of Literature
2 New Road, Oundle, Peterborough, Northants PE8 4LA
tel (01832) 273050
email liz@oundlelitfest.org.uk
website www.oundlelitfest.org.uk
Contact Liz Dillarstone (Publicity)
Takes place March

Featuring a full programme of author events, poetry, philosophy, politics, story-telling, biography, illustrators and novelists for young and old. Includes events for children.

Poetry-next-the-Sea
Rowans, Warham Road, Wells-next-the-Sea, Norfolk NR23 1NE
tel (01328) 710193
email enquiries@poetrynextthesea.com
website www.poetrynextthesea.com
Contact Helen Flanagan
Takes place April

An annual festival attracting poets of international standing to perform their work in the beautiful North Norfolk countryside.

Poetry International
Literature Section, Royal Festival Hall, Southbank Centre, London SE1 8XX
tel (0871) 663 2501 *fax* (0871) 663 2500
website www.southbankcentre.co.uk
Contact Martin Colthorpe *tel* 020-7921 0904
Takes place October 2008 (biennial)

The biggest poetry festival in the British Isles, bringing together a wide range of poets from around the world. Includes readings, workshops and discussions. The Literature + Talks also runs a year-round programme of readings, talks and debates.

Poet's Letter London Poetry Books Festival
mobile (07931) 357109
email Editor@poetsletter.com
website www.poetsletter.com

Takes place May

Celebrating the craft of poetry, poetry publications of each and every sort, and poetry books.

Port Eliot Literary Festival
Port Eliot Estate Office, St Germans, Cornwall PL1Z 5ND
tel (01503) 232783
website www.porteliotlitfest.com
Contact Shelley Worthy Eveleigh
Takes place July

ProudWords Festival
mobile (07973) 894912
email pwcwf@hotmail.com
website www.proudwords.org.uk

Promotes all kinds of writing by lesbian, gay and bisexual writers. The organisation was established in 1997 and runs an annual writing festival in Newcastle and Gateshead featuring poets, playwrights, novelists, singer-songwriters and performers.

R: Runnymede International Literary Festival
tel (01784) 477304
email info@rfest.co.uk
website www.rfest.co.uk
Takes place March

Redbridge Book and Media Festival
London Borough of Redbridge, Arts & Events Team, 3rd Floor, Central Library, Clements Road, Ilford IG1 1EA
tel 020-8708 2857
website www.redbridge.gov.uk
Contact Arts & Events Team
Takes place May

Features author talks, performances, panel debates, Urdu poetry events, an exhibition, workshops, children's activities and events, and a schools outreach programme.

Richmond Book Now Literature Festival
The Arts Service, Orleans House Gallery, Riverside, Twickenham TW1 3DJ
tel 020-8831 6000 *fax* 020-8744 0501

email artsinfo@richmond.gov.uk
website www.richmond.gov.uk/literature
Takes place November

Scottish Book Town Festival

County Buildings, Wigtown,
Dumfries & Galloway DG8 9JH
tel (01988) 403222
email mail@wigtownbookfestival.com
website www.wigtownbookfestival.com
Festival Chair Michael McCreath
Takes place 28th September to 5th October
2008

An annual festival in Scotland's national Book
Town, which boasts 23 bookshops and book-
related businesses. Readings and talks take
place in the County Buildings, festival
marquee, bookshops and nearby Bladnoch
Distillery.

Snape

The Poetry Trust, The Cut, 9 New Cut,
Halesworth, Suffolk IP9 8BY
tel (01986) 835950
email info@thepoetrytrust.org
website www.aldeburghpoetryfestival.org/html/
the_trust1.htm
Takes place August

Annual poetry prom at Snape Maltings
Concert Hall.

Southwell Poetry Festival

Nottinghamshire County Council 4th Floor,
Arts Nottingham NG2 7QP
tel 0115-977 4435
email http://www.southwellpoetryfestival.co.uk
Literature Officer Ross Bradshaw
Takes place March

Poetry events based at the historic Southwell
Minster.

Spit-Lit; the Spitalfields Literary Festival

c/o Alternative Arts, Top Studio,
Montefiore Centre, Hanbury Street,
London E1 5HZ
tel 020-7375 0441
email info@alternativearts.co.uk
website www.alternativearts.co.uk
Frequency/price Annual (March)

Celebrates women's writing.

Split the Lark Poetry Festival

1 King Edward Road, Deal, Kent CT14 6QL
tel (01304) 367625
Contact Liz Turner
Takes place June

Festival organised by the Split the Lark Poets in
Deal, Kent.

StAnza: Scotland's Poetry Festival

The Byre Theatre, St Andrews, Fife KT16 9LA
email info@stanzapoetry.org
website www.stanzapoetry.org
Contact Brian Johnstone, Festival Director
Takes place 12th to 16th March 2008

The only regular festival dedicated to poetry in
Scotland, StAnza is international in outlook.
Held in the ancient university town of St
Andrews, the festival presents world-class poets
and writers performing in exciting,
atmospheric venues. "For Scotland's finest
poetry festival, bouquets and bucketfuls of
deserved applause." *The Scotsman*

Stoke Newington Festival

tel 020-8356 6410
email info@stokenewingtonfestival.co.uk
website www.stokenewingtonfestival.co.uk
Contact Fiona Fieber
Takes place June

A 10-day multi-arts programme, including
'WordontheStreet', which focuses on literature,
spoken work, performance, texts and readers.

Stop All The Clocks at The Marlborough

The Marlborough, Prince's Street, Brighton,
East Sussex
tel (01273) 207562
email simon@stopalltheclocks.co.uk
website www.stopalltheclocks.co.uk
Contact Simon Clayton
Takes place May

The highlight of Brighton's poetry year,
including more traditional readings,
performance events and 'fringe of the fringe'
nights like 'All Mouth No Trousers' – a
combined poetry/striptease performance.

Stratford-upon-Avon Poetry Festival

Shakespeare Centre, Henley Street,
Stratford-upon-Avon CV37 6QW

tel (01789) 204016 *fax* (01789) 296083
email info@shakespeare.org.uk
website www.shakespeare.org.uk
Takes place July–August

Now in its 55th year, this festival features weekly recitals given by established poets and by actors who present themed evenings of verse. Full details available on the website from late May. Sponsored by the Shakespeare Birthplace Trust.

The Sunday Times Oxford Literary Festival

301 Woodstock Road, Oxford OX2 7NY
tel (01865) 514149 *fax* (01865) 514804
email oxford.literary.festival@ntlworld.com
website www.sundaytimes-oxfordliteraryfestival.co.uk
Festival Directors Angela Prysor-Jones, Sally Dunsmore
Takes place March/April

An annual 6-day festival for both adults and children. Presents topical debates, fiction and non-fiction discussion panels, and adult and children's authors who have recently published books. Topics range from contemporary fiction to discussions on politics, history, science, gardening, food, poetry, philosophy, art and crime fiction. An additional 2 days of events for schools.

Swindon Festival of Literature

Lower Shaw Farm, Shaw, Swindon, Wiltsshire SN5 5PJ
tel (01793) 771080 *fax* (01793) 771080
email swindonlitfest@lowershawfarm.co.uk
website www.swindonfestivalofliterature.co.uk
Festival Director Matt Holland
Takes place Starts at dawn on 7 May for 14 days

An annual celebration of literature – prose, poetry, drama and storytelling – by readings, discussions, performances, talks, etc, indoors and out.

Tears in the Fence Festival

38 Hod View, Stourpaine, Blandford Forum, Dorset DT11 8TN
tel (01258) 456803
email david@davidcaddy.wanadoo.co.uk
website www.wanderingdog.co.uk

Contact David Caddy
Takes place July

A themed international poetry festival that includes readings, talks, writing workshops, art exhibits, music, children's workshops and events, bookstalls and signings.

Text Festival

Exeter Phoenix, Bradninch Place, Gandy Street, Exeter EX4 3LS
tel (01392) 667080
email director@exeterphoenix.org.uk
website www.textfestival.org
Takes place April/May

Exeter-based writing festival.

The Brighton Fringe Literature Festival

12A Pavilion Buildings, Castle Square, Brighton, East Sussex BN1 1EE
tel (01273) 260804 *fax* (01273) 722996
email info@brightonfestivalfringe.org.uk
website www.brightonfestivalfringe.org.uk
Takes place May

An alternative programme to the Brighton Festival.

Dylan Thomas Festival

Dylan Thomas Centre, Somerset Place, Maritime Quarter, Swansea SA1 1RR
tel (01792) 463980
email dylanthomas.lit@swansea.gov.uk
website www.dylanthomas.com
Contact David Woolley
Takes place October/November

Annual festival of contemporary writing and art.

Torbay Weekend Festival of Poetry

The Mount, Higher Furzeham Road, Brixham, Devon TQ5 8QY
tel (01803) 851098
Contact Patricia Oxley
Takes place October

Audience participation is actively encouraged, with 8 events having space for the audience to join in.

Tŷ Newydd Festival

Tŷ Newydd, Llanystumdwy, Gwynedd LL52 0LW

tel (01766) 522811
email post@tynewydd.org
website www.tynewydd.org
Contact Sally Baker, Executive Director
Takes place 2009

Events are centred on the writing centre at Llanystumdwy in Gwynedd, and feature a mix of Welsh and English events including Poetry Stomps and guest readers. The Academi, the Welsh National Literature Promotion Agency, supports Ty Newydd to create this festival.

Warwick International Festival

Pageant House, 2 Jury Street,
Warwick CV34 4EW
tel (01926) 410018
email director@warwickmusiclive.org.uk
Festival Director Esther Blaine
Takes place 21st June to 6th July 2008

A multi-arts festival which includes some literature and poetry events: readings, performances and workshops.

Wells Festival of Literature

25 Chamberlain Street, Wells,
Somerset BA5 2PQ
tel (01749) 670929
website www.somersite.co.uk/wellsfest.htm
Takes place Mid-October

An annual week-long festival featuring leading writers and poets. It includes theatre and cinema events, writing workshops and short story and poetry competitions. Events take place in the historic Bishop's Palace and other venues around the historic city of Wells.

Wonderful Words Book Festival

Penzance Library, Morrab Road,
Penzance TR18 4EY
tel (01736) 350206
email agunderson@cornwall.gov.uk
website www.cornwall.gov.uk/library
Library Outreach Officer & Festival Organiser
Alison Gunderson
Takes place Sept/Oct

A biennial festival organised by the Cornwall Library Service. Events take place throughout the county, including talks, discussions, workshops, poetry and storytelling. The festival attracts high-profile authors.

Word – University of Aberdeen Writers Festival

University of Aberdeen,
Office of External Affairs,
University of Aberdeen, King's College,
Aberdeen AB24 3FX
tel (01224) 273874 *fax* (01224) 272086
website www.abdn.ac.uk/word
Artistic Director Alan Spence, *Festival Producer* Fiona Christie, *Festival Co-ordinator* Jill Burnett
Takes place May

Over 70 of the world's finest writers and artists take part in a packed weekend of readings, music, art exhibitions and film screenings. The festival hosts some of the UK's best-loved children's writers and some of the richest talents in Gaelic literature.

Word About Town

The Foresters Arms, 2 Shepherd Street,
St Leonards-on-Sea, East Sussex TN38 0ET
tel (01424) 436513
email info@dontfeedthepoets.co.uk
website www.dontfeedthepoets.co.uk
Contact John Knowles
Takes place November

Live literature, poetry, music, comedy, film, workshops and competitions.

Wordfringe

email info@wordfringe.co.uk
Director Haworth Hodgkinson
Takes place May

A new community-based festival showcasing writers and writing in the North East of Scotland. The festival takes place both before and after the weekend of Word 06, the University of Aberdeen Writers' Festival. The 2 festivals complement each other, with Word bringing some highly respected writers to Aberdeen, and Wordfringe providing opportunities for many more new writers to appear alongside some more established names. Events range from poetry readings and storytelling sessions to events combining the spoken word with music, dance and video. Many of the writers taking part live and work in the North East of Scotland, but visiting guests from Shetland, Lewis, Northumberland and Devon also feature.

Wordsworth Trust Poetry Season

The Wordsworth Trust, Dove Cottage,
Grasmere, Cumbria LA22 9SH
tel (01539) 435544
email events@wordsworth.org.uk
website www.wordsworth.org.uk
Contact Julie Nattrass
Takes place May-October

A programme of readings by major poets.

World Book Day

c/o The Booksellers Association,
272 Vauxhall Bridge Road, London SW1V 1BA
tel 020-8987 9370
email cathy.schofield@blueyonder.co.uk
website www.worldbookday.com
Contact Cathy Schofield
Takes place 6th March 2008

An annual celebration of books and reading
aimed at promoting their value and creating
the readers of the future. Every schoolchild in
full-time education receives a £1 book token.
Events take place all over the UK in schools,
bookshops, libraries and arts centres. World
Book Day was designated by UNESCO as a
worldwide celebration of books and reading,
and is marked in over 30 countries. It is a
partnership of publishers, booksellers and
interested parties who work together to
promote books and reading for the personal
enrichment and enjoyment of all.

Writers' Week

24 The Square, Listowel, Co. Kerry,
Republic of Ireland
tel (068) 21074 *fax* (068) 22893
email info@writersweek.ie
website www.writersweek.ie
Administrators Eilish Wren, Máire Logue
Takes place 31st May to 4th June 2008

Aims to promote the work of Irish writers in
both the English and Irish language, and to
provide a platform for new and established
writers to discuss their works. Events include
readings, seminars, lectures and book launches.

Writing On the Wall

60 Duke Street, Liverpool L1 5AA
tel 0151-707 4313
email info@writingonthewall.org.uk
website www.writingonthewall.org.uk
Contact Janette Stowell
Takes place May

An annual programme of events culminating in
an annual festival, which – with schools, young
people, local communities and broader
audiences – celebrates writing, diversity,
tolerance, storytelling and humour through
controversy, inquiry and debate.

Supporting your work
The Poetry Book Society

The Poetry Book Society (PBS) is both book club and poetry promotion agency, doing fine work –
in these days of invisibility for poetry titles in bookshops – in getting poetry to its readership.
Chris Holifield explains the work of the Society.

When TS Eliot and friends set up the Poetry Book Society in 1953, its remit was to support
and develop the sales of poetry books. To this day the organisation, now regularly funded
by the Arts Council, is focused on maximising poetry book sales, although it has also taken
on the task of promoting the reading of poetry. The PBS functions as a book club for
poetry lovers, and the *Bulletin* magazine provides its members with an overview of the best
newly published poetry.

Four times a year the PBS requests submissions from poetry publishers, in accordance
with the eligibility criteria for the Choice. Books are submitted by publishers, and the PBS's
Poet Selectors choose the best new single-author poetry collection of the quarter. This title
is then ordered from the publisher (with the words 'Poetry Book Society Choice' proudly
emblazoned on the cover) and sent to all full PBS members.

The Selectors also make four Recommendations, and choose a Special Commendation,
which need not be a single-author collection and is sometimes a non-fiction book. The
Bulletin, which is sent to the members quarterly with their books, is in effect a review of
the best new poetry, with comment from the Selectors and from the poets themselves. It
also features the Translation Choice, chosen by the Translation Selector. The fairly newly
established Pamphlet Choice, which has proved a successful way of bringing interesting
new work to a wider audience, is chosen by two Pamphlet Selectors. This is the only
category for which self-published work is eligible. Other new books are featured in the
Bulletin, which also lists every poetry book submitted by publishers for that quarter.

During 2007 the Bulletin has received a fresh new design; a new web version of the
magazine enables members to order their books online from anywhere in the world.

Poetry Book Society members are knowledgeable and enthusiastic about poetry; they
are extremely loyal; and many of them have been with the PBS for years. As well as full
membership, the PBS offers Associate membership: Associates receive only the *Bulletin*
each quarter, but can still buy books at the members' discount of 25 per cent. Then there
is the Charter membership for libraries: Charter members receive the Choice and all the
Recommendations – i.e. five books a quarter. Finally, there is the Education membership,
which is designed for secondary school teachers and includes teaching tips on poems from
the books chosen. The PBS also has special expertise in finding poetry titles from smaller
presses and can often track down a hard-to-find title.

The PBS website is at **www.poetrybooks.co.uk**; here members get their 25 per cent
discount on all the poetry books in print in the UK.

The PBS also runs the Children's Poetry Bookshelf, offering poetry written for children
in the 7-11 year-old age group. The CPB has a lively child-friendly website at
www.childrenspoetrybookshelf.co.uk, providing quizzes and poetry puzzles for children,

as well as the chance for children to send their own poems and reviews to go on the site. The adult part of the site recruits new members, including teachers, parents and grandparents, and libraries. Members receive books every term and teaching tips are freely available to all members. The new gift membership allows the member to send the books straight to the child they nominate, making it possible for any poetry lover to give the gift of poetry to a child throughout the year. Members can buy all the children's poetry titles available in the UK through the website at a discount of 25 per cent, with a further discount for class sets.

In 2006 the CPB ran its first national children's poetry competition for 7-11year-olds from its website over National Poetry Day. This was repeated in 2007 with the new Children's Laureate, Michael Rosen, as chair of the judges.

In 2004 the PBS launched **www.poetrybookshoponline.com**, a niche online bookselling site which offers all the poetry titles in print in the UK. This new website was launched in response to the difficulty many readers have experienced with locating a good selection of poetry in bookshops. We intend to develop the website into a poetry portal, with reviews, news and events – a wide range of information of interest to poetry readers – as well as a strong emphasis on books.

Every January, the PBS awards the annual T S Eliot Prize for the best new single-author poetry collection published in the previous year. Titles are entered by the publishers, and there is keen interest in the winner. The Prize is sponsored by the broadcaster Five, and Mrs Valerie Eliot provides the winner's cheque for £10,000. In 2007 the Prize money was increased to £15,000, making it the richest UK poetry prize, and the ten shortlisted poets each received £1000. The evening before the award ceremony the shortlisted poets are invited to take part in the annual T S Eliot Readings in London, which is an electrifying evening of superb poetry.

In 2006 the PBS, working in association with the English and Media Centre, launched the first T S Eliot Prize School Shadowing Scheme, the first of its kind for a major poetry prize. This enables teachers to download poems from the ten shortlisted poets from the website, so that their students can study the best new poetry whilst shadowing the judges.

For more information, contact:
The Poetry Book Society
Fourth Floor, 2 Tavistock Place,
London WC1H 9RA
tel 020-7833 9247
email info@poetrybooks.co.uk
website www.poetrybooks.co.uk

In 2004 the PBS also ran the Next Generation Poets promotion. The judging panel, chaired by the Poet Laureate Andrew Motion, chose, from amongst the poets whose first collections were published in the previous decade, the 20 poets who in their opinion were the most exhilarating new voices.

In 2005 the Poetry Bookshop Online took on the exclusive sales of the CDs from the Poetry Archive **www.poetryarchive.org**, featuring 60-minute recordings from 90 poets. The Archive is dedicated to making recordings of living poets, so that their voices will not be lost to posterity. Its superb new digital recordings enable everyone to enjoy the luxury of listening to their favourite poets.

There is great concern in the poetry world about the poor sales of poetry books. In the current retail climate many bookshops struggle to maintain a reasonable stockholding of poetry titles, and all too often there is only a small selection of poetry available. Faced with this problem, the Poetry Book Society's mission to serve readers and support poets by maximising the sales of poetry books becomes even more important. The Society is also unique in a global context, as is the Children's Poetry Bookshelf, as they are the only poetry book clubs in existence. With this in mind, future plans will involve growing the PBS membership internationally, promoting the T S Eliot Prize and selling as many poetry books as possible both in the UK and all over the world.

Chris Holifield is the Director of the Poetry Book Society.

The Poetry Society

The Poetry Society was founded in London almost a hundred years ago, as a small membership organisation to promote "a more general recognition and appreciation of poetry". Since then it has grown into one of Britain's most high-profile arts organisations, representing British poetry both nationally and internationally. Today, it has more than 3000 members around the world. If you read, write or enjoy poetry, the Poetry Society can help open up the world of contemporary poetry for you.

Membership benefits include a subscription to *Poetry Review* magazine, a free information directory, a discount on entry to the National Poetry Competition, 'partner' discounts at bookshops and events around the UK, and *Poetry News* – a members' newsletter that explores the contemporary landscape of poetry. Membership is open to all, with special categories of membership for libraries, schools and young poets.

Poetry Review

The place in which to get published, and the place to find out about the best in contemporary poetry, *Poetry Review* has been a part of the Poetry Society's membership benefits since 1912. Ripped eagerly from the envelope each quarter by readers and writers of good poetry, *Poetry Review* puts you at the heart of what's happening, with a diverse selection of poems by contemporary writers – from the famous and established to promising newcomers; from the formally traditional to the modernist and avant-garde. It's a literary magazine with authority and vision, and a forum for intelligent reviews. One feature of the magazine is the annual Geoffrey Dearmer Prize, which was established to enable *Poetry Review* to award £400 to the 'new poet of the year'. This goes to the best poem published in the *Review* by a poet who has not yet published a book.

Poetry News

Poetry News is the Poetry Society's quarterly newsletter. Members are invited to send in poems on a particular theme each quarter, and six of the best are included on a regular dedicated members' page as well as on the Poetry Society's website. There is also a 'close-up' on the nuts and bolts of poetic craft; a Q&A on the route to a first collection; interviews with rising stars; profiles of poetry publishers and magazines; features on poetry overseas; news of prize-winners; and details of current activities at the Poetry Society. Each year the Hamish Canham Poetry Prize awards £300 for the best member's poem to appear in *Poetry News* during the year.

Poetry Directory

When you join the Poetry Society, you'll receive the indispensable *Poetry Directory* absolutely free of charge. This is packed with information on everything from copyright law to courses, reference books to residential workshops. In it you'll find the answers to many of the questions an interest in poetry raises.

The website

For poetry events and activities around the country, visit the Poetry Society website at **www.poetrysociety.org.uk**. Have the poetry world at your fingertips; look up specific poetry locations (more than 500 and growing) on 'Poetry Landmarks of Great Britain'; explore how to celebrate National Poetry Day; keep in touch with what's been happening with poetry in the news; find out who UK publishers are publishing in 'Forthcoming Publications'; discover an ever-changing range of lively poetry links; enter the National Poetry Competition; and of course, keep up to date with everything the Poetry Society is doing. The members' page on the website provides a guide to Poetry Society Stanzas, listings of members' books, discounts for Poetry Society members at bookshops, and special offers on tickets to poetry events nationwide.

Stanzas

In these days of virtual communication, the local poetry group still thrives. Years ago we had the nationwide Poetry Secretariat; today we have the nationwide (potentially world-wide) Poetry Society Stanzas. We're committed to developing local links between Poetry Society members on a voluntary basis, whereby the members constitute themselves a Poetry Society 'Stanza' so that they can exchange information, meet, and contribute to the local poetry scene more effectively. Our aim is to connect members with what is happening in their locality – our local 'stanzas' can circulate news and 'happenings' from groups, competitions, journals, publishers and readings in your area.

The Poetry Café

The Poetry Café (22 Betterton Street, Covent Garden) is the public face of the Poetry Society. It's a great place to meet other poetry-lovers and to pick up news and information. The range of events at the Café gives you the opportunity to try out a number of different poetry activities to see which suits your interests best. You can hear both complete beginners and internationally renowned poets. As a Poetry Society member you'll enjoy a discount on all events.

The Café has different moods: from quiet in the morning and mid-afternoon, when members come to write and talk to friends, to busy lunches with excellent, reasonably priced, freshly cooked food, culminating in buzzing evenings that might feature a visit by 15 poets from Birmingham, an open mic evening, a book launch, or an opportunity to catch one of the leading lights of the poetry world as they pass through London.

Poetry Prescription

For an honest, unbiased critical appraisal of your poetry, you can have your work looked at by our team of published poets. The Poetry Prescription service is an invaluable opportunity to get constructive advice from a professional poet; and as a member you will get a 20 per cent discount.

National Poetry Competition

Since it was established in 1978 by the Poetry Society, the National Poetry Competition has become the biggest and most prestigious poetry competition of its kind. It offers the chance to get your poetry read by some of the most distinguished writers of our time. The entry fee is £5 for the first poem submitted, and £3 for subsequent entries. Poetry Society members get a *free* second entry. All entries are judged anonymously. Past winners have been both well known and previously unpublished poets.

The Foyle Young Poets Award

This is one of the leading competitions for writers between 11 and 17 years old. Funded by the Foyle Foundation, and commonly referred to as the 'Young National', the award stands out for not only recognising but also nurturing talented young poets. The 15 overall winners are invited to attend a residential writing course at the Arvon Lumb Bank centre, where they are tutored by the very same poets who judged the competition. Previous winners have enjoyed the long-term benefits from this extraordinary opportunity to form a tightly knit writing community, and some have gone on to be published by Carcanet Press, in established poetry journals, and as part of Young Poets on the Underground. The competition is free to enter, with entries accepted from February to July each year.

Poems on the Underground

Travellers on London's Underground don't have to open a book to enjoy poetry: Poems on the Underground is Britain's most popular public art project. And the Poetry Society is happy to announce that you don't have to be a traveller on the London Underground to enjoy these wonderful posters displaying the history of English and world poetry, and featuring poets from William Blake to Don Paterson, from Carol Rumens to anonymous medieval scribes. With our special 'Underground Membership' we'll send you six new Poems on the Underground posters three times a year. NB: If you are affiliated with a school, Poems on the Underground is a benefit of school membership.

Slam

The 'respect slam' is aimed at young people in Greater London, aged between 12 and 18. Slam is the competitive art of performance poetry, and the Poetry Society's respect slam showcase team is chosen from over a hundred participants. The showcase team of young poets shares the stage with professional performance poets in a spectacular finale of original work on the theme of 'respect' at the Mayor of London's annual anti-racism festival. Out of this project we now have a team of 'Poetry Slambassadors' who are available to travel to communities across the UK to perform and discuss their work.

The Poetry Society, 22 Betterton Street, London WC2H 9BX

Apples & Snakes

Apples & Snakes works with emerging performance poets, commissioning and producing new work. Schools, prisons and libraries are just some of the organisations with which it forms partnerships, keeping education at the core of its mission, alongside programming events.

When Apples & Snakes was founded back in 1982 its purpose was to host, facilitate and promote performance poetry through live events. Over the past 25 years there has been a considerable increase in the number and geographical span of regular events that Apples & Snakes organises. In addition to a central office in London, there are offices in Cumbria, Leicester, Wolverhampton and Plymouth, each helping to curate projects in and around the regions, with a strong emphasis on working in partnership with other literature and arts organisations. In the future, Apples & Snakes will expand into the northeast, East Anglia and southern regions to create new opportunities for poets and to ensure that the reach and impact of its work is truly national.

Apples & Snakes views education in its broadest context, as the act of inspiring and motivating people within their environments. Finding innovative ways to develop the use of poetry within education is an integral part of communicating the enduring power of the art form. In nurseries, primary and secondary schools, the aim is to nurture a love of poetry within children from an early age that will become a life-long interest. Schools often work with a poet year after year as an established part of teaching, bringing the curriculum to life. A poet may find that s/he is facilitating a workshop with a class of 30 pupils, or performing in front of an assembly of 300 pupils.

Performance poetry is a vital gateway in working with communities who lack direct access to or feel alienated by the presentation and teaching of 'page' poetry. Performance poetry in education can challenge their negative preconceptions and break down perceived barriers to learning. Workshops are a process of discovery. It is often a revelation to young people, in particular, that poetry can take on many forms, one example being the use of poetic metre in modern day hip-hop tracks. This recognition of a link between traditional and modern styles has the potential to reconnect young people with words on a page – they may feel inspired to write, and words become a source of expression and empowerment. Long-term project work spanning weeks and sometimes months in Pupil Referral Units, with young offenders, adult inmates and in refugee centres can be critical for the development of these traditionally disenfranchised voices. Over the next five years, Apples & Snakes aims to increase the number of poets working in education by setting up high-quality training initiatives for aspiring and existing practitioners.

For most performance poets, education is just one outlet for their work that fits alongside other opportunities. Over the years, in partnership with poets, Apples & Snakes has produced a range of works-in-progress, or 'scratch' shows that have subsequently been developed into full-length theatrical productions. Every year Apples & Snakes produces and tours a one-person show in addition to a National Project, which commissions the work of poets from different regions in England with a view to bringing them together to tour in venues across the country. The frequent touring of shows necessitates extensive collaboration with fellow arts organisations.

On tour, audiences vary in their size, age and ethnicity as performers are brought to city theatres as well as rural village halls. Evening performances are often supplemented with same-day workshops that can establish a unique intimacy with a poet. It is an effective way of stripping down the mystique of the performer and the idea that poetry is a lofty art form, the preserve of the uniquely gifted. Workshop participants perform their work as part of the evening shows. Such grass-roots input can create a sense of common ownership over an event.

The Apples & Snakes marketing team works tirelessly to develop audiences and has the constant challenge of finding new ways to raise the profile of poetry in performance. Often performance poets prefer to place themselves under the more encompassing banner of 'spoken word artist' to attract a wider spectrum of people, but as performance and published poet Malika Booker (co-founder of Malika's Poetry Kitchen, an innovative London-based poetry collective) points out, "My work remains the same in essence, regardless of whether it is marketed as a 'one-woman show', a 'performance poetry show', or a 'spoken word event'. What is important is that I'm not billed as an actor, but recognised as a writer."

Shows by performance poets can and have been toured internationally as a progression from national touring. Apples & Snakes works in partnership with the British Council to provide the opportunity for contemporary performance poets to tour their work in schools and entertainment venues across the world, to eager audiences in Slovenia, India, Singapore and Ghana just to name a few.

Apples & Snakes holds regular open mic events across the country as part of its commitment to providing showcase opportunities for emerging artists (details of events can be found on the website **www.applesandsnakes.org/events**). The open mic circuit is a useful way for performance poets to get their work heard and noticed. It guarantees a more immediate response compared to submitting written poems. Apples & Snakes has a small staff team who can be found whiling away their evenings at a whole range of spoken-word events in search of promising performers. Moreover, the availability of slick self-promotion tools on the Internet such as MySpace, YouTube and Sky Cast offer reasonably easy ways for poets to showcase their performance skills, by downloading their video-recorded work from a camera or a mobile phone. An increasing number of poets are networking with Apples & Snakes through this very useful medium.

Performance poetry as a 'professional career'?

Although there is no formal career ladder in poetry, having a collection of poems printed by a mainstream publisher is still viewed by many as the apex. But the popular belief that publishing poetry will automatically grant a poet access to a wider audience (with more lucrative results) is at odds with declining poetry book sales. Over the years, performance poetry as an art form has not received a lot of support from a literary establishment that often dismisses it as an outlet for frustrated writers waiting to get their 'big break' in the world of print.

Financial necessity means that performance poets have to diversify in terms of what they do, getting a foothold through the open mic circuit and then building up to other possibilities. Being a professional has as much to do with attitude as it does a flexibility of approach. Alongside writing their material, performance poets facilitate workshops in schools, community centres and corporations; they set up poetry nights, publishing initiatives, collectives, or work in other areas entirely unrelated to poetry and the arts sector. For many performance poets, career progression is about focusing on the quality of output and being in touch with the key ideas that their poems are trying to capture and express. To travel along the road of the performance poet is to embark on a journey that is at once parallel to and transcendent of poetry on the page.

Chikodi Nwaiwu works as an administrator for Apples & Snakes, having previously served as a volunteer. She is also a writer and a poet.

Poetry organisations

Academi – The Welsh National Literature Promotion Agency and Society for Writers

Mount Stuart House, Mount Stuart Square,
Cardiff CF10 5FQ
tel (02920) 472266
email post@academi.org
website www.academi.org
Contact Peter Finch

The Welsh Academi is the Welsh National Literature Promotion and Society of Writers. The Academi runs events, courses, competitions, conferences, tours by authors, events for schools, readings, literary performances and festivals. Has responsibility for offering financial bursaries and critical advice, and administers the annual Book of the Year award. Publishes a number of magazines including *A470*, *What's On In Literary Wales*, and *Taliesin*, a literary journal in the Welsh language.

Academy of American Poets

The Academy of American Poets,
584 Broadway, Suite 604, New York,
NY 10012-5243
tel (001212) 2740343 *fax* (001212) 2749427
email academy@poets.org
website www.poets.org

The Academy of American Poets was founded in 1934 to support American poets at all stages of their careers, and to foster the appreciation of contemporary poetry. To fulfill this mission, the Academy administers a wide variety of programmes, including: National Poetry Month (April) – the largest literary celebration in the world; online educational resources providing free poetry lesson-plans for high school teachers; the Poetry Audio Archive, a collection of nearly 500 recordings dating back to the 1960s; and **Poets.org**, an award-winning website which provides a wealth of content on contemporary American poetry and receives an average of 400,000 unique users each month.

Apples & Snakes

Battersea Arts Centre, Lavender Hill,
London SW11 5TN
tel 020-7924 3410
email info@applesandsnakes.org
website www.applesandsnakes.org,
www.myspace.com/applesandsnakespoetry
Contact Chikodi Nwaiwu

Works nationwide to promote popular, high-quality and cross-cultural poetry; programmes live events for new and established poets, including open mic events; operates a Poets in Education scheme where poets run workshops and perform in schools, prisons and community settings; coordinates the professional development of poets, with opportunities for training, mentoring, national touring and residencies.

Arts Council England

Details The Literature Dept,
Arts Council England, 14 Great Peter Street,
London SW1P 3NQ
tel 0845-300 6200 *textphone* 020-7973 6564
fax 020-7973 6590
email enquiries@artscouncil.org.uk
website www.artscouncil.org.uk

Arts Council England presents national prizes rewarding creative talent in the arts. These are awarded through the Council's flexible funds and are not necessarily open to application: the Children's Award, the David Cohen Prize for Literature, the Independent Foreign Fiction Prize, John Whiting Award, Meyer Whitworth Award and the Raymond Williams Community Publishing Prize.

Arts Council England, East

Eden House, 48-49 Bateman Street,
Cambridge CB2 1LR
tel 0845-300 6200 *fax* 0870-242 1271
textphone (01223) 306893

Area covered: Bedfordshire, Cambridgeshire, Essex, Hertfordshire, Norfolk, Suffolk; and unitary authorities of Luton, Peterborough, Southend-on-Sea, Thurrock.

Arts Council England, East Midlands

St Nicholas Court, 25-27 Castle Gate,
Nottingham NG1 7AR

tel 0845-300 6200 *fax* 0115-950 2467

Area covered: Derbyshire, Leicestershire, Lincolnshire (excluding North and North East Lincolnshire), Northamptonshire, Nottinghamshire; and unitary authorities of Derby, Leicester, Nottingham, Rutland.

Arts Council England, London

Details David Cross, Literature Administrator, Arts Council England, London, 2 Pear Tree Court, London EC1R 0DS
tel 020-7608 6184 *fax* 020-7608 4100
website www.artscouncil.org.uk

Arts Council England, London, is the regional office for the Capital, covering 33 boroughs and the City of London. Grants are available through the 'Grants for the arts' scheme throughout the year to support a variety of literature projects, concentrating particularly on:

• original works of poetry and literary fiction and professional development for individual writers, including writers of children's books;
• touring and live literature;
• small independent literary publishers; and
• literary translation into English.

Contact the Literature Unit for more information, or see website for an application form.

Arts Council England, North East

Central Square, Forth Street, Newcastle upon Tyne NE1 3PJ
tel 0845-300 6200 *fax* 0191-230 1020
textphone 0191-255 8585

Area covered: Durham, Northumberland; metropolitan authorities of Gateshead, Newcastle upon Tyne, North Tyneside, South Tyneside, Sunderland; and unitary authorities of Darlington, Hartlepool, Middlesbrough, Redcar and Cleveland, Stockton-on-Tees.

Arts Council England, North West

Manchester House, 22 Bridge Street, Manchester M3 3AB
tel 0845-300 6200 *fax* 0161-834 6969
textphone 0161-834 9131

Area covered: Cheshire, Cumbria, Lancashire; metropolitan authorities of Bolton, Bury, Knowsley, Liverpool, Manchester, Oldham, Rochdale, St Helens, Salford, Sefton, Stockport, Tameside, Trafford, Wigan, Wirral; and unitary authorities of Blackburn with Darwen, Blackpool, Halton, Warrington.

Arts Council England, South East

Sovereign House, Church Street, Brighton BN1 1RA
tel 0845-300 6200 *fax* 0870-242 1257
textphone (01273) 710659

Area covered: Buckinghamshire, East Sussex, Hampshire, Isle of Wight, Kent, Oxfordshire, Surrey, West Sussex; and unitary authorities of Bracknell Forest, Brighton & Hove, Medway Towns, Milton Keynes, Portsmouth, Reading, Slough, Southampton, West Berkshire, Windsor and Maidenhead, Wokingham.

Arts Council England, South West

Senate Court, Southernhay Gardens, Exeter EX1 1UG
tel 0845-300 6200 *fax* (01392) 229229
textphone (01392) 433503

Area covered: Cornwall, Devon, Dorset, Gloucestershire, Somerset, Wiltshire; unitary authorities of Bath and North East Somerset, Bournemouth, Bristol, North Somerset, Plymouth, Poole, South Gloucestershire, Swindon, Torbay.

Arts Council England, West Midlands

82 Granville Street, Birmingham B1 2LH
tel 0845-300 6200 *fax* 0121-643 7239
textphone 0121-643 2815
website www.artscouncil.org.uk
Literature Officer Adrian Johnson *Literature Assistant* Maeve Haughey

Area covered: Shropshire, Staffordshire, Warwickshire, Worcestershire; metropolitan authorities of Birmingham, Coventry, Dudley, Sandwell, Solihull, Walsall, Wolverhampton; and unitary authorities of Herefordshire, Stoke-on-Trent, Telford and Wrekin. Supports Ledbury Poetry Festival, *Poetry on Loan* in public libraries, and individual writers through grant aid, which can be applied for by using the organisation's *Grants for the Arts* pack. Telephone for a full application pack.

Arts Council England, Yorkshire

21 Bond Street, Dewsbury, West Yorkshire WF13 1AX

tel 0845-300 6200 *fax* (01924) 466522
textphone (01924) 438585

Area covered: North Yorkshire; metropolitan
authorities of Barnsley, Bradford, Calderdale,
Doncaster, Kirklees, Leeds, Rotherham,
Sheffield, Wakefield; and unitary authorities of
East Riding of Yorkshire, Kingston upon Hull,
North Lincolnshire, North East Lincolnshire,
York. Premises are wheelchair-user friendly.
For information on disabled parking, please
phone in advance.

Arts Council/An Chomhairle Ealaíon

Literature Adviser, 70 Merrion Square,
Dublin 2, Republic of Ireland
tel (01) 6180200 *fax* (01) 6761302
website www.artscouncil.ie
Arts Programme Director John O'Kane

The national development agency for the arts
in Ireland. Founded 1951.

Arts Council of Northern Ireland

MacNeice House, 77 Malone Road,
Belfast BT9 5JW
tel 028-9038 5200 *fax* 028-90661715
website www.artscouncil-ni.org
Chief Executive Roisín McDonough, *Literature
Officer* Damian Smyth, *Visual Arts Officers* Iain
Davidson, Suzanne Lyle

Promotes and encourages the arts throughout
Northern Ireland. Artists in drama, dance,
music and jazz, literature, the visual arts,
traditional arts and community arts can apply
for support for specific schemes and projects.
The value of the grant will be set according to
the aims of the application. Applicants must
have contributed regularly to the artistic
activities of the community, and been resident
for at least 1 year in Northern Ireland.

Arts Council of Wales

9 Museum Place, Cardiff CF10 3NX
tel 029-2037 6500 *minicom* 029-2039 0027
fax 029-2022 1447
email info@artswales.org.uk
website www.artswales.org.uk
Chairman Prof. Dai Smith, *Arts Director* David
Alston, *Head of Communications* Sian Phipps,
Wales Arts International Director Eluned Haf

National organisation with specific
responsibility for the funding and development

of the arts in Wales. ACW receives funding
from the National Assembly for Wales and also
distributes National Lottery funds for the arts
in Wales. From these resources, ACW makes
grants to support arts activities and facilities.
Some of the funds are allocated in the form of
annual revenue grants to full-time arts
organisations such as the Academy. It also
operates schemes which provide financial and
other forms of support for individual artists or
projects. ACW undertakes this work in both
the English and Welsh languages. Wales Arts
International is the unique partnership between
the Arts Council of Wales and British Council
Wales, which works to promote knowledge
about contemporary arts and culture from
Wales and encourages international exchange
and collaboration.

The Arvon Foundation

Lumb Bank, The Ted Hughes Arvon Centre,
Heptonstall, Hebden Bridge,
West Yorkshire HX7 6DF
tel (01422) 843714 *fax* (01422) 843714
email l-bank@arvonfoundation.org
website www.arvonfoundation.org
Contact Ilona Jones
Moniack Mhor, Teavarran, Kiltarlity, Beauly,
Inverness-shire IV4 7HT
tel (01463) 741675 *fax* (01463) 741733
email m-mhor@arvonfoundation.org
Contact Lyndy Batty
The Arvon Foundation, Totleigh Barton,
Sheepwash, Beaworthy, Devon EX21 5NS
tel (01409) 231338 *fax* (01409) 231144
email t-barton@arvonfoundation.org
Contact Julia Wheadon
The Hurst – The John Osborne Arvon Centre
Clunton, Craven Arms, Shropshire SY7 0JA
tel (01588) 640658 *fax* (01588) 640509
email hurst@arvonfoundation.org
Contact Dan Pavitt

Founded in 1968, the Arvon Foundation run 5-
day residential courses throughout the year for
anyone over the age of 16, providing the
opportunity to live and work with professional
writers. Writing genres explored include
poetry, narrative, drama, writing for children,
song-writing and the performing arts. Bursaries
are available.

Association for Scottish Literary Studies (ASLS)

c/o Dept of Scottish Literature,
9 University Gardens,
University of Glasgow G12 8QH
tel 0141-330 5309
email office@asls.org.uk
website www.asls.org.uk
Hon. President Alan Riach, *Hon. Secretary*
Lorna Borrowman Smith, *Publishing Manager*
Duncan Jones
Membership £38 p.a. individuals, £10 UK
students, £67 corporate

Promotes the study, teaching and writing of
Scottish literature and furthers the study of the
languages of Scotland. Publishes annually an
edited text of Scottish literature, an anthology
of new Scottish writing, a series of academic
journals and a Newsletter (2 p.a.). Also
publishes *Scotnotes* (comprehensive study
guides to major Scottish writers), literary texts
and commentary CDs designed to assist the
classroom teacher, and a series of occasional
papers. Organises 3 conferences a year.
Founded 1970.

Australia Council

PO Box 788, Strawberry Hills, NSW 2012,
Australia
located at 372 Elizabeth Street, Surry Hills,
NSW 2010, Australia
tel (02) 9215 9000 *fax* (02) 9215 9111
email mail@ozco.gov.au
website www.ozco.gov.au
Chairperson David Gonski

Provides a broad range of support for the arts
in Australia, embracing music, theatre,
literature, visual arts, crafts, Aboriginal arts,
community and new media arts. It has 8 major
Boards: Literature, Visual Arts/Craft, Music,
Theatre, Dance, New Media, Community
Cultural Development, Major Performing Arts,
as well as the Aboriginal and Torres Strait
Islander Arts Board.

The Literature Board's chief objective is to
support the writing of all forms of creative
literature – novels, short stories, poetry, plays
and literary non-fiction. It also assists with the
publication of literary magazines, has a book

publishing subsidies programme, and initiates
and supports projects of many kinds designed
to promote Australian literature both within
Australia and abroad.

Big Mouth

18 Allington Road, Southville, Bristol BS3 1PS
mobile (07771) 546919
email rosemary.dun@virgin.net
website www.rosemarydun.co.uk
Contact Rosemary Dun

Has been promoting poetry, poets and poetry
events in Bristol for 5 years. Regular Big Mouth
Cabaret nights see poetry mixed with music,
comedy, visuals – anything. Big Mouth has an
ethos of bringing on new poets, and has run
master classes with top international poets as
well as slams. It organises the Big Mouth poetry
tent at Bristol's Ashton Court Festival, with
audiences of between 200 and 400. Also
supports education in schools projects, which
can and often do include football poetry.

Big Word Performance Poetry

72 Roseburn Street, Edinburgh EH12 5PL
tel 0131-476 3822
email jemrolls@bigword.fsnet.co.uk
Co-ordinator Jem Rolls

Organises regular poetry performances and
competitive 'slams' around Scotland, as well as
undertaking international tours, including
yearly visits to fringe festivals in Canada. Its
aim is to aid the development of a vibrant and
diverse live poetry scene in Edinburgh and
beyond, by presenting high-quality work at
accessible prices.

Blue Nose Poets

204 Horsenden Lane South, Perivale,
Greenford UB6 7NU
email bluenose@athelstan.netkonect.co.uk
website www.netkonect.net/~athelstan/
who.html

National poetry organisation based in London.
Provides workshops, cross-artform events,
residential courses, platforms for new writing,
correspondence workshops, poetry
competitions, and services to schools. Aims to
bring new audiences to poetry by forming
collaborations with groups working in other
fields, especially the visual arts.

Booktrust

(formerly the National Book League, founded 1925)
Book House, 45 East Hill, London SW18 2QZ
tel 020-8516 2977
email query@booktrust.org.uk
website www.booktrust.org.uk
Chairman Alison Morrison, *Executive Director* tbc

An independent charity dedicated to promoting books and reading to people of all ages. Booktrust is responsible for a number of successful reading promotions, sponsored book prizes and creative reading projects aimed at encouraging readers to discover and enjoy books. These include the Orange Prize for Fiction, the Children's Laureate, the Short Story Competition, Get London Reading campaign, the Nestle Children's Book Prize, the Booktrust Teenage Prize, and Bookstart – the national programme that works through locally based organisations to give a free pack of books to young children, with guidance materials for parents and carers.

Booktrust is responsible for the Booktrust website, which carries reviews, features and news on adults' books; and the Booktrusted website, which offers information on all aspects of children's reading and books. Booktrust also produces materials for Children's Book Week and the Best Book Guide.

Booktrust administers Bookstart, which gives 3 free packs of books to every child in the UK. The success of the Bookstart programme has led to the formation of 2 further book gifting schemes: Booktime, which is run in association with Pearson, gives a free book to every 5-year-old in the UK; and Booked Up, which gives a free book to every 11-year-old in the UK.

The Bridlington Heritage Poets

c/o Spindrift, 7 George Street, Kingsgate, Bridlington, East Yorkshire YO15 3PH
Contact J Sykes

Promotes poetry throughout the region, including involvement with schools and societies. Runs poetry competitions and works with established poets and musicians in concert; raises funds for many worthwhile charities.

Brightside

33 Churchill Street, Leicester LE2 1FH
tel (07974) 694605
email brightside@ntlworld.com
website www.brightside.mcmail.com

Opened in April 1996 as a poetry cabaret event in Leicester, the Brightside is now a performance poetry organisation made up of professional performance poets who have backgrounds in teaching, youth work, theatre, mental health and stand-up comedy.

The British Council

10 Spring Gardens, London SW1A 2BN
tel 020-7930 8466 *fax* 020-7839 6347
website www.britishcouncil.org,
www.britishcouncil.org/arts-literature,
http://literature.britishcouncil.org,
www.contemporarywriters.com,
www.encompassculture.com,
www.literarytranslation.com
Chair The Rt Hon. Lord Kinnock, *Director-General* Martin Davidson, *Director of Literature* Susanna Nicklin, *Director of Arts* Venu Dhupa

The British Council connects people worldwide with learning opportunities and creative ideas from the UK, and builds lasting relationships between the UK and other countries. It works in 109 countries, where it has over 122 libraries and information centres, each catering to the needs of the local community with print and electronic resources. In 2006–7, 290,000 library members borrowed over 6 million books and videos. British Council libraries not only provide information and materials to users, but also promote the latest UK publications.

Working in close collaboration with book trade associations, British Council offices participate in major international book fairs.

The British Council is an authority on teaching English as a second or foreign language. It also gives advice and information on curriculum, methodology, materials and testing.

The British Council promotes British literature overseas through writers' tours, academic visits, seminars and exhibitions. It publishes *New Writing*, an annual anthology of unpublished short stories, poems and extracts from works in progress and essays; and a series of literary bibliographies, including *Tbooks: UK Teenage Literature, Crime Literature* and *Reading in the City*. Through its Literature Department, the British Council provides an overview of UK literature and a range of online resources (see above). This includes a literary portal, information about UK and Commonwealth authors, including translation workshops, and a worldwide online book club and reading group for adults, teenagers and children with over 10,000 books plus reading group advice.

The Visual Arts Department, part of the British Council's Arts Group, develops and enlarges overseas knowledge and appreciation of British achievement in the fields of painting, sculpture, printmaking, design, photography, the crafts and architecture, working closely with the British Council's overseas offices and with professional colleagues in the UK and abroad.

Further information about the work of the British Council is available from Press and Public Relations at the above address, or from British Council offices overseas.

The British Haiku Society
38 Wayside Avenue, Hornchurch,
Essex RM12 4LL
tel (01708) 475774
website www.britishhaikusociety.org
General Secretary Dr Doreen King

Promotes the appreciation and writing of haiku and related forms; welcomes overseas members. Provides tutorials, workshops, readings, critical comment and information. Specialist advisers are available. Runs a library, and administers a contest. The journal, *Blithe Spirit*, is produced quarterly. The Society has active local groups and it issues a regular newsletter. Current membership details can be obtained from the website. Founded 1990.

The Browning Society
Hon. Secretary 38b Victoria Road,
London NW6 6PX
tel 020-7604 4257
email pamela@tvdox.com
website www.browningsociety.org

Contact Dr Vicky Greenaway
Membership £15 p.a.

Aims to widen the appreciation and understanding of the lives and poetry of Robert Browning (1812–89) and Elizabeth Barrett Browning (1806–61), as well as other Victorian writers and poets. Founded 1881; refounded 1969.

Byron Society (International)
Byron House, 6 Gertrude Street,
London SW10 0JN
website www.internationalbyronsociety.org
Hon. Director Mrs Elma Dangerfield CBE
Membership £20 p.a.

Aims to promote research into the life and works of Lord Byron (1788–1824) by seminars, discussions, lectures and readings. Publishes *The Byron Journal* (annual, £6.50 plus postage). Founded 1971.

Centerprise Literature
Centreprise, 136–138 Kingsland High Street,
London E8 2NS
tel 020-7249 6572
email literature@centerprisetrust.org.uk
website www.centerpriseliterature.com
Contact Susan Yearwood

Runs courses and workshops in creative writing, organises poetry and book readings, discussions and debates on literary and relevant issues, writers' surgeries, and telephone information on resources for writers in London. Publishes *Calabash* newsletter for writers of Black and Asian origin. Funded by ACE London. Founded 1995.

The City Chapter
Library HQ, 1 Markethill Road,
Armagh BT60 1NR
tel (02837) 520754
email gerry.burns@ni-libraries.net
website www. citychapter.org
Contact Gerry Burns
Takes place October

A partnership of the main library providers in the Armagh City area. Organises a programme of literary events throughout the year to mark World Book Day, National Poetry Day, Children's Book Week etc. with readings and workshops held in the various local libraries.

Commonword

6 Mount Street, Manchester M2 5NS
tel 0161-832 3777
website www.commonword.org.uk

Along with its sister organisation, Cultureword, co-ordinates a range of Writing Development and Publishing Projects, often in collaboration with other organisations. The aim of these projects is to encourage specific sections of the community to engage in creative writing and reading activities.

Creative Arts East

Griffin Court, Market Street, Wymondham, Norfolk NR18 OGU
tel (01603) 774789
email lisa.d'onofrio@cae.norfolk.gov.uk
website www.creativeartseast.co.uk
Contact Lisa D'Onofrio

A fast-growing arts development agency, which provides practical support to the arts community in Norfolk; directly promotes tours, exhibitions, and one-off performances and readings by professional artists and companies; and develops community-based arts projects which address social issues around isolation and disadvantage. The agency was formally launched in 2002, and was set up to combine the collective expertise and energy of 4 smaller arts organisations: Rural Arts East, Norfolk Arts Marketing, Norfolk Literature Development, and Create!. Whether you are a writer or a reader. join the Norfolk Literature Network newsletter for information, news, events listings and competitions.

Dead Good Poets Society

96 Bould Street, Liverpool, Merseyside L1 4HY
tel 0151-709 5221
email dgps@blueyonder.co.uk
Contact Cath Nichols

Organises Open Floors for new writers to try out their material, as well as Guest Nights for audiences to hear established poets. Also arranges workshops plus various projects to increase everyone's enjoyment of poetry.

Disability Writes

Just Services Ltd, Beaumont Enterprise Centre, 72 Boston Road, Beaumont Leys, Leicester LE4 1HB
tel 0116-229 3102
email www.disabilitywrites.org.uk
website info@disabilitywrites.org.uk.

A website where disabled writers and would-be writers can get support and feedback, specific to them, from people who recognise the barriers faced by disabled people. Actively supports and encourages disabled writers, whatever their previous writing experience. Promotes the work of disabled writers to a wide audience of disabled and non-disabled people, through the website and printed publications.

Don't Feed the Poets Productions

The Foresters Arms, 2 Shepherd Street, St Leonards-on-Sea, East Sussex TN38 0ET
tel (01424) 436513
website www.dontfeedthepoets.co.uk
Contact John Knowles

Organises year-round poetry events, open mics and theatrical readings as well as the Word About Town Festival, which runs in Hastings from late April to early May.

Driftwood Publications

5 Timms Lane, Formby, Merseyside L37 7DW
tel 0151-525 0417
email janet.speedy@btinternet.com
Contact Janet Speedy

One of the most active poetry organisations in Merseyside. First registered as a poetry publishing press in the 1970s, it began by publishing booklets by (then) new and neglected poets. It has recently been revived to include promotions (poetry readings at The Freshfield Ho) and has just announced its new programme of events. The organisation also produces spoken-word CDs by many of the poets whose work is published in its book series. Driftwood works closely with Sefton Arts Development and is involved in its annual poetry competition and in many of the promotions, including the recent visits/ readings in Southport and Crosby, Merseyside by Andrew Motion, Brendan Kennelly, Paul Durcan, UA Fanthorpe, John Cooper Clarke and the late Miroslav Holub, among others.

The Dylan Thomas Society of Great Britain

Fernhill, 24 Chapel Street, Mumbles, Swansea SA3 4NH

tel (01792) 363875
Chair Mrs Cecily Hughes

The society aims to foster an interest in Dylan Thomas's writings, and those of other Welsh writers in English.

Dylan Thomas Centre

Somerset Place, Swansea SA1 1RR
tel (01792) 463980
email dylanthomas.lit@swansea.gov.uk
website www.dylanthomas.com
Contact David Woolley/Jo Furber

Opened by former US President Jimmy Carter in 1995, the Dylan Thomas Centre is home to a permanent exhibition on Dylan Thomas and a year-round programme of literary events. It also hosts the annual Dylan Thomas Celebration, from 27th October to 9th November.

English Association

University of Leicester, University Road, Leicester LE1 7RH
tel 0116-252 3982 *fax* 0116-252 2301
email engassoc@le.ac.uk
website www.le.ac.uk/engassoc/
Chair Peter J Kitson, *Chief Executive* Helen Lucas

Aims to further knowledge, understanding and enjoyment of English literature and the English language, by working towards a fuller recognition of English as an essential element in education and in the community at large; by encouraging the study of English literature and language by means of conferences, lectures and publications; and by fostering the discussion of methods of teaching English of all kinds.

Exiled Writers Ink

31 Hallswelle Road, London NW11 0DH
tel 020-8458 1910
email jennifer@exiledwriters.fsnet.co.uk
website www.exiledwriters.co.uk
Director Jennifer Langer

Provides a platform for the work of artists living in exile in the UK and Mainland Europe through performance, publishing and training activities.

Farrago Poetry

108 High Street, West Wickham, Kent BR4 0ND

mobile (07905) 078376
email farragopoetry@yahoo.co.uk
website http://london.e-poets.net
Contact John O'Neill

A spoken-word and performance poetry organisation based in London. Runs a range of different events, from Spanish language poetry nights to events for elders, but is best known for pioneering slam poetry in the UK and for its links to the international performance poetry scene.

Guernsey Arts Council

Mitton House, Round Chimney, St Sampsons, Guernsey GY2 4NX
Chairman Mrs Terry Domrille, *Secretary* Ann Wilkes-Green

Hammer & Tongue

16b Cherwell Street, Oxford OX4 1BG
tel (01865) 200550
email events@hammerandtongue.co.uk
website www.hammerandtongue.co.uk
Contact Steve Larkin

A not-for-profit organisation that promotes some of the best spoken-word artists that the world has to offer, and engages diverse communities, promoting open poetry slams. The organisation was responsible for the first UK tour of international slam poets – 'The 4 Continents Slam'. Regular events take place in Oxford, London and Brighton. Hammer & Tongue also places poets in educational settings such as schools, universities and prisons.

Seamus Heaney Centre for Poetry

46-48 University Road, Belfast BT7 1NN
tel (02890) 273319
email shc@qub.ac.uk
website www.qub.ac.uk/heaneycentre

Designed to celebrate and to build upon Seamus Heaney's enormous contribution to contemporary poetry, as well as the achievements of poets from Northern Ireland more generally. The centre will house an extensive library of contemporary poetry volumes and journals, which will be open to the public. It will host regular creative writing workshops, a fortnightly poetry reading group, and an ongoing series of readings and lectures by visiting poets and critics from all over the world.

Independent Northern Publishers

Aidan House, Sunderland Road,
Gateshead NE8 3HU
tel 0191-478 8431
email info@northernpublishers.co.uk
website www.northernpublishers.co.uk,
www.literaturenortheast.co.uk

A collective of poetry and fiction publishers, including magazines based in the North East of England. Members include: *Mslexia*, *Other Poetry* and *Bullet* magazines; Arrowhead Press, Biscuit Publishing, Blinking Eye, Diamond Twig, Dogeater, Flambard, Iron Press, Ek Zuban (including *Kenaz* magazine), Mudfog, Morning Star, Sand, Smokestack, Vane Women Press and Zebra Publishing.

Independent Publishers Guild

PO Box 93, Royston, Herts SG8 5GH
tel (01763) 247014 *fax* (01763) 246293
website www.ipg.uk.com
Membership £160 + VAT p.a. min. Open to new and established publishers and book packagers; supplier membership is available to specialists in fields allied to publishing (but not printers and binders)

Provides an information and contact network for independent publishers. The IPG also voices the concerns of member companies with the book trade. Founded 1962.

Inpress

Northumberland House, 11 The Pavement, Popes Lane, Ealing, London W5 4NG
tel 020-8832 7464
email info@inpressbooks.co.uk
website www.inpressbooks.co.uk

Provides sales, marketing and technical support for independent publishers in the UK. Funded by Arts Council England, Inpress offers practical support and gives members a strong collective voice, helping small presses to achieve healthy sales and wider exposure for their published output each year. This is achieved by providing sales representation through Troika, distribution via Central Books Ltd, attendance at fairs and events across the UK, and by offering secure transactions for purchasers, via the Inpress Books website, which allows purchasers to deal directly with independent publishers.

Irish Writers' Centre

19 Parnell Square, Dublin 1,
Republic of Ireland
tel (01) 8721302 *fax* (01) 8726282
email info@writerscentre.ie
website www.writerscentre.ie
Director Cathal McCabe

National organisation for the promotion of writers and writing in Ireland. Runs an extensive programme of events at its headquarters; operates the Writer in Community Scheme, which funds events throughout Ireland; runs an education programme offering courses and workshops in writing; and operates an International Writers' Exchange Programme. See website for further details. Founded 1991.

Keats-Shelley Memorial Association

Bedford House, 76A Bedford Street,
Leamington Spa CV32 5DT
tel (01926) 427400 *fax* (01926) 335133
Chairman Hon Mrs H Cullen, *Hon. Secretary* David Leigh-Hunt
Membership £12 p.a. minimum

Owns and supports house in Rome where John Keats died, as a museum open to the public; celebrates the poets Keats (1795–1821), Shelley (1792–1822) and Leigh Hunt (1784–1859). Regular meetings; poetry competitions; annual *Review;* 2 literary awards; and progress reports. Founded 1903.

Kent and Sussex Poetry Society

39 Rockington Way, Crowborough,
East Sussex TN6 2NJ
tel (01892) 662781
email john@kentandsussexpoetrysociety.org
website www.kentandsussexpoetrysociety.org
Publicity Officer John Arnold

A lively society founded in 1946. Monthly meetings feature readings by major poets. There are monthly workshop meetings to discuss members' poems; also an annual folio of members' work and an annual open poetry competition.

League of Canadian Poets

920 Yonge Street, Suite 608, Toronto,
Ontario M4W 3C7, Canada
tel 416-504-1657 *fax* 416-504 0096
email info@poets.ca
website www.poets.ca
Executive Director Joanna Poblocka
Membership $175 p.a.

Aims to promote the interests of poets and to
advance Canadian poetry in Canada and
abroad. Administers 3 annual awards; operates
the 'Poetry Spoken Here' webstore; runs
National Poetry Month; publishes a newsletter
and *Poetry Markets for Canadians, Who's Who
in The League of Canadian Poets*, and *Poets in
the Classroom* (teaching guide). Promotes and
sells members' poetry books. Founded 1966.

The Literary Consultancy

Diorama Arts, No 1 Euston Centre,
London NW1 3JG
tel 020-7813 4330
email info@literaryconsultancy.co.uk
website www.literaryconsultancy.co.uk
Contact Rebecca Swift, Jess Porter

While working as an editorial assistant in her
early years at Virago Press, Rebecca Swift,
founder of TLC, realised that there was no
professional, trustworthy body for authors to
send work to before they approached
publishers and agents. TLC provides detailed
critiques and invaluable advice to writers,
including poets.

Literature Southwest

website www.literaturesouthwest.co.uk

A one-stop portal for what's happening in the
world of literature in the southwest of England.

Litfest

PO Box 751, Lancaster, Lancashire LA1 9AJ
tel (0152) 462166
email all@litfest.org
website www.litfest.org
Contact Steve Lewis, Sarah Hymas

The literature festival and development agency
for Lancashire. Litfest also develops literature
through projects across the county.

Mini Mushaira

c/o 11 Donnington Road, Sheffield,
South Yorkshire S2 2RF
tel 0114-272 3906, (01743) 245004
email simon@shrews1.fsnet.co.uk,
debjani@chatterjee.freeserve.co.uk
Contact Simon Fletcher, Debjani Chatterjee

Mushaira is the Arabic word for 'a gathering of
poets', and the Mini Mushaira writers (Debjani
Chatterjee in Sheffield, Simon Fletcher in
Shrewsbury, Basir Sultan Kazmi in Manchester
and Brian G D'Arcy in Sheffield) are a group of
multicultural poets and storytellers who seek to
build cultural bridges through their work with
both children and adults. Mini Mushaira have
given excellent multilingual poetry
performances and run poetry workshops
throughout the country. All the writers are well
published; some of their poetry may be
sampled in *A Little Bridge* (Pennine Pens).

National Association of Writers' Groups

Headquarters The Arts Centre, Biddick Lane,
Washington, Tyne and Wear NE38 2AB
tel (01262) 609228
email nawg@tesco.net
Secretary Diane Wilson, 40 Burstall Hill,
Bridlington, East Yorkshire YO16 7GA
website www.nawg.co.uk
Membership £30 p.a. plus £5 registration per
group; £14 Associate individuals

Aims "to advance the education of the general
public throughout the UK, including the
Channel Islands, by promoting the study and
art of writing in all its aspects". Publishes *Link*
bimonthly magazine. Annual Festival of
Writing held in Durham in September. Annual
Creative Writing Competition. Founded 1995.

National Literacy Trust

68 South Lambeth Road, London SW8 1RL
tel 020-7587 1842
email contact@literacytrust.org.uk
website www.literacytrust.org.uk,
www.rif.org.uk, www.readon.org.uk,
www.readingthegame.org.uk,
www.talktoyourbaby.org.uk
Director Jonathan Douglas

"An independent charity that changes lives
through literacy. 1 in 5 people in the UK
struggles to read and write. Poor skills

compromise the health, confidence, happiness and employability of individuals, and have a negative impact on the national economy. To make a real difference, whole communities need to work together. The National Literacy Trust helps to make this happen.

The National Literacy Trust links home, school and the wider community to inspire learners and create opportunities for everyone. It brings together key organisations to lead literacy promotion in the UK and support those with learners through information, research, and innovative programmes – Reading is Fundamental, UK; the National Reading Campaign; Reading the Game; and Talk to Your Baby."

National Poetry Day

Poetry Society, 22 Betterton Street, London WC2H 9BX
tel 020-7420 9880
email npd@poetrysociety.org.uk
website www.poetrysociety.org.uk

Takes place in October of each year. A day of poetry events and performances all over the country at venues and in schools.

New Forest Poetry Society

Forest Arts, New Milton, Hants BH25 6DS
tel (01590) 675409
email keithbennett532@hotmail.com
Contact Keith Bennett

Forest Arts, an arts centre in the New Forest, hosts the monthly Poems and Pints evenings organised by the New Forest Poetry Society, and runs an ambitious literary programme of book groups, readings, performances, workshops and literary happenings.

New Writing North

2 School Lane, Whickham NE16 4SL
tel 0191-488 8580 *fax* 0191-488 8576
email mail@newwritingnorth.com
website www.newwritingnorth.com

The writing development agency for the North East of England (the area covered by Arts Council England, North East). It aims to create an environment in the North East of England in which new writing in all genres can flourish and develop. It is a unique organisation within

the UK, merging individual development work with writers across all media with educational work and the production of creative projects. It works with writers from different genres and forms to develop career opportunities, new commissions, projects, residencies, publications and live events.

New Writing Partnership

4-6 Netherconesford, 93-95 King Street, Norwich NR1 1PW
tel (01603) 877177
email info@newwritingpartnership.org.uk
website www.newwritingpartnership.org.uk
Contact Chris Gribble

The New Writing Partnership promotes, develops and celebrates new writing, building on the East of England's reputation as a national and international centre of literary excellence.

New Zealand Poetry Society

PO Box 5283, Lambton Quay, Wellington
email info@poetrysociety.org.nz
website www.poetrysociety.org.nz
President James Norcliffe

For more than 30 years the New Zealand Poetry Society has been supporting New Zealand poets and poetry in its many forms.

Northern Voices

93 Woodburn Square, Whitley Lodge, Whitley Bay, Tyne & Wear NE26 3JD
tel 0191-252 9531
email KeithArmstrongnv@aol.com

Aims to: offer a platform for the views and experiences of those people living in the North East of England who are normally denied a voice; contribute to the culture of the region, through a publishing and events programme; develop links with like-minded people and institutions; establish specific projects of interest to Northern Voices' members and their associates; offer help and advice to local people seeking to develop a voice. Membership is open to anyone who shares these objectives, and who is engaged in creative writing and community publishing activity in the North East of England. For further details, contact Keith Armstrong.

Outlook

Mount View Cottage, Mousehole Lane, Paul,
Penzance, Cornwall TR19 6TY
tel (01736) 732508
email outlook@easynet.co.uk
Contact Roger Butts

An agency for artists who work in education;
also organises cross-curricular and language-
based projects through Outlook, which are
inspired by the out-of-doors and in which
schools (mainly Cornish Primary) can take
part.

Wilfred Owen Association

29 Arthur Road, London SW19 7DN
website www.1914-18.co.uk/owen
Membership £6 p.a. (£10 overseas), £15 groups/
institutions, £4 concessions

Aims to commemorate the life and work of
Wilfred Owen (1893–1918), and to encourage
and enhance appreciation of his work through
visits, public events, a newsletter and journal.
Founded 1989.

Oxford University Poetry Society

Magdalen College, Oxford OX1 4AU
mobile (07973) 249419
email jonathan.taylor@magd.ox.ac.uk
website users.ox.ac.uk/~magd1931
Contact Jonathan Taylor

Society run for, and by, students of Oxford
interested in the reading and writing of poetry.
The Society meets once a week for readings,
workshops and other events, and produces *The
Reader* – a biannual poetry pamphlet.

Pass on a Poem

112 Elgin Crescent, London W11 2JL
tel 020-7229 9152
email enquiries@passonapoem.com
website www.passonapoem.com

Exists to provide entertainment and to create
enthusiasm for poetry, by bringing people
together to read out loud poems which have a
special personal significance and to explain,
briefly, why. Some readings take place in
private homes, with group membership being
by invitation. Others are organised at regular
intervals in public venues, so that anybody who

enjoys or who would like to try reading or
simply listening to poetry can be included. No
previous experience of reading out loud is
necessary. Anybody is welcome to submit a
poem they would like to share. The
adminstration of the project is based in
London, but the idea is to promote local live
readings nationwide, using them as a resource
and support.

PEN, International

Brownlow House, 50–51 High Holborn,
London EC1V 6EK
tel 020-7405 0338 *fax* 020-7405 0339
email intpen@dircon.co.uk
website www.internationalpen.org.uk
Executive Director Caroline McCormick
Membership Apply to Centres

A world association of writers. PEN was
founded in 1921 by C.A. Dawson Scott under
the presidency of John Galsworthy, to promote
friendship and understanding between writers
and to defend freedom of expression within
and between all nations. The initials PEN stand
for Poets, Playwrights, Editors, Essayists,
Novelists – but membership is open to all
writers of standing (including translators),
whether men or women, without distinction of
creed or race, who subscribe to these
fundamental principles. PEN takes no part in
state or party politics. The International PEN
Writers in Prison Committee works on behalf
of writers imprisoned for exercising their right
to freedom of expression, a right implicit in the
PEN Charter to which all members subscribe.
The International PEN Translations and
Linguistic Rights Committee strives to promote
the translations of works by writers in the
lesser-known languages and to defend those
languages. The Writers for Peace Committee
exists to find ways in which writers can work
for peaceful co-existence in the world. The
Women Writers' Committee works to promote
women's writing and publishing in developing
countries. The Writers in Exile Network helps
exiled writers. International Congresses are
held annually.

Membership of any one Centre implies
membership of all Centres; at present 144
autonomous Centres exist throughout the

world. Associate membership is available for writers not yet eligible for full membership and for persons connected with literature. The English Centre has a programme of literary lectures, discussion, dinners and parties.

Penned in the Margins
53 Arcadia Court, 45 Old Castle Street,
London E1 7NY
tel 020-7375 0258
email info@pennedinthemargins.co.uk
website www.pennedinthemargins.co.uk
Contact Tom Chivers

Celebrates the power of words in performance and on the page with live poetry events. Also manages spoken-word artists, publishes new work by emerging writers, creates innovative projects, and provides research and consultancy services to the live literature sector.

Performing Right Society Ltd (PRS)
Copyright House, 29–33 Berners Street,
London W1T 3AB
tel 020-7580 5544 *fax* 020-7306 4455
website www.prs.co.uk

Pirandello
9 Jew Street, Brighton, East Sussex BN1 1UT
tel (01273) 735353
email pirandello@newwritingsouth.com
website www.pirandello.org.uk

A database of writers, all published and/or performed. They cover all genres – novels, biography, poetry and playwrighting, with books published by major mainstream publishers as well as cutting-edge small presses like Two Rivers Press and Arc. Their work has been broadcast on radio and television and played on national stages. From a writing workshop for youngsters to a commissioned poem, from a reading to a live literature performance, you can find the writer that could be invaluable to your workshop, workplace, school or event.

Poems on the Underground
c/o The Poetry Society, 22 Betterton Street,
London WC2H 9BX
tel 020-7420 9880 *fax* 020-7240 4818
email info@poetrysociety.org.uk
website www.poetrysociety.org.uk
Contact Angel Dahouk

Poems on the Underground was launched in 1986. The programme was the brainchild of American writer Judith Chernaik, whose aim was to bring poetry to the wide-ranging audience of passengers on the Underground. In 2000, more than 3.5 million journeys were made each day. Judith Chernaik, together with poets Cicely Herbert and Gerard Benson, continues to select poems for inclusion in the programme.

Poeticise
PO Box 2147, Bristol BS99 7SF
email base@poeticise.co.uk

The UK's first interactive performance forum, fusing cutting-edge spoken word, new media and live beats from a black perspective. Since the organisation was founded in 1999, Poeticise has developed a reputation for pushing back the boundaries of 'performance poetry' by introducing progressive, high-profile cross-arts platforms that project emerging and established live black artists to new audiences.

Poetry Australia Foundation
School of Creative Arts,
University of Melbourne,
Parkville VIC 3010 Australia
email rpretty@unimelb.edu.au
website www.poetryaustraliafoundation.org.au

The Poetry Australia Foundation was established in 2002 to promote the reading, writing, reviewing and appreciation of poetry in all its forms. It is a not-for-profit, community-based organisation.

The Poetry Can
20-22 Hepburn Road, Bristol BS2 8UD
tel 0117-942 6976
email info@poetrycan.co.uk
website www.poetrycan.co.uk
Contact Colin Brown

A poetry development agency based in Bristol. Provides advice and support in matters relating to poets and poetry, organises events such as the Bristol Poetry Festival, and runs a lifelong learning programme.

The Poetry Cubicle
28 Burton Stone Lane, York YO30 6BU
email sara@thepoetrycubicle.org.uk
website www.thepoetrycubicle.org.uk
Contact Sara Wingate Gray

A not-for-profit educational resource base, shop, library and interactive performance centre, dedicated to making poetry more accessible.

The Poetry House

The Scores, St Andrews, Fife KY16 9AL
tel (01334) 462666
email english@st-andrews.ac.uk
website www.thepoetryhouse.org
Contact Donovan McAbee

The Poetry House is based in the School of English at the University of St Andrews, and promotes a programme of public readings and events with Scottish and international poets throughout the year. It is also home to a leading MLitt in Creative Writing, and publishes *Scores* and *The Red Wheelbarrow*. Some of Scotland's major poets work at the Poetry House, including John Burnside, Robert Crawford, Douglas Dunn, Kathleen Jamie and Don Paterson. The Poetry House website is designed to be an authoritative guide to information about poetry across the English-speaking world. Its coverage is both historical (from Old English to the present) and geographical, taking in all the world's major English-speaking areas. Its authority derives from the acumen of its international team of editors, each an expert in his or her subject area. The Poetry House may not be the largest site on the web devoted to poetry, but it aims to be one of the most helpful and easy to use.

Poetry International Foundation

William Boothlaan 4, 3012 VJ Rotterdam, The Netherlands
tel (00311) 0282 2777
email poetry@luna.nl
website www.poetry.nl

Poetry International is a government-sponsored foundation working to promote interest in and foster love for the art of poetry, and to encourage contacts between poets, poetry translators, poetry lovers and publishers from all countries. It does so by organising the annual Poetry International Festival, the Children's Poetry Festival, a National Poetry Day and various international exchange projects. Poetry International also tries to bring poetry to a wider public by posting poems in public areas, on building, in railway carriages, even on garbage trucks.

Poetry Ireland/Éigse Éirann

2 Prouds Lane, off St Stephen's Green, Dublin 2
tel (+353 1) 478 9974 *fax* (+353 1) 478 0205
email poetry@iol.ie
website www.poetryireland.ie
Director Joseph Woods

Poetry Ireland is the national organisation dedicated to developing, supporting and promoting poetry throughout Ireland. A resource and information point for any member of the public with an interest in poetry; works towards creating opportunities for poets working or living in Ireland.

Main activities are: Publications, Readings, Education and Resource Services.

The Poetry Society – see page 166

The Poetry Society (India)

L-67 A, Malviyar Nagar, New Delhi-110017, India
tel 989 101 6667
email hkkaul@delnet.ren.nic.in
website www.indianpoetry.org
Secretary-General Dr HK Kaul

Promotes poetry in India written in the Indian languages. Organises workshops, readings, lectures, conferences and competitions.

The Poetry Society of America

15 Gramercy Park, New York, NY 10003
tel (212) 254-9628
email anita@poetrysociety.org
website www.poetrysociety.org
Executive Officer Alice Quinn

WH Auden, Robert Frost, Langston Hughes, Edna St Vincent Millay, Marianne Moore and Wallace Stevens were among the original members, who envisioned a society that would not only be a local meeting place for poets, but also a centre from which a national poetry renaissance would emerge. Current members, such as John Ashbery, Rita Dove, Kimiko Hahn, Brenda Hillman, Yusef Komunyakaa, Stanley Kunitz, Sharon Olds, Robert Pinsky and Adrienne Rich, carry on their great tradition.

Poetry Translation Centre

Room 404,
School of Oriental & African Studies,
Thornhaugh Street, London WC1H 0XG
tel 020-7898 4367
email ptc@soas.ac.uk
website www.poetrytranslation.soas.ac.uk

The Poetry Translation Centre at the School of Oriental & African Studies was established in February 2004. Concentrates on translating contemporary poetry from non-European languages into English to the highest literary standards, through a series of innovative collaborations between leading international poets and poets based in the UK. Visitors to the Centre's website will be able to read translations of contemporary poets in a wide variety of languages, and to take part in lively debates about poetry and translation with people from all over the world.

The Poetry Trust

The Cut, 9 New Cut, Halesworth,
Suffolk IP19 8BY
tel (01986) 835950
email info@thepoetrytrust.org
website www.aldeburghpoetryfestival.org/html/
the_trust1.htm

An arts organisation which runs the UK's leading annual festival of international contemporary poetry at Aldeburgh on the Suffolk coast (established 1989), and promotes the reading, writing and enjoyment of poetry to a wide variety of children and adults. Delivers a year-round programme of events, creative education opportunities, prizes and publications.

ProudWords Festival

mobile (07973) 894912
email pwcwf@hotmail.com
website www.proudwords.org.uk

Promotes all kinds of writing by lesbian, gay and bisexual writers. The organisation was established in 1997 and runs an annual writing festival in Newcastle and Gateshead featuring poets, playwrights, novelists, singer-songwriters and performers.

Royal Society of Literature

Somerset House, Strand, London WC2R 1LA
tel 020-7845 4676 *fax* 020-7845 4679
email info@rslit.org
Chairman of Council Maggie Gee, FRSL,
Secretary Maggie Fergusson, FRSL
Membership £40 p.a.

For the promotion of literature and encouragement of writers by way of lectures, discussions, readings, and by publications. Administers the VS Pritchett Memorial Prize, the Royal Society of Literature Ondaatje Prize, and the Royal Society of Literature/Jerwood Awards. Founded 1820.

Scottish Book Trust (SBT)

Sandeman House, 55 High Street,
Edinburgh EH1 1SR
tel 0131-524 0160 *fax* 0131-524 0161
email info@scottishbooktrust.com
website www.scottishbooktrust.com

With a responsibility towards Scottish writing, SBT exists to inspire readers and writers, and through the promotion of reading, to reach and create a wider reading public. Programmes include: management of Live Literature Scotland, a national initiative enabling Scottish citizens to engage with authors, playwrights, poets, storytellers and illustrators; Writer Development, offering mentoring and professional development for writers; a national touring programme; the network of Scottish writers and illustrators (BRAW); Royal Mail Scottish Children's Book Awards; and a growing international programme showcasing Scottish writing abroad. An information service for readers, writers and occasional exhibitions and publications all contribute to SBT's mission to bring readers and writers together.

Sentinel Poetry Movement

60 Titmuss Avenue, Thamesmead,
London SE28 8DJ
tel (07940) 249812
email info@sentinelpoetry.org.uk
www.sentinelpoetry.org.uk
Administrator Nnorom Azuonye

Sentinel Poetry Movement is a non-profit free-to-join poetry society open to writers of all levels of accomplishment, regardless of racial or religious background.

The South

PO Box 145, Brighton, East Sussex BN1 6YU
tel (01273) 242850
email info@thesouth.org.uk
website www.thesouth.org.uk
Contact John Davies

An independent, not-for-profit, literary arts development group and promoter which has emerged from the 'grass roots' of poets and writers in Brighton and along the south coast. Through its readings and presentations, writers' workshops, hosting international poets, building links with publishers, cross art-form collaborations, promoting networks and commissioning special projects, the South has quickly established itself as an organisation which makes things happen. In addition to supporting the production of new high-quality work, it has successfully sought to build new audiences and to respond to their interests through its programming, communication and other activities. The South has stimulated a dramatic renaissance in poetry activity in the south of England.

Speaking Volumes

Ground Floor, Marshall Court,
1 Marshall Street, Leeds LS11 9YP
tel 0113-394 4840
email info@speakingvolumesonline.org.uk
website www.speakingvolumesonline.org.uk

Aims to bring the enjoyment of reading and involvement in reading activities to people with a visual impairment, through the public libraries in all 15 local authorities throughout the Yorkshire and Humber region.

Stop All the Clocks

The Marlborough Theatre, Prince's Street, Brighton, East Sussex
tel (01273) 207562
email simon@stopalltheclocks.co.uk
website www.stopalltheclocks.co.uk
Contact Simon Clayton

Formed as an amalgamation of the 3 best poetry-promotion stables in Brighton: Don't Feed The Poets, Holy! Holy! Holy! Holy!, and Wanderlust Wonderlust. Organises year-round, genuinely grass-roots events as well as the Brighton fringe literature festival every May.

Suffolk Poetry Society

9 Gainsborough Road, Felixstowe IP11 7HT
email suffolkpoetry@aol.com
website www.blythweb.co.uk/sps
Secretary Maureen Butler

During the summer, occasional meetings are held on Sunday afternoons at various places in Suffolk. Speakers include foremost poets and critical writers of the day (see website for details of the 2006 programme). From November to March inclusive, local groups meet in members' homes to read and discuss poetry. Further details from the Membership Secretary. Membership, £10 p.a.

Survivors' Poetry

Studio 11, Bickerton House,
25-27 Bickerton Road, London N19 5JT
tel 020-7281 4654
email info@survivorspoetry.org.uk
website www.survivorspoetry.com
Contact Dr Simon Jenner

Promotes poetry for survivors of mental distress, through a programme of workshops, performances, readings, training and publications. There is a free subscription to the quarterly magazine, *Poetry Express*.

The Tennyson Society

Central Library, Free School lane,
Lincoln LN2 1EZ
tel (01522) 552851 *fax* (01522) 552858
email jeffersk@lincolnshire.gov.uk
website www.tennysonsociety.org.uk
Membership £10 p.a., £12 family, £15 institutions

Promotes the study and understanding of the life and work of the poet Alfred, Lord Tennyson (1809–92) and supports the Tennyson Research Centre in Lincoln. Holds lectures, visits and seminars; publishes the *Tennyson Research Bulletin* (annual), Monographs and Occasional Papers; tapes/recordings available. Founded 1960.

Time Haiku

Basho-An, 105 King's Head Hill,
London E4 7JG

Contact Erica Facey

Promotes haiku and haiku-related forms. Aims to increase accessibility through education, and encourages school and college activities as well as providing a biannual journal and newsletter.

Toddington Poetry Society

tel (01582) 723500
website www.toddingtonpoetrysociety.co.uk
Contact Jean Janes

Open to all who enjoy reading, writing or hearing poetry. Meets on the second and fourth Tuesdays of the month, in Luton. Meetings usually alternate between a visiting poet or an informal evening, with impromptu contributions of members' and other poems.
   Jean Janes

The Windows Project

Liver House, 96 Bold Street, Liverpool L1 4HY
tel 0151-709 3688 *fax* 0151-707 8722
email windowsproject@btinternet.com
website www.windowsproject.demon.co.uk

Since 1976 the Windows Project has been making poetry fun – helping children to start writing, and providing support and advice for poetry-writing by and with all ages and abilities. Over the years, the Project has been involved in most aspects of poetry.

Word Market

PO Box 150, Barrow in Furness,
Cumbria LA14 3WF
mobile (07812) 172193
email janice@word-market.co.uk
website www.wordmarket.org.uk
Contact Janice Benson

Supports literary events in South Cumbria; organises a wide range of events aimed at encouraging the development of aspiring writers in the region; is committed to increasing employment opportunities for local writers, professional or amateur; organises workshops and training for writers.

Write Out Loud

11 Palace Court, Bolton, Lancs BL1 2DR
tel (01204) 398148
email julian@writeoutloud.net

website www.writeoutloud.net
Contact Julian Jordan

Aims to increase the opportunities for the widest range of the public to express themselves through the medium of poetry, in its broadest sense. Holds informal poetry open-floor nights on the third Sunday of every month at the Howcroft Inn, Bolton, and more formal readings bimonthly at the Octagon Theatre Bolton. Currently developing a strategy to take performance poetry to new audiences, as well as providing workshops for new poets.

Write Together

18 Penshaw View, Hebburn on Tyne,
Tyne & Wear
tel 0191-483 7071
Contact Mrs P Brown (Secretary)

A voluntary community group aiming to promote creative writing (including poetry) and to provide support, advice and benefit of experience to writers in the borough of South Tyneside.

Writing Together

Booktrust, Book House, 45 East Hill,
London SW18 2QZ
tel 020-8516 2976
email writingtogether@booktrust.org.uk
website www.booktrust.org.uk
Contact Nikki Marsh

Works to establish links with other organisations in the field of literature development; to devise models for writers and teachers to work together out of school; to pilot a new form of professional development for teachers based on The Poetry Society's Poetry class course, but using writers of different genres – drama, journalism and science writing; to sponsor training for writers organised on our behalf by the National Association of Writers in Education; to organise conferences for local authority staff, to help them promote the idea of working with writers to their schools; and to fund 8 residencies in schools that will be written up as case studies and will include teaching materials.

Funding organisations and grants

Academi (Welsh Academy)

Main Office 3rd Floor, Mount Stuart House, Mount Stuart Square, Cardiff CF10 5FQ
tel 029-2047 2266 *fax* 029-2049 2930
email post@academi.org
and Academi Glyn Jones Centre, Wales Millennium Centre, Cardiff Bay, Cardiff CF10 5AL
tel 029-2047 2266 *fax* 029-2047 0691
email post@academi.org
North West Wales Office Ty Newydd, Llanystumdwy, Cricieth, Gwynedd LL52 0LW
tel (01766) 522817 *fax* (01766) 523095
email post@tynewydd.org
South West Wales Office Dylan Thomas Centre, Somerset Place, Swansea SA1 1RR
tel (01792) 463980 *fax* (01792) 463993
website www.academi.org
Chief Executive Peter Finch
Membership Associate: £15 p.a. (waged), £7.50 (unwaged)

Academi is the trading name of Yr Academi Gymreig, the Welsh National Literature Promotion Agency and Society of Writers. With funds mostly provided from public sources, it has been constitutionally independent since 1978. It runs courses, competitions (including the Cardiff International Poetry and Book of the Year Competition), conferences, tours by authors, festivals and represents the interests of Welsh writers and Welsh writing both inside Wales and beyond. Its publications include *Taliesin* (3 p.a.), a literary journal in the Welsh language; *A470* (bi-monthly), a literature information magazine; *The Oxford Companion to the Literature of Wales*, *The Welsh Academy English–Welsh Dictionary*, and a variety of translated works.

Academi administers a range of schemes including Writers on Tour, Writers Residencies and Writing Squads for young people. Academi also runs services for writers in Wales such as bursaries, critical advice and mentoring. Founded 1959.

Arts Council England

Details The Literature Dept, Arts Council England, 14 Great Peter Street, London SW1P 3NQ
tel 0845-300 6200 *textphone* 020-7973 6564
fax 020-7973 6590
email enquiries@artscouncil.org.uk
website www.artscouncil.org.uk

Arts Council England presents national prizes rewarding creative talent in the arts. These are awarded through the Council's flexible funds and are not necessarily open to application: the Children's Award, the David Cohen Prize for Literature, the Independent Foreign Fiction Prize, John Whiting Award, Meyer Whitworth Award and the Raymond Williams Community Publishing Prize.

Arts Council England, London

Details David Cross, Literature Administrator, Arts Council England, London, 2 Pear Tree Court, London EC1R 0DS
tel 020-7608 6184 *fax* 020-7608 4100
website www.artscouncil.org.uk

Arts Council England, London, is the regional office for the Capital, covering 33 boroughs and the City of London. Grants are available through the 'Grants for the arts' scheme throughout the year to support a variety of literature projects, concentrating particularly on:

• original works of poetry and literary fiction and professional development for individual writers, including writers of children's books;
• touring and live literature;
• small independent literary publishers; and
• literary translation into English.

Contact the Literature Unit for more information, or see website for an application form.

The Arts Council/An Chomhairle Ealaíon

Details 70 Merrion Square, Dublin 2, Republic of Ireland

tel (01) 618 0200 *fax* (01) 676 1302
email artistsservices@artscouncil.ie
website www.artscouncil.ie

Publishes a guide for individuals and organisations to Arts Council bursaries, awards and schemes. It is also available online. This guide is called *Supports for Artists*.

Cholmondeley Awards

Awards Secretary, The Society of Authors, 84 Drayton Gardens, London SW10 9SB
tel 020-7373 6642
email info@societyofauthors.org
website www.societyofauthors.org

These honorary awards are to recognise the achievement and distinction of individual poets. Submissions are not accepted. Total value of awards about £8000. Established by the then Dowager Marchioness of Cholmondeley in 1965.

The Rhys Davies Trust

Details Prof Meic Stephens, The Secretary, The Rhys Davies Trust, 10 Heol Don, Whitchurch, Cardiff CF14 2AU
tel 029-2062 3359

The Trust aims to foster Welsh writing in English and offers financial assistance to English-language literary projects in Wales, directly or in association with other bodies.

The Eric Gregory Trust Fund

Awards Secretary, The Society of Authors, 84 Drayton Gardens, London SW10 9SB
tel 020-7373 6642
email info@societyofauthors.org
website www.societyofauthors.org

A number of substantial awards are made annually for the encouragement of young poets who can show that they are likely to benefit from an opportunity to give more time to writing. An eligible candidate must:

• be a British subject by birth, but not a national of Eire or any of the British dominions or colonies, and be ordinarily resident in the UK or Northern Ireland;
• be under the age of 30 on 31st March in the year of the Award (i.e. the year following submission). Send sae for entry form. Closing date, 31st October.

Hawthornden Fellowships

The Administrator,
International Retreat for Writers,
Hawthornden Castle, Lasswade,
Midlothian EH18 1EG
tel 0131-440 2180 *fax* 0131-440 1989

Applications are invited from novelists, poets, dramatists and other creative writers whose work has already been published by reputable or recognised presses. Four-week fellowships are offered to those working on a current project. Translators may also apply. Application forms are available from March for Fellowships awarded in the following year.

The John Masefield Memorial Trust

Details Awards Secretary,
The Society of Authors, 84 Drayton Gardens, London SW10 9SB
tel 020-7373 6642 *fax* 020-7373 5768
email info@societyofauthors.org
website www.societyofauthors.org

This trust makes occasional grants to professional poets who find themselves with sudden financial problems. Apply for an information sheet and application form.

New Writing North

Culture Lab, Grand Assembly Rooms, Newcastle University, King's Walk, Newcastle NE1 7RU
tel 0191-222 1332 *fax* 0191-222 1372
email mail@newwritingnorth.com
website www.newwritingnorth.com
Director Claire Malcolm

The literature development agency for the North East. Offers advice and support to writers of poetry, prose and plays. See website. Founded 1996.

The Saltire Society Awards

Details The Saltire Society, 9 Fountain Close, 22 High Street, Edinburgh EH1 1TF
tel 0131-556 1836 *fax* 0131-557 1675
email saltire@saltiresociety.org.uk
website www.saltiresociety.org.uk

Books published between 1 September and 31 August are eligible for the following awards:

The Welsh Academy

3rd Floor Mount Stuart House,
Mount Stuart Square, Cardiff CF10 5FQ

tel 029-2047 2266 *fax* 029-2049 2930
email post@academi.org
website www.academi.org
CEO Peter Finch

Wingate Scholarships

The Administrator, QABC, 28 Broadway,
London SW1H 9JX
website www.wingatescholarships.org.uk

Wingate Scholarships are awarded to
individuals of great potential or proven
excellence who need financial support to
undertake creative or original work of
intellectual, scientific, artistic, social or
environmental value; also to outstanding
musicians for advanced training. The
scholarships are designed to help with the costs
of a specific project, which may last up to 3
years. The average total of each award is £6500
and the maximum amount in any one year is
£10,000. Between 40 and 50 awards are made
each year. All information and application
materials can be found on the website.

Poetry and Arts Council England

Poetry is heavily dependent on the work and funding of Arts Council England; without it, many publishers would find it hard to exist. **Gary McKeone** explains the work of ACE in relation to poetry.

Poet Laureate, Poetry Society, Poetry Library, Poems on the Underground, Poems in the Waiting Room, poetry in schools, hospitals and prisons; poetry publishers, poetry magazines, poetry competitions; slam poetry, performance poetry. Enough. Poetry is not an invisible literary genre, yet its status, impact and reach are constantly debated. Who buys it? Do we publish too much? Who reads it? Why? Why not? Does poetry matter any more? Has it been buried in the avalanche of other demands on our time, its heartbeat hardly perceptible beneath the noise of contemporary life?

Yet, we still reach for it *in extremis*; for weddings, births and funerals, in grief and in wonder, in public and in private, as if we retain some residual, instinctive belief in its talismanic, perhaps sacred qualities. Why? A definitive answer to that question would be reductive. There are some things in this age of outputs and outcomes that rightly remain beyond scrutiny. That doesn't, of course, deter the scrutinisers.

Perhaps the essence of poetry is simply, "the best words in the best order" as Samuel Taylor Coleridge has it. Andrew Motion eloquently suggests that, "Poetry is sanctified by a sense that it helps us to enjoy and endure our existence." We needn't probe too deeply. Poetry can move us and amuse us; it can illuminate and confound; it can shout out loud in the public domain or whisper to us privately in that unique communion between writer and reader. A single, all-embracing definition eludes us, but no matter. We might just as well try to 'define' the blood that runs in our veins. Impossible, but without it, where would we be?

Arts Council England's role in all this is to nurture and develop an environment in which poetry, in its many shapes, can find its way in the world. There was a time when this would simply have meant supporting poetry publishers. We continue to do this, of course. Presses like Carcanet, Bloodaxe and Enitharmon, Anvil and Arc, magazines such as *Modern Poetry in Translation*, *Rialto*, *Agenda* and *Poetry Review* use Arts Council investment to bring new poets and new poetries to the notice of the reading world. Our support enables editors to take risks with new work, often poetry in translation, that the purely commercial sector might not countenance.

But there is more to poetry in the 21st century than words on a page. Any listings magazine worth the name advertises events that are happening in all sorts of places right across the country. This might mean a poetry festival in Ledbury or a Poetry Prom in Aldeburgh; a poetry tour, or National Poetry Day. In most cases, Arts Council support will have provided the necessary financial backing. And if heading out to enjoy poetry is not your thing, the Internet can keep you up to speed with its e-magazines and ever-increasing number of poetry websites. Click on **www.poetryarchive.org** and listen to poets reading their own work. Explore the site further and you'll find resources for teachers, students, librarians and children – in fact anyone with an interest in poetry. While you're surfing, try **www.poetrybooks.co.uk**, home of the Poetry Book Society. With a couple of clicks you can become a member and receive discounted poetry books all year round by post: poetry for adults and poetry for young people.

The Arts Council is both a funding agency and a development agency. What does that mean? In short, we make resources available through our open application programme, Grants for the Arts. This enables individuals, organisations and touring organisations to seek funding for a truly wide range of artistic programmes and initiatives. For a poet, that might mean buying time to write, funding for a period of research or travel, or support for a residency, to name but a few options; for an organisation, Grants for the Arts can support a programme of work, e.g. a series of poetry translations, set-up money for a literary magazine, or finance for organisational development that will help an organisation evolve and make it fit for purpose in a constantly changing environment. Support for touring does what it says on the tin, by making resources available for literature touring initiatives.

We also make good use of strategic budgets, i.e. resources not open to application that we invest in Arts Council-generated programmes of work. Often our financial input will lever resources from other partners, the commercial world, government departments, the education or library sectors, essentially any group or organisation that can help make literature a prominent and effective part of all our lives. This might mean work around children and young people, or arts and health; it might mean an international dimension or work on distribution. We rightly keep an eye on the cultural weather to identify those areas that need our intervention. In this way, we can function properly as a development agency.

The Arts Council, a national office and nine regional offices, has, of course, more strings to its bow than budgets. There is a wealth of experience and expertise in the organisation, people who are knowledgeable and passionate about the arts, people who work with individuals and organisations to maximise all opportunities and towards securing the long-term future of the sector with which we are involved. It is when we work *with* the sector that we work best.

The details can be found on our website, **www.artscouncil.org.uk** ... but let me finish, not with strategies or policies, not with funding programmes or priorities, but with a poem. It's by Jackie Kay. She once worked as a Literature Officer at the Arts Council. It's called *Promise*.

Remember, the time of year
when the future appears
like a blank sheet of paper
a clean calendar, a new chance.
You vow fresh footprints
then watch them go
with the wind's hearty gust.
Fill your glass. Here's tae us. Promises
made to be broken, made to last.

Gary McKeone was formerly Literature Director for Arts Council England.

A poetry tutor's experience

Poets are increasingly turning to teaching to supplement their income. An explosion of writing courses and summer schools has opened up many opportunities. **Myra Schneider** has a great deal of experience in teaching poetry, both on a one-to-one basis and in a classroom set-up; here she provides some useful methods and tips for those wanting to teach poetry.

It is true that it isn't possible to *teach* someone to be a poet. Nevertheless I believe profoundly in the value of poetry courses and workshops, especially those run by practising poets who like teaching. Good tutors may play a key role in helping a gifted participant develop his/her talent. They can also offer everyone the opportunity to learn about the craft of poetry, to use words more effectively and to share in the enjoyment of writing and reading poems. I love generating an enthusiasm for poetry and I find it immensely satisfying when I see a student's work flowering.

I began running poetry and creative writing workshops for local education authorities in 1988. At that time I had had three collections of poetry published, as well as a novel for children and two for teenagers. I had also had experience of teaching in comprehensive schools and had been a member of a poetry society. The former had taught me something about teaching and managing people. The latter I'd found very frustrating, because in meetings to workshop poems, members commented on a poem the moment it had been read, often referring to minor points. Sometimes there were arguments; only rarely, in-depth feedback. I left the group and started a much smaller one with a poet friend, Colin Rowbotham, who suggested that after a poem was read we should spend some minutes in silence re-reading it and writing our comments on the script before we began to discuss it.

This idea worked so well that I adopted it for my teaching. The method was very successful and I still use it. What participants in workshop classes want most is a focused response to their work, and they find it valuable to have everyone's considered points written on their poem. Moreover, asking students to crystallise their reactions to each piece of work discussed is a useful way to help them develop critical faculties to apply to their own writing. It's crucial, of course, to give rigorous and explanatory criticism, but important too that comments should be positive and constructive (and I impress this on groups). I also try to ensure that I offer feedback that is appropriate to the stage the writer is at and I try to remember there is always an ability range in any workshop. In the main I find that members of a group are very supportive of one another.

I think it is essential that a poetry class should open doors. Whatever a group's terms of reference, the relationship between reading and writing should always be stressed. I introduce published poets, look at their poems and the techniques they use, discuss possible approaches to material and the writing process. In some of my groups the setting of exercises, which encourage students to write in new ways, has been an important element.

When I began running poetry workshops, I realised that I must try to combine informality with management. Controlling a group of adults is trickier than controlling a class in a school. Unlike children, they cannot be *told*. Sometimes there is a workshop member who wants to utter his/her views or feelings about everything, or who is quickly on the defensive, however tactfully feedback is given. Quite soon I decided that I would not have a free-for-all even after a piece of work had been considered in silence. Instead I asked one person to make the opening comments, added my own and then invited general discussion. This structure has worked well. It means that everyone, not just the most articulate or dominating, has the opportunity to express their views. When problems have arisen, this framework has made it easier to deal with them.

After a few years I stopped working for local authorities, mainly because they wanted to make all courses accredited; I felt that this was inappropriate for creative work. For a while I ran monthly groups privately; I also gave one-to-one tutorials with detailed comments on about six pages of poetry, together with a general assessment and suggestions for developing work. When my friend, Mimi Khalvati, started The Poetry School in 1997 I was keen to be part of it, as I very much agreed with her vision. I currently run monthly workshops and a small seminar group for the School. In the main I now work with poets who have moved beyond the very early stages of writing. One of my workshops begins with an in-depth focus on an aspect of the writing process. The other is open to writers of serious prose as well as poetry.

For the last 15 years I have also run one-off poetry courses for poetry groups, colleges, literature departments and the Second Light Network of Women Poets. I have also co-tutored many residential weekends with poet John Killick (who has done a wide range of writing residencies, and for several years has used writing as a way to communicate with people suffering from dementia). The main aim in all these courses has been to help poets and sometimes prose writers develop their work by offering exercises and ideas which will stretch them. Longer workshops give participants space to try out different ideas and to exchange views with other aspiring writers.

To become a poetry tutor it is crucial to have a catholic taste, an ability to communicate, and a feeling of sympathy with people who are trying to develop their work. Ideally one should have had at least one collection published and a track record in good magazines. The best way of finding work is to approach adult education authorities which run or are willing to set up poetry workshops, or universities offering courses in creative writing. It may also be worth looking at education websites for information, or contacting The Poetry Society. The number of poetry workshops and courses is growing; poets interested in this field will probably be able to find work in it.

Myra Schneider's most recent books are *Images of Women: An Anthology of Contemporary Women's Poetry* (with Dilys Wood, Arrowhead Press 2006); *Multiplying The Moon* (Enitharmon 2004); *Insisting on Yellow* – new and selected poems (Enitharmon 2000); and *Writing My Way Through Cancer* – a journal with poem notes and poems (Jessica Kingsley 2003). She has also co-edited four anthologies of poetry by contemporary women poets.

Creative writing courses

Poets have realised that they can make a good living from teaching, while passing on some of their hard-earned experience. Many are now involved in creative writing courses, the venues for which range from community centres to the Greek Islands. However, there are also (literally) hundreds of university and college courses in creative writing, most of which will provide a poetry module or option. The website of the National Association of Writers in Education (**www.nawe.co.uk**) provides a comprehensive list of creative writing courses available throughout the country.

Alston Hall College
Alston Lane, Longridge, Preston PR3 3BP
tel (01772) 784661 *fax* (01772) 785835
email alston.hall@ed.lancscc.gov.uk
website www.alstonhall.com

The Arvon Foundation
Lumb Bank, The Ted Hughes Arvon Centre,
Heptonstall, Hebden Bridge,
West Yorkshire HX7 6DF
tel (01422) 843714 *fax* (01422) 843714
email l-bank@arvonfoundation.org
website www.arvonfoundation.org
Contact Ilona Jones
Moniack Mhor, Teavarran, Kiltarlity, Beauly,
Inverness-shire IV4 7HT
tel (01463) 741675 *fax* (01463) 741733
email m-mhor@arvonfoundation.org
Contact Lyndy Batty
The Arvon Foundation, Totleigh Barton,
Sheepwash, Beaworthy, Devon EX21 5NS
tel (01409) 231338 *fax* (01409) 231144
email t-barton@arvonfoundation.org
Contact Julia Wheadon
The Hurst – The John Osborne Arvon Centre
Clunton, Craven Arms, Shropshire SY7 0JA
tel (01588) 640658 *fax* (01588) 640509
email hurst@arvonfoundation.org
Contact Dan Pavitt

Founded in 1968, the Arvon Foundation run 5-day residential courses throughout the year for anyone over the age of 16, providing the opportunity to live and work with professional writers. Writing genres explored include poetry, narrative, drama, writing for children, song-writing and the performing arts. Bursaries are available.

The Ashburton Centre
A Taste of Travel Ltd, The Ashburton Centre,
79 East Street, Ashburton,
South Devon TQ13 7AL

tel (01364) 652784
email stella@ashburtoncentre.co.uk
website www.a-taste-of.com

Runs a range of creative writing holiday courses in Italy and Spain.

Blaze Online Writing Courses
University of Strathclyde, Livingstone Tower,
26 Richmond Street, Glasgow G1 1XH
tel 0141-552 3493
email alix.mcdonald@strath.ac.uk
website www.strath.ac.uk

The Centre for Lifelong Learning has been championing creative writing classes for a number of years. Due to demand, the Centre has launched 'Blaze' – a collection of online creative writing classes, developed to suit writers at all levels.

Bridgewater College
Bridgewater Arts Centre, Castle Street,
Bridgewater, Somerset TA6 3DD
tel (01278) 422700
email info@bridgewaterartscentre.co.uk,
gwmailbox@yahoo.co.uk
website www.bridgewaterartscentre.co.uk
Contact Genista Wheatley

A creative writing workshop – fiction/non-fiction, poetry, playwriting. All abilities welcome. £50 for a 10-week term.

Burton Manor
Burton, Neston, Cheshire CH64 5SJ
tel 0151-336 5172 *fax* 0151-336 6586
email enquiry@burtonmanor.com
website www.burtonmanor.com
Principal Keith Chandler

College offering a wide range of residential courses.

Centerprise Literature

Centreprise, 136–138 Kingsland High Street,
London E8 2NS
tel 020-7249 6572
email literature@centerprisetrust.org.uk
website www.centerpriseliterature.com
Contact Susan Yearwood

Runs courses and workshops in creative
writing, organises poetry and book readings,
discussions and debates on literary and relevant
issues, writers' surgeries, and telephone
information on resources for writers in
London. Publishes *Calabash* newsletter for
writers of Black and Asian origin. Funded by
ACE London. Founded 1995.

Cinnamon Press Writing Courses

Meirion House, Glan yr afon, Tanygrisiau,
Blaenau Ffestiniog, Gwynedd LL41 3SU
email jan@cinnamonpress.com
website www.cinnamonpress.com

Bespoke tuition for writers – from young
people to adults – both beginning writers and
those who want to develop skills further, or
who want specific input on a work-in-progress.
Tailor-made study can include an introduction
to writing skills across a range of genres, such
as journaling, non-fiction, poetry and fiction,
or a more specialist focus on novel-writing, a
work of non-fiction or poetry. New residential
courses in mindfulness and creative writing –
see website.

Creative in Calvados

1 Ormelie Terrace, Joppa,
Edinburgh EH15 2EX
tel 0131-669 5330
email steveharvey@creativeincalvados.co.uk
website www.creativeincalvados.co.uk
Contact Stephen Harvey

Mid-week and long weekend courses in poetry,
songwriting/music, scriptwriting, drama and
prose. Courses take place in Normandy.
Founded 2001.

Dingle Writing Courses

Ballintlea, Ventry, Co Kerry,
Republic of Ireland
tel 00 353 66 9159815
email info@dinglewritingcourses.ie
website www.dinglewritingcourses.ie
Contact Nicholas McLachlan

An annual residential poetry weekend set in a
stunning venue on the Atlantic Coast, west of
Dingle, Co Kerry. An intensive course led by an
experienced tutor (e.g. Mary O'Malley, Colette
Bryce, Eva Salzman). Numbers are limited to
14. Further details are available on the website.

Dorset East Street Poets

Garden Cottage, The Down House,
Blandford Forum, Dorset DT11 9AD
tel (01258) 454026
email westrow@cooper.co.uk
website www.theworldtravels.com
Contact Westrow Cooper

Organises weekend writing courses tutored by
established national and international poets
and writers, at hotels and other venues linked
to the literary landscape. See website for
current and forthcoming events and courses.

Far West

23 Chapel Street, Penzance,
Cornwall TR18 4AP
tel (01736) 363146
email angela@farwest.co.uk
website www.farwest.co.uk
Contact Angela Stoner

Offers a range of creative writing courses and
workshops.

Fire in the Head

PO Box 17, Yelverton, Devon PL20 6YF
tel (01822) 841081
email roselle.angwin@internet-today.co.uk
website www.fire-in-the-head.co.uk
Contact Roselle Angwin

Poetry and prose; journaling and personal
development; retreats and short courses;
correspondence courses.

Highgreen Arts

Highgreen, Tarset, Northumberland NE48 1RP
tel 020-7602 1363
email highgreenarts@aol.com
website www.highgreen-arts.co.uk
Contact William & Cynthia Morrison-Bell

Highgreen Arts runs residential writing and
arts courses with a strong emphasis on poetry.
Highgreen is in the heart of the
Northumberland National Park, and is also

home to Bloodaxe Books. Course tutors to date have included Brendan Kennelly and David Constantine, both Bloodaxe poets. Good teachers, friendly hosts, great food and accommodation.

Indian King Arts

Garmoe Cottage, 2 Trefrew Road, Camelford, Cornwall PL32 9TP
tel (01840) 212161
email indianking@btconnect.com
website www.indianking.org.uk
Contact Helen Jagger Wood

Following the sale of the Indian King Arts Centre in 2006, a number of literary groups continue to meet in Camelford. The Indian King Poets meet weekly; the Novel Surgery meets bi-monthly; Latin literary translators meet weekly; and there are occasional day or non-residential weekend poetry workshops led by guest poets (recent guests include Mimi Khalvati, George Wallace, Penelope Shuttle and John Greening).

La Muse

1 Rue de la Place, Labastide Esparbairenque, France
tel ++33 (0)4 68 26 33 93
email getaway@lamuseinn.com
website www.lamuseinn.com
Contact Kerry Eielson, John Fanning

Provides a peaceful space where artists and writers can work in a peaceful, isolated and inspiring setting. La Muse is a self-service establishment. The house is informal and comfortable, but a structure exists with the purpose of vigorous work and focus on a creative project. That structure consists of the house guidelines, which each guest is asked to consult before applying. The purpose is to support a true retreat from life back home.

Missenden Abbey

Great Missenden, Bucks HP16 0BD
tel (01296) 383582 *fax* (01753) 783756
email dcevreham@buckscc.gov.uk
website www.arca.uk.net/missendenabbey

Weekend and summer-school writing courses.

National Association of Writers in Education

PO Box 1, Sheriff Hutton, York YO60 7YU
tel (01653) 618429
email paul@nawe.co.uk
website www.nawe.co.uk
Director Paul Munden

The only organisation supporting the development of creative writing of all genres and in all educational and community settings throughout the UK.

NorthCourt Manor

Shorwell, Isle of Wight
tel (01983) 740980
email lydia_fulleylove@lineone.net
website www.shorewomen.org.uk
Contact Lydia Fulleylove

This ancient manor house with its beautiful garden has inspired many writers and artists, including the poet Swinburne who often stayed there. Now, writing weekends are run at the house, Arvon style, for keen young writers – an opportunity to work alongside professional writers (for example, Philip Gross, Mimi Khalvati, Jane Draycott) and artists intensively for 2 days. Each year a publication, often with a strong cross-arts emphasis (poetry and artwork), is produced. These weekends are organised by Literature Development Worker & Writer in Healthcare, Lydia Fulleylove. Lydia also runs poetry days to refresh and restore teachers' creative energies; writing days for able writers in primary schools; and independent writing days for adults and for Healing Arts clients. Northcourt is, as one young writer commented, "A world of its own, a writer's paradise."

Old Olive Press

Old Olive Press,
C/ de la Mare de Deu del Miracle,
56 Relleu 03578, Spain
tel (00349) 66 856 003
email oldolivepress@tiscali.es
website www.oldolivepress.com/

Designed as a home and as a centre for residential writing, art and other cultural courses. Runs a variety of workshops, activities and creative writing courses.

The Open College of the Arts

Registration Department, OCA,
The Michael Young Arts Centre,

Unit 1B Redbrook Business Park,
Wilthorpe Road, Barnsley S75 1JN
tel 0800-731 2116
email open.arts@ukonline.co.uk
website www.oca-uk.com

An open-access college dedicated to artistic development. No formal qualifications are required, there are no age limits and students can enrol at any time of the year. The poetry course explains and illustrates the essential elements of the art and craft of poetry; and a tutor, who is a poet with a good record of publication, will assess students' poems and help them to develop their skills. There are 9 creative writing courses offered in total, covering most genres. Request a free *Guide to Courses*.

Open Studies – Part-time Courses for Adults: Office of Lifelong Learning

University of Edinburgh, 11 Buccleuch Place, Edinburgh EH8 9LW
tel 0131-650 4400 *fax* 0131-667 6097
email oll@ed.ac.uk
website www.lifelong.ed.ac.uk

Offers a large number of creative writing courses.

Open University

PO Box 197, Milton Keynes MK7 6BJ
tel (08703) 334340
email general-enquiries@open.ac.uk
website www.open.ac.uk

Start Writing Poetry course. This course will introduce students in a gradual and accessible way to the basic 'tools of the trade'. Through examples, exercises, and games, they will practise poetic devices and methods, get ideas for subject matter, and learn how to edit their work. They will eventually write in a variety of forms from the haiku to the sonnet and in a range of styles including satire and parody. The course will also enhance reading skills and increase the ability to appreciate contemporary poetry. This is a 12-week course.

Poetry: Writing Our Lives

Missenden Abbey, Great Missenden HP16 0BD
tel (08450) 454040
Contact Gerard Benson

A writing course with tutor Gerard Benson. Residential or tuition-only.

Poetry & Writing

World Spirit, 12 Vale Road, Bowden, Cheshire WA14 3AQ
tel 0161-928 5768
email worldspirit99@aol.com
website www.worldspirit.org.uk/writers.html

Exploring artistic creativity within the inspiring natural resource of South West Crete. Courses take place over 5 days. Short private tutorials may be offered. Each course offers short-course summaries upon application and, unless stated otherwise, takes place irrespective of numbers.

Poetry Class

Poetry Society, 22 Betterton Street, London WC2H 9BX
tel 020-7420 9889
email poetryclasss@poetrysociety.org.uk
website www.poetryclass.org
Contact Andrew Bailey

An online poetry classroom and unique INSET training provides teachers with a 'nuts and bolts' insight into how poetry works. A training team of poets – all of whom are highly experienced with work in schools, and have between them hundreds of tried and tested ideas – is available to work with teachers to overcome their problems and concerns with teaching poetry.

Poetry Dorchester

School Lane, The Grove, Dorchester, Dorset DT1 1XR
tel (01305) 266926 (Box Office), (01300) 320826
email pam@zhope.co.uk
website www.dorchesterarts.org.uk
Contact Pam Zinnemann-Hope, Zenobia Venner

Founded in 2001. Has an expanding programme, offering weekly workshops, occasional Saturday workshops and Poetry Cafes with well-known guest poets and open mic. Has links with the Poetry School and is funded by ACESW.

Poetry Otherwise

Emerson College, Forest Row, East Sussex RH18 5JX

tel (01342) 822238
email mail@emerson.org.uk
website http://www.poetryotherwise.org
Contact Paul Matthews

A creative summer gathering for poets, creative writers and lovers of language.

The Poetry School
1a Jewel Road, Walthamstow,
London E17 4QU
tel 0845-223 5274 *fax* 020-8223 0439
website programme@poetryschool.com

The Poetry School was founded in 1997 and now offers a comprehensive programme of courses, workshops and tutorials. The tutors are celebrated poets. Courses, workshops and Special Events take place at various venues in London, Manchester, York, Exeter and Lewes. Fees vary. A generous Bursary Scheme is available for all UK courses and workshops.

Poetry Surgery with Carole Satyamurti at the Poetry Café
Poetry Society, 22 Betterton, Street,
London WC2H 9BX
tel 020-7420 9887
email poetrycafe@poetrysociety.org.uk
website www.poetrysociety.org.uk/cafe
Contact Jessica Yorke

One-to-one surgeries for anyone writing poetry who wants to talk to an experienced poet about their work. For £20 (£15 for Poetry Society members) you will be able to talk to Carole for 30 minutes about your work. Surgeries happen quarterly. When enough people have asked to see her, Carole comes in to the Café for an afternoon.

The Poets' House
Clonbarra, Falcarrash, Co. Donegal,
Republic of Ireland
tel (353) 746 5470 *fax* (353) 746 5471
Contact John Fitzsimmons

Residential writing courses, weekends and week-long or 2-week workshops; also MA programme in Creative Writing in English and Irish.

Salmon Poetry Courses
Cliffs of Moher, County Clare, Ireland
tel (003536) 5708 1941

email jessie@salmonpoetry.com
website www.salmonpoetry.com

Runs regular weekend creative writing workshops at the Salmon premises. The workshops include all aspects of writing and publishing. Creative writing residencies lasting 1-4 weeks are also available.

School of English, Newcastle University
Percy Building, Newcastle upon Tyne NE1 7RU
tel 0191-222 7619
email melanie.birch@ncl.ac.uk
website www.ncl.ac.uk/elll/creative
Contact Melanie Birch

The School of English hosts poetry readings and book launches. Offers various creative writing courses – short evening classes, one-week intensive spring and summer schools, and Postgraduate Certificate (via distance learning as well as on campus), MA and PhD degrees.

South Hill Park Poetry Workshop
South Hill Park Arts Centre, Ringmead,
Birch Hill, Bracknell, Berks RG12 7PA
tel (01344) 416206
email gail.babb@southhillpark.org.uk
website www.southhillpark.org.uk
Contact Gail Babb

Regularly hosts day-long poetry and creative writing workshops; has started 5-week courses for adults and young people with published poets.

Swanwick, The Writers' Summer School
Contact Jean Sutton, The Secretary
email jeanfsutton@btinternet.com
website www.wss.org.uk

Has been in existence for 60 years, teaching new skills to (and honing old ones for) poets, playwrights, journalists and songwriters.

Trinity College, Carmarthen
Trinity College, Carmarthen SA31 3EP
tel (01267) 676721 *fax* (01267) 676863
email p.wright@trinity-cm.ac.uk
website www.trinity-cm.ac.uk
Contact Dr Paul Wright

Trinity College offers University of Wales degrees in creative writing at undergraduate and postgraduate level, with a particular emphasis on poetry. The writing director is Menna Elfyn, and the course has a growing relationship with a number of publishers, including Parthian. Applications to MA course on request.

Ty Newydd

Llanystumdwy, Cricieth, Gwynedd LL52 0LW
tel (01766) 522811 *fax* (01766) 523095
email post@tynewydd.org
website www.tynewydd.org
Contact Sally Baker

Residential 5-day poetry courses for all levels of expertise and experience, tutored by poets of the highest calibre. Ty Newydd is a beautiful, historic house, situated in stunning surroundings overlooking the sea in North West Wales. Has run residential creative writing courses for the past 16 years and has recently re-opened, with greatly improved facilities including disabled access. There are a variety of courses in all genres – poetry, fiction, scriptwriting and drama etc. The maximum number on any course is 16. Students work with 2 tutors who are experienced writers in their field. Nearly all courses run from Monday evening to Saturday morning and are a combination of workshops, individual tutorials and readings, with time in between for writing. A bursary fund exists and it is the aim to enable everybody who would benefit from a course at Ty Newydd to do so. Ty Newydd also offers courses with a similar format to groups of young writers from schools and colleges. Details of all the courses are available on the website. Course cost is approximately £430.

University of St Andrews Creative Summer Writing Programme

St Katharine's West, 16 The Scores,
St Andrews, Fife KY16 9AX
tel (01334) 462238 *fax* (01334) 462158
email crsp@st-andrews.ac.uk
website www.st-andrews.ac.uk/admissions/
CWSPweb.htm
Director Dr MIS Hunter

Now well established, the Creative Writing Summer Programme has proved as popular as the successful Scottish Studies Summer Programme, and incorporates many of its features. A series of master classes and workshops with leading Scottish writers allow students to develop skills of authoring, oral presentation, editing and analysis. In addition to the stimulating environment of St Andrews, there is a full programme of excursions and social and cultural activities to provide additional inspiration for students' poetry and prose. Come and experience what it is like to live and study in one of the most atmospheric and beautiful universities in the world, while honing your writing skills.

The Virtual Writing School

Manchester Metropolitan University Writing School, Geoffrey Manton Building, Oxford Road, Manchester M15 6LL
tel (01612) 471735
email h.beck@mmn.ac.uk
website www.hlss.mmn.ac.uk/english/
writingschool/
Contact Heather Beck

Campus or online MA/PGDip in Poetry or Novel-Writing, full- or part-time. Practitioners include Simon Armitage, Heather Beck, Andrew Biswell, Carol Ann Duffy, Michael Symmons Roberts, Jeffrey Wainwright.

Write Away

Arts Training Central (Arts Council, East Midlands), 16 New Street, Leicester LE1 5NR
tel 0116-242 5202
email bonnie@artstrainingcentral.co.uk
website www.artstrainingcentral.co.uk
Contact Bonnie James

The ATC programme of Write Away courses runs each summer. The programme consists of 4 residential writing courses for writers of all levels, which run from Friday afternoon to Sunday afternoon. Each course offers workshops, surgeries and individual writing time to a small and informal group. The fee for each course is £145, which includes all meals, accommodation and tuition. The exact course topics vary each year: courses in 2007 included Writing Romantic Fiction (tutors Kate Walker, Julie Cohen); Writing for Sound and Vision (tutors Stephen Loveless, Charlotte

Thompson); and Breaking Boundaries (for all writers of prose and poetry – tutors Rombert Hamberger, River Wolton). Register to receive details of the next programme.

Write Away in Tuscany

99 Via Della Fonte, Monticiano 53015, Siena, Italy
tel (0039) 3334149837
website wwwthewordworks.org.uk
Contact Sandra Stevens

Flexible week-long courses by special appointment only. For small groups or individuals who want to stretch themselves as writers and have a holiday in the hills of Tuscany, mentored by a professional and experienced tutor. A real retreat – and a stimulating retreat. The focus is usually on the local environment, nature, and art and language. Ring to discuss your particular needs: they can be met!

The Writers Bureau

Sevendale House, 7 Dale Street, Manchester M1 1JB
tel 0161-228 2362
email studentservices@writersbureau.com
website www.writersbureau.com

Home-study courses in Creative Writing, Journalism, Poetry and Writing Biographies, Memoirs and Family Histories.

Poets in education

Paul Munden describes how NAWE (the National Association of Writers in Education) supports poets working in educational contexts.

Poets, perhaps more so than any other writers, have a long tradition of working in education. Many of them seem to have a natural gift for this type of work, an instinct for how their own poetic strategies can be usefully shared to spark and sustain other people's efforts. Instinct, however, is not always enough. Poets, like anyone else, need help in negotiating the territory: finding the opportunities, improving their practice, devising effective collaborations with other partners. This was why NAWE was first set up and has grown into an association offering practical support to over a thousand members.

As the number of university writing courses continues to grow, and as 'creativity' is once again being taken seriously in the school curriculum, there are many opportunities for poets to work in formal educational settings, helping others to develop their craft. Within NAWE, however, we use the word 'education' in the very broadest sense, referring not only to the formal education system but also the many other community contexts in which learning takes place: writing groups, youth centres, hospices, prisons – anywhere, in fact, that people can get together and learn from each other in pursuing their writing. A professional writer is often key to making these gatherings work. The NAWE website, updated daily, provides a detailed listing of all opportunities for poets working – and learning – in these ways.

Even with the vast expansion of courses, jobs for poets in universities, as full time creative writing lecturers, are still relatively scarce. Only those poets with a substantial track record are likely to get a look in. It is, however, worth making contact with a university in your area, in case any smaller opportunities should arise. Universities pride themselves on giving students a broad experience of literary culture and engaging with their local community.

Working in schools is, in one sense, easier. Teachers are being actively encouraged to bring artists into their classes, so there really has never been a better time for poets to find this sort of work. If you wish to work in schools, make sure you are listed in our directory, artscape, the national directory for arts in education. Teachers are inevitably bombarded with all sorts of self-publicity from artists, and only by using a directory with rigorous standards can they be sure of what they are going to get. NAWE ensures that all individuals listed have Enhanced Disclosure checks and appropriate insurance. We also publish two references from previous employers as part of each directory entry. We encourage writers to be very specific about their experience, so that teachers can find someone to work, say, with a particular key stage group or specific aspect of the curriculum.

If you have not worked in education before, the very idea can be daunting. Schools, especially, can be scary places for those who haven't been there for some time. Besides, not all writers are natural workshop leaders. NAWE provides training opportunities through which writers new to educational work can gain the necessary knowledge and skills. Our single day seminars introduce relevant aspects of the school curriculum and tried and tested ways of working as writers in the classroom. We also run mentoring schemes, which enable new writers to gain valuable insight through working alongside those with more experience. Other events explore working with particular age groups or other specific contexts – including those outside of formal education. We also hold conferences, bringing together writers and other education professionals to share practice and learn from each other in a focused and supportive environment. Members have the chance to learn from each other's workshops and demonstrate to teachers the type of work they might introduce to their schools.

Our programme of events is just one part of NAWE's work. Our magazine, *Writing in Education*, is sent to all members three times a year and features lively articles on critical issues and workshop techniques. We encourage both our writer and teacher members to provide accounts of the projects they undertake, so that others can learn from their experience and gain inspiration and practical advice when planning projects of their own. Every writer is different, not just in the obvious way of being a poet rather than a dramatist, journalist or novelist, but in the very different ways they go about their own writing and the different ideas they have for encouraging others to write too. So the way in which we publish accounts of these writers' activities is not really for others to copy, but to make them think about unique ways in which they too could share their particular working practices. The NAWE archive, on our website, describes many different models.

Further information

NAWE membership is £20 per annum and brings three issues of the magazine, regular newsletters and reduced-rate booking for all events. For details of membership, journal, conferences and other events and resources, please visit the NAWE website, www.nawe.co.uk. Writers available for work in schools are listed in NAWE's online directory, www.artscape.org.uk.

The National Association of Writers in Education (NAWE)
PO Box 1, Sheriff Hutton, York YO60 7YU
tel (01653) 618429
email info@nawe.co.uk

Working effectively as a poet in education takes genuine commitment. It can be well paid but it is not easy money. We don't recommend that every poet should run workshops. Some are simply not cut out for it. If, however, you feel that you would find it rewarding and have something to offer, NAWE is here to help. Through a range of publications, events and online resources, NAWE assists its members in becoming as confident and well prepared in their work as possible, and promotes that work where it is really needed - in formal education at every level, and in the great variety of other contexts where poets and other writers can contribute to people's personal and professional development.

Paul Munden is a poet and Director of NAWE, the National Association of Writers in Education.

Poets in schools

Many poets take their poetry, and the poetry of others, into our schools. Not only does this provide welcome income for the poet; it also helps, if the poet does a good job, to create a future audience for poetry. **Mandy Coe** tells us how it works, and provides some handy resources.

Every week in the UK a poet is invited into a school to deliver workshops, answer questions or give a reading. The schools benefit by gaining new teaching ideas and having their pupils work alongside a published writer. Poets benefit by supplementing their income and – if they write for young people – having instant feedback on their work. That's the bare bones of it. But there is more ... If there weren't, most poets would have thrown away their copies of the A to Z years ago (I'm partial to spending my time writing, not setting the alarm for 6am so I can get to a school three counties away). But having enjoyed working with young people for many years, I am fascinated by what draws poets to this unpredictable formula of poet and school; poem and child.

The curriculum (for secondary schools in particular) leaves little room to explore the writing of poetry in any depth. Pupils study set forms and texts, but looking at the recipe is not the same as eating the food, and dissecting verse without placing it firmly in the context of mystery or pleasure can immunise a child against the enjoyment of poetry for life. A poet's visit, on the other hand, creates time 'out of school' – within the school, where teacher, writer and pupils have space to explore poetry in a more dynamic way. A time where literacy outcomes are secondary. When this happens, pupils develop not just their language skills and confidence levels; they also learn to think differently. They discuss, they ask questions. They take up their pens and paper and go away inside themselves to formulate thoughts and ideas. This act of *doing* is a very powerful one, and the feedback universal: *We learned to use our imagination.*

There is real pleasure to be found in this process – witnessing young people discovering a voice through poetry. Fortunately for poets, schools know that it's pleasure, not SATs, that keeps children plugged in to literacy. Poetry has mystery, narrative and humour and can be *about* anything. It has both a visual and an oral dynamic, it's short, re-readable and – with children taking turns to compose and listen – utterly democratic. I believe that poetry is one of the most child-centred, literacy-friendly artforms there is.

Readers of the future

It's hard to read a newspaper or listen to the BBC without being told that poetry exists in a small world inhabited by a handful of academics and the ghosts of dead writers. This is puzzling, especially when we recognise the long tradition of poets working in schools, and the vibrant relationship this builds with the readers and writers of tomorrow. When he was the Children's Laureate, Michael Morpurgo said he believed an author's visit could "help a child become a reader for life". He is not alone in believing this. Many of the best-known poets in the UK know that there is no better way to encourage a child to read than to let them meet the author.

Residencies and visits

So how does it work? The one-day visit will always remain a staple for schools and poets, but through organisations such as Writing Together (writingtogether@booktrust.org.uk) the shape and breadth of this work is evolving in exciting ways: year-long residencies; projects based in museums; poets working across the curriculum; poets working with writers in other genres. Through residencies with schools I have collaborated with photographers, dancers and musicians in venues such as the Tate Gallery, the Royal Festival Hall, Mersey Ferries and of course, the classroom.

Making it work

When asked what three things would make her work in schools more rewarding, Jackie Kay said: "Small workshop groups; teacher participation and students reading at least one poem of mine before I get there," (**www.poetryclass.net**). This is sound advice. The poet's role is different from that of the teacher – the passion s/he brings as a practising writer is both contagious and slightly dangerous. The poet should always be presented in the context of their poetry.

In his keynote address to Writing Together, Andrew Motion said: "It's vital for us to be prepared to look for 'relevance', or even 'irrelevance', in the widest possible array of talents. Not that we should begin to look on writers merely as passive collaborators, who might be co-opted to shore up existing ambitions and intentions. We should look at them instead as people who can help to change the landscape. The fact of their difference in the classroom is crucial – however complementary it might be to teachers' own efforts."

Partnerships

• In addition to local projects and Arts Council regional offices, the following national organisations can offer information on partnership and employment options, training and good practice:
• The National Association of Writers in Education (**www.nawe.co.uk**);
• The National Association for Literature Development (**www.nald.org**);
• The Poetry Society (**www.poetrysociety.org**);
• Live Literature Scotland (**www.scottishbooktrust.com**);
• Poetry Ireland/Éigse Éireann (**www.poetryireland.ie**);
• Apples and Snakes (**www.applesandsnakes.org**).

Resources

A comprehensive guide for writers is *Our thoughts are bees: Writers Working with Schools* (Wordplay Press, **www.wordplaypress.com**). This handbook covers subjects such as writers finding work in schools, fees, planning and project ideas. For an introduction to poetry workshops in the classroom, try *Jumpstart Poetry in the Secondary School* (Poetry Society): edited by Cliff Yates, this book is full of insight on how to encourage young people to read and write poetry. For primary years, *The Poetry Book for Primary Schools* (Poetry Society), edited by Anthony Wilson and Siân Hughes, provides a wonderful selection of poems, interviews, games and lesson ideas.

If you are interested in other ways of encouraging poetry in the classroom (books, worksheets, lesson plans), take a look at the Poetry Society's *Poetryclass* (**www.poetryclass.net**); The Poetry Archive (**www.poetryarchive.org**); the Children's Poetry Bookshelf (**www.childrenspoetrybookshelf.co.uk**) and the Barbican's award-winning *Can I Have A Word* e-learning site (**www.canihaveaword.org.uk**).

Mandy Coe writes poetry for children and adults. She works for Poetryclass, Writing Together, NAWE and the Children's Poetry Bookshelf. Her work has been widely published and broadcast on radio and television, and her latest collection is *The Weight of Cows* (Shoestring Press). She received a Hawthornden Fellowship in 2005.

Minding the poet's business

Writer and brand consultant, **John Simmons**, teaches people in business to write better and, consequently, communicate more effectively. Why should poets not take their skills into the world of business, he argues.

No one becomes a poet to make a fortune. It's a generally accepted truth that born poets were born to be poor. Even though, here and there across the centuries, there have been a few exceptions to this golden rule.

But what about you and me? Is there a way that poetic skills can be put to profitable use in the business world? Can some skill in rhyme earn an honest shilling in time?

All I can do is write about my own experience. But then I write not as a poet (I'm sure you'll have noticed) but as a writer who enjoys poetry and uses some of its techniques. Let me explain.

I've been a writer in the business world for the last 20 years. In that time I've worked in design and branding consultancies, and more recently as a freelance. I've carried out activities that business people might describe as 'marketing' or 'communications'; I've trained people in those business communities to write more creatively; and I've even written the odd poem. In fact, I've earned a living and poetry has been an important part of it.

Things really started to take off for me – at least in terms of personal satisfaction – when I decided to write books about 'how to write more powerfully for business'. The first of these (*We, Me, Them & It*, 2000) drew on work I'd been writing for clients over the previous decade – for people like Waterstone's and Royal Mail, for example. In analysing and writing about this work in the book, it became clear to me that the best of my writing for business drew for inspiration on the examples of writers I enjoyed reading – not business writers but poets, novelists, storytellers.

Other books followed and the theme was reinforced. Another book (*The Invisible Grail*) described my experiences as 'writer-in-residence' alongside Jackie Wills as 'poet-in-residence' at Unilever's Kingston offices. There we worked with the brand marketing teams (Persil, Dove, Domestos, etc.) to help release more of their creativity through writing. You will find, as you get closer to the business world, that individuals and corporations share a yearning to be more creative. Because it's liberating for the individual who might be bored and inert for much of the time at work; and because all companies are desperately trying to find an edge that will differentiate them from competitors. Most companies, of every size and every type, will recognise that they need more creative people to work for them; it's good for innovation, motivation, company culture and all sorts of business buzzwords.

So here is the opportunity for poets. Companies are interested in the potential of poetry to play a part in personal development. For that, think of the 'human resources' function in a company – they are fond of acronyms and programmes that are labelled with alliterative mnemonics like the *5 Ps*. Companies are even more interested, though, in helping their own people to be more productively creative. For that, think of areas like 'marketing' where people feel more pressure at least to try thinking laterally.

If you approach a business to offer your poetic skills, you will need to research a little. Company websites give you all the information you need. Read the language of the website.

Does it communicate well? If not, what's wrong with it? How is it different from poetry? How might poetry improve it? Perhaps, without needing to write a sonnet, you could rewrite it as you would wish to read it. Perhaps that becomes your introductory gambit.

Of course you will also need to think through your own approach to a company. What will your first line be? How will you keep their attention after that? What might be a satisfying conclusion; one that opens up the corporate door for you like a well-oiled couplet? In thinking through these questions you will also find that actually there is not such an enormous divide between poetry and persuasive writing to or for a business. Put aside any prejudices you might have, show a little compassion, and you will be more likely to succeed.

People in companies are subjected to all sorts of pressures so they won't necessarily see the immediate attraction of your approach. You might need to compromise a little, as you would like them to. Try understanding what makes people write in jargon and corporate-speak. You might find a good argument to suggest why poetry could be the perfect antidote to all that stuff.

Clarity is one compelling answer. To be able to offer greater clarity in writing is an attractive incentive for a business. Most companies would be interested in that, because most companies are not even clear in their own heads about some fundamental things – what is this business really about? How can we tell what we do more engagingly to our customers?

It's all about connecting with audiences. To do that we need to speak and to listen. We learn those fundamental skills from the very earliest age and the way we learn them is through stories. Then we grow up and forget this essential truth. Businesses have certainly forgotten it, but many of them are starting to wake up to the possibilities of storytelling. And, business being business and always conscious of short attention spans, the one-page poem is a more relevant storytelling model than *War and Peace*.

Businesses like short, sharp chunks of information. They also like to take training in similar short, sharp chunks. Here is an area for the would-be 'poet in business' to focus attention. Think through carefully what you might usefully pass on from your experience of writing poetry. Think of the poor manager who has to write an investment case to the Board by tomorrow lunchtime. And if your business is to be a good poet, show it can also be good for business.

John Simmons is a writer and brand consultant. He was recently writer-in-residence at King's Cross tube station. His latest book is *Dark Angels: How writing releases creativity at work*, Cyan Books, £9.99.

Poetry writers' groups

It is all very well to scribble away in your lonely garret, but there comes a point at which you need to share your work with others. Writers' groups are ideal for this: they not only provide a wonderful support group, but will also help you to improve the quality of your work. A number of these groups also publish books or magazines, providing you with a printed outlet for your work. To find out where your nearest writing group is, visit the website of the National Association of Writers' Groups (www.nawg.co.uk), where you will find a comprehensive, countrywide list. It also provides information about how to set up and run your own writers' group.

4th Monday Poets

tel (07834) 150523
Contact Linda Graham

Meets at the new venue of The King's Arms Upstairs, King Street, Ulverston, at 7.30pm. Anyone who is serious about pursuing the craft of poetry writing, in any style – whether a beginner or experienced – is welcome to join. Please bring 10 copies of your poem and be prepared for critical feedback.

Aberdeen Writers' Circle

c/o Aberdeen Arts Centre, 33 King Street, Aberdeen AB24 5AA

Meets every Wednesday morning from 10am to 12pm (summer and Christmas/New Year holidays excepted). The venue is the Arts Centre, King Street, Aberdeen.

Aberystwyth Arts Centre Writing and Poetry Group

Penglais, Aberystwyth, Ceredigion SY23 3DE
tel (01970) 621512
email ggo@aber.ac.uk
website www.aber.ac.uk
Contact Gill Ogden, Performing Arts Officer

An informal group that meets every month to discuss and share each other's poetry and writing. Open to all adults and led by a professional tutor.

Airedale Writers' Circle

20 Glenhurst Avenue, Park Lane, Keighley BD21 4RJ
tel (01535) 603119
email lesley@annelesley.freeserve.co.uk
Contact Maureen O'Hara

Meets on the second Tuesday of every month, at the Social Centre for the Association for the Blind in Keighley (7.30pm) for a meeting with speakers; also on the last Thursday of the month at 15 Manor Road, Utley, Keighley, for a manuscript evening.

Alford Writers Group

Clifton, 2 Station Road, Sutton on Sea, Lincs LN12 2HN
tel (01507) 450630
email hazelbogg@aol.com
Secretary Mrs Pamela Charret

Founded in 2000. Meetings are held in the Alford Library on the first Wednesday evening of every month. Average attendance is 12-15 people per month. A list of topics is distributed for each month and members usually write on the selected theme. The group is informal and aims to get writers together and share one another's creations, with critiques on request. A guest speaker attends once or twice a year and there are occasional workshops, either in-house or with a paid speaker or workshop leader. Members have enjoyed successes in various competitions and the group produces small anthologies.

Alsager Writers' Circle

35 Fields Road, Alsager, Stoke-on-Trent, Staffs ST7 2NA
email inkspot@tiscali.co.uk
Contact John Statham

Meets alternate Thursday evenings to share and evaluate members' work. Writing in any genre is welcome. Meetings include a writing workshop. Evenings are friendly, sociable events.

Angus Writers' Circle

email kfarrow@mateng.co.uk

Meets on the evenings of the first and third

Wednesday of each month. The venue is the Viewfield Hotel, Viewfield Road, Arbroath, Angus.

Ashton Writers' and Literary Group

3 Shared Street, Wigan WN1 3BA
tel (01942) 204571
email blem_white@hotmail.com
Contact Evelyn Crompton (Secretary)

Members enjoy writing/reading poetry. Holds competitions; submissions welcome. Contact the Secretary for more information.

Ayr Writers' Club

16 Yorke Road, Troon, Ayrshire KA10 6LB
tel (01292) 316009
email awc@rowenamlove.co.uk
website www.ayrwriters.co.uk
Contact Rowena M Love

Founded in 1970, this well-established group is strong on encouraging its members towards achieving success in various genres; many of them have been published. Meetings are held every Wednesday from September to May at 7.30pm in Prestwick Community Centre, Caerlaverock Road. There are at least 2 poetry workshops and 1 poetry speaker per year.

Back Room Poets

6 Princes Street, Oxford
email enquiries@brpoets.org
website www.brpoets.org

Ballycastle Writers

45a Drumavoley Road, Ballycastle BT54 6PQ
Contact Heather Newcombe

Meets at the Sheskburn Recreation Centre, Ballycastle.

Bank Street Writers

16-18 Mill Lane, Horwich, Bolton BL6 6AT
tel (01204) 669858
email bswscribe@aol.com
website http://hometown.aol.co.uk/bswscribe/myhomepage/writing.html
Secretary Rod Riesco

An independent writers' group for those living in the Bolton area. Meets monthly, covering writing of all kinds but mostly poetry and short stories. All interested writers are invited to attend on a free-trial basis.

Bards in the Park

Winter Gardens, Tollcross Park, Glasgow
email mail@poets-writers.co.uk
Contact R Sherland

Meets to read work and to encourage participation in the spoken word. Poetry, short stories and comment always welcome. On the first Saturday of the month, 1-3pm.

Bassetlaw Writers' Group

149 Galway Crescent, Retford,
Notts DN22 7YR
tel (01777) 700307
Secretary Mrs P Mann

Meeting of like-minded people with an interest in writing – any type, any level. Poetry competition annually, around September/October.

Battle Writers' Group

21 Oxshott Court, Sutton Place,
Bexhill TN40 1PH
Contact Geoffrey Hume

A friendly group that has been in existence since 1979. Members have had several publications in various forms, many with poetry. The biggest group effort was *The Tapestry of Battle*, which is still on sale. All members are from Battle, Hastings and Bexhill.

The Beehive Poets

The New Beehive, Westgate, Bradford,
West Yorks
tel (01274) 490561
Contact John Sugden

The Beehive Poets meet in the back room of the last gas-lit pub in the UK – the New Beehive, Westgate, Bradford, on a Monday night. The sessions are either read-arounds, or invited poets from almost anywhere, but somehow they have a Yorkshire connection. On every fourth Monday Bradford Poetry Workshop offers a critical and constructive forum for poets wishing to get feedback on their work.

Berwick-upon-Tweed Writers' Group

6 The Glebe, Gavinton TD11 3QU
tel 013-188 3297
Contact Francis Blacklock

Meets fortnightly, Wednesdays, 7pm at The Maltings, Berwick-upon-Tweed.

Bexley Poets

Civic Centre, Bexleyheath, Kent
tel (01322) 431997
email bexleypoets@ukf.net
Contact Paul Seymour

A great 'meeting place' for local poets and poetry enthusiasts. The group meets up once a month (normally on the first Monday of each month) and is both popular and entertaining.

The Black Horse Poets

25 Wyecliffe Street, Ossett, Wakefield, West Yorkshire WF5 9ER
email blackhorsepoets@hotmail.com

A group based in the city of Wakefield. Meets twice monthly at Henry Boons Pub, Westgate, to workshop, perform and promote new poetry. Twice-yearly magazine and annual competition. New members welcome.

Bracknell: Poetry Workshop at South Hill Park Arts Centre

Ringmead, Bracknell, Berkshire RG12 7PA
tel (01344) 484858
website www.southhillpark.org.uk

Meets on the third Wednesday of the month.

Bracknell Library Writers' Group

Bracknell Library, Town Square, Bracknell RG12 1BH
tel (01344) 423149
email jill.harvey-brown@bracknwell-forest.gov.uk
website www.bracknell-forest.gov.uk/learning/learn-libraries.htm
Contact Jill Harvey-Brown, Community Services Librarian

Meets once a month on a Friday lunchtime. Both poets and writers of prose are welcome to receive feedback on work in progress, and to find support and inspiration from like-minded people.

Bradford Poetry Workshop/Beehive Poets

c/o 37 Wilmer Road, Heaton, Bradford BD9 4RX

tel (01274) 223665
email bruce.poetbradford@blueyonder.co.uk
Contact Bruce Barnes/John Sugden

Meets weekly on Mondays at the New Beehive pub, Westgate, Bristol from 8.30pm onwards. Provides a programme of reading and read-arounds, and on the fourth Monday of the month a critical, constructive workshop for the consideration of members' poetry (bring 6 copies, at least).

Brewery Poets

Brewery Arts Centre, Highgate, Kendal, Cumbria LA9 4HE
tel (01539) 821304
Contact Patricia Pogson

Bridlington Writers' Group

40 Burstall Hill, Bridlington YO15 7GA
tel (01262) 609228
email Anne.Mullender@tesco.net
Contact Diane Wilson (Secretary)

Meets on Tuesdays at 7.30pm at the Jamroz Centre, North Street, Bridlington. A mixed group, always with a warm welcome for new members.

Bristol Black Writers' Group

Kuumba Project, 20-22 Hepburn Road, St Pauls, Bristol BS2 8QT
website www.discoverybristol.org.uk
Contact Bertle Martin

For black writers in the Bristol area. Monthly newsletter and active performance groups and workshops.

Burton Poets' and Writers' Group

86 Beamhill Road, Burton-on-Trent, Staffordshire DE13 0AD
email bpws2001@yahoo.com

BWSG Book Project

c/o 11 Donnington Road, Sheffield S2 2RF
tel (01142) 723906
email debjani@chatterjee.freeserve.co.uk
Contact Dr Debjani Chatterjee

Part of the Bengali Women's Support Group in South Yorkshire. Its members are very friendly and meet on the first Saturday of the month at the Space Centre above Park Library, Duke

Street, Sheffield S2, for workshops and readings. BWSG Book Project is also an exciting community publisher and publishes bilingual poetry in Bengali and English. Any woman who is interested in Bengali culture and is living, studying or working in South Yorkshire is welcome to join.

Café Writers
tom@cafewriters.org.uk
Contact Tom Corbett

Meets on the second Monday of each month from 7.15pm at Jurnet's Bar, Wensum Lodge, King Street, Norwich. All welcome. Free entry (voluntary collection). Presents a wide range of writers performing a variety of styles – poetry, drama, prose – in an atmosphere that both welcomes new work and invites professional polish. There are opportunities to read from the floor.

Cambridge Writers Poetry Group
48 Bishop's Road, Cambridge CB2 2NH
tel (01223) 512133
email tpl@eng.cam.ac.org
website www.cambridgewrites.org
Contact Tim Love

Cambridge Writers is a fairly large writing group with a poetry sub-section. This meets monthly on the evening of the third Tuesday in the month. The Cambridge Writers' website has a poetry anthology and the group holds an annual open poetry competition.

Camden Poetry Group
64 Lilyville Road, London SW6
Contact Hannah Kelly

Meets on Saturdays, once a month.

Cannon Poets
22 Margaret Grove, Harborne, Birmingham B17 9JH
tel 0121-426 6413
email martin@cannonpoets.co.uk
website www.cannonpoets.co.uk
Contact Martin Underwood

Meets at MAC (Midlands Arts Centre), Hexagon Room, on the first Sunday in the month (2-5.30pm), except August.

Century Poets
Century House, 99-101 Sutton House, Birmingham B23 5XA

tel 0121-382 0109
Contact Prof Kopan Mahadeva

Meets on the last Sunday in the month (2-6pm).

Circle in the Square
45 Totterdown Road, Weston-Super-Mare, Somerset BS23 4LJ
tel (01934) 628994 (for details of meetings)
Contact Bill Pickard

Meets on alternate Thursdays, from 7.45pm until 10.30pm. Over-18s only; admission 50p. No meetings in August or over Christmas. Has been running for 46 years and held more than 2000 meetings. Ex-members now live worldwide.

Cootehill Writers' Group
Station Road, Cootehill, County Cavan, Ireland
tel (00353) 495552321
email kphelan04@eircom.net
Contact Kay Phelan

A small group that meets occasionally to discuss poetry and prose.

Coventry Live Poets Society
Earlsdon Library, Earlsdon Avenue North, Coventry CV5 6FZ
tel (02476) 675359
email info.follib@covnet.co.uk
Contact C Jones

Meets on the first Wednesday of the month.

Cumbria Poets Workshop
25 High Hill, Keswick CA12 5NY
tel (01768) 773814
email chrispilling@onetel.com
Contact Chris Pilling

Meets at the above address.

Dean Clough Writers Group
227 Stirling Street, Halifax, West Yorkshire HX3 5AZ
Contact Gaia Hughes

Derby Poetry Society
Friends Meeting House, St Helens Street, Derby
tel (01332) 553430

Meets at 7.30pm in Room 4, Friends Meeting House, St Helens Street, Derby.

Dialstone Writers
90 Hillcrest Road, Offerton, Stockport,
Cheshire SK2 5SE
tel (01614) 835958
email cliffjim7@aol.com

A creative writing group meeting in a room in
the local church. Encourages all types of
writing, and takes its work out into the local
community.

Dorset East Street Poets
38 Hod View, Blandford Forum,
Dorset DT11 8TN
Contact David Caddy

Monthly meetings with workshops and talks
from visiting poets and writers.

Dublin Writers' Workshop
email dubwriter@indigo.ie
website www.dublinwriters.org

Dublin's longest-running writers' group.

East Anglian Writers
email chair@eastanglianwriters.org.uk
Chairman Benjamin Scott

Aims to bring together – and help promote the
work of – professional writers working or living
in Norfolk, Suffolk, Essex, Cambridgeshire and
Bedfordshire. Runs a number of social events
throughout the year to help break the isolation
of writing and to share experiences; also
organises a number of speaker events. To join
the EAW you must be a professional writer
living, or planning to live, in Norfolk, Suffolk,
Essex, Cambridgeshire, or Bedfordshire. You
must have had a work published, performed or
broadcast, but not vanity-published.
Illustrators, self-published and retired writers
are also welcome.

East Coker Poetry Group
The Helyar Arms, East Coker, Yeovil,
Somerset BA22 9JR
tel (01935) 863573
email info@eastcokerpoetry.org.uk
website www.eastcokerpoetry.org.uk
Contact Sue McKerracher

The village of East Coker, home to TS Eliot's
ancestors, was immortalised in his *Four
Quartets*; the poet's ashes are buried in the

churchyard of St Michael's. This heritage
prompted the formation of the East Coker
Poetry Group, meeting 6 times a year to share
favourite verse in the informal, relaxed
environment of the village inn, the Helyar
Arms.

Eastwood Writers' Group
c/o Eastwood Library, Wellington Place,
Nottingham Road, Eastwood,
Nottingham NG16 3GB
tel (01773) 788752
email gorbutler@hotmail.com
website www.eastwoodwriters.co.uk/
eastwho.htm
Contact Gordon Butler

Meets every Tuesday at the Catholic Social
Centre, Nottingham Road, Hilltop, Eastwood,
Nottingham, from 1.30 to 3.30pm, to share and
appraise each other's short stories, novels and
poetry.

Erewash Writers' Group
631 Tamworth Road, Long Eaton,
Nottingham NG10 3AB
tel 0115-849 8519
Secretary Janet Devereux

The group's main aim is to promote the art of
creative writing, including poetry. Most
members write some poetry.

Falmouth Poetry Group
Falmouth Library, Municipal Offices,
The Moor, Falmouth TR11 3QA
tel (01736) 763803
email tozer.jane@virgin.net
website www.falmouthpoetrygroup.org.uk
Contact Jane Tozer

Falmouth Poetry Group was founded 30 years
ago, by the later Peter Redgrove. It meets
fortnightly at Falmouth Library, for critical
workshops; also acts as a discussion forum for
work-in-progress. It still follows the method
used by The Group, founded by Philip
Hobsbaum, of which Redgrove was a founder
member. FPG endures as a dynamic and
influential source of inspiration and
encouragement to poets in Cornwall, and has
an excellent record of achievement. When
funds allow, it runs readings, creative

workshops and other poetry events, and publishes a quarterly newsletter featuring poems by members.

Fareham WordWrights

20 Laurel Gardens, Locks Heath SO31 6QH
tel (01329) 846480
email liza@look828.fsnet.co.uk
Contact Rosa Johnson Sylvie Whitaker, Secretary

A group for budding writers in Hampshire. Help, discussion and constructive criticism always available. Meets at Litchfield Community Centre, Litchfield, Hants.

Fire River Poets

2 Deane View, Bishops Hull Road, Bishops Hull, Taunton, Somerset TA1 5EG
tel (01823) 252486
email enquiry@fireriverpoets.org.uk
website www.fireriverpoets.org.uk
Contact John Stuart

A group of poets who meet about 20 times a year to read their own poetry critically, and sometimes other people's. Occasionally offers workshops and public readings. Local poets are welcomed regardless of preferred style, but numbers are limited; those who cannot be accommodated may become corresponding members or set up a separate group which Fire River can support. Beginners are advised to join a writing class, as Fire River does not offer a taught curriculum. Contact John Stuart for details of local poetry appreciation groups.

Flint Creative Writers

10 Hillcourt Avenue, Bagillt, Flintshire CH6 6DW
tel (01352) 735302
Contact EM Hudson

Group includes several members who write poetry and enter competitions.

Flowerfield Arts Centre

185 Coleraine Road, Portstewart, County Derry, Northern Ireland
tel 028-7083 1400
email info@flowerfield.org
Contact Bernie McGill

Meets once a week on a 10-week term basis, October-December and January-March, with a short 6-week term after Easter each year. Enrol at Flowerfield Arts Centre at the start of each new term. The group tackles short writing exercises in-session, and each member produces a piece at home for the following week's meeting. 12 members write poetry and fiction. New members welcome.

Footwork

Flat 1, 30 Pembroke Avenue, Hove, East Sussex BN3 5DB
email info@footwork.org.uk
Contact Robert Walton

A collective of Sussex poets.

Fosseway Writers

Ashleigh, 5 Main Street, Upton, Notts NG23 5ST
tel (01636) 812484
Contact Kirsty Adlard

Galway Writers' Workshop

Galway Language Centre, Bridge Mills, Galway, Ireland
website www.crannogmagazine.com/gww.htm

Meets each Saturday in The Bridge Mills building. It is a peer-led workshop, i.e. we do not use a facilitator. Members bring copies (usually 10-12) of their work (poetry, fiction, drama), read it aloud and have it critiqued by the other members. Usually about 15 minutes allotted to each reader. New members to the workshop must be nominated in advance by an existing member. Also publishes *Crannog Magazine*.

Hereford Poetry Group

tel (01684) 576445
Contact Amanda Attfield

Herga Poets

10 Runnelfield, Harrow on the Hill, Middx HA1 3NY
tel 020-8864 3149
Contact Dorothy Pope

Meets on the third Sunday of every month (second Sunday in December), 2-5.15pm in the Library of Orley Farm School, South Hill Avenue, Harrow on the Hill. (Please call before attending.)

Highgate Poets

9 Western Road, London N2 9JB
email 020-8883 8095
Contact Jill Bamber

Meets on the first Sunday of the month, in members' homes in the North London area. Would-be joiners must submit a sample of work with an sae. The group offers common ground for exchange, criticism and help for poets keen to find a platform for their work.

Hope Valley Writers
89 Castleton Road, Hope, Hope Valley, Derby S33 6SB
Contact Elizabeth Lunston

The Indian King Poets
Garmoe Cottage, 2 Trefew Road, Camelford, Cornwall PL32 9TP
tel (01840) 212161
email indianking@btconnect.com
website www.indianking.org.uk
Contact Helen Jagger Wood

Meets from 10am to 12.30pm most Tuesdays to write together, share work in progress for critical comment, and support each other in submitting work for publication. Members are available to lead workshops or give readings, singly or in groups.

Islington Poetry Workshops
FPHC, 12 Pine Grove, London N4 3LL
tel 020-7272 9023/020-8340 5974
Contact Brian Docherty

Offers opportunities to present and discuss poetry in a supportive and friendly group.

Keele Writers
52 The Moorings, Stone, Staffordshire ST15 8QZ
tel (01785) 811353
email rog.bradleythefirst@tiscali.co.uk
Contact Betty Titley

Based on a poetry writing group at Keele University, with the assistance of Harry Owen, Cheshire's first Poet Laureate, the group meets out of term time at other venues. It consists of about 16 poets at present, many having contributed to poetry magazines, both local and national.

Kelso Writers' Group
Lammercote, 7 Hadden Farm Cottages, Sprouston, nearr Kelso TD5 8HU
tel (01890) 830364

Contact Maureen Still

Meets Mondays, fortnightly, at the Abbey Road Centre, Kelso.

Kent & Sussex Poetry Society
The Camden Centre, Market Square, Tunbridge Wells, Kent TN1 2SW
email info@KentAndSussexPoetrySociety.org
website www.kentandsussexpoetrysociety.org

Established for 60 years in Tunbridge Wells. Activities include: monthly open poetry readings from a wide range of contemporary poets, including a short open mic slot for readings from the floor; monthly poetry workshops; biannual Saturday all-day 'master poet' workshops for igniting new inspiration; annual writing retreat for members, which is highly subsidised by the Society; annual open poetry competition, with £1000 in prizes.

Kick Start Poets
c/o 11 St Ann's Court, Friary Lane, Salisbury SP1 2HB
tel (01722) 329687
website www.kickstartpoets.freeuk.com
Contact Ruth Marden

An independent group of poets, founded in 1997. Meetings are normally on the first Monday of every month, at Sarum College, in members' homes, by arrangement.

King's Lynn Writers
The Friends' Meeting House, 38 Bridge Street, King's Lynn, Norfolk PE30 5AB
tel (01553) 67563

Meets on the second Thursday of every month at the Friends' Meeting House, 28 Bridge Street, King's Lynn.

Lampeter Writers' Workshop
tel (01570) 422351 ext 297
email writersworkshop@lamp.ac.uk

Meets on Tuesday nights, 7pm (term time only) in Lecture Room 7, Canterbury Building, University of Wales Lampeter.

Leicester Poetry Society
tel (01162) 567074
email e.lee@bssgroup.com
Contact Emma Lee

Runs workshops at the Leicester Adult Education College, Friday evenings at 7-9.30pm.

Leigh and Atherton Writers
54 Orchard Close, Leigh, Lancs WN7 1NY
tel (01942) 678454 or (01942) 876279
email nopampen@supanet.com
Joint Secretaries H Wellings, P Buxton

A group of writers interested in poetry, drama, short stories, articles and novels.

Lichfield Poetry Writers' Group
Lichfield Library, The Friary, Lichfield, Staffordshire WS13 6QG
tel (01543) 510700
email valerie.lovatt@staffordshire.gov.uk
Contact Val Lovatt

A venture in writing that is at the forefront of a poetry revival in the city of Lichfield. The group promotes opportunities for writers of all ages and experience to develop their craft through workshops, events, performances, readings and publication. Thus a natural part of this work is to reach out to a wider audience, and to turn the joy of verse into a more mainstream attraction. LPWG's monthly meetings are hosted at, and generously supported by, Lichfield Library. All are welcome to attend. Admission is free of charge, with refreshments provided.

Ligden Poetry Society
34 Lineacre, Grange Park, Swindon, Wiltshire SN5 6DA
email pulsar.ed@btopenworld.com
website www.pulsarpoetry.com
Contact David Pike

The performance-poetry wing of *Pulsar*. Holds regular 'free entry' poetry evenings in the Swindon, Wiltshire area.

Llandudno Writers' Club
tel (01492) 540855, (01492) 860156
Telephone the Club for full details.

Llanelli Writers' Circle
20 Rectory Close, Loughor, Swansea SA4 6JU
tel (01792) 891679
email cazleucarum@tesco.net
Secretary Carole Ann Smith

Aims to stimulate and encourage the craft of writing, including poetry. Several members of the group are published poets. Welcomes beginners and more experienced writers, providing a network of support.

London Voices Poetry Workshop
70 Holden Road, London N12 7DY
tel 020-8445 0090 *fax* 020-8445 6663

Friendly discussion of members' poetry and prose; produces an annual anthology. The group encourages young people and all ages; meets on the second-last Friday of the month (except December and July) at the Lambs Pub, Lambs Conduit Street, London WC1 (nearest tube, Holborn). A collection is taken.

Longford Writers
Norwood House, 2 Bowling Green Road, Gainsborough, Lincolnshire DN21 2QA
tel (01427) 612414
email john_silkstone@yahoo.co.uk
website http://groups.yahoo.com/group/longfordwriters
Contact John A Silkstone

A poetry group that publishes an A5 quarterly magazine of members' work (£16, €25, $30 p.a.).

Ludlow Poetry Cafe
Ludlow Library, 7/9 Parkway, Ludlow, Shropshire SY8 2PG
tel (01584) 813600
Contact Gill Mortimer

Meets on the first Wednesday each month at the Assembly Rooms, Ludlow.

Magnetic North Writers
email magneticnorthse10@yahoo.co.uk
website www.geocities.com/magnorth_writing

An open writers' group, based in South London and covering poetry, short fiction and non-fiction.

Manky Poets
15 Cross Road, Manchester M21 9DH
tel 0161-1881 3179
email manky@toucansurf.com
Contact Copland Smith

Continuing a tradition of Friday poetry readings that began in 1978, Manky usually meets on the 3rd Friday of each month. There is a guest poet and there are opportunities for others to read. For up-to-date information, see www.myspace.com/coanco.

Market Rasen Writers' Group
'Cobwebs', Middlefield Lane, Glenthm, Market Rasen LN8 2ET
tel (01673) 878633
email cobwebs1@tiscali.co.uk
Contact CF Green

A group of local writers who meet monthly to discuss each other's work.

Mendip and Somerton Writers
11 Chapman's Close, Wookey, Wells, Somerset BA5 1LU
email jmthom@tiscali.co.uk
Contact Judith Thomas

Classes are for Somerset County Council's Learning and Leisure groups. Poetry is included; some learners write nothing else.

Metroland Poets
Pucks Paigles, Burtons Lane, Little Chalfont, Bucks
tel (01494) 762290

Contact Christopher North

A poetry appreciation group with workshop elements for members' original work.

National Association of Writers' Groups
Headquarters The Arts Centre, Biddick Lane, Washington, Tyne and Wear NE38 2AB
tel (01262) 609228
email nawg@tesco.net
Secretary Diane Wilson, 40 Burstall Hill, Bridlington, East Yorkshire YO16 7GA
website www.nawg.co.uk
Membership £30 p.a. plus £5 registration per group; £14 Associate individuals

Aims "to advance the education of the general public throughout the UK, including the Channel Islands, by promoting the study and art of writing in all its aspects". Publishes *Link* bimonthly magazine. Annual Festival of Writing held in Durham in September. Annual Creative Writing Competition. Founded 1995.

New Rivers Writers Group
The Wenlock Arms, 26 Wenlock Road, Islington, London N1 7TA

tel (07949) 621288
email Dffusjjg@hotmail.com
website www.foxglove.co.uk/newrivers
Contact Julian Duffus

A workshop-based group that meet weekly (Thursday evenings, 8.30-11pm) to read out work-in-progress of any type and give each other supportive feedback. Also runs a programme of social events during the summer in and around London. Particularly welcomes visitors passing through London. No fee is charged.

Newquay Library Poetry group
Newquay Library, Marcus Hill, Newquay, Cornwall
tel (01872) 241106
Contact Zeeba Ansari

Meets on the second Friday of the month from 11-1 in Newquay Library.

Norwich Writers' Circle
1 Osbert Close, Lakenham, Norwich NR1 2NL
tel (01603) 479342
Contact Sean Hindle

Established in 1943, to serve a growing need for writers and would-be writers in the City of Norwich. Since then it has enjoyed the support of many individuals with varying involvements in the art, craft and hard-nosed business of writing. Today, membership is widely dispersed, throughout the region of East Anglia and beyond. Membership fee, £20.

Otley Poets
The Black Horse Hotel, Westgate, Otley, West Yorkshire
tel (01943) 870344
Contact Alan Holdsworth

Meets every first Monday in the month (second Monday Bank Holidays) at 8pm, for read-arounds and occasional guest poets: pass the pot, £1 each. Contact as above.

OU Poets
email adrian@greenad.co.uk
website www.oupoets.org.uk
Contact Adrian Green

A poetry group for students and staff, past or present, of the Open University, Milton Keynes

UK. Currently has about 120 members. Like other poetry groups, members submit poems for others to read and comment on; unlike most other poetry groups, they do this by post and not face-to-face, because they are scattered all across the country, with some in Ireland and in other parts of Europe. The magazine (strictly for members only) contains poems, criticisms and comments, and is issued 5 times a year.

Peebles and Innerleithen Writers' Group

Craig View, 4 Ballantyre Street, Innerleithen, Peeblesshire EH44 6LN
tel (01896) 830396
Contact Joan Hailstones

Meets Thursdays, fortnightly. Telephone for venue information.

Pennine Ink Writers' Workshop

The Gallery, Mid-Pennine Arts, Yorke Street, Burnley, Lancs BB11 1HD

Established in 1983. Meets every Monday night from 8-10pm at the Woodman Inn, Todmorden Road, Burnley. Programme is stimulating and varied and includes workshops on articles, short stories, poetry and plays.

Pentland Writers' Group

Amulree, Carlops, Penicuik EH26 9NF
tel (01968) 660727
email annamulree@cs.com
Contact Ann Smith

Meets in the Carlops area.

Penwith Poets and Writers Group

Newburn, Cockwells, Penzance, Cornwall TR20 8DB
Contact Patricia Bishop

Meets on the third Wednesday of every month from 11.30-3.30pm. One-to-one help for beginners is possible.

Penzance Poetry Group

tel (01872) 241106
Contact Zeeba Ansari

Meets on the first Monday and third Thursday of each month at Trevelyan House, Chapel Street, Penzance, Cornwall.

Phrase Writers

c/o Mrs Kathleen Lewis (Chairman), 48 Hughes Road, Hayes, Middlesex UB3 3AP

c/o Mrs Beatrice Holloway (Secretary), 31 Parkfield Crescent, Ruislip, Middlesex HA4 0RD
email beatriceholloway@yahoo.co.uk

Pitshanger Poets

Questors Theatre, Mattock Lane, Ealing, London W5 5BQ
tel 020-8567 7234 or 020-8567 0011
email nala.ques@virgin.net or pitshangerpoets@virgin.net
website pitshangerpoets.co.uk
Contact Alan Chambers/Nigel Lawrence

A weekly workshop-cum-discussion evening at Questor Theatre, every Tuesday except during August. Runs special events and readings with guest poets. Also runs a national poetry competition. *Poetry Ealing* is an occasional magazine, now in its 16th issue, devoted largely to West London poetry.

Poetry Ireland

2 Prouds Lane, off St Stephen's Green, Dublin 2
tel (00353) 1478 9974
email poetry@iol.ie
website www.poetryireland.ie

Provides a comprehensive list of writers' groups and workshops throughout Ireland.

Poetry Round

Finborough Arms PH, Finborough Road, London SW10
email info@poetryround.8m.com
website http://poetryround.8m.com

Meets Mondays at 7.30pm.

The Poetry Society of Cheltenham

Contact Roger Turner, Chairman (01242) 515595, Gerald O'Shaughnessy, Treasurer (01452) 862416, Michael Newman (01242) 675028

A lively, growing group which meets twice a month at Parmoor House, Lypiatt Road, Cheltenham. Several of the members are published extensively in magazines, or have had volumes of their poetry published. The Poetry Writing Group meets on a Tuesday; membership is by invitation. The Poetry Reading Group meets on a Thursday; readings, which are from an anthology or by Members' Choice, are followed by a short informal discussion. Also holds an annual lecture and social events. Further details are obtainable from the contacts listed above.

Poetry Wednesbury
25 Griffiths Road, West Bromwich,
West Midlands B71 2EH
tel (07950) 591455
email geoff@poetrywednesbury.co.uk
website www.poetrywednesbury.co.uk
Contact Geoff Stevens

A group of poets who meet at The George in Wednesbury on the last Wednesday of each month.

Poets Anonymous
70 Aveling Close, Purley, Surrey CR8 4DW
tel 020-8645 9956
email poets@poetsanon.org.uk
website www.poetsanon.org.uk
Contact Peter Evans

Holds 2 meetings a month: on the first Friday of the month at the Dog and Bull, Surrey Street, Croydon from 8pm; and on the second Saturday of the month in the Primary Room, United Reformed Church, Addiscombe Grove, Croydon, 2.30-4pm.

Poets of London
PO Box 4YP, London W1A 4YP
email sallycrawford@poetsoflondon.com
website www.poetsoflondon.com

A workshop and collegiate base for poets visiting London. Open to poets and those interested in poetry and the built environment. Monthly 'Creating Poetic Space' meetings on the first Saturday of the month at Waterstone's Gower Street. Ongoing poetry of city project to encourage more poetry of place and places of poetry in cities.

Rathmines Writers' Workshop
8 Brighton Gardens, Rathgar, Dublin 8, Ireland
tel 08 6402 5578 (08 6492 6980, evenings and weekends)
email rathmineswritersworkshop@eircom.net
website www.rathmineswritersworkshop.com
Contact James Conway

Meets every second Thursday at 7.30pm; reviews original work by writers who attend. Established in 1990, membership numbers around 40. Fee of €5 per workshop.

Saint Johns Library Poetry Workshops
41 Buckleys Green, Alvechurch,
Birmingham B48 7NG
tel 0121-445 2110
Contact Charles Johnson

Meets Saturdays, 1pm, bi-monthly.

Salisbury Poetry Café
Salisbury Arts Centre, Bedwin Street,
Salisbury SP1 3UT
website www.salisburypoetrycafe.org.uk

Meets on the last Thursday of every month at Salisbury Arts Centre. Guests are welcome to attend and listen to the poet and/or take part.

Salisbury Writers
4 Rosedale, Cholderton Road, Newton Tony,
Salisbury, Wilts SP4 0EU
tel (01980) 629440
email Susandown5@aol.com
website www.susanfrench.co.uk
Contact Susan Down

Many members write poetry, in both free verse and traditional forms; holds readings and enables group criticism of work-in-progress. Aims to produce an anthology annually, which includes short stories, non-fiction articles and poems. Meetings are on the first Thursday of each month at 7-9pm at the United Reformed Church, Salisbury.

Scarborough Poetry Workshop
19 Trinity Road, Scarborough,
North Yorkshire YO11 2TD
tel (01723) 365562
email ritasherriff-hammond@tiscali.co.uk
Contact Rita Sherriff-Hammond

A group that promotes all aspects of poetry and its performance, and encourages new and experienced poets to develop their existing talent and discover their hidden talents.

Scriveners
The Secretary, Ty Beirdd, 53 Church Street,
Ebbw Vale NP23 6BG

tel (01495) 305463
email scriveners@yahoo.co.uk
website www.scriveners.co.uk
Contact The Secretary

A group of published and unpublished writers who meet fortnightly on Wednesday evening, to give constructive criticism on work-in-progress. Work is circulated before meetings to enable in-depth criticism. 50-75% is poetry, but other genres are also welcome.

Southend Poetry Group

c/o Adrian Green (Secretary), Railway Hotel, Clifftown Road, Southend-on-Sea
email dorothy@southendpoetry.co.uk (Chair), adrian@greenad.co.uk (Secretary)
website http://www.southendpoetry.co.uk/
Contact Adrian Green

Meets at 8pm on the first Wednesday of each month, upstairs in the Railway Hotel, Clifftown Road, Southend. Meetings usually take the form of a presentation and discussion of a poet or topic, followed, if time allows, by a brief workshop session at which members can read their own work. At least 3 times a year, a whole evening is devoted to workshops. There is no formal membership; anyone is welcome to the meetings and the first time is free!

Southwest Writers

Shortlees Community Centre,
Blacksyke Avenue, Kilmarnock KA1 4SR
Contact Alan J Dixon

Meets every second Monday throughout the year to discuss all sorts of literature, including books, short stories, poems and articles.

Speakeasy: Milton Keynes Writers' Group

c/o 46 Wealdstone Place, Springfield,
Milton Keynes MK6 3JG
tel (01908) 663860
email speakeasy@writerbrock.co.uk
website www.mkweb.co.uk/speakeasy
Contact Martin Brocklebank

Welcomes writers of all genres. See website for further details.

Survivor Poets Leeds

94 Cherry Tree Walk, East Ardsley,
Wakefield WF3 2AJ
website www.survivorspoetry.com
Contact Tom Ireland

Leeds Survivors' Poetry has been running workshops and staging performances since 1994.

Survivor Poets Manchester

Manchester Survivors, Commonword,
6 Mount Street, Manchester M2 5NS
website www.survivorspoetry.com
Contact Rosie Garland

Runs 2 groups that meet for writing workshops and performances. The mixed group meets every Monday from 2-4pm, and the women's group meets on Thursdays from 1-3pm. Workshops are either run by guest facilitators or are a time for the group to receive positive feedback in 'open' writing/reading sessions.

Survivors' Poetry Bristol

26 Bradley Avenue, Shirehampton,
Bristol BS11 9SL
tel 0117-983 2790
email steve.hy@blueyonder.co.uk
website www.steppingouttheatre.co.uk
Contact Steve Hennessy

Runs creative writing and drama groups for mental-health-service users.

Survivors' Poetry Scotland

4C4 Templeton Centre, 62 Templeton Street,
Glasgow G40 1DA
tel 0141-556 4554
email www.spscot.co.uk
website www.spscot.co.uk

Sutton Coldfield Poetry Society

Sutton Coldfield Library, Lower Parade,
Sutton Coldfield B72 1XX
tel 0121-354 3860
Contact Mrs WM Mottram

Meets on the third Tuesday in the month, from 10am onwards.

Thin Raft

Reading International Solidarity Centre,
35-39 London Street, Reading RG1 4PS
tel (01189) 786678
website www.centrepoint.ch/ThinRaft
Contact Susan Utting

Regular poetry workshop sessions are open to anyone looking for structured feedback from a supportive, eclectic poetry group. Poets at all levels of experience are welcome – from absolute beginner to bestsellers. Also arranges dayschools led by visiting poets, as well as public poetry readings.

Tigh Fili Writers Group

Tigh Fili Art Centre, Thompson House, McCurtain St, Cork, Ireland
tel 086 8585558
website www.tighfili.com/literature.asp
Contact Eoin Ryan

Meets once a month at Tigh Filí Arts Centre from 6.30-8.30pm.

Toddington Poetry Society

82 Marston Gardens, Luton LU2 7DY
tel (01582) 723500
website www.toddingtonpoetrysociety.co.uk
Contact Jean Janes

Open to all who enjoy reading, writing or hearing poetry. Meets on the second and fourth Tuesdays of the month, in Luton. Meetings usually alternate between a visiting poet or an informal evening, with impromptu contributions of members' and other poems.

Torquay Writers' Group

18 Cedar Road, Preston, Paignton, Devon TQ3 2DD
tel (01803) 520165
Coordinator Danny Pyle

Weekly group meeting at St Marychurch Precinct Centre, Torquay, on Thursdays, 2-4pm, covering short stories, articles and poems which make up 75%. No age bar, but mailnly middle-age to senior.

Tottington Writers

30 Beryl Avenue, Tottington, Bury, Lancashire BL8 3NF
tel (01204) 882950
Contact Bettina Jones

A small, tutor-led group; tackles all kinds of creative writing, including poetry, which is the special interest of the tutor.

Truro Library Poetry Group

Truro Library, Union Place, Truro, Cornwall TR1 1EP
email mtwose@cornwall.gov.uk
website www.cornwall.gov.uk
Contact Maureen Twose

Meets on the second Thursday of the month to read, discuss and enjoy their own work and that of other poets.

Tynesidepoets

189 Stamfordham Road, Newcastle upon Tyne NE5 3JL
tel 0191-2421 565
email alantynepoet80@aol.com
Contact Alan C Brown

Has been in existence since 1960; has had cultural exchange with poets from the US, Germany, Bulgaria, Sweden, Norway, Iceland, Russia and elsewhere. Helps writers in all fields of literature and most European languages to learn, discuss and share ideas, and those who do not write but like English poetry or prose. Meets on the second and last Tuesdays of the month at 7.30pm at The Old George, Cloth Market, Newcastle upon Tyne.

Ulverston Writers

tel (01229) 582399
email maggie@townbank1.fsnet.co.uk
Contact Maggie Norton

Short story writers, novelists, poets and playwrights meet to discuss work each fortnight, on Wednesdays, at Owl Barn, Back Lane (first left off Church Walk), Ulverston, at 10.30-1pm.

Ver Poets

Secretary Daphne Schiller, 15 Brampton Road, St Albans, Herts AL1 4PP
email daphne.schiller@virgin.net
Contact Daphne Schiller
Membership £15 p.a. UK, £20 overseas, £10 students

Was founded in 1996 by May Badman and has both local and postal members. Encourages the writing and study of poetry. Holds evening meetings and daytime workshops in the St Albans area. Local and postal members. Holds members' competitions and the annual Open Competition.

Ware Poets

c/o David Perman, 11 Musley Lane, Ware, Herts SG12 7EN

email david@rockpress.freeserve.co.uk
website www.rockingham-press.co.uk
Contact David Perman

Ware Poets meet on the first Friday of each month in the Ware Arts Centre. There is a guest poet and readings from the floor. For further information, see **www.rockingham-press.co.uk**.

Westway Writers' Workshop
1 Thorpe Close, Ladbroke Grove,
London W10 5XL
tel 020-8964 1900
email mail@openage.co.uk
website www.openage.co.uk
Contact Mary Callaghan

Poetry, prose, playwriting; a group that is open to new ideas and new members.

Wimbledon and Merton Poetry Group
tel (07969) 597967
email zznsh@yahoo.co.uk
Contact Russell Thompson

Workshop/group with no fixed house style. Open to anyone who wishes to discuss their work, share some constructive criticism, or simply lend an ear and meet other poets.

Worcester Writers' Circle
4 Nixon Court, Callow End,
Worcester WR2 4UU
tel (01905) 830660
email phyll@handley606.wanadoo.co.uk
Contact Phyllis Handley

Welcomes all kind of writing.

Word for Word
Hornsey Library, Haringey Park, Crouch End,
London N8 9JA
website www.wforw.org.uk
Contact Laurence Scott, c/o Hornsey Library

A friendly, mixed group of poets, prose writers, filmmakers and musicians who meet in Hornsey Library to write. Tuesday is poetry; Wednesday is poetry and prose. Word for Word, Wood Green meets on Saturday morning. See website for details.

Write Direction
Bedford Central Library, Harpur Street,
Bedford MK40 1PG
tel (01234) 269519
Contact Peter Salt

Writers' and Poets' Circle
tel 020-8763 2692
email veronicaspaintbox@yahoo.co.uk
Contact Veronica Aldous

Meets on the second Friday of each month at 7pm at the Friends Meeting House.

Writers' Group
6 The Innings, Observatory Lane,
Lr. Rathmines Road, Dublin 6, Ireland
tel (01) 4910034
email phylherbert@hotmail.com
Contact Phyl Herbert

A group comprising of people who write in all genres.

Resources
Getting there

Poet, **Jeremy Reed**, writes about how he became a poet, and pleads for poets to follow their own voices.

My initiation into being a published poet, soon after I left school in Jersey at the age of 18, came about in events as extraordinary as those that have continued to characterise my life as a prolific poet, novelist and non-fiction writer, who is proud never to have worked in any other capacity than that of a writer.

After unsuccessfully attempting to overdose on tranquillisers on a beach in the pouring September rain, the slow-moving bottle-green sea slowly encroaching on my comatose body, I was, after being discovered by a dog-walker, resuscitated in hospital and appointed a Samaritan who visited me twice a week. By some felicitous accident it turned out that my Samaritan, Michael Armstrong, not only wrote poetry, but was in the process of setting up Andium Press, a small self-financed project devoted to publishing poetry. After reading my juvenilia, Michael, who wore chunky Pringle lambswool jumpers in ivory, oatmeal and navy blue, decided to make the poems I was writing at the time the first book to be published by Andium. It was called *Target*, and as a jacket image had a red, white and blue roundel silk-screened on its white covers, like the one popularised by the Mods as their parka logo as they burned through the West End in a raft of chrome and mirror-stacked Vespa and Lambretta scooters in the 1960s.

My first little book sunk without trace, but was picked up on by Asa Benveniste who ran the cutting-edge Trigram Press, a poetry publisher which gravitated towards innovative work that was more American-influenced than British, and who published the likes of Tom Raworth, Jim Dine, Anselm Hollo and Nathaniel Tarn. The spin-off from my first book was the collection *The Isthmus of Samuel Greenberg*, a book typically distinguished by Asa's superb eye for typography, good paper and a smudgy green, grey and purple cover design of the New York harbours hazed into cloudy sea fog.

I was still living in Jersey at the time and took little or no interest in circulating poems to small magazines, except on the rare occasions when I was contacted for contributions. One such magazine, *Joe DiMaggio*, published by John Robinson on an old mimeograph from his bedroom, and stapled together with silk-screened covers, proved not only to be a home for my poetry, but was, through the resulting correspondence, to instigate a lifelong friendship that persists to this day. John proved that a devotion to poetry matched by a practical economic way of producing it could affect wonders, and soon poets like Barry MacSweeney, Lee Harwood and Tom Raworth were regular contributors to the magazine.

At the same time I was publishing small press booklets, which have today become collectors' items, amazed at the ingenuity of the individuals who published work in this form, the money usually being put up by friends to facilitate the costs of production. Today the process has been simplified by desktop publishing and Internet distribution. The problem here is saturation – anyone can publish their own book now – but how do you get anything to stand out, good from bad, in the surfeit of self-published poetry that floods the net?

I suppose the only method of attempting to get published in a way that attracts a small readership is instinctual. Go to somewhere like Borders, or the Poetry Library at the South Bank, and just browse through the magazines on display to see if anything appears to fit with your own style and sympathies in poetry. If it seems to, then chance a submission. Don't be drawn to the idea of being published in a particular journal because it has a reputable name; it may not be the right place for your work at all. My sympathies are always with the underground and not the mainstream milieu, so take your talent where it belongs. You'll find that writers like William Burroughs often published work in the most obscure places. Poetry appeals to a minority, and if its readership comprises a microcosm, then the magnitude of its expression transforms it into a macrocosm in terms of cultural significance. I tend to agree with Oscar Wilde when he wrote, "A man can exist three days without water but not one without poetry."

But don't expect instant feedback when you are published. If work is good it travels slowly through a sort of subterranean network. And it's a fallacy to think that success in your chosen field is dependent on publishing with large houses. The Cambridge poet, JH Prynne, considered in certain circles to be the most important poet writing in Britain today, has remained so consistently hermetic in his approach to publishing his work that his poetry has to be assiduously searched for in often small, self-published booklets, excepting his *Collected Poems* published by Bloodaxe, and is rarely if ever to be discovered in magazines like *Poetry Review*. Prynne is just one example of a writer who has established a reputation through doing his own thing, and consistently avoiding all notions of celebrity, including readings – relying on the work itself to generate a slow but unstoppable momentum.

My advice is always to place the work before the idea of recognition. It's the doing of course, the engagement with creativity that is important; and if there's a small payback later, then that's a bonus. But poetry's essentially a solitary engagement, so before anything else you need to get used to your own company, and to working regularly and with discipline at your writing. Because of his demanding job at New York's Metropolitan Museum of Modern Art, and his recklessly excessive social life, the American poet Frank O'Hara used to write his poems in every available free moment, often standing up at parties, in taxis gunning across town, and of course in his lunch hours. O'Hara's *Lunch Poems*, published by City Lights in 1964, are precisely that, the marvellous synthesis of his sensory perceptions of fragmented New York life put into the fast visual imagery takes permitted him in his lunchtime strolls around the city. Like Bob Dylan, who rarely bothers with a second take of a song, O'Hara seldom rewrote, trusting his instincts as having got it right first time.

Poets can be too over-precious about letting a poem go. To my mind, writing workshops serve little purpose unless it's the sharing of group energies as a positive instructor to work that you are seeking. I feel if a poem is going to come out right it does so independent of commentary or academic analysis as the dissection of the living organism. Reading your work to sympathetic friends is probably the best criterion as to whether the poem you have written works or not. Try it on your own pulses first and then on people you trust. Somewhere between the two you'll find the poem's natural resting point.

I write poetry every day. To me it's an addiction like a drug, the rush of adrenalin I experience each time I fire-up imagery promoting a dopamine high. I write always by hand in exercise books. That way, rather like Frank O'Hara, I can write anywhere: on buses across London, in cafes, sitting outside in squares; and always, because of that, be directly in the moment. The idea of writing at a desk seems to me to be so formal as to be inhibitive. Better to take your laptop or notebook with you anywhere and write when the moment comes up almost as a providential accident. Imagination needs to be open to all experience and kept very separate from any received notions of what literature comprises. You should be able to write a poem about anything if you have the imaginative capacity. And in this respect it's important if you are thinking about magazine publication to look at the editorial policy. There is in mainstream British poetry the constrictive belief that the subject matter of poetry should be confined to a self-limiting radius of domestic issues, nature and socially realist commentary, a circumscribed ethic that in Thom Gunn's words subscribes to a "total lack of ambition". Don't be dragged into the obligatory grey post-Larkin undertow. There are many other outlets. Pete Doherty for instance sometimes publishes his poetry in online magazines. Look for broader horizons. You wouldn't have imagined William Burroughs bothering to submit work to the *TLS*. Choose your canvas, and like the artist Francis Bacon, throw your paint at it in a detonation of colour. Sooner or later you'll find the metier in which you feel most comfortable.

Follow your own voice and you'll find that in time it comes through, and that it makes a little mark with someone. We all need to feel that we have shared the experience of writing a poem and that it has communicated to the reader, so research a prospective outlet and go for it. I tend to write poetry, principally because little I read in British poetry excites me, so I have to create it for myself. That's one reason for writing; but you'll have your own. Whatever it is, value the impulse as central to your life and nurture it. It's up to you to react against Auden's negative belief that "poetry makes nothing happen", and to prove the opposite – that it changes the world every single moment with the tang of biting into a ripe orange.

Jeremy Reed has written a number of books of poetry and prose. *Orange Sunshine: The Party That Lasted a Decade* is published by SAF.

Poetry bookshops

It is increasingly difficult to find a good selection of poetry in many of our high-street booksellers. EPOS, the technology that keeps retailers up to date on what they are selling, has never been kind to poetry and the range of books sold has suffered terribly as a result. Thankfully, most of the shops listed here provide a wider selection of poetry titles than the average bookseller. The Internet, of course, provides an ideal solution, but most bookshops can now get their hands on any book in print. So, if you wish to keep your local bookshop going, you may wish to order through them. At least you will not have the added postage cost to consider.

Any Amount of Books

56 Charing Cross Road, London WC2H 0BB
tel 020-7836 3697 *fax* 020-7240 1769
email charingx@anyamountofbooks.com
website www.anyamountofbooks.com
Contact Nigel Burwood

Traditional Charing Cross Road bookshop with a wide-ranging stock, including a bargain basement and an antequarian section. The shop has a very high turnover with new books added every day. There is a yearly catalogue and a website with many unusual items.

Arnolfini Bookshop

16 Narrow Quay, Bristol BS1 4QA
tel 0117-917 2304
email bookshop@arnolfini.org.uk
website www.arnolfini.org.uk
Contact Katie Teasdale

Arnolfini is home to one of the best specialist arts bookshops in the country. Has more than 100 magazines and periodicals on art, design, literature and film, as well as an exceptional range of books on contemporary art and culture. The bookshop showcases books by independent publishers.

Blackwells, Broad Street, Oxford

8-51 Broad Street, Oxford OX1 3BQ
tel (01865) 792792 *fax* (01865) 794143
email oxford@blackwell.co.uk

Vast selection of poetry titles as well as a comprehensive range of poetry magazines, and spoken word. Second-hand titles are also available. Poetry and other readings take place throughout the year.

Blackwells Bookshop, Charing Cross Road

100 Charing Cross Road, London WC2H 0JG
tel 020-7292 5100 *fax* 020-7240 9665

email orders.london@blackwell.co.uk
Manager Andrew Chart

Situated in the heart of bookland. Although the focus of the shop is academic, being in the middle of the West End of London, it also stocks a good range of poetry titles. Also stocks a good range of poetry magazines.

The Bookshop, Launceston

10 Church Street, Launceston,
Cornwall PL15 8AP
tel (01566) 774107
website www.launceston-bookshop.co.uk

Bookshop at Queens

91 University Road, Belfast BT7 1NL
tel (028) 90 666 302
email info@queensbookshop.co.uk
website www.queensbookshop.co.uk

The oldest independent academic and general bookseller in Belfast. Specialises in history, politics and literature. The bookshop is also proud of its extensive collection of British and Irish poetry. Signed editions of local poets such as Michael Longley, Adrian Rice, etc. frequently in stock. A mail order service is available.

Borders Books, Music, Video and Cafe, Oxford Street

203-207 Oxford Street, London W1D 2LE
tel 020-7292 1600

Borders' flagship store in the heart of London's West End, with a large selection of poetry titles and a varied and interesting events programme. Stocks a good range of literary and poetry magazines.

Centreprise Bookshop

136-138 Kingsland High Street, Dalston,
London E8 2NS

tel 020-7254 9632

Specialises in Black writing, contemporary fiction and books for children, plus cards, giftwraps and book tokens. Orders accepted for any book in print; the bookshop can supply books on invoice to schools and libraries.

Children's Poetry Bookshop

tel 020-7833 9247
website www.childrenspoetrybookshelf.co.uk

Website set up by the Poetry Book Society to support poetry written for children. Its aim is to encourage children to read and enjoy poetry, and it operates as a book club. The books offered are chosen by a panel of expert Selectors, whose task is to find the very best children's poetry. The site also runs the Children's Poetry Bookshelf Competition for poems written by 8-11 year olds. Chair of the 2007 judges was Children's Laureate, Michael Rosen.

Cogito Books

5 St Mary's Chare, Hexham,
Northumberland NE46 1NQ
tel (01434) 602555
email alan.grint@btinternet.com
website www.cogitobooksonline.co.uk
Contact Alan and Julia Grint

An independent bookshop run by poetry-loving owners, Alan and Julia Grint. Their poetry section is exceptionally well stocked and has many volumes and anthologies with which the bigger stores no longer bother.

David's Bookshop

14 Eastcheap, Letchworth Garden City,
Hertfordshire SG6 3DE
tel (01462) 684631
website www.davids-bookshops.co.uk

Open since 1963, David's Bookshop, Music Shop and Gift Shop are all located in 3 shops in Eastcheap, Letchworth Garden City. Comprehensive range of books of all kinds.

The Derwent Bookshop

10 Finkle Street, Workington,
Cumbria CA14 2BB
website www.cumbriabooks.com/product.cfm
Contact John Bailey

The Derwent Bookshop is the largest independent bookseller in West Cumbria, serving a huge geographical area between Barrow in the South and Carlisle in the North – a distance of some 100 miles.

Diehard Books

91-93 Main Street, Callander FK17 8BQ
tel (01877) 339449
email sally.king4@btinternet.com
website www.zen39641.zen.co.uk/ps/diehard.htm

Bookshop and publisher of books and the magazine, *Poetry Scotland*.

Ellwood Books

38 Winchester Street, Salisbury,
Wiltshire SP1 1HG
tel (01722) 322975
email info@ellwoodbooks.com
website www.ellwoodbooks.com
Contact Marc Harrison

Large selection of poetry and plays, from fine first editions to paperback reading copies.

Foyles

113-119 Charing Cross Road,
London WC2H 0EB
tel 020-7434 1580
email webmaster@foyles.co.uk
website www.foyles.co.uk

The famous London bookshop has a large selection of poetry titles and hosts a large, year-round events programme.

G David

16 St Edward's Passage, Cambridge CB2 3PJ
tel (01223) 354619

Poetry lovers are particularly well-served with an extensive section that covers hard-to-find small press editions as well as the usual sets of complete works and anthologies.

Hatchards

187 Piccadilly, London W1
tel 020-7439 9921 *fax* 020-7494 1313
email books@hatchards.co.uk
website www.hatchards.co.uk
Manager Gavin Pilgrim

Stocks a broad range of poetry titles. The emphasis is on the classic, but also keeps a good selection of contemporary writing. A Mail Order Department sends books to destinations worldwide.

Heffers Booksellers

20 Trinity Street, Cambridge CB2 1TY
tel (01223) 568568
email heffers@heffers.co.uk
Manager David Robinson

Extensive book range, including over 1000 titles covering contemporary poetry from all over the world, along with criticism and biographies. Also offers a comprehensive range of anthologies.

Hellenic Bookservice

91 Fortess Road, London NW5 1AG
tel 020-7627 9499
email info@hellenicbookservice.com
website www.hellenicbookservice.com

Specialises in the poetry of 3 distinguished cultures: Greek, ancient and modern, including 2 Nobel Prize winners, Seferis and Elytis; and Roman. Runs a mail-order service.

John Sandoe (Books) Ltd

10 Blacklands Terrace, Chelsea,
London SW3 2SR
tel 020-7589 9473
email sales@johnsandoe.com
website www.johnsandoe.com/

One of London's leading independent bookshops, with books crammed into every bit of available space.

Joseph's Bookstore

2 Ashbourne Parade, 1257 Finchley Road, Temple Fortune, London NW11 0AD
tel 020-8731 7575
email info@josephsbookstore.com
website www.josephsbookstore.com

One of North London's leading independents, offering an events programme, a good range of magazines and a wide selection of books.

Loch Croispol Bookshop and Restaurant

17c Balnakeil, Durness, Sutherland IV27 4PT
tel (01971) 511777
email lochcroispol@btopenworld.com
website www.scottish-books.net
Contact Kevin Crowe

The most north-westerly bookshop on the British mainland, selling a wide range of poetry titles, from classic texts to contemporary work. There is a large selection of Scottish poets writing in English, Gaelic and Scots. Customers can browse the shelves while enjoying food and drink. Car parking, disabled access and facilities for children.

London Review Bookshop

14 Bury Place, London WC1A 2JL
email books@lrbshop.co.uk
website www.lrbshop.co.uk
Contact Andrew Stilwell

Situated round the corner from the British Museum, offering a wide range of contemporary and classic poetry, with particular strengths in contemporary European and American verse. Also hosts regular poetry readings and other events.

News From Nowhere

96 Bold Street, Liverpool L1 4HY
tel 0151-708 7270
email nfn@pop3.pop.org.uk
website www.newsfromnowhere.org.uk

A women's co-operative committed to social change. Apart from poetry, a wide range of books are stocked. Subjects include: Black Britain and America, Children, Course books, Fiction, Ireland, Politics, Self-Help, Sexuality and Women. There is also a fast, friendly ordering service.

Owl Bookshop

209 Kentish Town Road, London NW5
tel 020-7485 7793
email owlbookshop1@btconnect.com

Organises regular literary events. Poetry readings have included Margaret Atwood, John Hegley and Tobias Hill. Can supply books by mail order. As well as any British book in print, can also order American books.

The Palmers Green Bookshop

379 Green Lanes, London
tel 020-8882 2088
email pgreenbooks@aol.com

Stocks an extensive range of adult and children's books. Regular poetry readings and children's storytelling events.

The Poetry Bookshop

The Ice House, Brook Street, Hay-on-Wye,
Powys HR3 5BQ
tel (01497) 821812
email info@poetrybookshop.co.uk
website www.poetrybookshop.co.uk
Contact Melanie Prince

The only bookshop in the UK devoted entirely
to poetry; covers every aspect, from the
antiquarian and the scholarly to contemporary
work, and supplies rare, out-of-print and now
new books (to order or via the website). Also
stocks criticism, biography, small and fine
press, Beat, war, illustrated, poetry in
translation and much more. Booksearch, Postal
Service and Books Bought.

Poetry Bookshop Online

Poetry Book Society, Fourth Floor,
2 Tavistock Place, London WC1H 9RA
tel 020-7833 9247 *fax* 020-7833 5990
email customerservice&commat
etrybookshoponline.com
website www.poetrybookshoponline.com
Director Chris Holifield

An online bookshop run by the Poetry Book
Society. Not only does it sell poetry books and
books about poets and poetry, it also sells
Poetry Achive CDs.

Roundstone Books

29 Moor Lane, Clitheroe, Lancashire BB7 1BE
tel (01200) 444242
email joharbooks@aol.com
website www.roundstonebooks.co.uk
Contact Jo Harding

A town centre shop which specialises in all the
Arts (including poetry, fiction and literary
studies) but has books in most categories.
Described as "a haven of peace" and has
friendly, helpful staff.

Sharston Books

Unit 15, Wearlee Works, Longley Lane,
Sharston, Manchester M22 4WT
tel 0161-945 8604
website www.sharstonbooks.com

Bookshop with a large range, situated on
modern warehouse premises.

Soma Books

38 Kennington Lane, London SE11 4LS
tel 020-7735 2101
email books@somabooks.co.uk
website www.somabooks.co.uk

Specialises in books from Asia (including Urdu
poetry with English translations), Africa and
the Caribbean. Selection of poetry for children
and adults. Imports from USA, Indian
subcontinent, etc.

Subterranean Books

270 Hackney Road, London E2 7SJ
email eddie@subterraneanbooks.com
website www.subterraneanbooks.com

Shop selling only poetry. Has great selection;
informative content on its website and in its
newsletter.

Sweetens of Bolton

86 Deansgate, Bolton, Lancashire BL1 1BD
tel (01204) 528457

Supports the work of local writers, and offers a
good stock of poetry titles.

Talking Book Shop

11 Wigmore Street, London W1H 9LB
tel 020-7491 4117
email support@talkingbooks.co.uk
website www.talkingbooks.co.uk

Has the most comprehensive stock of poetry
available on tape and CD. Famous poets
reading their work, e.g. Betjeman, Eliot,
Hughes, Auden, and celebrated readers giving
their own individual interpretations of
favourite poems. Publishes a yearly catalogue,
has an efficient mail-order service and offers an
exciting Internet site with sound bites!

Truro Bookshop

RCM, 25 River Street, Truro TR1 2SJ
tel (01872) 272185
website www.cornwallbooks.com

Stocks more than 20,000 titles and a wide range
of gifts in the foyer of the Royal Cornwall
Museum. The range of poetry, plays and
literary criticism is the most extensive in the
South West, and includes large Cornish section.
Student discount of 10% on stock lines and a
full ordering service.

Ulysses Bookshop

40 Museum Street, London WC1A 1LT
tel 020-7831 1600
email ulyssesbooks@FSBDial.co.uk
Contact Peter Jolliffe

Independent bookshop, dedicated to keeping important copies of major British poets in stock.

Waterstone's, Brighton

71-74 North Street, Brighton,
East Sussex BN1 1ZA
tel (01273) 206017

A good selection of poetry books and magazines.

Waterstone's, Deansgate, Manchester

91 Deansgate, Manchester M3 2BW
tel 0161-832 1992

Extensive range of poetry titles, and exciting programme of events and readings.

Waterstone's, Gower Street

82 Gower Street, London WC1E 6EQ
tel 020-7636 1577 *fax* 020-7580 7680
email enquiries@gowerstreet.waterstones.co.uk

Stocks work by outstanding contemporary and classical poets, men and women, from every continent, in tranlation, bilingual editions, and original English. The anthologies section ranges from African to Zen School. Also stocks Poetry Journals, Audiobooks, Secondhand/Out of Print, Poetry Criticism and Creative Writing. Full mail-order service.

Waterstone's, Hampstead

68/69 Hampstead High Street,
London NW3 1QP
tel 020-7794 1098

A large, successful and wide-ranging section covering everything from the classics to new titles, with a strong range of imports and poetry in translation. Specialist staff and recommendations. Regular poetry events also held in store.

Waterstone's, Sauchiehall Street

154/160 Sauchiehall Street, Glasgow G2 3EW
tel 0141-353 2484

A large poetry section including a wide range of Scottish poetry.

Word Power Books

43 West Nicholson Street, Edinburgh EH8 9DB
tel 0131-662 9112
email books@word-power.co.uk
website www.word-power.co.uk
Contact Elaine Henry

An independent bookshop, with a comprehensive range of books of all sorts.

Poetry libraries

The services available from our libraries are quite staggering. Often they are also so understated that we are not fully aware of what is on offer – and it is well worth investigating. Many of the libaries below provide a wonderful resource for poets, whether it be in the form of a collection of small magazines or, simply, in reference material with a specific connection to poetry.

Bangor Library

80 Hamilton Road, Bangor, Down BT20 4LH
tel (02891) 270591
email bangor.library@ni-libraries.net
Contact Stephen Hanson

Has a well-stocked poetry collection concentrating mainly on post-1950 poetry and Irish poets. Runs poetry events nearly every month, with readings, workshops, and a poetry reading group. One poet has described it as "the Best poetry library in Northern Ireland". Also has Poetry Unlimited, a Children's Poetry library with masses of poetry books and tapes of poems for young people. There are competitions, readings and workshops, even producing poems on computers to put on the library walls.

Barbican Library

Barbican Centre, Silk Street,
London EC2Y 8DS
tel 020-7382 7098
email barbicanlib@cityoflondon.gov.uk
website www.cityoflondon.gov.uk/
barbicanlibrary
Contact John Lake

Excellent collection of poetry books for loan. Also runs poetry readings and workshops throughout the year.

Birmingham Central Library

Chamberlain Square, Birmingham,
West Midlands B3 3HQ
tel 0121-303 4227
Contact Paul Woodward

Large library with an extensive poetry collection.

The British Library

96 Euston Road, London NW1 2DB
tel 0870-444 1500 (Switchboard), 020-7412 7676 (Advance Reservations, St Pancras

Reading Rooms and Humanities enquiries), 020-7412 7702 (Maps), 020-7412 7513 (Manuscripts), 020-7412 7772 (Music), 020-7412 7873 (Asia, Pacific & Africa Collections)
website www.bl.uk

The national library of the UK and a legal deposit library. The collection includes in excess of 150 million items, in most known languages. Online catalogues.

Chesterfield Library

New Beetwell Street, Chesterfield,
Derbyshire S40 1QN
tel (01246) 209292
email ann.ainsworth@derbyshire.gov.uk
Contact Janet Scott

Runs regular poetry events.

Halifax Central Library

Northgate, Halifax, Yorkshire HX1 1UN
tel (01422) 392628
email shymas@one.com
website www.calderdale.gov.uk
Contact Sarah Hymas

Runs a poetry book of the month promotion, bringing national and international contemporary poets to users' attention. Also runs poetry reading groups at Central Library, and at branch libraries in Sowerby Bridge and Brighouse. Committed to highlighting the value poetry and poets have to everyday life.

Hall Green Library, Birmingham

Hall Green Library, 1221 Stratford Road,
Birmingham, West Midlands B28 9AD
tel 0121-464 6633
email hall.green.library@birmingham.gov.uk_:
website www.birmingham.gov.uk/
hallgreenlibrary
Contact Mike Reed

A large selection of poetry books for loan; also runs a poetry group on the first Monday evening of each month.

The Little Magazines, Alternative Press and Poetry Store Collections

The Library, University College London, Gower Street, London WC1E 6BT
tel 020-7380 7796
website www.ucl.ac.uk/Library/special-coll/litmags.shtml

Extensive holdings from mid-1960s of UK little magazines, small press and underground publications in particular, and large but less comprehensive holdings of US publications. There is also a selection of magazines and books from the Commonwealth, Europe and other countries and a small collection of reference material either about little-magazine and small-press activities or of a more general critical or background nature. The library currently subscribes to around 200 little magazine titles. Over 3500 little magazine and alternative press titles are held in all.

Manchester Central Library

St Peters Square, Manchester M2 5PD
tel 0161-234 1981
email libbtt@libraries.manchester.gov.uk
Contact Libby Tempest

Has been organising poetry readings and events for a number of years, and has seen a growing audience for live poetry. Extensive collection of poetry books.

Mitchell Library

North Street, Glasgow G3 7DN
tel 0141-287 2838
email catherine.mcinerney@cls.glasgow.gov.uk
Contact Catherine McInerney

Houses the largest available collection of Burns poetry and songs, as well as an extensive collection of Scottish poetry.

Norfolk and Norwich Millennium Library

The Forum, Millennium Plain, Norwich, Norfolk NR2 1AW
tel (01603) 774774
email millennium.lib@norfolk.gov.uk
website www.norfolk.gov.uk

A huge range of poetry books available to borrow. Numerous poetry-related events, bringing poetry alive in the heart of Norwich.

Northern Poetry Library

Morpeth Library, Gas House Lane, Morpeth, Northumberland NE61 1TA
tel (01670) 534524
email pahallam@northumberland.gov.uk
Contact Pat Hallam

The largest collection of contemporary poetry in England outside London, consisting of 17,000 volumes plus magazines covering English-language poetry published since 1968. Adult and children's poetry available. All items are available for loan.

The Poetry Archive

PO Box 286, Stroud, Gloucestershire GL6 1AL
website www.poetryarchive.org
Editor Esther Morgan, Andrew Bailey

The world's premier online collection of recordings of poets reading their work. Here you can enjoy listening, free of charge, to the voices of contemporary English-language poets and of poets from the past. The Archive is growing all the time.

The Poetry Cubicle Library

5 Wrights Court, Elm Hill, Norwich NR2 2RA
tel (07789) 514655
email Sara@thepoetrycubicle.org.uk
website www.thepoetrycubicle.org.uk
Contact Sara Wingate Gray

The Poetry Cubicle is a not-for-profit organisation dedicated to making poetry more accessible. As part of its remit it has established an independent poetry library, with the aid of a Millennium Award, in Norwich. Specialises in stocking the mad, bad, deranged, denounced poet, the lost, forgotten and renounced poet, and has a wealth of poetical material veering from a William Burroughs APO-33 pamphlet to a Linton Kwesi Johnson spoken-word vinyl LP to *The Illustrated Ape* magazine to Bob Cobbing concrete poetry prints, plus the unusual gamut of pamphlets, books and DIY poetry booklets from the 1960s onwards. Also has a small children's poetry library and is beginning to convert some of its collection into braille and large print format. Almost free to join, and hopes to provide access to under-supported and under-funded poetry and poets.

The Poetry Library

Royal Festival Hall, Level 5, London SE1 8XX
tel 020-7921 0943/0664 *fax* 020-7921 0939
email info@poetrylibrary.org.uk
website www.poetrylibrary.org.uk,
www.poetrymagazines.org.uk

Comprehensive collection of poetry written in
or translated into English since 1912. The
biggest collection of its type with around
100,000 items. A first-rate information service
relating to all aspects of modern and
contemporary poetry is also provided –
available via email, the website, and by letter.
The Poetry Library provides up-to-date listings
of competitions, publications, magazines and
workshops, either on its excellent website or if
you send an sae to the postal address.

The Poetry Store Collection

UCL Library Services,
UCL (University of London), Gower Street,
London WC1E 6BT
tel 020-7679 7700 *fax* 020-7679 7373
email library@ucl.ac.uk
website www.ucl.ac.uk

Contains small press publications, mostly of
poetry, now totalling more than 7000 titles.

Scottish Poetry Library

5 Crichton's Close, Canongate,
Edinburgh EH8 8DT
tel 0131-557 2876
email reception@spl.org.uk
website www.spl.org.uk,
www.splreadingroom.org.uk
Robyn Marsack, Julie Johnstone (Librarian)

The Scottish Poetry Library is a unique national
resource, funded by the Scottish Arts Council.
It is the place for poetry in Scotland for the
regular reader, the serious student or the casual
browser. It has a remarkable collection of
contemporary poetry with an emphasis on
Scottish writing in English, Scots and Gaelic;
works from Europe and almost every part of
the world feature too. It also has collections of
audio-visual material, cuttings, Braille,
periodicals, and a children's section. Borrowing
is free to all. Services include a postal lending
scheme; enquiries; schools workshops;

exhibitions and events; publications; reading
groups; poetry reading website; an online
catalogue and index to Scottish poetry
periodicals; and the Edwin Morgan Archive.

Shirley Library

Church Road, Shirley, Solihull,
West Midlands B90 2AX
tel 0121-744 1076
email libraryarts@solihull.gov.uk
Contact Barbara Clarke

A poetry-friendly library which hosts regular
Poetry Coffee Mornings for its readers. At these
sessions poetry lovers can hear contemporary
poetry by published poets and can also read
some of their own work.

Solihull Central Library

Homer Road, Solihull,
West Midlands B91 3RG
tel 0121-704 6965
website www.solihull.gov.uk/wwwlib
Contact Nickie Thomas

Hosts poetry slams, performances and
workshops as part of the Live Literature
Programme in conjunction with Solihull Arts
Complex. Runs a Young People's Writing
Group that meets every other month.
Committed to the promotion of contemporary
poetry.

South Yardley Library

Yardley Road, Birmingham,
West Midlands B25 8LT
tel 0121-464 1944
e-mail south.yardley.library@birmingham.gov.uk
website www.birmingham.gov.uk/
southyardleylibrary
Contact Pat Gisbourne

Committed to providing a wide range of
poetry, particularly modern poetry. A member
of both the Poetry Society and the Poetry Book
Society.

Walsall Central Library

Lichfield Street, Walsall,
West Midlands WS1 1TR
tel (01922) 653121
email CentralLendingLibrary@walsall.gov.uk
website www.walsall.gov.uk/libraries
Contact Annie Wood

Committed to promoting poetry to a wide audience.

Warwick Library

Barrack Street, Warwick,
Warwickshire CV34 4TH
tel (01926) 748900
email warwicklibrary@warwickshire.gov.uk
website www.warwickshire.gov.uk/libraries
Contact Kate Mackie

Has a wide selection of poetry books for loan.

Wolverhampton Central Library

Snow Hill, Wolverhampton WV1 3AX
tel (01902) 552061
email simon.fletcher@dial.pipex.com
website www.wolverhampton.gov.uk/
leisureculture/libraries/centrallibrary
Contact Simon Fletcher

The focus of much poetic activity in the city.
The Poetry Readers' Group meets regularly,
and poetry events are held.

Useful books

There are many books that will help you to write better poetry. Here are just a few:

101 Ways to Make Poems Sell: The Salt Guide to Getting and Staying Published by Chris Hamilton-Emery

An Introduction to English Poetry by James Fenton (Penguin)

A Poetry Handbook by Mary Oliver (Harcourt)

The Art and Craft of Poetry by Michael J Bugela

The Art of Haiku 2000 by Gerald England, Jean M Kahler (Illustrator)

The Creative Writing Coursebook: Forty Authors Share Advice and Exercises for Fiction and Poetry by Andrew Motion (Pan)

Getting into Poetry: A Readers' and Writers' Guide to the Poetry Scene by Paul Hyland (Bloodaxe Poetry Handbooks)

How Poetry Works by Philip Davies Roberts (Penguin)

How to be Well-Versed in Poetry edited by EO Parrott (Penguin)

How to Publish Your Poetry by Peter Finch (Allison & Busby)

How to Write a Poem by John Redmond (Blackwell Publishing)

In the Palm of Your Hand: The Poet's Portable Workshop by Steve Kowit (Atlantic Books)

Ode Less Travelled: Unlocking the Poet Within by Stephen Fry (Hutchinson)

Our Thoughts Are Bees: Working with Writers and Schools by Mandy Coe (Wordplay Press)

The Poetry Handbook by John Lennard (Oxford University Press)

The Practice of Poetry: Writing Exercises from Poets Who Teach by Robin Behn (HarperCollins)

Poetry: The Basics by Jeffrey Wainwright (Routledge)

Poets' Handbook – A Guide to Building Great Poems by Kenneth C Steven (Writers' Bookshop)

Strong Words: Modern Poets on Modern Poetry by WN Herbert (Bloodaxe)

Taking Your Poetry Further – The Poetry Society's guide for the novice poet, available free by sending an sae to The Poetry Society, 22 Betterton Street, London WC2H 9BU

Writing Poems by Boisseau, Wallace & Mann (Longman)

Writing Poems by Peter Sansom (Bloodaxe Poetry Handbooks)

Writing Poetry by John Whitworth (A&C Black)

Writing Poetry by Matthew Sweeney & John Hartley Williams (Teach Yourself)

Writing the Bright Moment: Inspiration and Guidance for Writers by Roselle Angwin (Fire in the Head)

Poetry websites

The Internet was made for poetry, whether to publish e-magazines or create communities where poets can gather virtually to discuss mutual interests or just share their work. It also provides invaluable resources. Below are some of the websites the poet may turn to for information about the world of poetry.

57 Productions
www.57productions.com

57 presents an extensive and diverse programme of promotional events, and an expanding catalogue of productions – CDs and cassettes, videos and specials for the Internet – featuring popular poets and performers. It offers agency and advisory services to venues and festivals, educational institutions and the general media on a wide range of popular poetic activity.

Askaboutwriting.net
www.askaboutwriting.net

A news and resource site for writers of all abilities everywhere. It updates on Saturdays. A free update notice is emailed on Mondays.

Britain In Print
www.britaininprint.net

Set up to promote the wealth of pre-1700 printed materials that exists within some of Britain's major libraries. A core part of the site is an e-learning project based on Robert Henryson's medieval Scot's poem, *The Testament of Cresseid*. The materials have been piloted in Queen Anne High School in Dunfermline, Fife (birthplace of Henryson), and the innovative online support tools have helped bring the poem alive for school students. Through visits to major libraries, the project has also introduced school students to primary source materials, ranging from first editions of Shakespeare to early works of Chaucer, Gavin Douglas and other writers.

Cambridgepoetry
www.cambridgepoetry.org

A website for presses and events running in Cambridge, including the poetry summit and Cambridge series readings, featuring new and innovative poetry by young writers.

Can I Have a Word
www.canihaveaword.org.uk

An interactive resource aimed at primary age children's skills in creative writing. The website captures the spirit of the live project and makes it available to all. The resource offers teachers new ideas to stimulate creative thinking, newly commissioned poems and top writing tips from a range of leading poets, exciting new animated and aural stimuli for the classroom, and downloadable worksheets with specific curriculum links developed by the NLT.

Contemporary Writers
www.contemporarywriters.com

UK and Commonwealth poet biographies, bibliographies, critical reviews, prizes and photographs. A British Council/Booktrust Initiative.

Everypoet
www.everypoet.com

Poems and poetry resources.

Guardian Poetry Workshop
books.guardian.co.uk/poetryworkshop/

Hosted every month by a different poet who sets an exercise, chooses the most interesting responses and offers an appraisal of them.

hEar4Words
uk.groups.yahoo.com/group/hEar4Words

Online poets meet. News and dates of events.

Lines On the Map
www.cheshire.gov.uk/ReadersAndWriters/ Writers/linesonthemap/home.htm

A local project set up by Andrew Rudd, the Cheshire Poet Laureate for 2006. It is a clickable map of Cheshire: each place-name leads to a poem, gradually building into a poetry map of the County. People have been asked to submit poems; more are added each month – currently the total is about 75 poems. Gives people a chance to write about the places they know best, and share that work with others.

Lit-Net
www.lit-net.org

A virtual literature centre for the West Midlands with stacks of poetry landmarks, including Poetry of Place with poems about places in the West Midlands, and poetry on loan in public libraries.

New Hope International
www.geraldengland.co.uk

Reviews of hard-copy poetry-related publications, and much more.

Poetry Can
www.poetrycan.co.uk

A one-stop portal to the world of poetry in the south-west of England.

Poetry Foundation
www.poetryfoundation.org

An independent US literary organisation committed to a vigorous presence for poetry in our culture. It exists to discover and celebrate the best poetry and to place it before the largest possible audience.

Poetry International Web
www.poetryinternationalweb.org

A worldwide forum for poetry on the Internet. PIW offers news, reviews, essays, interviews and discussions as well as hundreds of poems by acclaimed modern poets from all around the world, both in the original language and in English translation. In keeping with the spirit of the Web, it is a truly international collaboration of 12 editors in 12 different countries. Each of these countries maintains its own national domain within PIW, with its chosen 'Poet of the Quarter', news and other articles.

Poetry Jukebox
www.57productions.com

A unique production for the Internet from the 57 organisation. The jukebox features more than 40 poets – and expands in time. It features exclusive works from artists such as Benjamin Zephaniah, Zena Edwards & Brian Patten ... including works-in-progress and those that can only be understood in terms of recent events in the Middle East and the USA (for instance from Moniza Alvi and Michael Rosen). The jukebox also offers rare archive material from poets including Kamau Brathwaite and Christopher Logue, dating from the 60s.

Poetry Landmarks
www.poetrysociety.org.uk/landmark

The Poetry Society's extremely useful Landmarks project – a database of poetry organisations, venues, writing groups, publishers, magazines, etc.

poetrymagazines.org
www.poetrymagazines.org.uk

A full text digital library of British 20th-century and contemporary poetry magazines from the Poetry Library's collection based in London's Royal Festival Hall. New issues and new titles are added all the time.

Poetry On Loan
www.poetryonloan.org.uk

A virtual gateway to over 20 public libraries in the West Midlands, which specialise in poetry – from books on the shelves to poets in between them.

Poetry pf
www.poetrypf.co.uk

The site is principally intended to be a showcase for modern poets, and to provide a focused point for members to take advantage of the visibility and searchable presence the Internet provides. Each member has his/her own pages within the site, and feature articles and reviews (of others' books) are invited. There is a members' events listing, including competitions advised by members associated with them.

Poetry Portal
www.poetry-portal.com

A directory of worldwide poetry online; a simple-to-use and detailed overview of the fascinating variety of literary productions on the Internet.

Poets' Graves
www.poetsgraves.co.uk

An online guide to the graves of famous poets, with photographs!

Poet's Letter
www.poetsletter.com

Website offering lots of poetry material.

Poets On Fire
http://poetsonfire.blogspot.com

A website filled with news and discussion about poetry in performance across the UK.

Spoiled Ink
www.spoiledink.com

Designed to help writers get more readers, improve their craft, get published and promote any already-published work.

The British Electronic Poetry Centre
www.soton.ac.uk/~bepc

A reference guide to the work of contemporary British poets from the parallel tradition. Launched in May 2002, it provides information on poets and their publications, and audio files to accompany examples of their work. The site is particularly dedicated to increasing the understanding of the role of oral performance in poetry, and will be supported by research projects on the history and theory of performance. Its development was supported by an AHRB small grant for the study of the history of poetry readings in post-war Britain.

The Staffordshire Learning Net for Geography
www.sln.org.uk/geography/poem.htm

An award-winning initiative to celebrate geography for young people and to celebrate good practice between teachers. Using poetry in geography-teaching helps by developing a sense of place – through descriptive vocabulary of sights, sounds, smells and even tastes,

relating the emotions of experiences, relaying polemic opinions about issues, and illustrating in words, geographical shapes and patterns.

The Poetry Kit
www.poetrykit.org

Incredibly useful and comprehensive website set up in 1997 to provide an information resource for poets. Lists courses, competitions, events, festivals, venues, magazines, poetry organisations, publishers, workshop groups and more. Coverage is full and international. There is also a magazine section that provides an outlet for poetry, reviews, articles and interviews.

The South
www.thesouth.org.uk

Poetry in the south of England, and especially Brighton.

UK Authors
www.ukauthors.com

A writers' showcase and resource site, which has grown hugely over the past three years, and now has almost 2000 members. The resource pages contain thousands of resources for writers of all levels, and the site regularly runs (prose and poetry) competitions and publishes an annual anthology. There are also flourishing forums, poetry workshops and prose and poetry discussions.

writersartists.net
www.writersartists.net

A collaborative of globally and socially minded poets, writers and artists, many of whom specialise in cross-arts work, and who perform, teach and work internationally, especially in the UK, Europe and in the US.

WritersServices
www.writersservices.com

A website for writers, including invaluable resources and help, as well as a self-publishing service.

Poetry forums, chatrooms and message boards

It can be a lonely business being a poet. Unless you are lucky enough to find a publisher or win a competition, how do you know if what you are writing is any good? One way is to take part in the increasing number of poetry boards and forums. Some are discussion sites, where you can debate the weighty poetic issues of the day. On others you can put your work up for public scrutiny which, although scary, can be very helpful.

ABC Tales
www.abctales.com

Discussion forum about stories and poems; you can start a conversation with fellow readers about the latest book or article, or chat with others and share experiences with fellow authors or would-be-authors.

Able Muse: Eratosphere
http://eratosphere.ablemuse.com

One-stop online destination for the post and critique of poems, fiction and artwork.

About.com Poetry Forum
http://poetry.about.com

Solicits questions about and reviews of submitted poems.

Alien Flower
http://www.sonic.net/web/

An interactive medium where poets share ideas about poetry and its place in society.

Allpoetry
http://allpoetry.com

Forum where poets can post and customise the look of their poetry, accept feedback, and make comments about others' poetry.

Artist Corner
www.artistcorner.com

Multiple boards on which to post poetry, short stories, song lyrics and quotes.

Blueline Poetry Forum
http://blueline.goobertree.com/forum/index.php

A full-featured forum, including various contests, boards, games, chats, and discussions. Readers may nominate poetry for awards.

Burgundy
www.robgodfrey.com/burgundy

A small, friendly poetry discussion board for British poets, with the ethos that poetry is, first and foremost, fun.

Captain Cynic: Prose and Poetry
http://www.captaincynic.com/forum/15/poetry.htm

Poetry and prose forum offering critique and useful feedback.

The Critical Poet
http://www.criticalpoet.com/forum/

Multiple boards, including how to critique poetry and individual member archives.

Friendly Musings
http://p219.ezboard.com/bfriendlymusings

Multiple active poetry boards, including critique, holiday thoughts, nature, and poetry writing instruction.

The Gazebo
http://alsopreview.com/cgi-bin/gazebo/discus.cgi

Dedicated, experienced writers who have spent years studying their craft meet at this forum.

HaikuTalk
http://clara.net/nhi/hktalk.htm

A general discussion list for writers and others interested in haiku and related genres such as tanka, senryu, renga, sijo, haibun, sedoka, etc.

Just Our Love
www.justourlove.com/poetry/

User submissions and critique forum featuring love poetry.

Magma Poetry Forums
http://magmapoetry.com/phpBB2/index.php

Discussions about poetry.

Moontown Cafe
www.moontowncafe.com

Multiple poetry boards including free verse, metered, rhyming, and spiritual. Moontown Cafe also includes a chat room.

NewPoetry List
http://wiz.cath.vt.edu/mailman/listinfo/new-poetry

Announcements, reviews, essays, open letters, quotes, news items, calls for submissions, poems and commentary.

Paradise Poets Society
http://groups.msn.com/ParadisePoetsSociety

An MSN community including chat, submissions, featured poetry, and an online novel in progress.

ThePoem.co.uk
www.ThePoem.co.uk

A taster of contemporary poetry in Britain and Ireland, plus a discussion board.

Poems & Quotes: Poetry Forum
www.poems-and-quotes.com/discussion/

Poetry and general writing forum offering user interaction and critique.

Poetic Muse
www.daypoems.net/nodes/5168.html

Affiliated with Poetictricity and Beatnik Poetry Journal. Includes a poet of the month and opportunities to get a poetry folio published.

Poetry Circle
www.poetrycircle.com/

Poems, criticism and discussion.

The Poetry Club
www.poetryclub.com/

A community for poets to post and review written works. User-based community offers critiques, tips, and exercises.

Poetry Critical
http://poetry.tetto.org/

An open online poetry workshop where anyone can read, critique and numerically rate poetry, with over 3000 poems, 20,000 comments, and 260 active amateur poets.

poetryetc
www.jiscmail.ac.uk/lists/poetryetc.html

A venue for discussing poetry and poetics.

The Poetry Pages
www.poetrypages.com

Offers message and critique boards, as well as webspace for poets.

The Poets Place
http://groups.msn.com/ThePoetsPlace/

MSN group community forum for poets and writers.

Poets Anonymous
http://poetsanon.proboards10.com/

Poetry message boards featuring different styles of poetry such as haikus and tankas.

Sonnet Central
www.sonnets.org

Everything you need to know and say about the sonnet form.

Starlite Cafe's Poet Corner
www.thestarlitecafe.com

General poetry forum offering a variety of selections in poetry types.

Unknown Poets
http://poets.unknowncommunity.com/

Poetry community where poets can post their work into different categories such as 'love' and 'observation'.

Wild Poetry Forum
www.wildpoetryforum.com/

Discussion board for poets and writers providing constructive critiques in a supportive atmosphere.

Word Doctors Forum
http://www.worddoctors.co.uk/phpBB2/

Resources for writers.

The Writer's Block
www.the-writers-block.net/forum/

Forum for critiquing and discussing poetry. Includes publication, chapbook information, and writing programmes.

Writers' Dock
www.writersdock.co.uk

A writing community, incorporating forums and chat rooms. It has articles about writing, news about the writing industry, and discussion forums on the art of writing.

Index